Lecture Notes in Computer Science   13591

More information about this series at https://link.springer.com/bookseries/558

Mohamed Sellami · Paolo Ceravolo ·
Hajo A. Reijers · Walid Gaaloul ·
Hervé Panetto (Eds.)

Cooperative Information Systems

28th International Conference, CoopIS 2022
Bozen-Bolzano, Italy, October 4–7, 2022
Proceedings

 Springer

Editors
Mohamed Sellami ⓘ
Telecom SudParis - Institut Polytechnique de
Paris
Evry, France

Hajo A. Reijers ⓘ
Utrecht University
Utrecht, The Netherlands

Hervé Panetto ⓘ
University of Lorraine
Vandoeuvre-les-Nancy, France

Paolo Ceravolo ⓘ
University of Milan
Milan, Italy

Walid Gaaloul ⓘ
Telecom SudParis - Institut Polytechnique de
Paris
Evry, France

ISSN 0302-9743   ISSN 1611-3349 (electronic)
Lecture Notes in Computer Science
ISBN 978-3-031-17833-7   ISBN 978-3-031-17834-4 (eBook)
https://doi.org/10.1007/978-3-031-17834-4

This Springer imprint is published by the registered company Springer Nature Switzerland AG
The registered company address is: Gewerbestrasse 11, 6330 Cham, Switzerland

General Co-chairs and Editors' Message for CoopIS 2022

The International Conference on Cooperative Information Systems (CoopIS 2022), held during October 4–7, 2022, in Bozen-Bolzano, Italy, further consolidated the importance of the series of annual conferences that were started in 2002 in Irvine, California. The conference then moved to Catania, Sicily, in 2003, Cyprus in 2004 and 2005, Montpellier in 2006, Vilamoura in 2007 and 2009, Monterrey, Mexico, in 2008, Heraklion, Crete, in 2010 and 2011, Rome in 2012, Graz in 2013, Amantea, Italy, in 2014, Rhodes in 2015, 2016, 2017, and 2019, and in Valletta in 2018.

Cooperative Information Systems (CISs) facilitate the cooperation between individuals, organizations, smart devices, and systems of systems by providing flexible, scalable, and intelligent services to enterprises, public institutions, and user communities. As a result, people and smart devices can interact, share information, and work together across physical barriers. The domain of CISs integrates research results from different related computing areas, such as distributed systems, coordination technologies, collaborative decision making, enterprise architecture, business process management, and conceptual modeling.

In recent years, several innovative technologies have emerged: cloud computing, service oriented computing, the Internet of Things, linked open data, semantic systems, collective awareness platforms, block chain, processes as a service, etc., which enable the next generation of CISs. In developing the next generation CISs, research is needed towards (1) the applicability and use of the above-mentioned innovative technologies, (2) approaches to develop CISs in particular catering to the multitude of stakeholders involved in the development of socio-cyber-physical systems, and (3) associated modeling techniques to express and analyze the different aspects of these systems in cohesion.

The CoopIS conference series is an established international event for presenting and discussing scientific contributions to technical, economical, and societal aspects of distributed information systems at scale. This 28th edition was collocated with the 26th edition of the Enterprise Design, Operations and Computing (EDOC) conference, and its guiding theme was "Information Systems in a Digital World."

As with the earlier CoopIS editions, the organizers wanted to stimulate this cross-pollination with a program of engaging keynote speakers from academia and industry. We are quite proud to list for this year:

- Daniel R. Isaacs, Digital Twin Consortium (CoopIS keynote)
- Stephen Mellor, Industry IoT Consortium (CoopIS/EDOC joint keynote)
- Jordi Cabot, ICREA, Spain (EDOC keynote)
- Carliss Y. Baldwin, Harvard Business School, (EDOC keynote)
- Giovanni Sartor, University of Bologna and the European University Institute of Florence (EDOC keynote)

We were once again able to develop a high-quality conference program for this edition. A total of 68 papers were submitted and a reviewing process by the CoopIS Program Committee (PC) was performed to professional quality standards: each paper review was assigned to at least three referees, with arbitrated email discussions in the case of strongly diverging evaluations. After this process, 15 submissions were accepted as regular papers and five as research in progress papers. In keeping with the international nature of CoopIS, the authors of the accepted papers originate from a variety of nations around the world.

We would like to express our thanks to everyone who helped make CoopIS 2022 a success. We especially want to express our thanks to the EDOC 2022 organization committee who helped us in organizing CoopIS 2022 and the authors who contributed papers on their research to CoopIS 2022, as well as the PC members and additional reviewers who promptly assessed the submissions and offered the authors insightful feedback.

October 2022

Mohamed Sellami
Paolo Ceravolo
Hajo A. Reijers
Walid Gaaloul
Hervé Panetto

Organization

Honorary Chair

Robert Meersman   University of Graz, Austria

General Chairs

Hervé Panetto   Université de Lorraine - TELECOM Nancy, France

Walid Gaaloul   Institut Polytechnique de Paris - Télécom SudParis, France

Program Committee Chairs

Hajo A. Reijers   Utrecht University, The Netherlands

Paolo Ceravolo   Università degli Studi di Milano, Italy

Website Chair

Mohamed Sellami   Institut Polytechnique de Paris - Télécom SudParis, France

Publicity Chairs

Jean M. Simão   Federal University of Technology – Parana, Brazil

Zhangbing Zhou   China University of Geosciences, China

Program Committee

Marco Aiello   University of Stuttgart, Germany

Joao Paulo Almeida   Federal University of Espirito Santo, Brazil

Abel Armas Cervantes   University of Melbourne, Australia

Nour Assy   Télécom SudParis, France

Ahmed Awad   University of Tartu, Estonia

Imed Abbassi   ISIM Monastir, Tunisia

Banu Aysolmaz   TU Eindhoven, The Netherlands

Eduard Babkin   National Research University Higher School of Economics, Russia

Sylvio Barbon Junior   University of Trieste, Italy

Ingmar Baumgart	Karlsruhe Institute of Technology, Germany
Khalid Belhajjame	Université Paris Dauphine-PSL, France
Salima Benbernou	Université Paris Cité, France
Mario Luca Bernardi	University of Sannio, Italy
Javier Berrocal	University of Extremadura, Spain
Xavier Blanc	University of Bordeaux, France
Hayet Brabra	Télécom SudParis, France
Uwe Breitenbücher	University of Stuttgart, Germany
Cristina Cabanillas	University of Seville, Spain
Paolo Ceravolo	University of Milan, Italy
Richard Chbeir	Université de Pau et des Pays de l'Adour, France
Carlo Combi	Università degli Studi di Verona, Italy
Marco Comuzzi	UNIST, South Korea
Silvia Inês Dallavalle de Pádua	Universidade de São Paulo, Brazil
Johannes De Smedt	KU Leuven, Belgium
Jochen De Weerdt	Katholieke Universiteit Leuven, Belgium
Bruno Defude	Télécom SudParis, France
Adela Del Río Ortega	University of Seville, Spain
Giuseppe Desolda	University of Bari, Italy
Claudio Di Ciccio	Sapienza University of Rome, Italy
Chiara Di Francescomarino	Fondazione Bruno Kessler-IRST, Italy
Khalil Drira	LAAS-CNRS, France
Mahendrawathi Er	ITS, Indonesia
Rik Eshuis	TU Eindhoven, The Netherlands
Ernesto Exposito	Université de Pau et des Pays de l'Adour, France
Marcelo Fantinato	University of São Paulo, Brazil
Walid Gaaloul	Télécom SudParis, France
Luciano García-Bañuelos	Tecnológico de Monterrey, Mexico
Chirine Ghedira Guegan	Université Jean Moulin Lyon 3, France
Maria Teresa Gómez López	University of Seville, Spain
José González Enríquez	University of Seville, Spain
Mohamed Graiet	ISIM Monastir, Tunisia
Daniela Grigori	Université Paris Dauphine-PSL, France
Georg Grossmann	University of South Australia, Australia
Mohad-Saïd Hacid	Université Claude Bernard Lyon 1, France
Mirian Halfeld Ferrari	Universite d'Orleans, France
Armin Haller	Australian National University, Australia
Lazhar Hamel	ISIM Monastir, Tunisia
Martin Hepp	Universität der Bundeswehr München, Germany
Anett Hoppe	Leibniz Universität Hannover, Germany
Stijn Hoppenbrouwers	HAN University of Applied Sciences, The Netherlands

Natalia Sidorova	Technische Universiteit Eindhoven, The Netherlands
Jean M. Simão	Federal University of Technology – Paraná, Brazil
Pnina Soffer	University of Haifa, Israel
Jacopo Soldani	University of Pisa, Italy
Farouk Toumani	Blaise Pascal University, France
Nick van Beest	CSIRO, Australia
Inge van de Weerd	Utrecht University, The Netherlands
Han van der Aa	University of Mannheim, Germany
Boudewijn van Dongen	Eindhoven University of Technology, The Netherlands
Sebastiaan van Zelst	RWTH Aachen University, Germany
Maria Esther Vidal	TIB Leibniz Information Center for Science and Technology, Germany
Georg Weichhart	PROFACTOR GmbH, Austria
Lena Wiese	Fraunhofer ITEM, Germany
Karolin Winter	Technical University of Munich, Germany
Guido Wirtz	University of Bamberg, Germany
Moe Thandar Wynn	Queensland University of Technology, Australia
Jian Yu	Auckland University of Technology, New Zealand
Zhangbing Zhou	China University of Geosciences, China

Additional Reviewers

Abdulwahab Aljubairy
Elie Chicha
Olena Chornovol
Ehsan Emamirad
Fernanda Gonzalez-Lopez
Mamadou Gueye
Mohammad Mustafa Ibrahimy
Elena Jaramillo
Suhwan Lee
Robin Lichtenthäler
Yuchen Liu Faiza Loukil
Adnan Mahmood

Johannes Manner
Maria Moreno
Rebecca Morgan
Hadi Nowandish
Mohammadmehdi Peiro
Madhawa Perera
Thiago Richter
Adrian Rebmann
Sareh Sadeghianasl
Salma Sassi
Mokhtar Sellami
Jan Martijn van der Werf

CoopIS 2022 Keynotes

Understanding the Nature of Digital Twin – Digital Twin Challenges & Values; Empowering Businesses

Daniel R. Isaacs

Chief Technical Officer, Digital Twin Consortium

Short Bio

Dan Isaacs is Chief Technology Officer of Digital Twin Consortium, where he is responsible for setting the technical direction for the Member Consortium, liaison partnerships and business development support for new memberships. Previously, Dan was Director of Strategic Marketing and Business Development at Xilinx where he was responsible for emerging technologies including AI/Machine Learning, including defining and executing the ecosystem strategy for the Industrial IoT. Prior to joining the Digital Twin Consortium, Dan was responsible for Automotive Business Development focused on Automated Driving and ADAS systems. Dan represented Xilinx to the Industrial Internet Consortium (IIC). He has more than 25 years of experience working in automotive, Mil/Aerospace and consumer-based companies including Ford, NEC, LSI Logic and Hughes Aircraft. An accomplished speaker, Dan has delivered keynotes, presentations and served as panellist and moderator for IIC World Forums, Industrial IOT Global conferences, Embedded World, Embedded Systems, and FPGA Conferences. He is a member of international advisory boards and holds degrees in Computer Engineering: EE from Cal State University, B.S. Geophysics from ASU.

Talk

The term digital twin is being used with increasing frequency, but with little consistency, across multiple industries today. Digital Twin Consortium is working to address this and help industries better understand the advantages and value over the continuum of digital twins from discrete to complex.

Learn about the challenges the Digital Twin Consortium membership is working to address and its priorities. Gain a clear understanding through real-world use cases how businesses are recognizing value today through use of digital twins an enbaling technologies.

Trustworthiness in Industrial IoT Systems: trends and issues for the future Collaborative and Computing Enterprise

(Joint session with EDOC 2022)

Stephen Mellor

Chief Technical Officer, Industry IoT Consortium

Short Bio

Stephen Mellor is the Chief Technical Officer for the Industry IoT Consortium, where he aligns groups for business, technology, trustworthiness and industry for the Industrial Internet. He is a well-known technology consultant on methods for the construction of real-time and embedded systems, a signatory to the Agile Manifesto, and one-time adjunct professor at the Australian National University in Canberra, ACT, Australia. Stephen is the author of Structured Development for Real-Time Systems, Object Lifecycles, Executable UML, MDA Distilled and Models to Code. Stephen was Chief Scientist of the Embedded Software Division at Mentor Graphics, and founder and past president of Project Technology, Inc., before its acquisition. He participated in multiple UML and modeling-related activities at the Object Management Group (OMG), and was a member of the OMG Architecture Board, which is the final technical gateway for all OMG standards. Stephen was the Chairman of the Advisory Board to IEEE Software for ten years and a two-time Guest Editor of the magazine.

Talk

Trustworthiness, the combination of security, privacy, resilience, reliability and safety, is especially critical in industrial systems. Life, limb and the environment are at risk.

Unfortunately, these trustworthiness characteristics often conflict. Security would suggest locking that door, but safety demands it be able to be opened in case of emergency. This is resolvable, but often further factors must then be considered. (A bad actor could open the door from the inside. Now what?)

The Industry IoT Consortium has published the Trustworthiness Foundation, which outlines eleven principles to help guide you through the maze. This presentation will show how these principles can help you build a trustworthy system.

Contents

Research in Progress Papers

Regular Papers

Bi2E: Bidirectional Knowledge Graph Embeddings Based on Subject-Object Feature Spaces

Zhe Wang$^{(\boxtimes)}$, Xiaomei Li, and Zhongwen Guo

Ocean University of China, Qingdao, China
iiilannn9527@gmail.com

Abstract. In high connectivity knowledge graph, distance based knowledge graph embedding methods show promising performance on link prediction task, and are capable of encoding complex relations and key relation patterns. However, the existing methods fail to achieve excellent results in knowledge graph with poor context structure information. To mitigate this problem, we propose Bi2E, a bidirectional model based on subject-object feature spaces. To enhance the efficiency of data utilization and perceive more potential semantic links, we utilize the bidirectionality of relation to model from both forward and reverse directions. And Bi2E represents triples in the subject-object feature spaces, which enables it to capture richer feature information from rare data. In addition, Bi2E employs adaptive margin γ which makes embedded representation more flexible by only using a small amount of feature information. Experiments on link prediction benchmarks demonstrate the proposed key capabilities of Bi2E. Moreover, we set a new state-of-the-art on two low connectivity knowledge graph benchmarks.

Keywords: Knowledge graph embeddings · Low connectivity · Bidirectionality of relation · Subject-object feature spaces · Adaptive margin

1 Introduction

The knowledge graph is a collection of a large number of fact triples. A triple (h, r, t) indicates that there is a certain relation r between entity h, t. There are many examples of knowledge graphs, such as WordNet [1], Freebase [2] and YAGO [3]. These knowledge graphs have many applications in reality, such as question answering [4], recommender systems [5], natural language processing [6] and so on.

Since many implicit relations in most knowledge graphs are not found, predicting the missing links between entities becomes a fundamental work. This problem is named as link prediction or knowledge graph completion. Recently, massive work has focused on the research of knowledge graph embedding method, which embeds all entities and relations into a low dimensional space.

From TransE [7] to RotatE [8], and then to the recent state-of-the-art PairRE [9], the distance based embedding method has made great progress and demonstrated its effectiveness in link prediction. The research focuses on two problems, the first is encoding

© The Author(s), under exclusive license to Springer Nature Switzerland AG 2022
M. Sellami et al. (Eds.): CoopIS 2022, LNCS 13591, pp. 3–18, 2022.
https://doi.org/10.1007/978-3-031-17834-4_1

1-to-N, N-to-1, and N-to-N complex relations [7, 10]. Taking the 1-to-N relation as an example, a triple (*QuentinTarantino, DirectorOf*, ?), through the transformation of *DirectorOf* relation, the distance based model should make all entities corresponding to the film name, such as *InglouriousBasterds* and *PulpFiction*, closer to entity *Quentin-Tarantino*. The latter is based on the existing triple encoding relation patterns, as the success of link prediction heavily relies on this capability [7, 8]. There are various types of relation patterns: symmetry (e.g., *_similar_to*), antisymmetry (e.g., *_has_part*), inverse (e.g., *_hypernym* and *_hyponym*), composition (e.g., my father's brother is uncle) and so on.

Previous methods can solve these problems well in high connectivity, while performance declines in the absence of data. TransE, TransR [10], TransD [11] only show limited encoding ability in the case of sufficient data. RotatE and the recent state-of-the-art PairRE have achieved gratifying performance on knowledge graphs with rich context structure information, but they have not continued strong performance in low connectivity environment.

Here we propose Bi2E, which is capable of encoding complex relations and key relation patterns in low connectivity. Bi2E employs the bidirectionality of relation to model from both forward and reverse directions. And we map the triples to two different Euclidean spaces to capture richer feature information. In addition, Bi2E uses the adaptive margin parameter γ to adjust the distance between entities flexibly. These provide three important benefits:

- Bi2E models from both forward and reverse directions, which improves the efficiency of data utilization and discovers more potential semantic links that are not easily found in the unidirectional model.
- Our method captures semantic links in two different spaces, which not only improves the utilization of data, but also makes the model more flexible to adjust the distribution of knowledge graph embedding.
- Adaptive γ makes the model more flexible and more realistic to represent the relations between entities in the real world.

We evaluate Bi2E on three knowledge graph benchmarks. The experimental results show that Bi2E achieves state-of-the-art in low connectivity. Besides, further analysis confirms the effectiveness of methods proposed in Bi2E.

2   Background and Notation

Given a knowledge graph that is represented as a list of fact triples, knowledge graph embedding methods define scoring function to measure the plausibility of these triples. We utilize (h, r, t) to denote a triple, where h and t denote the head and tail entity in the triple, and r denotes the relation. The column vectors of entities and relations are represented in bold lowercase letters, belonging to sets E and R respectively. All triples that really exist in the world belong to set T and $f_r(h, t)$ is used to denote the scoring function.

We calculate average number of edges per entity(**epe**) to measure the connectivity of knowledge graphs. The smaller the epe is, the poorer context structure information the knowledge graph has.

In addition, we utilize the method in [9, 12] to define complex relations. For each relation r, we divide it into corresponding complex relations type by calculating the average number of tails per head(**tphr**) and the average number of heads per tail(**hptr**). If tphr < 1.5 and hptr < 1.5, r is divided into 1-to-1 type; if tphr > 1.5 and hptr > 1.5, r is divided into N-to-N type; if tphr > 1.5 and hptr < 1.5, r is treated as 1-to-N type.

We analyze three relation patterns:

1. **Symmetry/Antisymmetry.** A relation r is symmetric if $\forall e_1, e_2 \in E$, $(e_1, r, e_2) \in T$ $\Longleftrightarrow (e_2, r, e_1) \in T$ and is antisymmetric if $(e_1, r, e_2) \in T \Rightarrow (e_2, r, e_1) \notin T$;
2. **Inverse.** If $\forall e_1, e_2 \in E$, $(e_1, r_1, e_2) \in T \Longleftrightarrow (e_2, r_2, e_1) \in T$, then r_1 and r_2 are inverse relations;
3. **Composition.** If $\forall e_1, e_2, e_3 \in E$, $(e_1, r_1, e_2) \in T \land (e_2, r_2, e_3) \in T \Rightarrow (e_1, r_3, e_3) \in T$, then r_3 can be seen as the composition of r_1 and r_2.

3 Related Work

Distance Based Models. The distance based models evaluate the rationality of triples by the distance between entities. TransE interprets the relation as a translation vector r, and connect entities to achieve the balance of triple by r, i.e., $h + r \approx t$. TransE is effective, but it cannot encode symmetric relations and has problem in dealing with complex relations. After TransE, a series of models have been proposed to solve the problem, including TransR, TransD, TranSparse [13] and so on. These methods project the entities to specific relation hyperplanes or spaces first, and then use the method similar to TransE to translate projected entities with relation vectors. However, simple translation cannot make it obtain the ability to encode composition relations. In addition, the lack of its ability to capture features will be exposed in data set with poor context structure information.

Inspired by Euler's identity, RotatE interprets the relation as a rotation vector r in complex space, and rotates an entity into another to achieve the balance of triple, i.e., $h \circ r \approx t$. Although RotatE can encode multiple important relation patterns, it still faces challenge in encoding complex relations, and its performance on low connectivity knowledge graphs still needs to be improved. After RotatE, GC-OTE [14] proposes a method to enhance the ability of RotatE to encode complex relations by introducing graph context to entity embedding, but calculating graph context for entities brings huge amounts calculation costs. Different from RotatE, PairRE embeds the relation into a pair of vectors ($[r^H, r^T]$). r^H, r^T project the head and tail entities to Euclidean space respectively, i.e., $h \circ r^H \approx t \circ r^T$. In the case of rich context structure information, PairRE shows excellent modeling ability, which is able to encode key relation patterns and complex relations, but its ability of encoding will encounter challenges in low connectivity.

Semantic Matching Models. Semantic matching model exploit similarity-based scoring functions to measure the rationality of triples. According to the network structure, it can be divided into bilinear models and neural network models. Over time, new semantic matching models have emerged, such as RESCAL [15], DistMult [16], HolE [17], ComplEx [18] and QuatE [19], which constantly enhance the encoding ability of key relation patterns. However, these models will encounter challenges in encoding composition patterns [8].

When the embedding dimension satisfies, RESCAL, ComplEx and SimplE [20] are capable of representing the real triples. However, the embedding dimension is difficult to meet in reality. [21] has proved that, to achieve complete expressiveness, the embedding dimension should be greater than N/32, where N is the number of entities in dataset.

Neural networks based method, e.g., convolutional neural networks [22, 23], graph neural network [24, 25] achieve remarkable performances, which is as exciting as magic, but also makes them difficult to understand and analyze.

4   Methodology

In order to encode complex relations and key relation patterns better in knowledge graphs with poor context structure information, we propose a bidirectional model based on subject-object feature spaces. We employ three methods to enhance the encoding ability of the Bi2E: subject-object feature spaces, bidirectionality of relation, and adaptive γ.

4.1   Subject-Object Feature Spaces

Inspired by the relation between subject and object in philosophy, we believe that entities and relations are represented from two different perspectives, which are named as subject attribute and object attribute. Specifically, given a triple (h, r, t), we represent h, r, t as $[h^S, h^O]$, $[r^S, r^O]$ and $[t^S, t^O]$. h^S, h^O are the subject attribute and object attribute of h. Inspired by RotatE, we map h^S, t^S to the same Euclidean space, and we name it as the subject feature space; and h^O, t^O are mapped to another space, named as object feature space. Then we define the functional mapping induced by each relation r^S/r^O as an element-wise scaling from the head entity h^S/h^O to the tail entity t^S/t^O. We expect that

$$t^S = h^S \circ r^S,$$

$$t^O = h^O \circ r^O,$$

and $\circ$ is the Hadmard (or element-wise) product. Specifically, for each element in the embeddings, we have $t_i^S = h_i^S \circ r_i^S$.

4.2   Bidirectionality of Relation

We observe a property of the relation: $\forall r_f \in R$, if $(e_1, r_f, e_2) \in T$, then $\exists! r_r \in R$, making $(e_2, r_r, e_1) \in T$, i.e., r_r appears in pairs with r_f. In this paper, we name this property as **the bidirectionality of relation**. We employ this property to improve the utilization efficiency of data and find more semantic connections. The adjoint relation r_r of r_f can perceive more potential semantic connections from the opposite direction. Obviously, r_f and r_r are a pair of inverse relation, which means that Bi2E has the innate ability to encode the inverse relation. We represent r_f as $[r_f^S, r_f^O]$ and r_r as $[r_r^S, r_r^O]$.

When (h, r, t) holds, we expect in forward direction:

$$t^S = h^S \circ r_f^S,$$

$$t^O = h^O \circ r_f^O,$$

we expect in reverse direction:

$$h^S = t^S \circ r_r^S,$$

$$h^O = t^O \circ r_r^O.$$

To represent triples more realistically, we do not add too much constraints to entities and relations embedding, which enables them to adjust more flexibly. In this paper, we use L1-norm to measure the distance.

The distance in the forward direction subject-object feature space is defined as follows:

$$d_{r_f}^S \left(h^S, t^S \right) = h^S \circ r_f^S - t^S, \tag{1}$$

$$d_{r_f}^O \left(h^O, t^O \right) = h^O \circ r_f^O - t^O, \tag{2}$$

The distance in the reverse direction subject-object feature space is defined as follows:

$$d_{r_r}^S \left(h^S, t^S \right) = t^S \circ r_r^S - h^S, \tag{3}$$

$$d_{r_r}^O \left(h^O, t^O \right) = t^O \circ r_r^O - h^O. \tag{4}$$

The scoring function is defined as follows:

$$f_r(h, t) = d_{r_f}^S \left(h^S, t^S \right) + d_{r_f}^O \left(h^O, t^O \right) + d_{r_r}^S \left(h^S, t^S \right) + d_{r_r}^O \left(h^O, t^O \right). \tag{5}$$

Illustration of the proposed Bi2E is shown in Fig. 1. Compared with RotatE and PairRE, Bi2E's subject-object feature spaces have better flexibility to adjust the distributed representations of entities and the scaling ratio of relations, which plays an important role in low connectivity environment. As Fig. 1d shows, Bi2E learns and infers the relations between entities from two different directions, which makes it more likely to perceive some potential semantic connections.

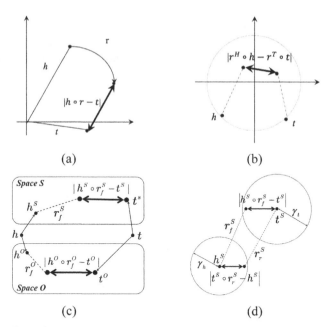

Fig. 1. Illustrations of RotatE, PairRE and Bi2E. (c) is the illustration of subject-object feature spaces in forward direction. (d) is the illustration of bidirectionality of relation in subject feature space. The illustrations of RotatE and PairRE are from [9].

4.3 Adaptive γ

We take a 1-to-N relation as an example to further illustrate the work of Bi2E. We set the embedding dimension to 1 for better illustration. Given triples $(h, r, ?)$, where the correct tail entities belong to set $S = \{t_1, t_2, \ldots, t_N\}$, Bi2E predicts tail entities by letting

$$f_r(h, t_i) = d_{r_f}^S\left(h^S, t_i^S\right) + d_{r_f}^O\left(h^O, t_i^O\right) + d_{r_r}^S\left(h^S, t_i^S\right) + d_{r_r}^O\left(h^O, t_i^O\right) < \gamma_i \qquad (6)$$

where γ_i is an adaptive margin for our distance based embedding model and $t_i \in S$. The previous methods use fixed γ to add constraints to the models so that the distance between different entities is at the same level, but that is contrary to reality. Such as the distance between the United States and China and the distance between California and Texas at the same level, which is obviously unreasonable. Bi2E employs adaptive γ to make each entity have an independent γ, which makes embedded representation more flexible and closer to the real world.

To illustrate our model concisely and clearly, we use $d_{r_f}^S\left(h^S, t_i^S\right)$ as $f_r(h, t_i)$, then Eq. 6 is expressed as

$$\|h^S \circ r_f^S - t_i^S\| < \gamma_i,$$

The value of t_i should stay in the following range:

$$t_i^S \in \left(h^S \circ r_f^S - \gamma_i, h^S \circ r_f^S + \gamma_i\right).$$

The above analysis shows Bi2E can adjust the value of γ to fit the entities in S. When the context structure information of the knowledge graph is sparse, the individual γ of each entity can flexibly adjust the distribution distance between entities using a small amount of feature information. For RotatE, fixed γ limits its ability to encode complex relations. When S has rich context structure information, PairRE can effectively encode complex relations. However, its ability of encoding will encounter challenges in low connectivity.

Meanwhile, Bi2E is capable of encoding several key relation patterns.

Lemma 1. Bi2E can infer the symmetry/antisymmetry pattern.

Proof. If $(e_1, r_1, e_2) \in T$ and $(e_2, r_1, e_1) \in T$, we have

$$\begin{cases} e_1^S \circ r_1^S = e_2^S \\ e_1^O \circ r_1^O = e_2^O \end{cases} \wedge \begin{cases} e_2^S \circ r_1^S = e_1^S \\ e_2^O \circ r_1^O = e_1^O \end{cases} \Rightarrow r_1^{S2} = r_1^{O2} = 1 \qquad (7)$$

if $(e_1, r_1, e_2) \in T$ and $(e_2, r_1, e_1) \notin T$, we have

$$\begin{cases} e_1^S \circ r_1^S = e_2^S \\ e_1^O \circ r_1^O = e_2^O \end{cases} \wedge \begin{cases} e_2^S \circ r_1^S \neq e_1^S \\ e_2^O \circ r_1^O \neq e_1^O \end{cases} \Rightarrow \begin{cases} r_1^{S2} \neq 1 \\ r_1^{O2} \neq 1 \end{cases} \qquad (8)$$

Lemma 2. Bi2E can infer the inversion pattern.

Proof. If $(e_1, r_1, e_2) \in T$ and $(e_2, r_2, e_1) \in T$, we have

$$\begin{cases} e_1^S \circ r_1^S = e_2^S \\ e_1^O \circ r_1^O = e_2^O \end{cases} \wedge \begin{cases} e_2^S \circ r_2^S = e_1^S \\ e_2^O \circ r_2^O = e_1^O \end{cases} \Rightarrow r_1^S \circ r_2^S = r_1^O \circ r_2^O = 1 \qquad (9)$$

Lemma 3. Bi2E can infer the composition pattern.

Proof. If $(e_1, r_1, e_2) \in T$, $(e_2, r_2, e_3) \in T$ and $(e_1, r_3, e_3) \in T$, we have

$$\begin{cases} e_1^S \circ r_1^S = e_2^S \\ e_1^O \circ r_1^O = e_2^O \end{cases} \wedge \begin{cases} e_2^S \circ r_2^S = e_3^S \\ e_2^O \circ r_2^O = e_3^O \end{cases} \wedge \begin{cases} e_1^S \circ r_3^S = e_3^S \\ e_1^O \circ r_3^O = e_3^O \end{cases}$$

$$\Rightarrow r_1^S \circ r_2^S \circ r_3^O = r_1^O \circ r_2^O \circ r_3^S = 1 \qquad (10)$$

4.4 Optimization

To optimize the model, we employ the self-adversarial negative sampling loss [8] as objective for training:

$$L = -\log\sigma(\gamma - f_r(h, t)) - \sum_{i=1}^{n} p\left(h_i', r, t_i'\right) \log\sigma\left(f_r\left(h_i', t_i'\right) - \gamma_i\right), \qquad (11)$$

where γ, γ_i are adaptive margin as we mentioned earlier and σ is the sigmoid function. (h_i', r, t_i') is the ith negative triple and $p\left(h_i', r, t_i'\right)$ represents the weight of this negative sample. $p\left(h_i', r, t_i'\right)$ is defined as follows:

$$p\left(\left(h_i', r, t_i'\right) | (h, r, t)\right) = \frac{exp\alpha f_r\left(h_i', t_i'\right)}{\sum_j exp\alpha f_r\left(h_j', t_j'\right)}. \qquad (12)$$

5   Experimental Results

5.1   Experimental Setting

Dataset. Three commonly used benchmark datasets are employed to evaluate the performance of Bi2E on link prediction. WN18RR [22] is derived from WN18 [7], which is a subset of WordNet. Since some drawbacks, such as information leakage [26], WN18RR is more persuasive than WN18 when evaluating the encoding ability of model. YAGO3-10 is a subset of YAGO3 [27]. Most triples are descriptions of human attributes. FB15k-237 [28] is a knowledge graph containing general world knowledge with high connectivity.

Table 1. Statistics of datasets.

Dataset	WN18RR	YAGO3-10	FB15k-237
Entities	40,943	123,182	14,541
Relations	11	37	237
Train Edges	86,835	1,079,040	272,115
Valid Edges	3,034	5,000	17,535
Test Edges	3,134	5,000	20,466
Epe	2.1	8.8	18.7

The statistics of three datasets are summarized at Table 1. Each dataset is split into three sets for: training, validation and testing, which are same with the setting of [8]. WN18RR is a low connectivity knowledge graph dataset with epe is 2.1; Compared with WN18RR, YAGO3-10 is a larger dataset with better connectivity (epe is 8.8); FB15k-237 represents the knowledge graph with rich context structure information (epe is 18.7).

Evaluation Protocol. Following the evaluation protocol in [8, 22], we test the triples in two scenarios: head focused $(?, r, t)$ and tail focused $(h, r, ?)$. We evaluate the ranking of each possible entity in the test triple. Five evaluation metrics, including Mean Rank (MR), the Mean Reciprocal Rank (MRR) and top 1, 3, 10 (Hits@1, Hits@3 and Hits@10).

Implementation. We implement our model based on the implementation of RotatE [8]. Our model is implemented by PyTorch and runs on a NVIDIA RTX-3090. Bi2E takes 2 h with 120,000 steps on WN18RR, 4.5 h with 150,000 steps on YAGO3-10 and 5 h with 120,000 steps on FB15k-237. Our code is available at: https://github.com/iiilannn9527/Bi2E.

We use Adam [29] as the optimizer and finetune the hyperparameters on the validation dataset. The ranges of the hyper-parameters for the grid search are set as follows: embedding dimension $k \in \{200, 500, 1000, 1500\}$, batch size $b \in \{256, 512, 1024\}$, self-adversarial sampling temperature $\alpha \in \{0.5, 0.75, 1.0, 1.25, 1.5\}$, negative sample size $n \in \{128, 200, 256, 400, 512, 800, 1024\}$ and initial adaptive margin $\gamma \in \{2.5, 5, 7.5, 10, 15, 20, 24, 28, 32\}$.

We list the best hyperparameter setting of Bi2E w.r.t the test dataset on several benchmarks in Table 2.

Table 2. The best hyperparameter setting of Bi2E on WN18RR, YAGO3-10 and FB15k-237.

Benchmark	k	b	n	α	γ
WN18RR	500	512	512	1.5	2.5
YAGO3-10	500	1024	400	0.5	24
FB15k-237	1500	1024	256	1.25	7.5

5.2 Main Results

Since our model shares the same hyper-parameter settings and implementation with RotatE [8] and PairRE [9], comparing with them is necessary and fair. In addition, there are several leading models involved in the comparison, including distance based TransE [7]; Semantic matching based DistMult [16], ComplEx [18], PROCRUSTEs [30]; Convolutional neural network based ConvE [22], InteraceE [23] and graph neural network based SACN [24], CompGCN [25]. Table 3 compares the performance of Bi2E and several state-of-the-art models on WN18RR, YAGO3-10 and FB15k-237.

From Table 3, we observe that:

1. On YAGO3-10, Bi2E achieves state-of-the-art performance. On WN18RR, Bi2E outperforms all other models on MR, MRR and Hist@10 metrics. Especially on MR metric of two datasets, Bi2E improves at least **10%** compared with other leading methods, which means that Bi2E has a significant progress in the overall representation of low connectivity knowledge graph;
2. With the same number of parameters, **Bi2E outperforms RotatE on all metrics**. These results show the effectiveness of the proposed Bi2E for the task of predicting missing links in knowledge graph.
3. Compared with other leading methods, Bi2E also shows highly competitive performance on FB15k-237;

In addition, compared with other models, Bi2E has more obvious improvement on low connectivity WN18RR and YAGO3-10 than on FB15k-237, which demonstrates the effectiveness of Bi2E in low connectivity knowledge graphs. FB15k-237 has rich context structure information, which makes learn complex relations and relation patterns easier. However, the feature information on WN18RR and YAGO3-10 is not easy to obtain. Bi2E improves the efficiency of utilizing data to capture more feature information, and uses limited feature information to learn and infer the relations between entities efficiently.

Table 3. Link prediction results on WN18RR, YAGO3-10 and FB15k-237. Results of TransE, DistMult, ComplEx and ConvE are taken from [8, 31]. Other results are taken from the corresponding papers. Best results are in bold.

Model	WN18RR					YAGO3-10					FB15k-237				
	MR	MRR	Hits@1	Hits@3	Hits@10	MR	MRR	Hits@1	Hits@3	Hits@10	MR	MRR	Hits@1	Hits@3	Hits@10
TransE	3384	.226	–	–	.501	–	–	–	–	–	357	.294	–	–	.465
DistMult	5110	.430	.390	.440	.490	5926	.34	.24	.38	.54	254	.241	.155	.263	.419
ComplEx	5261	.440	.410	.460	.510	6351	.36	.26	.40	.55	339	.247	.158	.275	.428
ConvE	4187	.430	.400	.440	.520	1671	.44	.35	.49	.62	244	.325	.237	.356	.501
InteraceE	5202	.463	.430	–	.528	2375	.541	.462	–	.687	172	.354	.263	–	.535
PROCRUSTEs	–	.474	.421	**.502**	.569	–	–	–	–	–	–	.345	.249	.379	.541
SACN	–	.470	.430	.480	.540	–	–	–	–	–	–	.350	.260	**.390**	.540
CompGCN	3533	.479	**.443**	.494	.546	–	–	–	–	–	197	**.355**	**.264**	**.390**	.535
PairRE	–	–	–	–	–	–	–	–	–	–	**160**	.351	.256	.387	**.544**
RotatE	3340	.476	.428	.492	.571	1767	.495	.402	.550	.670	177	.338	.241	.375	.533
Bi2E	**2978**	**.480**	.432	.498	**.574**	**1496**	**.550**	**.468**	**.603**	**.697**	169	.346	.249	.384	**.544**

5.3   Further Experiments of Bi2E Under Low Connectivity

We make further experiments to explore three sources of model enhancement: bidirectionality of relation, subject-object feature spaces and adaptive γ.

Analysis on Bidirectionality of Relation. We further validate the role of modeling by bidirectionality of relation. In this group of experiments, we employ single forward relation to replace the two-way relations in Bi2E and name it Si2E. All experiment settings remain the same, and the embedding dimension is 500. The experimental results on WN18RR are summarized in Table 4.

Table 4. Comparison of Link Prediction Results between Bi2E and Si2E on WN18RR.

–	WN18RR				
Model	MR	MRR	Hits@1	Hits@3	Hits@10
Si2E	4489	.450	.396	.473	.551
Bi2E	**2978**	**.480**	**.432**	**.498**	**.574**

From Table 4 we can easily conclude that bidirectional Bi2E has a breakthrough in encoding capacity compared to Si2E. These significant improvements verify the effectiveness of modeling by bidirectionality of relation. We analyze the reasons:

1. The utilization efficiency of bidirectional model for each triple is higher than unidirectional model, which means that Bi2E can capture more feature information in low connectivity;
2. Bi2E is modeled from both forward and reverse directions to discover more potential semantic links that are not easily found in the unidirectional model, which enhances the ability to learn and infer implicit relations.

Analysis on Subject-Object Feature Spaces. To verify the effectiveness of modeling in the subject-object feature spaces, we project entities and relations into one space and four spaces, and name them Bi1E and Bi4E. We set γ as the fixed value, and other settings remain the same. The embedding dimension is 500, and the experimental results on WN18RR are shown in Table 5.

It can be clearly seen from Table 5 that Bi2E is superior to Bi1E on all metrics, with the increase of 6.1% on MR and about 2% on other metrics. Compared with BI2E, BI4E has no significant improvement with doubling the number of parameters. These verify that, Bi2E is effective and efficient for the task of predicting missing links in low connectivity knowledge graph by introducing the subject-object feature spaces. Bi2E benefits from projecting entities and relations into different spaces, which enables it to capture more feature information and makes the embedded representation of knowledge graph closer to reality.

Table 5. Link prediction results of Bi1E, Bi2E and Bi4E on WN18RR.

–	WN18RR				
Model	MR	MRR	Hits@1	Hits@3	Hits@10
Bi1E	3366	.467	.420	.483	.562
Bi2E	3160	.476	.428	**.493**	**.572**
Bi4E	**3101**	**.478**	**.429**	.493	.570

Analysis on Adaptive γ. We further explore the influence of adaptive γ. Except the different modes of γ, the experiments share the same hyper-parameters. The experimental results on WN18RR and FB15k-237 are shown in Table 6.

Table 6. Comparison between different modes of γ on WN18RR and FB15k-237.

	WN18RR					FB15k-237				
Mode	MR	MRR	Hits@1	Hits@3	Hits@10	MR	MRR	Hits@1	Hits@3	Hits@10
Fixed γ	3160	.476	.428	.493	.572	**169**	**.346**	**.249**	**.384**	**.544**
Adaptive γ	**2978**	**.481**	**.433**	**.498**	**.574**	170	.345	**.249**	.383	.543

As shown in Table 6: compared with fixed γ, adaptive γ effectively improves the encoding ability of the model on the WN18RR. However, there is only a slight gap on FB15k-237.

We believe that in the knowledge graph with rich context structure information, such as FB15k-237, the embedding models are able to capture abundant feature information, and the saturated feature information can be used to well infer the relation patterns and complex relations. At this time, the effect of adaptive γ will be weakened. When the feature information is sparse, adaptive γ will use a small amount of feature information to infer the implicit relations. These indicate that adaptive γ is effective in low connectivity.

We instantiate some examples of adaptive γ, which are shown in Fig. 2. It can be seen that entities with larger semantic scope have larger γ, which is obviously consistent with our cognitive understanding.

5.4 Analysis on Complex Relations

We analyze the performance of Bi2E in dealing with complex relations on WN18RR, and the experimental results are summarized in Table 7. For comparison, we also test the ability of TransE, RotatE and PairRE to handle complex relations on WN18RR, and all experiments are carried out in accordance with [8] under the same experimental settings.

It is easy to observe that Bi2E performs well in the N-to-1 and N-to-N relation. Especially in the N-to-1 relation, Bi2E significantly leads other models. Bi2E improves MR

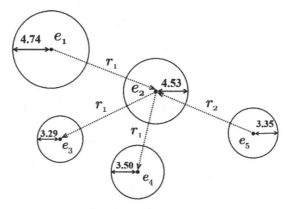

Fig. 2. Illustration of adaptive γ.

Table 7. Experimental results on WN18RR by relation category. All experiments followed the settings in RotatE.

–	WN18RR(Hits@10)				WN18RR(MR)			
Model	1-to-1	1-to-N	N-to-1	N-to-N	1-to-1	1-to-N	N-to-1	N-to-N
TransE	**0.976**	0.391	0.251	0.952	29.1	**1819.1**	6272.2	165.8
RotatE	**0.976**	**0.424**	0.322	0.960	28.8	1848.9	6128.2	157.1
PairRE	**0.976**	0.374	0.295	0.955	32.0	2206.2	5752.8	278.3
Bi2E	**0.976**	0.420	**0.330**	**0.961**	**25.4**	1828.9	**5454.6**	**155.4**

by **11%** compared with RotatE. On other metrics, Bi2E maintains high competitiveness. All these show that Bi2E can effectively encode complex relations in low connectivity.

5.5 Analysis on Relation Patterns

To verify whether Bi2E can implicitly represent relation patterns in knowledge graph, we visualize some examples of different relation patterns. The learned relation embedding histogram is shown in Fig. 3. The embedding dimension of relations in these examples is 1000. Since there is no inverse pattern in WN18RR, YAGO3-10 and FB15k-237, we also test some relations in WN18.

Symmetry/Antisymmetry. Figure 3a shows a symmetry relation _derivationally_-related_form in WN18RR. For Bi2E, symmetry relation can be encoded when r satisfies $r_1^{S2} = r_1^{O2} = 1$. Figure 3a and Fig. 3b indicate that the absolute values of most elements in r_1^S and r_1^O are 1. Figure 3c shows an antisymmetry relation _hypernym in WN18. We can see from Fig. 3c and Fig. 3d that the absolute values of most elements of r_2^S and r_2^O are not 1, indicating that Bi2E can implicitly infer antisymmetry relation.

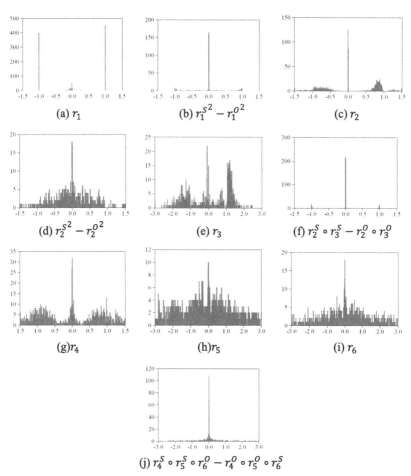

Fig. 3. Histograms of relation embeddings for different relation patterns. r_1 is relation _derivationally_related_form. r_2 is relation _hypernym. r_3 is relation _hyponym. r_4 is relation award_nominee/award_nominations./award/award_nomination/nominated_for. r_5 is relation award_category/winners./award/award_honor/award_winner. r_6 is relation award_category/nominees./award/award_nomination/nominated_for.

Inverse. Figure 3c and Fig. 3e show a pair of inverse relations _hypernym(r_2) and _hyponym(r_3) in WN18. It can be seen from Fig. 3f that the paired relations are very close to satisfy $r_2^S \circ r_3^S = r_2^O \circ r_3^O = 1$.

Composition. Figure 3g, 3h, 3i show a set of composition relation in FB15k-237. The third relation r_6 can be regarded as the combination of the first relation r_4 and the second relation r_5. Figure 3j shows that these three relations satisfy $r_4^S \circ r_5^S \circ r_6^O = r_4^O \circ r_5^O \circ r_6^S = 1$.

6   Conclusion

To represent the knowledge graph with poor context structure information more effectively, we propose Bi2E, which employs the bidirectionality of relation and the subject-object feature spaces to improve the efficiency of data utilization and perceive more potential semantic links. Bi2E utilizes adaptive γ to flexibly adjust the embedding distribution between entities. In addition to various complex relations, Bi2E can also encode four key relation patterns in low connectivity. Bi2E achieves state-of-the-art results on the low connectivity knowledge graph benchmarks. In addition, further experiments verify the effectiveness of the methods proposed in Bi2E.

References

1. Miller, G.A.: Wordnet: a lexical database for English. Commun. ACM **38**(11), 39–41 (1995)
2. Bollacker, K., Evans, C., Paritosh, P., Sturge, T., Taylor, J.: Freebase: a collaboratively created graph database for structuring human knowledge. In: Proceedings of the 2008 ACM SIGMOD International Conference on Management of Data, pp. 1247–1250 (2008)
3. Suchanek, F.M., Kasneci, G., Weikum, G.: Yago: a core of semantic knowledge. In: Proceedings of the 16th International Conference on World Wide Web, pp. 697–706. ACM (2007)
4. Bordes, A., Weston, J., Usunier, N.: Open question answering with weakly supervised embedding models. In: Calders, T., Esposito, F., Hüllermeier, E., Meo, R. (eds.) ECML PKDD 2014. LNCS (LNAI), vol. 8724, pp. 165–180. Springer, Heidelberg (2014). https://doi.org/10.1007/978-3-662-44848-9_11
5. Zhang, F., Yuan, N.J., Lian, D., Xie, X., Ma, W.-Y.: Collaborative knowledge base embedding for recommender systems. In: Proceedings of the 22nd ACM SIGKDD International Conference on Knowledge Discovery and Data Mining, pp. 353–362. ACM (2016)
6. Yang, B., Mitchell, T.: Leveraging knowledge bases in LSTMS for improving machine reading. In: Proceedings of the 55th Annual Meeting of the Association for Computational Linguistics (Volume 1: Long Papers), vol. 1, pp. 1436–1446 (2017)
7. Bordes, A., Usunier, N., Garcia-Duran, A., Weston, J., Yakhnenko, O.: Translating embeddings for modeling multi-relational data. In: Advances in Neural Information Processing Systems, pp. 2787–2795 (2013)
8. Sun, Z., Deng, Z.-H., Nie, J.-Y., Tang, J.: Rotate: knowledge graph embedding by relational rotation in complex space. arXiv preprint arXiv:1902.10197 (2019)
9. Teo, T.W., Choy, B.H.: In: Tan, O.S., Low, E.L., Tay, E.G., Yan, Y.K. (eds.) Singapore Math and Science Education Innovation. ETLPPSIP, vol. 1, pp. 43–59. Springer, Singapore (2021). https://doi.org/10.1007/978-981-16-1357-9_3
10. Lin, Y., Liu, Z., Sun, M., Liu, Y., Zhu, X.: Learning entity and relation embeddings for knowledge graph completion. In: Twenty-Ninth AAAI Conference on Artificial Intelligence (2015)
11. Ji, G., He, S., Xu, L., Liu, K., Zhao, J.: Knowledge graph embedding via dynamic mapping matrix. In: Proceedings of the 53rd Annual Meeting of the Association for Computational Linguistics and the 7th International Joint Conference on Natural Language Processing (Volume 1: Long Papers), pp. 687–696 (2015)
12. Wang, Z., Zhang, J., Feng, J., Chen, Z.. Knowledge graph embedding by translating on hyperplanes. In: Twenty-Eighth AAAI Conference on Artificial Intelligence (2014)
13. Ji, G., Liu, K., He, S., Zhao, J.: Knowledge graph completion with adaptive sparse transfer matrix. AAAI **16**, 985–991 (2016)

14. Tang, Y., Huang, J., Wang, G., He, X., Zhou, B.: Orthogonal relation transforms with graph context modeling for knowledge graph embedding. In: Proceedings of the 58th Annual Meeting of the Association for Computational Linguistics (2019)
15. Nickel, M., Tresp, V., Kriegel, H.-P.: A three-way model for collective learning on multi-relational data. ICML **11**, 809–816 (2011)
16. Yang, B., Yih, W., He, X., Gao, J., Deng, L.: Embedding entities and relations for learning and inference in knowledge bases. arXiv preprint arXiv:1412.6575 (2014)
17. Nickel, M., Rosasco, L., Poggio, T.: Holographic embeddings of knowledge graphs. In: Thirtieth AAAI Conference on Artificial Intelligence (2016)
18. Trouillon, T., Welbl, J., Riedel, S., Gaussier, É., Bouchard, G.: Complex embeddings for simple link prediction. In: International Conference on Machine Learning, pp. 2071–2080 (2016)
19. Zhang, S., Tay, Y., Yao, L., Liu, Q.: Quaternion knowledge graph embedding. arXiv preprint arXiv:1904.10281 (2019)
20. Kazemi, S.M., Poole, D.: Simple embedding for link prediction in knowledge graphs. In: Advances in Neural Information Processing Systems, pp. 4284–4295 (2018)
21. Wang, Y., Gemulla, R., Li, H.: On multi-relational link prediction with bilinear models (2018)
22. Dettmers, T., Minervini, P., Stenetorp, P., Riedel, S.: Convolutional 2D knowledge graph embeddings. In: Thirty-Second AAAI Conference on Artificial Intelligence (2018)
23. Vashishth, S., Sanyal, S., Nitin, V., Agrawal, N., Talukdar, P.: Interacte: improving convolution-based knowledge graph embeddings by increasing feature interactions. In: Proceedings of the AAAI Conference on Artificial Intelligence (2020)
24. Shang, C., Tang, Y., Huang, J., Bi, J., He, X., Zhou, B.: End-to-end structure-aware convolutional networks for knowledge base completion. In: Proceedings of the AAAI Conference on Artificial Intelligence (2019)
25. Vashishth, S., Sanyal, S., Nitin, V., Talukdar, P.: Composition-based multi-relational graph convolutional networks. In: 8th International Conference on Learning Representations (2020)
26. Akrami, F., Saeef, M.S., Zhang, Q., Hu, W., Li, C.: Realistic re-evaluation of knowledge graph completion methods: an experimental study. In: Proceedings of the 2020 ACM SIGMOD International Conference on Management of Data (2020)
27. Mahdisoltani, F., Biega, J., Suchanek, F.M. Yago3: a knowledge base from multilingual wikipedias. In: CIDR (2015)
28. Toutanova, K., Chen, D.: Observed versus latent features for knowledge base and text inference. In: Proceedings of the 3rd Workshop on Continuous Vector Space Models and their Compositionality, pp. 57–66 (2015)
29. Kingma, D.P., Ba, J.: Adam: a method for stochastic optimization. arXiv preprint arXiv:1412.6980 (2014)
30. Peng, X., Chen, G., Lin, C., Stevenson, M.: Highly efficient knowledge graph embedding learning with orthogonal procrustes analysis. In: Proceedings of the 2021 Conference of the North American Chapter of the Association for Computational Linguistics: Human Language Technologies (2021)
31. Kadlec, R., Bajgar, O., Kleindienst, J.: Knowledge base completion: baselines strike back. arXiv preprint arXiv:1705.10744 (2017)

Relevance-Based Big Data Exploration for Smart Road Maintenance

Devis Bianchini, Valeria De Antonellis, and Massimiliano Garda[✉]

Department of Information Engineering, University of Brescia,Via Branze 38,
25123 Brescia, Italy
{devis.bianchini,valeria.deantonellis,massimiliano.garda}@unibs.it

Abstract. In the latest years, the progressive digitalisation of Smart City ecosystems has fuelled an increasing availability of data from sensor networks, which is considered as a valuable asset for improving mobility resilience. In particular, data coming from sensors in vehicles can be leveraged to obtain useful information about the quality of the area-wide road surface in near real-time, and may be used by road maintainers to focus monitoring and maintenance activities on urban and public infrastructure. To bring such application scenario into the field, road maintainers should be equipped with valuable tools to gain insights from the data and ensure a safer and more efficient infrastructure. In this paper, we present a methodological approach, based on big data exploration techniques, applied to support road maintainers in analysing and assessing surface conditions of roads. Specifically, the proposed approach is grounded on three components: (i) a multi-dimensional model, apt to represent the road network and to enable data exploration; (ii) data summarisation techniques, in order to simplify overall view over high volumes of data collected by vehicles; (iii) a measure of relevance, aimed at focusing the attention of the maintainers on relevant data only. The paper illustrates the design and implementation of multiple exploration scenarios on top of the three components and their implementation and preliminary evaluation in an ongoing research project on sustainable and resilient mobility.

Keywords: Multi-dimensional model · Data summarisation · Big data exploration · Sustainable and resilient mobility

1 Introduction

In the landscape of the economic growth of the latest years, data has become an intangible asset for worldwide Smart Cities, which are progressively transforming into data-driven ecosystems. In particular, the increasing availability of data has paved the way to new methods and tools that address business problems that would not have been possible to tackle so far [1,9]. Nowadays, smart mobility is being affected by tremendous changes, taking advantage from big data generated with sensor networks and IoT devices to improve the organisation of the city

© The Author(s), under exclusive license to Springer Nature Switzerland AG 2022
M. Sellami et al. (Eds.): CoopIS 2022, LNCS 13591, pp. 19–36, 2022.
https://doi.org/10.1007/978-3-031-17834-4_2

and the transportation logistics [11]. Through such data, issues that can arise may be promptly noticed and tackled, enhancing the quality and the efficiency of services delivered to users [5]. For instance, data coming from sensors in vehicles can be leveraged to obtain in near real-time useful information about the quality of the area-wide road surface and may be used by road maintainers to focus monitoring and maintenance activities on urban and public infrastructure, for enhancing mobility resilience. In this landscape, road maintainers should be equipped with valuable tools to gain insights from the data and ensure a safer and more efficient infrastructure. Nevertheless, the variety and volume of collected data call for models, tools and methods for data representation and exploration [6]. In this paper, we present a methodological approach, based on big data exploration techniques, to support road maintainers in analysing and assessing surface conditions of roads. The proposed approach has been defined in the scope of the MoSoRe project[1] (Italian acronym for "Mobilità Sostenibile e Resiliente"), whose aim is to investigate the resilience of mobility systems and infrastructure in the city of Brescia (Italy). The approach is grounded on three components defined in [3], specifically conceived to support exploration of massive data streams: (i) *data summarisation techniques*, based on incremental clustering, to provide a synthetic view over massive data streams, which evolve over time; (ii) a *multi-dimensional model*, apt to organise data streams with respect to multiple exploration facets; (iii) a *measure of relevance*, aimed at focusing the explorers' attention on portions of the data streams that present substantial changes over time (e.g., to plan corrective actions).

The contribution of this paper is three-fold: (a) the aforementioned big data exploration components have been declined, with respect to [3], in the context of sustainable and resilient mobility, where data streams are collected through accelerometers to let road maintainers monitor road surface conditions and are organised according to a multi-dimensional model, based on distinguishing features such as the type of the road, area/district, mileage extent; (b) multiple *exploration scenarios* have been defined on top of the components, representing different challenges in road surface monitoring, and employed as the main pillars of a multi-step exploration methodology to assist road maintainers in mobility data exploration; (c) exploration scenarios have been implemented and a preliminary evaluation has been performed within the MoSoRe project. Noteworthy, the definition of scenarios and the exploration methodology are conceived to be general enough to be applied in any application context permeated by the presence of big data.

The remainder of the paper is organised as follows: in Sect. 2 the application context and research challenges are introduced; Sect. 3 presents the multi-dimensional model, data summarisation techniques and the relevance evaluation metric. Exploration scenarios are formalised in Sect. 4, whereas the exploration methodology based on them is illustrated in Sect. 5. Section 6 describes implementation and experimental evaluation. Related work and novel contributions

---

[1] Funded by Lombardy Region (Italy), POR FESR 2014-2020.

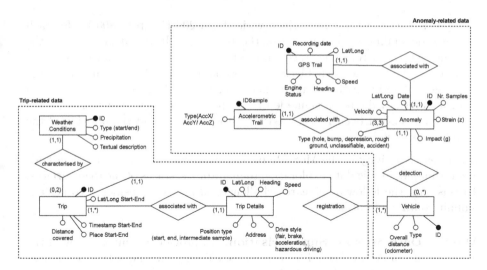

Fig. 1. E-R model for monitoring road surface conditions (only meaningful attributes are displayed).

with respect to the literature are discussed in Sect. 7. Finally, Sect. 8 closes the paper, sketching future research directions.

2 Application Domain and Research Challenges

In the MoSoRe project, a fleet of commercial vehicles has been equipped with black boxes, gathering data when vehicles transit on specific *road portions* (i.e., delimited sections of roads covered during daily trips). Collected data regards both contextual information (e.g., details of the journey, weather conditions) and measures of accelerometers over the X, Y and Z axes, which can be used to infer road surface conditions. Collected data is represented through the conceptual model in Fig. 1 and grouped as follows:

- *Trip-related data* regards the journeys accomplished by vehicles during the monitored period (at the time of writing, data is transferred from vehicles on a daily basis); the trip is described through the GPS coordinates of start and end position, the timestamp in which the vehicle was positioned at the beginning/ending of the trip, the covered distance; trip details are collected by the black box at the beginning/ending of the trip, twice per kilometre and when some driving events occur (e.g., burst of speed, hard braking); moreover, also weather conditions for the start/end place are registered;
- *Anomaly-related data* concerns anomalies recorded by the black box of a vehicle; for privacy preservation issues, only few characteristics of the vehicle are recorded (e.g., the type, to denote either a private or a commercial vehicle), but they cannot be used to infer any information regarding the owner; for each anomalous event, the black box collects data from the accelerometers

on X-Y-Z axes, with a rate which varies from 200 Hz up to 800 Hz for each trace, depending on the model of the black box; hence, depending on the frequency, accelerometric traces from different vehicles may have a different number of samples; each black box assigns a probabilistic estimate to the cause that induced the event (either hole, bump, depression, rough ground or undetermined – not assignable to any specific category); noteworthy, upon anomalous event occurrence, a GPS trail is recorded and the position of the vehicle is sampled.

Our research activity in the MoSoRe project concerns the definition of methods and techniques for big data exploration to monitor the status of the road surfaces. To this aim, the following research challenges have been considered to achieve mobility data exploration.

Massive Data Streams Summarisation. To provide a compact view of the huge amount of data collected from vehicles, efficient summarisation techniques are advocated, thus enabling vehicles data to be observed in an aggregated way. Indeed, monitoring each single data record may be neither relevant, due to the high level of noise introduced by vehicles black boxes accelerometers (i.e., slight variations in the measured variables) nor feasible, due to the high data generation rates (which depend on the model of the black box as explained before) and, generally, on the dynamic nature of the application domain, which compels data aggregations to be observed on the fly.

Multi-dimensional Exploration of Data Streams. Data collected from vehicles may be explored according to different perspectives, identifying homogeneous portions of the road network upon which the data analysis must be focused on. This allows to cope with the complexity and the variety of the domain (the city road network is conceived as a composition of several road portions, with different spatial extensions, types, travel frequency, etc.) and to consider the different importance of portions characteristics for road maintainers (for instance, road maintainers may be more interested in analysing portions of the road network prone to high congestion levels).

Multi-perspective Exploration Scenarios. Road maintainers, depending on their expertise, may pursue different goals while exploring vehicles data to assure mobility resilience. For instance, common issues tackled by road maintainers could be: (i) monitoring the evolution of an anomalous event over time; (ii) comparing anomalous events of the same type, thus establishing a severity order among them; (iii) estimating the type of an undetermined event by assessing its similarity with respect to the known typologies. Depending on the goal, road maintainers should be suggested with the exploration of relevant data only, to enable the management of critical situations. Hence, relevance evaluation techniques are required, to ensure both the identification of relevant data and its exploration at the proper level of granularity, complying with road maintainers' objectives.

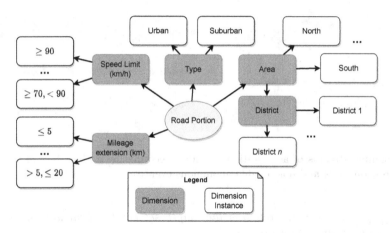

Fig. 2. Example of dimensions and corresponding instances from the MDM for exploration of vehicles data.

3 The Ingredients of the Big Data Exploration Approach

In this section, we briefly report the three building blocks of the big data exploration approach fostered in the MoSoRe project to let road maintainers monitor the status of the road surfaces and plan corrective actions, coping with variety, velocity and volume of anomaly-related data.

3.1 Multi-dimensional Model

The proposed Multi-Dimensional Model (in brief, MDM) is grounded on the definitions of *dimension* and *exploration facet*. With respect to the general formulation given in [3], one of the contributions in this paper has been the design of a MDM to organise and explore vehicles data, as shown in Fig. 2.

Definition 1 (Dimension). *A dimension d_i is an entity representing a single characteristic of a road portion (e.g., category, maximum speed limit, mileage extension) defined on a categorical domain $Dom(d_i)$. We denote with $\mathcal{D} = \{d_1, \ldots, d_p\}$ the finite set of dimensions. An instance $v_{d_i}^j$ of $d_i \in \mathcal{D}$ is a categorical or range value, belonging to the domain of d_i, that is, $v_{d_i}^j \in Dom(d_i)$, $\forall i = 1, \ldots, p$ and $\forall j = 1, \ldots, |Dom(d_i)|$. Dimensions with categorical values are organised into hierarchies $\{h_1, \ldots, h_m\}$ and each hierarchy is described with: (i) a subset of dimensions $Dim(h_k) \subseteq \mathcal{D}$, $\forall k = 1, \ldots, m$; (ii) a total order $\succeq_{h_k}$ over the set of dimensions.*

Definition 2 (Exploration facet). *An exploration facet ϕ_i (or, abbreviated, facet) is a combination of instances, belonging to different dimensions, apt to identify road portions with homogeneous characteristics. Let $\Phi = \{\phi_1, \ldots, \phi_k\}$ be the set of available facets. The cardinality of the set Φ, denoted as $|\Phi|$, spans over all the possible combinations of dimension instances ($|\Phi| \leq 2^N - 1$, where*

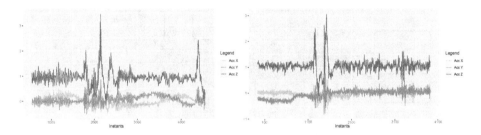

Fig. 3. Sample streams of acceleration measures recorded by a black box in the case of a depression (left) and hole (right) anomalous event.

$N = \sum_{i=1...p} |Dom(d_i)|$, *excluding the empty set combination and, generally, non combinable dimension instances).*

Example. Considering the dimensions and the corresponding instances reported in Fig. 2, an example of facet $\hat{\phi} \in \Phi$ may contain instances of the following four dimensions: { *Type, SpeedLimit, District, MileageExtension* }. For $\hat{\phi}$, *Type* = Urban and *District* = District1 are sample dimension instances. With reference to the figure, *Area* and *District* are two dimensions included in the hierarchy h_1 so that $Dim(h_1) = \{ALL, Area, District\}$ and $District \succeq_{h_1} Area \succeq_{h_1} ALL$ holds, where *ALL* denotes the coarsest aggregation level. Other hierarchies are h_2 ($Dim(h_2) = \{ALL, Type\}$), h_3 ($Dim(h_3) = \{ALL, SpeedLimit\}$) and h_4 ($Dim(h_4) = \{ALL, MileageExtension\}$).

Physical quantities recorded by black boxes on vehicles are referred to as *features*, whereas the values associated with features are denoted as *measures*. A feature f_i is a measurable quantity described by a name and a unit of measure (if any). Let $\mathcal{F} = \{f_1, \ldots, f_d\}$ be the overall set of measurable features. A measure is a scalar value for the feature $f_i \in \mathcal{F}$, expressed in terms of the unit of measure and the timestamp t, that represents the instant in which the measure has been collected. Measures are conceived as a data stream and are associated with specific road portions in the MDM. In the MoSoRe project, measures collected by each black box are values of X-Y-Z gravity accelerations and are provided as already classified with respect to a possible event associated with that stream, such as hole, bump, depression, rough ground. Figure 3 reports two examples of streams corresponding to the detection of a depression and hole event.

3.2 Clustering-Based Data Summarisation

Once focusing the attention on a specific facet, gathering road portions with homogeneous characteristics, the stream of records from a single black box can be used to ascertain whether road surface conditions are diverging from reference values. To obtain an effective representation of the temporal evolution of a road surface conditions, data summarisation based on an incremental clustering algorithm is applied. The algorithm has been described in [3] and is briefly sketched in the following. The algorithm takes as input the stream of measures related to the observed features and, at a given time t, produces as output a set of syntheses $\mathcal{S}(t)$, where each synthesis corresponds to a cluster of records that are close each other according to distance between measures. For a given road portion, the set $\mathcal{S}(t)$ is built considering records collected from timestamp $t - \Delta t$ to timestamp t and the previous set of syntheses $\mathcal{S}(t - \Delta t)$ through the assignment of records to existing syntheses, creation of new syntheses, merging/removal of existing ones. Roughly speaking, syntheses conceptually represent a specific state in the status of a road surface conditions. A set of syntheses at a given timestamp t corresponds to a *snapshot*, that is, a "picture" of the status of the road portion at time t, defined as follows.

Definition 3 (Snapshot). *A snapshot $SN_i(t)$, stored at time t, is defined as the following tuple:*

$$SN_i(t) = \langle \mathcal{S}_i(t), F_{SN_i}, \phi_i, \epsilon_{SN_i}, ID_{\epsilon_{SN_i}} \rangle \tag{1}$$

where: (i) $\mathcal{S}_i(t)$ is the set of syntheses generated at time t, (ii) F_{SN_i} is the set of the monitored features; (iii) ϕ_i is the facet that identifies the road portion; (iv) ϵ_{SN_i} is the type of anomalous event the snapshot refers to (i.e., either hole, bump, rough ground, depression, undetermined event); (v) $ID_{\epsilon_{SN_i}}$ is the identifier of the anomalous event as assigned by the black box of a vehicle.

Figure 4 shows the set of syntheses in two snapshots taken at time $t_1 + \Delta t$ and $t_1 + 2\Delta t$, where measured features are X-Z accelerations and the type of triggering event is *hole* (the identifier of the event is the same for both the snapshots). Specifically, syntheses refer to a road portion identified through a facet that groups urban roads in city downtown. From Fig. 4(a) to Fig. 4(b) changes in the two snapshots are evident. In fact, the set of syntheses moves towards higher values of Z axis acceleration, that physically corresponds to the identification of a hole on the road surface.

3.3   Identification of Relevant Data

Given two snapshots $SN_i(t_1)$ and $SN_j(t_2)$ (with $i \neq j$ and $t_2 > t_1$), changes between syntheses in the two snapshots are apt to identify *relevant data*, which can be proposed to road maintainers to start the exploration from. In particular, the measure of relevance is based on the notion of *distance* between snapshots formalised in [3] and reported in the following.

Definition 4 (Distance between snapshots). *The distance between two snapshots SN_i and SN_j is based on the sets $\mathcal{S}_i$ and $\mathcal{S}_j$ of syntheses in the two snapshots (containing n and m syntheses, respectively, where n and m do not necessarily coincide):*

$$d_{SN}(SN_i, SN_j) = \frac{\sum_{s_h \in \mathcal{S}_i} d(s_h, \mathcal{S}_j) + \sum_{s_k \in \mathcal{S}_j} d(\mathcal{S}_i, s_k)}{m + n} \tag{2}$$

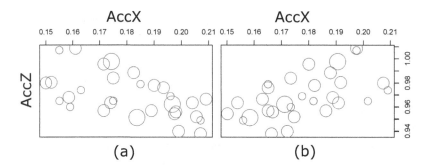

Fig. 4. Incremental clustering on a stream of records over X and Z axes acceleration for a *hole* event (higher values on the Z axis acceleration from (a) to (b)).

where $d(s_h, \mathcal{S}_j) = min_{k=1,...m} d_s(s_h, s_k)$ *is the minimum distance between the synthesis* $s_h \in \mathcal{S}_i$ *and a synthesis in* $\mathcal{S}_j$. *Similarly,* $d(\mathcal{S}_i, s_k) = min_{h=1,...n} d_s(s_h, s_k)$. *To compute the distance between two syntheses* $d_s(s_h, s_k)$, *different factors have been combined: (i) the Euclidean distance between syntheses centroids, to verify whether* s_k *moved with respect to* s_h; *(ii) the difference between syntheses radii, to verify whether there has been an expansion or a contraction of synthesis* s_k *with respect to* s_h; *(iii) the difference in the density of syntheses (i.e., number of aggregated records with respect to the hyper-volume occupied by each synthesis).*

Snapshots for which the distance value from a reference snapshot $\hat{SN}(t_0)$ falls within an interval $[val_{min}, val_{max}]$ are highlighted as *relevant*. The val_{min} and val_{max} are predefined thresholds set by road maintainers based on their experience and domain knowledge. Techniques to support road maintainers in the definition of the thresholds can be considered (e.g., learn-by-example approaches), but their application in the exploration methodology presented in the following sections is out of the scope of this paper. Focusing on the set of syntheses of a relevant snapshot, it is possible to check what are the syntheses that changed over time (namely, appeared, merged or removed), which contributed to make that snapshot relevant. The concepts formerly introduced become a key aspect for the definition of exploration scenarios and the methodological approach for data exploration, described in the next sections.

4   Exploration Scenarios

The components of the big data exploration approach presented in the former section are employed by road maintainers to explore vehicles data. However, depending on their exploration goals and expertise, different road maintainers may focus the exploration on different areas of the road network (e.g., to oversee the area that is under their responsibility). Moreover, different threshold intervals may be adopted by road maintainers to highlight relevant snapshots (e.g., since road surface repair interventions imply a huge economic expense, a road maintainer may be forced to limit the intervention on a subset of anomalous events, selecting them according to the relevance value). As a result, a plethora of exploration use cases, that we refer to as *exploration scenarios*, can be performed. An exploration scenario aims at capturing the essential elements demanded to perform data exploration, starting from the set of snapshots Σ, in order to fulfil a specific exploration goal. The formal definition of exploration scenario is given in the following.

Definition 5 (Exploration scenario). *An exploration scenario ES_i is a four-elements tuple $\langle focus_i, D_i, R_i, \Sigma_{\phi_i} \rangle$ where:*

- *$focus_i$ is a textual description of the goal of the scenario;*
- *$D_i = \langle \phi_i, \overline{\Sigma}_i \rangle$ is the domain of the scenario, containing the dimensions to be considered for exploration (in the exploration facet ϕ_i) along with a set of reference snapshots $\overline{\Sigma}_i$ to be used for detecting relevant ones;*
- *R_i is the set of rules holding within the scenario, consisting in numeric intervals $int_i^j = [v_{a_i}^j, v_{b_i}^j]$, $j = 1, \ldots, |R_i|$ defined by the road maintainers according to their expertise and domain knowledge and exploited as distance thresholds to highlight relevant snapshots;*
- *$\Sigma_{\phi_i} \subseteq \Sigma$ is the set of snapshots available within ES_i, labelled with the dimensions of ϕ_i.*

Example. To assure mobility resilience, a road maintainer's goal might be sorting anomalous events with respect to their severity, given several snapshots related to different anomalous events of the same type (e.g., holes) occurred on a specific portion of the road network. This exploration goal is modelled through an exploration scenario denoted as $ES_{severity}$ having as $focus_{severity}$ the description "determine the severity of anomalous events with type hole", whereas the road portion on which the exploration is focused on is identified by the facet $\phi_{severity}$ (e.g., {*Type*: Urban, *SpeedLimit*: *ALL*, *District*:District1, *Mileage-Extension*:*ALL*}). In $ES_{severity}$, the set of reference snapshots $\overline{\Sigma}_{severity}$ contains a unique reference snapshot, corresponding to a reference critical event. The reference snapshot $\overline{\Sigma}_{severity}$ and the set of rules $R_{severity}$ are used, leveraging the exploration methodology proposed in the following section, to identify relevant snapshots related to hole events. Such snapshots are then sorted according to an increasing value of distance from $\overline{\Sigma}_{severity}$, thus establishing an order from the most to the least critical (indeed, the lower is the distance value the higher is the similarity with the critical event).

5   The Proposed Relevance-Based Data Exploration Methodology

To assist road maintainers in finding relevant snapshots compliant with their exploration goals, we propose a methodology rooted on exploration scenarios and organised over the four phases detailed in the following (Fig. 5).

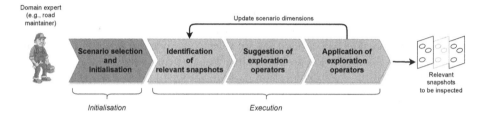

Fig. 5. Phases of the proposed data exploration methodology.

Phase 1 - Exploration Scenario Selection and Initialisation. Exploration of snapshots starts with the selection of an exploration scenario ES_i by the road maintainer. Before performing the exploration, the scenario has to be *initialised* (i.e., the rules R_i and the domain D_i have to be set, as they determine the relevant snapshots the exploration will be focused on). Initialisation is done by exploiting the information contained in the *profile* associated with each road maintainer. Let $\mathcal{M}$ be the set of road maintainers. The profile $p(m)$ of a road maintainer $m \in \mathcal{M}$ is a triple $\langle \mathcal{R}^m, \mathcal{SN}^m, \phi^m \rangle$ where: (i) $\mathcal{R}^m$ is a set containing the rules R_i^m to be considered within a specific exploration scenario ES_i; (ii) $\mathcal{SN}^m$ is a set containing the reference snapshots $\overline{\Sigma}_i^m$ to be considered to perform relevance evaluation according to Eq. (2) in Definition (4); (iii) ϕ^m is the facet containing the preferred dimensions of the road maintainer, to be considered for exploration of snapshots within the scenario.

Phase 2 - Identification of Relevant Snapshots. In an exploration scenario ES_i, relevant snapshots from Σ_{ϕ_i} can be identified by calculating the distance between each snapshot in Σ_{ϕ_i} and the reference snapshots in $D_i.\overline{\Sigma}_i$ (using the distance function d_{SN} from Eq. (2)), considering the set of rules R_i. Let us denote with $\Sigma_{\phi_i}^{rel} \subseteq \Sigma_{\phi_i}$ the set of identified relevant snapshots.

Example. Considering a road maintainer m_1 and recalling the exploration scenario $ES_{severity}$ introduced in Sect. 4, the domain $D_{severity}$ and the rules $R_{severity}$ sets of the scenario are populated using the profile $p(m_1)$. In particular, regarding the domain set $D_{severity}$, the preferred dimensions of the road maintainer in the facet ϕ^{m_1} (e.g., { *Type*: Urban, *SpeedLimit*: *ALL*, *District*:District-2, *MileageExtension*:≤ 5}) are used to populate the facet $\phi_{severity}$, and the initial set of snapshots $\Sigma_{\phi_{severity}}$ related to anomalous events is identified. Moreover, the snapshot to be used as a reference is $\overline{\Sigma}_{severity}^{m_1}$ and corresponds to a critical snapshot exploited for relevance evaluation using as thresholds the rules contained in the set $R_{severity}^{m_1}$, fixed by the road maintainer according to her expertise (e.g., for the road maintainer m_1 a snapshot is considered as relevant if the relevance value is in $[0.3, 0.6]$).

Phase 3 - Suggestion of Exploration operators. To explore the relevant snapshots in $\Sigma_{\phi_i}^{rel}$, a road maintainer may resort to several *exploration operators*, to change the dimensions instances in the facet $D_i.\phi_i$ according to both his/her exploration interests and the measure of relevance.

Definition 6 (Exploration operator). *An exploration operator is denoted as* $o(\tau_o, \iota_o, d_{h_j}^k)$, *where: (i)* τ_o *is the type of* o; *(ii)* ι_o *is a measure quantifying the impact of the application of* o *over the dimension* $d_{h_j}^k \in D_i.\phi_i$ *in the hierarchy* h_j *on the set of snapshots* $\Sigma_{\phi_i}^{rel}$. *The type of operator* τ_o *is inspired by the OLAP operators, and can be either: (i) roll-up/drill-down, to move across the dimension levels of the hierarchy* h_j; *(ii) bind/unbind dimension, to modify an instance of the dimension* $d_{h_j}^k$. *We denote with* $\mathcal{O}$ *the set of available exploration operators.*

Being guided by the measure of relevance, the road maintainer may be proactively suggested with exploration operators to be applied on dimensions in $D_i.\phi_i$. The suggestion of an operator o, amongst all the possible operators in $\mathcal{O}$ and depending on the set of available facets Φ, is made according to the measure ι_o which is calculated as $\frac{|\Sigma_{o(\phi_i)}^{rel}|}{max(1,|\Sigma_{\phi_i}^{rel}|))}$, which quantifies the extent of variation in the number of relevant snapshots before and after the application of the exploration operator. A value of ι_o in $[0,1)$ denotes a reduction in the number of snapshots, a value > 1 denotes an increment, whilst a value $= 1$ denotes no variations.

Example. While executing $ES_{severity}$, an example of exploration operator to be applied to update the facet $\phi_{severity}$ in the domain set of the scenario could be $o_1(\texttt{rollup}, 2.15, District_{h_1})$, a roll-up operator over the dimension $District$ of the hierarchy h_1 (with reference to the notation and examples made in Sect. 3.1). The operator o_1 is associated with the measure ι_{o_1} which, in this case, quantifies an increment in the number of relevant snapshots if o_1 would be applied over $\phi_{severity}$. Conversely, another operator $o_2(\texttt{bind}, 0.75, SpeedLimit_{h_3} : \{\geq 90\})$ would cause a reduction in the number of relevant snapshots since $\iota_{o_2} \in [0,1)$.

Phase 4 - Application of Exploration Operators. Through the ι_o measure, the road maintainer is proposed with different exploration operators, which are ranked according to a decreasing value of ι_o. Amongst the exploration operators suggested for application, the road maintainer selects one of the exploration operators, thus avoiding a trial-and-error approach while moving across the dimensions of the Multi-Dimensional Model. The selection of an exploration operator causes the update of the set $D_i.\phi_i$ of the scenario and the exploration process restarts from Phase 2, until the road maintainer has achieved her goal.

Algorithm 1 summarises the operative steps of the methodology in the scope of a generic exploration scenario ES_i. After setting the domain D_i and rules R_i of ES_i, according to the profile of the user $p(m)$ (lines 2–4), exploration is iteratively performed (lines 6–18), wherein relevant snapshots are highlighted exploiting the distance function d_{SN}, the reference snapshots $D_i.\overline{\Sigma}_i$, and the set

---

Algorithm 1: EXPLORATION SCENARIO BASED DATA EXPLORATION

> **Input**   : Set of snapshots Σ, Multi-Dimensional Model MDM, set of
>   exploration operators $\mathcal{O}$, exploration scenario ES_i, road
>   maintainer's profile $p(m)$
> **Parameters**: type of an anomalous event $\widetilde{\epsilon}$ (optional), identifier of an
>   anomalous event $\widetilde{ID}$ (optional)

1   $\triangleright$ *Initialisation of ES_i (domain and rules sets) with profile data*

2   $D_i.\phi_i \leftarrow p(m).\phi^m$;

3   $D_i.\overline{\Sigma}_i \leftarrow p(m).\overline{\Sigma}_i^m$;

4   $R_i \leftarrow p(m).R_i^m$;

5   $\triangleright$ *Iterative exploration*

6   **begin loop**

7   $\triangleright$ *Initialisation/update of Σ_{ϕ_i} – isset(*test; expr_if_true; expr_if_false*)*

8   $\triangleright$ *Select snapshots according to $D_i.\phi_i$ (and possibly other parameters)*

9   $\Sigma_{\phi_i} \leftarrow \{SN_j | SN_j.\phi_j \equiv D_i.\phi_i \wedge isset(\widetilde{\epsilon}; SN_j.\epsilon_j \equiv$
   $\widetilde{\epsilon};$ True$) \wedge isset(\widetilde{ID}; SN_j.ID_{\epsilon_j} \equiv \widetilde{ID};$ True$)\}, SN_j \in \Sigma$;

10   $\triangleright$ *Highlight relevant snapshots using distance function d_{SN} and rules set R_i –*
   *apply_fun(*func, src_snapshots, ref_snapshots, rules*)*

11   $\Sigma_{\phi_i}^{rel} \leftarrow apply\_fun(d_{SN}, \Sigma_{\phi_i}, D_i.\overline{\Sigma}_i, R_i)$;

12   $\triangleright$ *Exploration scenario specific operations*

13   [. . .]

14   $\triangleright$ *Suggestion of exploration operators (top-n operators ordered by decreasing ι_o*
   value)

15   $O^n \leftarrow suggest\_operators(\mathcal{O}, \Sigma_{\phi_i}^{rel}, D_i.\phi_i, MDM, n)$;

16   $\triangleright$ *Application of one of the suggested operators and update of $D_i.\phi_i$*

17   $apply\_operator(o_j \in O^n, D_i.\phi_i, MDM)$;

18 **end loop**

---

of rules R_i of ES_i. Moreover, depending on the focus of the scenario, specific operations may be performed on relevant snapshots and exploration operators are applied according to the aforementioned procedure. Apart from reference snapshots and rules sets, which are mandatory, exploration scenarios may be optionally parameterised considering: (a) the type $\widetilde{\epsilon}$ and/or (b) the identifier $\widetilde{ID}$ of an anomalous event to be monitored.

5.1 Additional Exploration Scenarios for Smart Road Maintenance

The exploration methodology presented in the former section is being applied within the MoSoRe project also on other scenarios, targeted to assist road maintainers when inspecting road surface conditions. In the following, we present two additional scenarios, beyond the $ES_{severity}$ scenario introduced in Sect. 4: (i) $ES_{evolution}$, concerning the analysis of the evolution over time of an anomalous event; (ii) $ES_{classification}$, to infer a classification for undetermined events.

Analysis of the Evolution Over Time of an Anomalous Event. In this exploration scenario, the road maintainer analyses a sequence of snapshots related to a single anomalous event, identified by $\widetilde{ID}$, for a monitored road portion $p(m).\phi^m$. For the same road portion, a reference snapshot, taken under normal conditions (i.e., not referred to an anomalous event) is considered. The goal of this scenario is to compare the evolution of syntheses in the sequence of snapshots against the reference snapshot. As a result, it is possible to understand the triggering causes of the anomalous event, focusing only on relevant snapshots and, for such snapshots, inspecting the evolution of syntheses that changed over time. To generalise the analysis, starting from the road portion identified by the preferred dimensions in $p(m).\phi^m$, a road maintainer may progressively update the set $D_1.\phi_1$ to discover the *Area* of the city with the highest percentage of relevant snapshots. Once found, he/she can then narrow down the exploration with a drill-down operator, enabling the inspection of anomalous events at *District* level for which a valuable increment of the relevance value occurs.

Classification of an Undetermined Event. The goal of this scenario is to determine the similarity of an undetermined event with respect to the known typologies, thus performing a classification task. In this respect, four reference snapshots are considered, one for each of the aforementioned types. Snapshots to be considered for analysis are the ones of an undetermined event ($\widetilde{\epsilon} = undetermined$), identified by $\widetilde{ID}$, for a monitored road portion $p(m).\phi^m$. Classification is accomplished by calculating the distances of snapshots considered for analysis from each of the four reference snapshots, focusing only on the relevant ones. The lowest distance corresponds to the highest similarity, which is used to properly classify the undetermined event. Similarly to the former scenarios, road maintainers may focus on road portions with a considerable rate of undetermined events occurrence to start the exploration from.

Generally speaking, the relevant snapshots identified in the scope of a scenario can be leveraged to feed another scenario, pursuing a complementary goal. In this respect, a road maintainer may perform a *combined execution* of two or more exploration scenarios to fulfil a complex exploration goal, which cannot be achieved by the execution of a single exploration scenario alone. For instance, the combination of $ES_{severity}$ with $ES_{evolution}$ enables to analyse, for a group of critical anomalous event(s), the temporal evolution of snapshots associated with such events, to infer additional information regarding the causes (observing syntheses evolution). Moreover, the combination of $ES_{classification}$ with $ES_{severity}$ and $ES_{evolution}$ can be leveraged to firstly ascertain the classification of undetermined events (through $ES_{classification}$), then assessing their severity with respect to reference critical events (by performing $ES_{severity}$ on the newly classified snapshots) and lastly applying $ES_{evolution}$ on the most critical events as explained before. To generalise, the combined execution of two scenarios ES_i and ES_j ($i \neq j$ and assuming that ES_i is executed before ES_j) entails that, when executing ES_j, in Phase 1 of the exploration methodology, the dimensions of ES_j are initialised with the dimensions of ES_i ($\phi_j \leftarrow \phi_i$) whilst the snapshots

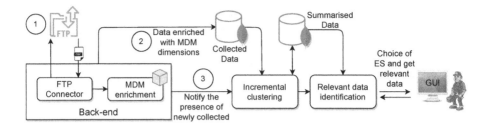

Fig. 6. Architecture overview.

to start the exploration from in ES_j are the relevant snapshots which are the output of Phase 4 of ES_i (i.e., $\Sigma_{\phi_j} \leftarrow \Sigma_{\phi_i}^{rel}$).

6 Implementation and Experimental Evaluation

6.1 Architecture

In Fig. 6, the architecture implementing the approach is reported. The numbers on the arrows in Fig. 6 denote the interactions flow between modules. Mobility data is made available by the vehicles black boxes provider on an FTP repository (in the form of CSV files). Once CSV files containing anomalous events, vehicles trips and accelerometric trails are available on the FTP repository, they are retrieved by the back-end (1), where records of measures are automatically associated with the dimensions of the MDM and stored within a MongoDB database (Collected Data) as JSON documents (one document for each record) and organised into collections (a collection contains documents grouped on a daily basis) (2). Then, the Incremental Clustering module is notified about the presence of available data to process from the Collected Data store (3). Clustering-based data summarisation modules have been implemented in R relying on the stream-MOA library. The output of the Incremental Clustering module is stored within a MongoDB database as well (Summarised Data) and then sent to the Relevance Data Identification module, which is in charge of: (i) identifying relevant snapshots according to the exploration scenario selected; (ii) sending relevant snapshots to be displayed on a GUI.

6.2 Preliminary Validation of the Approach

Experimental Setup. Experiments have been run on a Windows PC equipped with an Intel Core i5-3210M processor, CPU 2.50 GHz, 4 cores, 8 logical cores, RAM 8 GB. The goal of the experimental evaluation is two-fold: (i) assess the quality of data relevance evaluation, as the correlation between high relevance values in correspondence to time instants, where variations of the collected data occurred; (ii) test the processing time, to prove that data summarisation and relevance evaluation can be efficiently computed, thus facing high acquisition rates. Currently, the average number of daily anomalous events detected by the monitored fleet of vehicles is around 400, producing $\approx 3 \cdot 10^6$ records of measures.

Experiments on Data Relevance Evaluation Quality. Each exploration scenario ES_i is rooted on the relevance evaluation to highlight relevant snapshots (according to the rules set $R_i \in ES_i$) which, in turn, relies on incremental clustering results. Hereafter, we investigate the effects that the variation of two pivotal parameters of the clustering algorithm has on the quality of the relevance evaluation: (i) the time window size (Δt), retaining the next data points to be processed by the algorithm; (ii) the syntheses ageing threshold (τ), used to highlight least updated syntheses which are candidate to be discarded. Specifically, the goal is to evaluate whether the distance-based metric, apt to identify relevant snapshots, is able to capture variations in collected data. To this aim, a stream of 14160 samples (which is the maximum length of a stream related to an anomalous event in the context of the MoSoRe project) of a hole event has been employed. In particular, to generate the reference snapshot for calculating the measure of relevance, the first set of 1000 points from the stream has been considered. In Fig. 7(a) and (b) we report the values of relevance metric for different Δt values (a) and different values of the syntheses ageing threshold (b). The dashed line in light blue in Fig. 7 corresponds to the reference data stream. Regarding Δt variations, there is a reduction in sensitivity when Δt assumes larger values (Fig. 7(a)); the width of Δt influences not only the quality of the relevance evaluation, but also the processing time, as detailed in the next paragraph. Concerning the value of τ, it permits to tune the sensitivity of the algorithm to follow sharp variations in incoming data. Sensitivity is evaluated through the calculation of the distance value. Indeed, a value of τ too small prevents old syntheses from being eliminated, and sharp variations are more difficult to be perceived. In Fig. 7(b), fixing $\Delta t = 4$ s, variations are hardly intercepted as τ value decreases. Ongoing experiments are being conducted for determining, not in a blind way, the configuration of parameters to be used for running the clustering algorithm. In particular, the choice of the values for configuration parameters will be driven by the minimisation of the SSQ (sum of squared distance) metric, conceived for data stream clustering algorithms [10], which quantifies the error chargeable to the clustering operation.

Experiments on Processing Time. Regarding processing time, we performed tests varying the width of the time window Δt. Figure 7(c) shows the average time required to process a single record of measures for different Δt values, considering again the stream of measures composed of 14160 samples. The figure shows that lower Δt values demand more time to process data. Indeed, every time data summarisation and relevance evaluation are performed, some initialisation operations have to be executed (e.g., access to the set of syntheses previously computed). Therefore, to ensure lower processing time, the frequency of clustering execution and relevance evaluation must be reduced, that is, Δt value must be increased. On the other hand, higher Δt values indicate that clustering execution and relevance evaluation could be performed far from time instants where important variations occurred, thus reducing the quality of data relevance evaluation. This is evident in Fig. 7(a), where two different Δt values have been used.

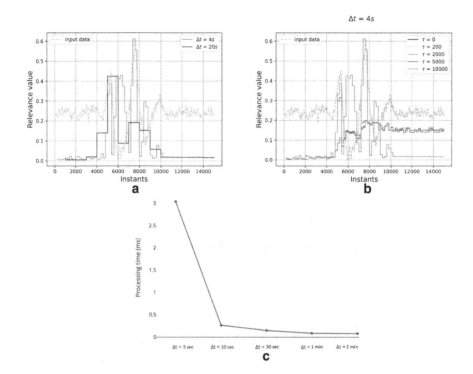

Fig. 7. (a) Relevance value for different Δt and (b) syntheses ageing thresholds τ. (c) Average processing time for each collected measure for different Δt.

The rationale is to adaptively increase/decrease Δt value according to the distance of relevant syntheses from warning and error thresholds for the observed features, depending on the road portion, since they correspond to potentially critical situations that must be monitored at finer granularity. This interesting result confirms what has been obtained in other application domains, different from the one of sustainable and resilient mobility [4]. The algorithm for adaptive tuning of Δt value will be further investigated in future research.

7   Related Work

In the literature, several research efforts proposed the adoption of comprehensive solutions for big data analysis and exploration to improve the resilience of Smart City mobility. In this respect, we surveyed an excerpt of the literature focusing on two different aspects: (a) how existing platforms and frameworks address big data issues, with a particular concern on data variety and volume, as tackled by our Multi-Dimensional Model and clustering-based data summarisation, respectively; (b) whether the approaches envisage the presence of techniques to attract users' attention on relevant data or not, and their possible employment in an exploration methodology. Authors in [8] propose a framework for analysing road accident data; therein, after data preprocessing, a clustering algorithm is applied and association rules are mined to obtain measures of interest, to find possible underlying patterns in the data set. With similar intents, the work in [7] combines IoT and big data to devise the Pavement Managements System (PMS), a road maintenance management structure composed of pavement detection and 3D modelling, data analysis and decision support. It also illustrates use cases for two main actors, the road maintenance company and a technical firm that offers smart solutions for road maintenance. In [12], a city traffic state assessment system is implemented using a big data cloud infrastructure, assuring high scalability, to host clustering methods to find areas of jam. Leveraging the recent advances in the field of computer vision and big data computing, authors in [2] developed a scalable framework for image-based monitoring of urban infrastructure, using both Web images and Google Street View imagery to train a CNN model. Pursuing the goal of analysing road traffic and pollution data for the city of Aaruhs (Denmark), in [13] big data technologies ease the calculation and the visualisation of the least polluted route.

Novel Contributions. With respect to the former state of the art approaches, we conceive the exploration of mobility data based on: (i) an exploration methodology, grounded on the three big data exploration ingredients described in Sect. 3, to support road maintainers exploration tasks; (ii) a formalisation for exploration scenarios, aimed at specialising the methodology according to the application context and the exploration goals of road maintainers. Regarding the exploration methodology, despite multi-dimensional data organisation, that is crucial to ensure data analysis across homogeneous road portions (e.g., characterised by the same type, mileage extent, etc.), is not envisaged in any of the former work, we share with [8] the introduction of metrics to identify relevant data for road maintainers. Furthermore, only [8,12] foster summarisation techniques, both of them relying on clustering but without eliciting considerations about the configuration parameters of the employed algorithms. Nevertheless, in [8] several clustering algorithms from the literature are cited, but none of them is conceived to be applied incrementally on a stream of data, whilst in [12] details on how the algorithm is applied are not provided. Regarding the formulation of exploration scenarios, only [13] sketches scenarios targeted to Smart Mobility, but details are coarsely given, without providing any formal definition.

8   Concluding Remarks

In this paper, we described our contributions in the scope of the MoSoRe research project, presenting a methodological approach, based on big data exploration techniques, to support road maintainers in analysing and assessing road surface conditions. The approach is grounded on a multi-dimensional model, apt to organise road portions with comparable characteristics and to enable data exploration, data summarisation techniques, in order to simplify overall view over high volumes of data collected by vehicles, and a measure of relevance aimed at focusing the attention of the road maintainers on relevant data only. The paper illustrates how the three components can be combined to design exploration scenarios of data in the sustainable and resilient mobility domain. Future work will be focused on an in-depth experimentation of the big data exploration techniques presented in this paper and on an extensive campaign of usability experiments, to be performed in the last phases of the MoSoRe project on the prototype GUI used for exploration purposes. Moreover, the adaptive setup of Δt values for dealing with evolving conditions of the data streams while ensuring good performance, will be investigated as well.

References

1. Albino, V., Berardi, U., Dangelico, R.M.: Smart cities: definitions, dimensions, performance, and initiatives. J. Urban Technol. **22**(1), 3–21 (2015)
2. Alipour, M., Harris, D.K.: A big data analytics strategy for scalable urban infrastructure condition assessment using semi-supervised multi-transform self-training. J. Civ. Struct. Heal. Monit. **10**(2), 313–332 (2020). https://doi.org/10.1007/s13349-020-00386-4
3. Bagozi, A., Bianchini, D., Antonellis, V.D., Garda, M., Marini, A.: A relevance-based approach for big data exploration. Futur. Gener. Comput. Syst. **101**, 51–69 (2019)
4. Bagozi, A., Bianchini, D., De Antonellis, V., Marini, A.: A relevance-based data exploration approach to assist operators in anomaly detection. In: Panetto, H., Debruyne, C., Proper, H.A., Ardagna, C.A., Roman, D., Meersman, R. (eds.) OTM 2018. LNCS, vol. 11229, pp. 354–371. Springer, Cham (2018). https://doi.org/10.1007/978-3-030-02610-3_20
5. Bibri, S.E.: The anatomy of the data-driven smart sustainable city: instrumentation, datafication, computerization and related applications. J. Big Data **6**(1), 1–43 (2019). https://doi.org/10.1186/s40537-019-0221-4
6. Campos-Cordobés, S., et al.: Big data in road transport and mobility research. In: Intelligent Vehicles, pp. 175–205 (2018)
7. Dong, J., Meng, W., Liu, Y., Ti, J.: A framework of pavement management system based on IoT and big data. Adv. Eng. Inform. **47**, 101226 (2021)
8. Kumar, S., Toshniwal, D.: A data mining framework to analyze road accident data. J. Big Data **2**(1), 1–18 (2015). https://doi.org/10.1186/s40537-015-0035-y
9. Lim, C., Kim, K.J., Maglio, P.P.: Smart cities with big data: reference models, challenges, and considerations. Cities **82**, 86–99 (2018)
10. Mansalis, S., Ntoutsi, E., Pelekis, N., Theodoridis, Y.: An evaluation of data stream clustering algorithms. Stat. Anal. Data Min. ASA Data Sci. J. **11**(4), 167–187 (2018)
11. Paiva, S., Ahad, M.A., Tripathi, G., Feroz, N., Casalino, G.: Enabling technologies for urban smart mobility: recent trends, opportunities and challenges. Sensors **21**(6), 2143 (2021)
12. Yang, C.-T., Chen, S.-T., Yan, Y.-Z.: The implementation of a cloud city traffic state assessment system using a novel big data architecture. Clust. Comput. **20**(2), 1101–1121 (2017). https://doi.org/10.1007/s10586-017-0846-z
13. Zenkert, J., Dornhofer, M., Weber, C., Ngoukam, C., Fathi, M.: Big data analytics in smart mobility: modeling and analysis of the Aarhus smart city dataset. In: 2018 IEEE Industrial Cyber-Physical Systems (ICPS), pp. 363–368 (2018)

At Design-Time Approach
for Supervisory Control of Opacity

Nour Elhouda Souid[1,2]($\boxtimes$), Kais Klai[2], Chiheb Ameur Abid[3],
and Samir Ben Ahmed[2]

[1] LIPN UMR CNRS 7030, University Sorbonne Paris Nord, Villetaneuse, France
`souid@lipn.univ-paris13.fr`
[2] LIPSIC Lab, Faculty of Sciences of Tunis, Université de Tunis El Manar,
Tunis, Tunisia
`kais.klai@lipn.univ-paris13.fr`, `samir.benahmed@fst.utm.tn`
[3] Mediatron Lab, Université de Tunis El Manar, Sup'Com, Tunis, Tunisia
`chiheb.abid@fst.utm.tn`

Abstract. Opacity is a property of information flow that characterizes
the ability of a system to keep a secret information hidden from a malicious external entity, called an attacker. Given a critical system that
may leak confidential information, an attacker with partial observation
of the system and a subset of controllable actions, we propose an approach to synthesize a controller that enforces the system's opacity. This
controller is designed as a function that applies, at run time, to the current execution to disable any controllable action that eventually leads
to the violation of the opacity of the system. The supervision function
is built at design time based on a new version of the symbolic observation graph that represents a reduced abstraction of the state space
graph of the system preserving the observation of both the attacker and
the controller. The language induced by this function is proven to be
controllable, observable and supremal no matter the relation that exists
between the observations of the attacker and the controller.

Keywords: Security · Information flow · Opacity · Supervisory
control theory · Formal methods

1 Introduction

As our daily lives become more and more dependent on the use of information
technology, more sensitive information is required to be shared to provide better services and the need to guarantee the security of such information grows
more critical. One of the most important categories of security requirements
is *information flow*. It is a class of security properties that characterizes the
way information flows between different entities of a system. *Opacity* [1] and
non-interference [2] are two of the main examples of information flow properties. Opacity aims at preserving unwanted retrievals of secrets by untrusted
users while observing the system [3]. It allows the protection of sensitive characteristics of the considered system and offers a general framework allowing to

M. Sellami et al. (Eds.): CoopIS 2022, LNCS 13591, pp. 37–54, 2022.
https://doi.org/10.1007/978-3-031-17834-4_3

specify a wide range of security properties. Indeed, it allows to characterize the plausible deniability of a system's secret in the presence of a malicious outside intruder. The opacity of a system is evaluated with reference to a predicate on its behaviour. This predicate is said to be opaque if for every behavior of the system satisfying the considered predicate, there is (at least) another behavior under which the same predicate is not satisfied such that both behaviors are indistinguishable by the attacker [4].

Enforcing (or reinforcing) the opacity property has been studied within the framework of Supervisory Control Theory (SCT). The objective is to synthesize a supervisor that restricts the behavior of the system by disabling events that lead to secret disclosure and hence, opacity violation. This behaviour restriction, however, needs to respect another key concept in Supervisory Control, which is permissiveness. A maximal supervisor has to enable the maximal number of events which means that the restriction of the behaviour of the system needs to involve as few disabled events as possible.

Our work investigates the problem of reinforcing the opacity of a Discrete Event System (DES) from a Supervisory Control perspective and suggests a novel methodology to synthesize a maximal supervisor that restricts the behavior of the considered system in the general case without any hypothesis on the relationship between the attacker and the supervisor observations of the system.

The main contribution of this paper is to propose a correct-by-construction abstraction algorithm for synthesizing a partial observation supervisor that enforces the opacity on-the-fly. Our approach is generic since the observations of the attacker and the supervisor are not necessarily comparable. This naturally leads to a more complex system to be considered with a larger state space to be explored. To deal with the state explosion problem, we propose a reduced abstraction of the state space, namely Hyper Symbolic Observation Graph (**HSOG**): a new version of the SOG approach [5] that reduces the complexity of the system by grouping sets of explicit states into symbolic nodes (encoded with binary decision diagrams [6]). We also prove that the language of the obtained system under supervision is prefix-close, controllable, observable and opaque. Our approach has been implemented in a C++ prototype.

The rest of the paper is organized as follows. In Sect. 2, we introduce some preliminary notions and models that are necessary to for the presented approach. The core contribution is presented in Sect. 3. Related work is presented and discussed in Sect. 4. Finally, our conclusions and some open questions are drawn in Sect. 5.

2   Preliminaries

Discrete event systems (DESs) are event driven dynamic systems with a discrete set of reachable states. Such systems can be modeled with Labeled Transition Systems. In this paper, we deal with finite state space systems only.

2.1   Labeled Transition System (LTS)

A Labeled Transition System, denoted by T, is a discrete transition structure that can be thought of as a generalization of an automaton with outputs.

Definition 1.   *Labeled Transition System*
A Labeled Transition System (LTS) is a four-tuple $T = (X, \Sigma, f_t, X_0)$ *where:*

- X *is a set of states;*
- Σ *is a set of actions;*
- $f_t : X \times \Sigma \to X$ *is a transition relation;*
- $X_0 \subseteq X$ *is a subset of initial states.*

A transition from a state s to a state $s\prime$ by an event or action e over a LTS T is denoted by $s \xrightarrow{e} s\prime$. A run of a LTS T is a finite sequence of transitions from an initial state $x_0 \in X_0$. The trace of a run $\pi = x_0 \xrightarrow{e1} x_1 \ldots \xrightarrow{e_n} x_n$, denoted by $tr(\pi)$, is the finite sequence of actions/events $\sigma = e_1 \ldots e_n$. By extension of the transition relation, the fact that the trace $tr(\pi)$ leads to state x_n from x_0 is denoted by $f_t(x_0, tr(\pi)) = x_n$. Given two traces α and β, $\alpha.\beta$ denotes the trace built by the concatenation of α and β. The language of a LTS T is defined as the set of its traces i.e. $L(T) := \{tr(\pi) \in \Sigma^* $ such that π *is a run of* $T\}$. Finally, ε denotes the empty trace.

An example of a LTS is presented in Fig. 1. It illustrates a *Secret Securing with Multiple Protections Problem* (inspired from [7]). We consider abstracting a dynamic system to a DES and we model this system using an LTS. States of the system are partitioned into two subsets: **secret** and **nominal** states. Secret states are states of the system that represent "accessing a component of the system that contains secret information". The set of states is $X = \{q_i \mid i \in \{0, 8\}\}$, with q_0 as initial state. Transitions between states represent events/actions that are actually happening in the plant. In other words, a transition from a state q_i to q_j labelled by e is interpreted as "the event e happened to the state q_i and hence the system moves to the state q_j". We denote the set of events of the system as Σ such that $\Sigma = \{\alpha_i, i \in [0, 10]\}$.

This system (in Fig. 1) models simplified system of a software application which has three restricted components. This application works according to the users permission levels. The users have to pass several authentication points to obtain the permission to reach the restricted component. The initial state q_0 indicates that no user is now logged into the system. Events α_0 and α_1 represent respectively logging into the system as a standard user (**User**) and as a system administrator (**Admin**) respectively. The event α_2 indicates switching permission from **Admin** to **User**. The application is, hence, launched by α_3 as **User** and by α_5 as **Admin**. α_4 is the event meaning that the **User** launches the application as **Admin**, e.g. sudo in Unix-like operating systems. The actions α_6, α_7 and α_9 indicate the authentication points to obtain access to the secret states q6, q7, and q8 respectively. α_8 is an optional authentication point at which administrators can apply a weaker protection than α_9. Finally, α_{10} is an event indicating a log-off function, which leads back the User/Admin to q_0.

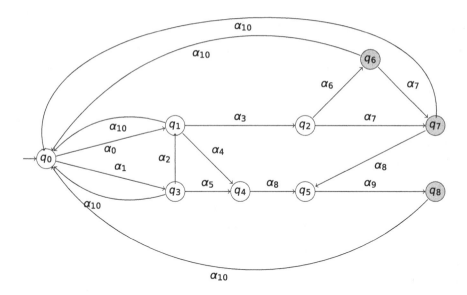

Fig. 1. Example of LTS

2.2 The Opacity Property

Opacity is a security property defined w.r.t a secret predicate (a set of secret states or runs) and an observer considered as an attacker. We assume that the attacker has a complete knowledge of the structure of the system and partially observes its actions. Before defining this security property, we introduce the notion of **projection function** on a subset of observable actions $\Sigma_o \subseteq \Sigma$.

Definition 2. *Projection Function*
For an alphabet $a \in \Sigma$ and a sequence $\sigma \in \Sigma^*$, the projection operation P_{Σ_o} : $\Sigma^* \rightarrow \Sigma_o^*$ is defined as follows:

$$P_{\Sigma_o}(\varepsilon) = \varepsilon; \quad P_{\Sigma_o}(a.\sigma) = \begin{cases} a.P(\sigma) & \text{if } a \in \Sigma_o \\ P(\sigma) & \text{if } a \notin \Sigma_o \end{cases}$$

Intuitively, a projection P_{Σ_o} takes a word from Σ^* and erases each action that does not belong to Σ_o. Given a set of sequences $T \subseteq \Sigma^*$, the projection function is extended as $P_{\Sigma_o}(T) = \bigcup_{\tau \in T} P_{\Sigma_o}(\tau)$. Finally, given a sequence $O \in \Sigma_o^*$, $P_{\Sigma_o}^{-1}(O)$ is the set of the sequence whose projection on Σ_o is equal to O.

In this work, Σ_a denotes the set of actions observed by the attacker, and P_{Σ_a} the corresponding projection function. Consider a LTS $T = (X, \Sigma, f_t, X_0)$, a regular predicate $\phi \subseteq \Sigma^*$ and a subset of actions Σ_a. The predicate ϕ is opaque if no attacker can ever conclude from its provided interface that the current **run** r of the system satisfies ϕ, denoted by $r \models \phi$ (i.e., the trace of r belongs to ϕ).

We say that a **state** $s \in X$ satisfies the predicate ϕ, denoted by $s \models \phi$, when it is reachable by a trace belonging to ϕ. A **set of states** X_S is said to be satisfying ϕ, denoted by $X_S \models \phi$, when all its states satisfy ϕ. In this context, the secret of the system can be indistinguishably represented by a set of traces $\phi \subseteq \Sigma^*$ or a set of states X_S (containing any state reachable by a secret trace in ϕ).

Definition 3. *Opacity*
A LTS T is opaque w.r.t. a secret predicate ϕ and a subset of actions Σ_a iff
$\forall r \in L(T) \mid r \models \phi$, *there exists* $r' \in L(T) \mid (P_{\Sigma_a}(r) = P_{\Sigma_a}(r')) \wedge (r' \not\models \phi)$.

As example, let us consider the plant of Fig. 1 and consider that it is observed by an external intruder aiming to reach secret state to obtain secret information about the system. We assume that $X_S = \{q_i, i \in \{6, 8\}\} \subseteq X$ is the subset of secret states of the system (Red/shaded circles in Fig. 1). Some of the events of the system are observed by the intruder and we define its observation as $\Sigma_a = \{\alpha_{10}, \alpha_6, \alpha_8\}$, which means that the attacker can observe the *log-off*, the authentication action to access the secret state $q6$ and the optional authentication point that lead to $q5$ (and eventually to the secret q_9) since we have a weak protection for this event. This system is not opaque w.r.t Σ_a and X_S since the trace $\alpha_0.\alpha_3.\alpha_6$ leads to the secret state q_6 and does not have an observably equivalent trace not leading to a secret state.

2.3 Symbolic Observation Graph (SOG)

The **Symbolic Observation Graph (SOG)** [5] is defined as a *deterministic* graph where each node (**aggregate**) is a set of states linked by unobservable actions and each arc is labeled with an observable action. Nodes of the SOG are called aggregates (Definition 4) and are represented and managed efficiently using decision diagram techniques (e.g., BDDs [6]).

Definition 4. *Aggregate*
Let $T = (X, \Sigma, f_t, X_0)$ be a LTS s.t., $\Sigma = \Sigma_o \dot{\cup} \Sigma_u$ s.t Σ_o is the set of observable actions and Σ_u the set of unobservable actions. An aggregate a is a non empty set of states satisfying: $\forall s \in X, s \in a \iff Saturate(s) \subseteq a$; *where* $Saturate(s) = \{s' \in X : \exists \sigma \in (\Sigma_u)^* \text{ such that } f_t(s, \sigma) = s'\}$

By extension to sets of states, $Saturate(S) = \underset{s \in S}{\cup} Saturate(s)$.

Definition 5. *Symbolic Observation Graph (SOG)*
A SOG G associated with a LTS $T = (X, \Sigma_u \dot{\cup} \Sigma_o, f_t, X_0)$ is a LTS $(A, \Sigma_o, \rightarrow, a_0)$ where:

- A *is a finite set of aggregates;*
- $\forall a \in A$, *and for each* $o \in \Sigma_o$, $\exists x \in a, x' \in X : x \overset{o}{\rightarrow} x' \implies$:
  $Saturate(\{x' \in X, \exists x \in a : x \overset{o}{\rightarrow} x'\}) = a'$ *for some aggregate a' s.t.*
  $(a, o, a') \in \rightarrow$;
- $\rightarrow \subseteq A \times \Sigma_o \times A$ *is the transition relation;*
- $a_0 \in A$ *is the initial aggregate s.t.* $a_0 = Saturate(X_0)$;

Since a single state can belong to several aggregates, the theoretical complexity of the size of a SOG is exponential w.r.t, the size of the underlying LTS. However, due to symbolic representation of the aggregates using BDDs, the SOG has a very moderate size in practice, especially for small sets of observable actions (see [5,8,9] for experimental results). Moreover, in [10] authors proved that a LTS is opaque iff its corresponding SOG is opaque.

Furthermore, they characterized the opacity of a SOG as follows: *SOG is opaque iff* **none of its aggregates is included in the set of secret states**. In fact, an aggregate a, that is reachable with a trace σ, includes all the states that are reachable, in the corresponding LTS, by a trace in $P_{\Sigma_o}^{-1}(\sigma)$. If $a \subseteq X_s$, then any trace in $P_{\Sigma_o}^{-1}(\sigma)$ leads to a secret state which violates the opacity.

Definition 6. *Opacity of a SOG* [10]
Given a LTS $T = (X, \Sigma_u \dot\cup \Sigma_a, f_t, X_0)$, Σ_a a subset of observable actions by the attacker and the set of secret states X_S, the corresponding SOG $(A, \Sigma_a, \rightarrow, a_0)$ is opaque iff $\forall a \in A, a \not\subseteq X_S$.

Theorem 1 *(Opacity Verification* [10]). *Let T be a LTS, X_S a subset of secret states, $\Sigma_a \subseteq \Sigma$ is the set of observable actions, and Γ the SOG of T w.r.t. Σ_a, then, T is opaque w.r.t. X_S and Σ_a if and only if Γ is opaque.*

2.4   Supervisory Control Background

The Supervisory Control Theory [11] (SCT) is a formal framework for modeling and control of Discrete Event Systems (DESs). Given a system modeled by a LTS T, the objective of the SCT is to synthesize a supervisor (also called a controller) in such a way that the controller can prevent some actions from occurring to enforce security properties. In this paper, $K \subseteq L(T)$ represents the opaque behavior of T. Assuming that the supervisor **observes** a subset of actions $\Sigma_m \subseteq \Sigma$ and **controls** only a subset of its observed actions $\Sigma_c \subseteq \Sigma_m$, its role is to enforce the behavior K on the system T by enabling or disabling each action in Σ_c. $\Sigma_u = \Sigma \setminus \Sigma_m$ is the set of **unobservable** actions (by the controller) and $\Sigma \setminus \Sigma_c$ is the set of **uncontrollable** actions.

In the running example of Fig. 1, our objective is to guarantee that the system is opaque and does not leak its secret information. Consider, then, that we are responsible to mitigate the risk that intruders reach secret states in the plant, and for this task we need to install protections at appropriate points on paths to secrets. We express installing protections at certain points as protecting events at certain states. Meanwhile, the costs to protect secrets must be minimum. We assume that protected events are events observed by the supervisor. Some of these events require more protection and we model them as controllable which means that the supervisor can not only observe these events, but control them. Hence, we define the set of protected/observed events by $\Sigma_m = \{\alpha_0, \alpha_1, \alpha_4, \alpha_6, \alpha_7, \alpha_8, \alpha_9\}$ and the subset of controllable events as $\Sigma_c = \{\alpha_0, \alpha_1, \alpha_4, \alpha_6, \alpha_9\}$. Figure 2 presents the Symbolic Observation Graph (Sect. 2.3) of the system w.r.t $\Sigma_a \cup \Sigma_m$.

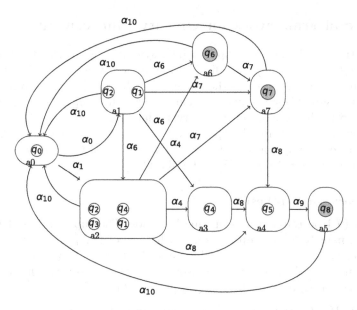

Fig. 2. SOG of Fig. 1 LTS

In the following, we introduce some key properties regarding the targeted language K where the languages of the considered systems (as well as K) are supposed to be *prefix-closed* (i.e., any prefix α of $\sigma \in L(T)$ belongs to $L(T)$). We start by defining the controllability of a prefix-closed language (Definition 7). A language K is controllable if any extension of its traces with uncontrollable actions leads to traces that are in K as well (as long as they belong to $L(T)$).

Definition 7. *Controllability of a Prefix-Closed Language*
A language K is controllable w.r.t. $L(T)$ and Σ_c iff, $K.(\Sigma \setminus \Sigma_c) \cap L(T) \subseteq K$.

Another key property SCT is **Observability**. Such a property is equivalent to another important one namely *normality* [12] when $\Sigma_c \subseteq \Sigma_m$ (which is our assumption in this paper). Intuitively, a language is observable if it can exactly be deduced from its projection P_{Σ_m}. Specifically, when a controller disables a controllable action c after the execution of a trace σ, then c has to be disabled after all execution traces equivalent to σ w.r.t P_{Σ_m}.

Definition 8. *Observability of a Language [13]*
A language K is observable w.r.t. $L(T)$ and Σ_m iff $P_{\Sigma_m}^{-1}[P_{\Sigma_m}(K)] \cap L(T) \subseteq K$

The purpose of the SCT is to find the *supremal* sublanguage of $L(T)$ that is controllable, observable, and s.t the specification (here, opacity) is respected. It has been proved that such a language exists if $\Sigma_c \subseteq \Sigma_m$ [13].

Definition 9. *Supremal Language*
A language K is supremal if $\nexists L \subseteq L(T)$ s.t L is a prefix-closed controllable, observable, opaque, and $K \subset L$.

3   General Framework for Opacity Enforcement

In this section, we design a new approach for synthesizing the **most permissive controller** (i.e., supremal) that disables any action when its execution, in the current run, eventually leads to the violation of the opacity of the system.

First, the supervisor behavior is defined through a supervision function γ. Then, we prove that the obtained supervisor language K is *controllable, observable, supremal* and ensures the opacity of $\mathcal{T}$. Finally, we propose an algorithm based on an on-the-fly construction of a new version of the SOG called *Hyper Symbolic Observation Graph* (HSOG for short).

3.1   Supervisor Synthesis

Let $K \subseteq L(\mathcal{T})$ be the system's opaque behavior. The supervisor is defined as a function, namely γ, that operates on each trace of $L(\mathcal{T})$ and gives the set of controllable actions in Σ_c to be disabled in order to reduce $L(\mathcal{T})$ to K.

The definition of the aimed supervisor γ of $\mathcal{T}$ is defined through an intermediate supervisor γ_0 on the runs of $L(\mathcal{T})$ projected on σ_m.

Definition 10. *Observed Trace-Based Supervision Function*
Let $\mathcal{T} = (X, \Sigma, f_t, X_0)$ be a LTS. Let ϕ be a secret predicate. The observed trace-based supervision function is defined as follows: $\gamma_0 : P_{\Sigma_m}[L(\mathcal{T})] \to 2^{\Sigma_c}$.
$\forall \sigma \in P_{\Sigma_m}[L(\mathcal{T})], \gamma_0(\sigma) = \{e \in \Sigma_c \mid \exists \alpha \in (\Sigma_a \setminus \Sigma_c)^* :$
$R(P_{\Sigma_a}(P_{\Sigma_m}^{-1}(\sigma.e)).\alpha) \models \phi\}$, *where* $R(P_{\Sigma_a}(P_{\Sigma_m}^{-1}(\sigma.e)).\alpha)$ *denotes the set of states reachable in* $\mathcal{T}$ *by any trace in* $P_{\Sigma_a}^{-1}(P_{\Sigma_a}(P_{\Sigma_m}^{-1}(\sigma.e)).\alpha)$ *from an initial state.*

γ_0 is defined on observable traces of the system $\mathcal{T}$ by the controller. It returns a set of actions to be disabled after the observation of a trace σ by the controller. Given an observable trace σ and a controllable action e, e is disabled iff any path in the original LTS having the path $P_{\Sigma_a}(\sigma.e)$ as projection on Σ_a can be completed with a sequence of uncontrollable actions α, that is observable by the attacker, such that any run in $L(\mathcal{T})$ having $P_{\Sigma_a}(\sigma.e).\alpha$ as projection on Σ_a leads to a secret state. Below, we can extend the supervision function to the complete runs of $\mathcal{T}$.

Definition 11. *Supervision Function*
Let $\mathcal{T} = (X, \Sigma, f_t, X_0)$ be a LTS and let ϕ be a secret predicate. The supervision function is defined as follows: $\begin{aligned}\gamma : L(\mathcal{T}) &\to 2^{\Sigma_c} \\ \gamma(tr) &= \gamma_0(P_{\Sigma_m}(tr)).\end{aligned}$

3.2   Properties of the Language Induced by Supervision

In this section, we prove that the language of the system controlled by the supervisor defined in the previous section is *prefix-closed, supremal, observable, controllable* and guarantees the opacity of the underlying system. We denote by K, the language obtained by applying the supervision function γ on all the traces of the system (abusively denoted by $\gamma(L(\mathcal{T}))$).

Theorem 2. *Let T be a LTS with the set of controllable actions Σ_c, the set of the controller's observed actions Σ_m, and the set of the attacker's observed actions Σ_a. Then, the language $K = \{\sigma \in L(T) \mid \nexists(\alpha, c) \in L(T) \times \Sigma_c :$ ($\alpha.c$ is a prefix of σ) $\wedge c \in \gamma(\alpha)\}$ is prefix-closed, controllable, observable, supremal and ensures the opacity of T.*

Proof.

1. K is prefix-closed i.e. the prefix of each element in K belongs to K:
   Let $\sigma \in K$ and let α be a prefix of σ. Let us prove that $\alpha \in K$.
   Assume $\alpha \notin K$. Then, there exists $(\alpha_1, c) \in L(T) \times \Sigma_c$ s.t. $\alpha_1.c$ is a prefix of α and $c \in \gamma(\alpha_1)$. Since α_1 is a prefix of α and α is a prefix of σ, α_1 is a prefix of σ as well. This is not possible, otherwise it contradicts, by definition, the membership of σ in K. Thus, $\alpha \in K$.
2. K is controllable i.e. $K.(\Sigma \setminus \Sigma_c) \cap L(T) \subseteq K$:
   Let $\sigma \in K$ and let $u \in (\Sigma \setminus \Sigma_c) \cap L(T)$. Let us prove that $\sigma.u \in K$.
   Assume the opposite. Then, there exists $(\alpha_1, c) \in L(T) \times \Sigma_c$ s.t. $\alpha_1.c$ is a prefix of $\sigma.u$ and $c \in \gamma(\alpha_1)$. Since $c \neq u$ ($c \in \Sigma_c$ while $u \in \sigma \setminus \sigma_c$), $\alpha_1.c$ is a prefix of σ which contradicts, by definition, the membership of σ in K. Thus, $\sigma.u \in K$.
3. K is observable i.e., $P_{\Sigma_m}^{-1}[P_{\Sigma_m}(K)] \cap L(T) \subseteq K$.
   Let $\sigma_1 \in K$ and let $\sigma_2 \in L(T)$ s.t. $P_{\Sigma_m}(\sigma_1) = P_{\Sigma_m}(\sigma_2)$. Assume that $\sigma_2 \notin K$. Then, there exists $(\alpha_2, c) \in L(T) \times \Sigma_c$ s.t. $\alpha_2.c$ is a prefix of $\sigma_2.u$ and $c \in \gamma(\alpha_2)$. Let α_1 be the prefix of σ_1 s.t. $P_{\Sigma_m}(\alpha_1) = P_{\Sigma_m}(\alpha_2)$. The fact that $c \in \gamma(\alpha_2)$ implies that the aggregate reached by $P_{\Sigma_m}(\alpha_2).c$ is included in the set of secret states. However, such an aggregate is also reached by $P_{\Sigma_m}(\alpha_1).c$ while $c \notin \gamma(\alpha_1)$ otherwise σ_1 would not belong to K. Thus, $\sigma_2 \in K$.
4. K is supremal i.e. $\nexists K \subset L \subseteq L(T)$ s.t. L is a prefix-closed language that is controllable, observable and opaque w.r.t. the secret predicate φ and the attacker observation Σ_a.
   Assume that such a language exists. Let $\sigma \in L \setminus K$. Then, there exists $(\alpha, c) \in L(T) \times \Sigma_c$ s.t. $\alpha.c$ is a prefix of σ and $c \in \gamma(\alpha)$. Thus, by definition, the aggregate reached by the trace $\alpha.c$ is included in the set of secret states. This contradicts the membership of α in L since L is a prefix-closed language. Thus, K is supremal.
5. K ensures the opacity of the system. This is guaranteed by construction of the supervisor and by using the result of [10] stating that a T is opaque iff the corresponding SOG does not contain any aggregate included in the set of secret states.

3.3 On-the-Fly Computation of the Supervision Function

To synthesize the previously defined supervisor, we propose to construct a *Hyper Symbolic Observation Graph* (HSOG) of an **LTS**. Informally, the **HSOG** is a graph where nodes, called *super aggregates*, are sets of aggregates (and not single states) connected with actions in $\Sigma_m \setminus \Sigma_a$. The arcs of HSOG are labeled with actions in Σ_a only. Such a graph can be trivially obtained for a *LTS* $\mathcal{T}$ by (1) Building the SOG $\mathcal{G}$ of $\mathcal{T}$ under the observation of $\Sigma_a \cup \Sigma_m$, then (2) building the SOG of (the *LTS*) $\mathcal{G}$ under the observation of Σ_a. There are two main differences between a SOG and a HSOG: First, nodes of the SOG represent sets of states encoded as a BDD, while the nodes of a HSOG are sets of aggregates. Then, links between states inside an aggregate of a SOG are not explicitly represented because irrelevant, while links between the elements inside a node of a HSOG are represented explicitly and used to opacify the system.

Figure 3 illustrates the HSOG of the considered running example. Clearly, the number of states decreases from 9 states to 3 nodes (super-aggregates). Similarly, the number of events passes from 17 to 6 events. The presented HSOG is not opaque [which is inline with the previously presented conclusion done for the LTS] since the super-aggregate S_2 is totally included in secret set of states.

To enforce the opacity of this system, we determine its corresponding *Observed Trace-Based Supervision Function* by γ_o and its corresponding *Supervision function* by γ:

$$\gamma_o(\sigma) = \begin{cases} \{\alpha_6\} & \text{if } \sigma = ((\alpha_1.\alpha_4.\alpha_8.\alpha_9)^*.(\alpha_1.\alpha_8.\alpha_9)^*.(\alpha_0.\alpha_4.\alpha_8.\alpha_9)^*)^*.(\alpha_0^+ \alpha_1) \\ \varnothing & \text{else} \end{cases}$$

$$\gamma(\sigma) = \begin{cases} \{\alpha_6\} & \text{if } \sigma = [[(\alpha_1 + \alpha_0).\alpha_{10}]^*.([\alpha_1.((\alpha_2.\alpha_4) + \alpha_5) + \alpha_0.\alpha_4].\alpha_8.\alpha_9.\alpha_{10})^*]^*.\alpha_0.\alpha_3 \\ \varnothing & \text{else} \end{cases}$$

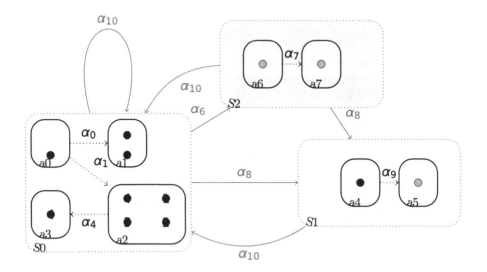

Fig. 3. HSOG Example

In the following, we propose algorithms to synthesise the supervision function γ_o of Definition 10 based on on-the-fly construction of the HSOG of a *LTS*.

Algorithm 1. On-the-Fly HSOG Construction and Opacification

1: **function** SOG-OPACIFICATION($\mathcal{T}, \Sigma_a, \Sigma_c, \sigma_m$) : Bool
2: **Begin**
3:      $a \leftarrow initAg(\mathcal{T}, \Sigma_{ua} \cap \Sigma_{um})$;
4:      $A \leftarrow initAg(\mathcal{T}, \Sigma_{ua}))$;
5:      **if** $A \subseteq X_S$ **then**
6:          return False;
7:      st.push $(A, \text{Enable}(A, \Sigma_a))$;
8:      **while** (st $\neq \varnothing$) **do**
9:          $(A, enb) \leftarrow \text{st.Top}()$;
10:         **if** $(enb = \varnothing)$ **then**
11:             st.Pop();
12:         **else**
13:             $t \leftarrow enb.pick()$;
14:             $A' \leftarrow SuccSupAg(A, t)$
15:             **if** $(\neg Treated(A'))$ **then**
16:                 **if** $(A' \subseteq X_S)$ **then**
17:                     $src \leftarrow Enable(A, t)$;
18:                     $dest \leftarrow Img(src, t)$
19:                     **if** $\neg(OpacifyByControl(st, src, dest, t, A'))$ **then**
20:                         return False;
21:                 addNodeToHSOG(A')
22:                 st.Push($A', Enable(A', \Sigma_a)$);
23:             addEdgeToHSOG(A, t, A')
24:     return True;

Definition 11 can then be used to obtain the general supervision function that applies on full traces of the system. Algorithm 1 describes this process.

The first step of Algorithm 1 is to construct the initial aggregate a (Line 3) and the initial super aggregate A (Line 4). We check if the latter is included in the secret set of states X_S (Line 5, 6). If it is the case, the opacification is not possible. Otherwise, we continue the construction of the **HSOG** (Line 7 to Line 24). Each time a super-aggregate is included in the secret, we call the OpacifyByControl function which is in charge of disabling the last controllable action leading to this secret disclosure (Lines 19). if OpacifyByControl returns False, then we cannot enforce the opacity of the system $\mathcal{T}$. Otherwise, we continue the construction of the HSOG by adding the calculated node A' to the HSOG (Line 21) and we save this information in the stack st (Line 23).

When calling the OpacifyByControl function with an input aggregate a', two cases are possible. Either it cuts all its already built branches [CutOldBranch] (see Line 4) in the case where the aggregate is totally included in the secret and must therefore be totally deleted [the first call to this function from Algorithm 1 is in this case], or it trims these branches [TrimOldBranches] (Line 7) in the case where an aggregate is going to be divided: a part leads to the secret and therefore it is deleted and we keep what respects the opacity. Then, this function backtracks (Line 12→17) to look for the last controllable action that leads to the secret to disable it.

The supervision function is defined through "Disable(st, t)" (OpacifyByControl Line 9). We recover the trace from the stack st. In fact, each element of the stack "st" contains an aggregate and the list of transitions enabled by this aggregate. Each time we compute a successor of an aggregate, we delete (top()) the transition that led to this aggregate. And so to have a complete trace, we also recover the arcs that led to the aggregate (from its predecessors).

When an aggregate (a) is secret, we must first delete it and then check if we have already built paths from it. These paths will not be deleted directly and our algorithm deletes only paths and aggregates that lead to the secret. The CutOldBranches function is used to disable already constructed branches (successors) of an aggregate entered as an input of the function (a). So, for every successor (a') of (a), we check if there is another path that can lead to this aggregate (which means that a' is reachable by another aggregate than a). If so, a' will not be deleted and we will only deactivate the arc $a \rightarrow a'$. Otherwise, the whole a' aggregate will be deleted too.

The TrimOldBranches function will be called with reduced aggregates. Let a be the input of the function. The aggregate a has already been reduced in previous steps of the algorithm. For each successor a' of a, we check if a' is no longer compatible with this reduction (Line 5→ 15). If so, this means that a'

```
1:  function OPACIFYBYCONTROL(st, src, dest, t, a'): Bool
2:  Begin
3:      if (a' ⊆ X_S) then
4:          CutOldBranches(a');
5:          delete a';
6:      else
7:          TrimOldBranches(a');
8:      if (t ∈ Σ_C) then
9:          Disable(st, t);
10:         return True;
11:     else
12:         if (st.size()>1) then
13:             a ← pop(st);
14:             t←getTrans(st.Top(), a);
15:             dest← SaturatePreImg(src)∩a ;
16:             a' ← a\ (dest ∪ src);
17:             src← PreImg (dest, t)∩ st.Top();
18:             if OpacifyByControl(st, src, dest, t, a') then
19:                 st.push(a', EnableObs(a'));
20:                 return True;
21:             else
22:                 return False;
23:         else
24:             return False;
```

must be modified after the steps previously done in the algorithm to reinforce the opacity. Then, we need to verify if it violates the opacity (Line 6→ 8) and if not we update it (Line 9 → 15).

To illustrate our approach, we consider the HSOG presented in Fig. 3. Super-aggregates, which illustrate the observation of the attacker, are represented by dotted-bordered rectangles, while the aggregates are represented by thick-bordered ones. The considered system is not opaque. We explain how to enforce its opacity by synthesizing a supervisor that restricts its behaviour. To this end, the supervisor disables some of its controllable events.

1: **procedure** CUTOLDBRANCHES(a)
2: **Begin**
3:     **for** ($a \xrightarrow{t} a'$) **do**
4:         **if** (a'.predecessors().size() > 1) or a' is initial aggregate **then**
5:             $E \leftarrow E \setminus (a \xrightarrow{t} a')$;
6:         **else**
7:             CutOldBranches(a')
8:             **if** (a') **then**
9:                 delete a';

1: **procedure** TRIMOLDBRANCHES(a)
2: **Begin**
3:     **for** ($a \xrightarrow{t} a'$) **do**
4:         $a'' \leftarrow$ Saturate(a, t);
5:         **if** ($a' \neq a''$) **then**
6:             **if** $a'' \subseteq X_S$ **then**
7:                 CutOldBranches(a')
8:                 delete a';
9:             **else**
10:                **if** (a'.predecessors().size() > 1) **then** /*a' is elsewhere accessible*/
11:                    $E \leftarrow E \setminus (a \xrightarrow{t} a')$;
12:                    save($a \xrightarrow{t} a''$);
13:                **else**
14:                    $a' \leftarrow a''$;
15:                    TrimOldBranches(a');

This leads to omitting some aggregates/super-aggregates of the system which will be represented in grey. Moreover, secret states are represented in red. Figure 4 illustrates a system G. We assume that the attacker observes the set of actions $\Sigma_a = \{A_1, A_2\}$, the supervisor observes $\Sigma_m = \{A_1, A_2, b, c, b', c'\}$,

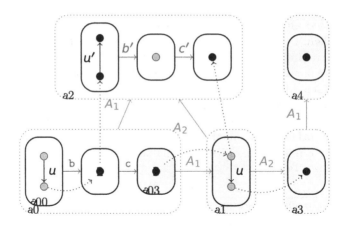

Fig. 4. Supervision G: $\gamma(ub) = c$

and controls $\Sigma_c = \{c\}$. The set of events of the system is $\Sigma = \Sigma_m \cup \Sigma_a \cup \{u\}$ and secret states are colored in red.

Although the aggregate $a_{00} \subseteq S_s$, the opacity is not leaked (at this level) since the super-aggregate a_0 is not totally included in the secret set of states. However, $a_1 \subseteq S_s$ which means that G is not opaque. To enforce the opacity of this system, the supervisor disables the controllable event c. Hence, the output of the algorithm is $\gamma(ub) = c$. This leads to omitting the super-aggregates a_1, a_3 and a_4 and the aggregate a_{03}. It should be noted that the super-aggregate a_2 will persist since it can be reached through the super-aggregate a_0 and hence, we delete only the arc $a_1 \xrightarrow{A_2} a_2$ [line 10 of trimOldBranches function]. It should also be mentioned that a_0 will be trimmed, deleting only the aggregate a_{03} using the trimOldBranches function.

3.4   Implementation

To conduct an experimental evaluation of our approach, we have developed a C++ prototype, namely the(G)eneral Framework for (O)pacity (Sup)ervision using the (S)ymbolic (O)bservation (G)raph (GoSup). The developed tool takes a Petri net model of a system as input (expressed through an XML Petri net oriented language) and returns the result of opacity checks. If the test is positive (system is opaque), the result is completed with the number of nodes and edges of the constructed SOG. If the test is negative (system is not opaque), it outputs the controlled events that the supervisor needs to disable are outputted, if the opacification is possible. Otherwise, a trace is displayed as a counterexample. Further implementation details can be found in https://depot.lipn.univ-paris13. fr/gosup/gosup. Theoretical complexity of our approach is exponential in time. Although experimentation haven't been done yet, but practical complexity of our approach is expected to be very moderate.

4   Related Work

Researches for investigating the opacity property are centered around the efficient verification of various notions of opacity [10,14–20], the enforcement of this property (for non opaque systems) [21] using a variety of techniques, and the quantification [22,23] which suggests that the opacity is not necessary a binary property. Much of work in this context has been carried out using **Petri nets** modeling formalism [15,16]. In [24], the authors extended the notion of opacity to **LTSs** and generalized this property to represent information flow concepts (anonymity and non interference). Different approaches were presented. However, implementation is the key limitation in this field of research. In fact, the implementation of any new approach in this field offers a testing environment, allowing a better vision and tangible results of the proposed solution. For the verification of opacity there exist tools such as **Takos** [25], **Umdes** [26] and the **SOG** [27]. However, to the best of our knowledge, there exists no accessible tools for the supervision of opacity except the work of [28]. Authors in this work assumed that the attacker observes a subset of actions of the supervisor. In this paper, the proposed approach revisit the SOG-based approach to reinforce the opacity based on the **SCT** and with no previous condition regarding the relationship between the attacker and the synthesized supervisor observations.

Here, we focus on existing approaches to enforce systems' opacity (which is the goal of this paper) and particularly those based on SCT.

In such approaches, we assume that the intruder (possibly more than one attacker) observes only a subset of the system's events. Let Σ_a, Σ_m and Σ_c be respectively the set of observable events of the intruder, observable events of the controller and controllable events. In [29] authors have shown that an optimal control always exists and provided sufficient conditions under which it is regular and effectively computable. Using the SCT, researchers in [30] presented a reduced-complexity approach to verify the opacity of modular systems, and proposed a method for computing a local supervisor to each module. Moreover, in [31] authors assumed that the system is associated with partial observers, each one having its predefined secret, and proved that an optimal control always exists but is not generally regular.

To sum up, it exists multiple approaches to ensure and enforce opacity. However, these techniques present some practical limitations preventing their applicability since most of them do not provide an implementation. Also, all the existing opacity verification tools can lead the state space explosion problem. It has been demonstrated, in [22], that the SOG-based approach largely outperforms the TAKOS-based approach in terms of run time and memory consumption. Thus, we claim that our extension of the SOG-based approach to enforce opacity, through HSOG, allows to tackle the state explosion problem while supplying a supremal supervisor.

5   Conclusion and Future Work

In this paper, we have proposed a general framework for enforcing the opacity of Discrete Event Systems. The aim is to synthesize a supervisor that disables some actions from occurring in order to preserve secret information from being revealed. This framework is said to be general since it does not take into consideration the relationship between the attacker and the supervisor. Moreover, our approach is on-the-fly, which means that the computation of the supervisor is performed while abstracting the system. For this purpose, we have proposed a new abstraction graph, called **Hyper Symbolic Observation Graph**, that is presented in this paper. Such a graph allows to alleviate the explosion state problem by representing the state space in a condensed manner. We have implemented our approach using C++ programming language which provides a user friendly framework to test the enforcement of this security property. As a use case sample, we have considered the security of a software application which has three restricted components, that works according to the users permission levels. Applying our approach allows to enforce opacity of the application and prevent the attacker from revealing some sensible information. Several perspectives of our approach are possible. For instance, the enforcement of opacity for modular systems using a unique or several attackers. Additionally, we aim to study the quantification of the opacity.

References

1. Bryans, J.W., Koutny, M., Mazaré, L., Ryan, P.Y.A.: Opacity generalised to transition systems. In: Dimitrakos, T., Martinelli, F., Ryan, P.Y.A., Schneider, S. (eds.) FAST 2005. LNCS, vol. 3866, pp. 81–95. Springer, Heidelberg (2006). https://doi.org/10.1007/11679219_7

2. O'Halloran, C.: A calculus of information flow. In: ESORICS 90 - First European Symposium on Research in Computer Security, 24–26 October 1990, Toulouse, pp. 147–159. AFCET (1990)

3. Falcone, Y., Marchand, H.: Enforcement and validation (at runtime) of various notions of opacity. Discr. Event Dyn. Syst. **25**(4), 531–570 (2014). https://doi.org/10.1007/s10626-014-0196-4

4. Falcone, Y., Marchand, H.: Enforcement and validation (at runtime) of various notions of opacity. Discr. Event Dyn. Syst. **25**(4), 531–570 (2015)

5. Haddad, S., Ilié, J.-M., Klai, K.: Design and evaluation of a symbolic and abstraction-based model checker. In: Wang, F. (ed.) ATVA 2004. LNCS, vol. 3299, pp. 196–210. Springer, Heidelberg (2004). https://doi.org/10.1007/978-3-540-30476-0_19

6. Bryant, R.E.: Symbolic Boolean manipulation with ordered binary-decision diagrams. ACM Comput. Surv. **24**(3), 293–318 (1992)

7. Matsui, S., Cai, K.: Application of supervisory control to secret protection in discrete-event systems. J. Soc. Instrum. Control Eng. Spec. Issue Event Based Control IoT **60**(1), 14–20 (2021)

8. Klai, K, Poitrenaud, D.: MC-SOG: an LTL model checker based on symbolic observation graphs. In: van Hee, K.M., Valk, R. (eds.) PETRI NETS 2008. LNCS,
vol. 5062, pp. 288–306. Springer, Heidelberg (2008). https://doi.org/10.1007/978-
3-540-68746-7_20

9. Klai, K., Petrucci, L.: Modular construction of the symbolic observation graph.
In: 8th International Conference on Application of Concurrency to System Design
(ACSD 2008), Xi'an, China, 23–27 June 2008, pp. 88–97. IEEE (2008)

10. Bourouis, A., Klai, K., Hadj-Alouane, N.B., Touati, Y.E.: On the verification of
opacity in web services and their composition. IEEE Trans. Serv. Comput. **10**(1),
66–79 (2017)

11. Ramadge, P.J., Wonham, W.M.: The control of discrete event systems. In: Proceedings of the IEEE; Special issue on Dynamics of Discrete Event Systems, vol.
77, no. 1, pp. 81–98 (1989)

12. Cassandras, C.G., Lafortune, S.: Controlled Markov chains. In: Introduction to
Discrete Event Systems, pp. 535–591. Springer, Cham (2021). https://doi.org/10.
1007/978-3-030-72274-6_9

13. Dubreil, J., Darondeau, P., Marchand, H.: Opacity enforcing control synthesis. In:
9th International Workshop on Discrete Event Systems, pp. 28–35 (2008)

14. Jacob, R., Lesage, J., Faure, J.: Overview of discrete event systems opacity: models,
validation, and quantification. Annu. Rev. Control. **41**, 135–146 (2016)

15. Bryans, J.W., Koutny, M., Ryan, P.Y.A.: Modelling dynamic opacity using petri
nets with silent actions. In: Dimitrakos, T., Martinelli, F. (eds.) Formal Aspects in
Security and Trust. IIFIP, vol. 173, pp. 159–172. Springer, Boston (2005). https://
doi.org/10.1007/0-387-24098-5_12

16. Bryans, J.W., Koutny, M., Ryan, P.Y.A.: Modelling opacity using petri nets. Electron. Notes Theor. Comput. Sci. **121**, 101–115 (2005)

17. Saboori, A., Hadjicostis, C.: Verification of k-step opacity and analysis of its complexity. In: IEEE Transactions on Automation Science and Engineering, vol. 8, pp.
549–559 (2011)

18. Saboori, A., Hadjicostis, C.N.: Verification of initial-state opacity in security applications of des. In: 2008 9th International Workshop on Discrete Event Systems,
pp. 328–333 (2008)

19. Saboori, A.: Verification and enforcement of state-based notions of opacity in discrete event systems. PhD thesis, University of Illinois at Urbana-Champaign (2011)

20. Saboori, A., Hadjicostis, C.N.: Verification of infinite-step opacity and complexity
considerations. IEEE Trans. Autom. Control. **57**(5), 1265–1269 (2012)

21. Bourouis, A., Klai, K., Hadj-Alouane, N.B.: Measuring opacity in web services. In:
Proceedings of the 19th International Conference on Information Integration and
Web-Based Applications Services, iiWAS 2017, New York, pp. 530–534. Association
for Computing Machinery (2017)

22. Bourouis, A., Klai, K., Hadj-Alouane, N.B.: Measuring opacity for non-
probabilistic DES: a sog-based approach. In: 24th International Conference on
Engineering of Complex Computer Systems, ICECCS 2019, Guangzhou, 10–13
November 2019, pp. 242–247. IEEE (2019)

23. Bérard, B., Mullins, J., Sassolas, M.: Quantifying opacity. In: QEST 2010, Seventh
International Conference on the Quantitative Evaluation of Systems, Williamsburg,
Virginia, 15–18 September 2010, pp. 263–272. IEEE Computer Society (2010)

24. Bryans, J.W., Koutny, M., Mazaré, L., Ryan, P.Y.A.: Opacity generalised to transition systems. Int. J. Inf. Sec. **7**(6), 421–435 (2008)

25. http://toolboxopacity.gforge.inria.fr/. Takos: a java toolbox for analyzing the k-
opacity of systems (2010)

26. S. Library. www.eecs.umich.edu/umdes/toolboxes.html (2009)
27. Klai, K., Hamdi, N., BenHadj-Alouane, N.: An on-the-fly approach for the verification of opacity in critical systems. In: 2014 IEEE 23rd International WETICE Conference, WETICE 2014, Parma, 23–25 June 2014, pp. 345–350. IEEE Computer Society (2014)
28. Souid, N.E., Klai, K.: A novel approach for supervisor synthesis to enforce opacity of discrete event systems. In: Gao, D., Li, Q., Guan, X., Liao, X. (eds.) ICICS 2021. LNCS, vol. 12919, pp. 210–227. Springer, Cham (2021). https://doi.org/10.1007/978-3-030-88052-1_13
29. Dubreil, J.: Monitoring and supervisory control for opacity properties. (Vérification et Synthèse de Contrôleur pour des Propriétés de Confidentialité). PhD thesis, University of Rennes 1, France (2009)
30. Zinck, G., Ricker, L., Marchand, H., Hlout, L.: Enforcing opacity in modular systems. In: IFAC 2020, IFAC World Congress, pp. 1–8 (2020)
31. Badouel, E., Bednarczyk, M.A., Borzyszkowski, A.M., Caillaud, B., Darondeau, P.: Concurrent secrets. Discr. Event Dyn. Syst. **17**(4), 425–446 (2007)

DATA-IMP: An Interactive Approach to Specify Data Imputation Transformations on Large Datasets

Michael Behringer[✉], Manuel Fritz, Holger Schwarz, and Bernhard Mitschang

Institute for Parallel and Distributed Systems, University of Stuttgart,
Universitätsstraße 38, 70569 Stuttgart, Germany
{michael.behringer,manuel.fritz,holger.schwarz,
bernhard.mitschang}@ipvs.uni-stuttgart.de

Abstract. In recent years, the volume of data to be analyzed has
increased tremendously. However, purposeful data analyses on large-scale
data require in-depth domain knowledge. A common approach to reduce
data volume and preserve interactivity are sampling algorithms. However, when using a sample, the semantic context across the entire dataset
is lost, which impedes data preprocessing. In particular data imputation
transformations, which aim to fill empty values for more accurate data
analyses, suffer from this problem. To cope with this issue, we introduce DATA-IMP, a novel human-in-the-loop approach that enables data
imputation transformations in an interactive manner while preserving
scalability. We implemented a fully working prototype and conducted
a comprehensive user study as well as a comparison to several non-
interactive data imputation techniques. We show that our approach significantly outperforms state-of-the-art approaches regarding accuracy as
well as preserves user satisfaction and enables domain experts to preprocess large-scale data in an interactive manner.

Keywords: Data imputation · Data cleansing · Interactive data
preprocessing · Human-in-the-loop

1 Introduction

Business processes and strategic decisions are often based on the analysis and
interpretation of data. Therefore, data analysis processes like the KDD process [8] and CRISP-DM [22] include a data preprocessing step. This is crucial
for data quality and hence for the reliability of analyses, which is why up to 80%
of the effort required for an analysis is spent on data preprocessing [5]. To define
the necessary preprocessing steps, knowledge about the relevant domain needs
to be considered. Typically, this is difficult to automate [24] and hence, domain
experts need to be involved [1,7]. They interactively define the data preprocessing steps, apply them to the data, evaluate the effects of individual steps based
on their domain knowledge and adjust them if necessary.

© The Author(s), under exclusive license to Springer Nature Switzerland AG 2022
M. Sellami et al. (Eds.): CoopIS 2022, LNCS 13591, pp. 55–74, 2022.
https://doi.org/10.1007/978-3-031-17834-4_4

Nevertheless, with today's data volumes, letting domain experts work on the entire dataset is not suitable. Response times for performed transformations would often be excessive and interactive work would be impossible. Therefore, existing approaches and tools frequently use a sampling approach and separate the specification of the necessary transformations in the frontend using a Programming-by-Demonstration [6] approach from the application of these transformations to the entire dataset in the backend [2]. Suppose the transformations are only applied to the sample dataset immediately, and their application to the data in the backend takes place not before the specification of the entire data preprocessing process has been completed. In that case, this results in a huge delay before potential issues can be detected.

An example approach to detecting issues at an early stage is the work done by Behringer et al. [2]. In addition to applying transformations to a sample in the frontend, the transformations are simultaneously started on the entire dataset in the backend. In contrast to state-of-the-art approaches, the domain expert is now notified about possible issues as soon as they occur, but before all transformations are specified. This prevents the long iteration cycles described above and thus promises to enable interactive data preprocessing even on large-scale datasets.

A particularly important part of data preprocessing is data imputation. Data imputation aims to recover missing values in the best possible way. In the following, we present a motivating scenario that draws attention to severe challenges which may occur when using the approach for data imputation mentioned above.

1.1 Motivating Scenario

In this motivating scenario, we use a publicly available dataset,[1] which contains reported crimes in boroughs of London for several years. To emphasize challenges of interactive data imputation, some values were removed or slightly adjusted. The left part of Fig. 1 shows an excerpt of the sample presented to the domain expert in the frontend, and the corresponding data available in the backend. Several values are missing in the data, so a data imputation is necessary to proceed with the analysis. Therefore, the domain expert specifies in the frontend a simple and illustrative data imputation transformation that fills previously empty cells (top left) with a constant value taken from the cell above (top right). As there are no missing values left, one can assume that the data quality has increased. This is confirmed by an acceptable relative error compared to the true value of only about 4%, that we obtain when comparing the imputed values with the actual values we removed beforehand to be able to calculate the relative error.

But, as shown in the lower left part of Fig. 1, the borough of Harrow is only present in the backend (bottom left). If the specified transformation is now applied to the entire dataset, the missing values only available in the backend, are imputed as well (bottom right). By doing so, we can see the first issue when using a state-of-the-art approach: The relative error which looks acceptable in the frontend increased to more than 66% resulting in massive data quality issues

---

[1] London Crime Data: https://www.kaggle.com/LondonDataStore/london-crime.

(Fig. 1, a). This is not perceivable by domain experts as they are only aware of data in the frontend while specifying imputation transformations.

In addition, a second issue can be observed in the figure when applying data imputation transformations. Even the simple and straightforward transformation *Fill from above* requires a reference to the preceding row. Since the domain expert is working on a sample, the preceding row is most likely not the same in frontend and backend. In our motivating scenario, this is why the value for Havering in 2008 is calculated in the frontend based on Haringey in 2012 (Fig. 1, b), but in the backend based on Harrow in 2012 (Fig. 1, c). As a result, the incidents for Havering in 2008 would be 22156 in the frontend, while in the backend this cell would be given the value 12803. Thus, two different values exist at the same time and again this is not perceivable for a domain expert.

Frontend

...	Borough	Year	Incidents	...
...	...	...	...	...
...	Haringey	2010	22156	...
...	Haringey	2011		...
...	Haringey	2012		...
...	Havering	2008		...
...	Havering	2009	21538	...
...	Havering	2010	21957	...
...	Havering	2011	21496	...
...	Havering	2012	21965	...
...	...	...	...	...

Backend

...	Borough	Year	Incidents	...
...	...	...	...	...
...	Haringey	2010	22156	...
...	Haringey	2011		...
...	Haringey	2012		...
...	Harrow	2008		...
...	Harrow	2009		...
...	Harrow	2010		...
...	Harrow	2011	12801	...
...	Harrow	2012	12803	...
...	Havering	2008		...
...	Havering	2009	21538	...
...	...	...	...	...

Transformation:
Fill from "above"
with "constant value"

Frontend

...	Borough	Year	Incidents	...
...	...	...	...	...
...	Haringey	2010	22156	...
Relative Error: 4,4%	...	Haringey	2011	22156	...
Relative Error: 4,6%	...	Haringey	2012	22156	...
Relative Error: 3,6%	...	Havering	2008	22156	...
...	Havering	2009	21538	...
...	Havering	2010	21957	...
...	Havering	2011	21496	...
...	Havering	2012	21965	...
...	...	...	...	...

Backend

...	Borough	Year	Incidents	...
...	...	...	...	...
...	Haringey	2010	22156	...
Relative Error: 4,4%	...	Haringey	2011	22156	...
Relative Error: 4,6%	...	Haringey	2012	22156	...
Relative Error: 60,9%	...	Harrow	2008	22156	...
Relative Error: 58,8%	...	Harrow	2009	22156	...
Relative Error: 58,9%	...	Harrow	2010	22156	...
...	Harrow	2011	12801	...
...	Harrow	2012	12803	...
Relative Error: 66,8%	...	Havering	2008	12803	...
...	Havering	2009	21538	...
...	...	...	...	...

Fig. 1. Discrepancy between perceived state in the frontend and the actual state in the backend applying a "Fill"-transformation to impute missing values. Gray shaded rows indicate data only contained in the backend, thus unperceived by a domain expert.

1.2 Problem Statement and Contribution

Our motivating scenario shows that state-of-the-art approaches have two fundamental issues regarding data imputation: (1) application of transformations on unintended cells and (2) differing values between frontend and backend for the same cell. In both cases, the reason is that the semantics of the data is not taken into account. In this example, the semantic context is defined by the borough, and the recorded incidents vary tremendously from one to the other borough. Hence, using a value from one borough to impute a value of another borough is mostly a bad idea. However, this is not perceivable for domain experts, who would continue with the analysis, resulting in entirely incorrect results.

A closer look reveals that data imputation transformations can be divided into three categories, as shown in Table 1. The first category describes data imputation transformations that do not require any reference(s) to other rows, such as replacing missing values with a fixed value like *null*. Applying such a transformation results in the expected behavior and can thus be considered as solved. The second category includes all transformations that reference their own row, for instance, to impute cities based on zip codes. Again, these data imputation transformations work well on a sample and with the expected behavior, since all the required information is contained in the sample.

Nonetheless, in most cases, a meaningful data imputation requires references to other cell values in the same column, e. g., to interpolate missing values across different months. Although the entire column is usually not required for this purpose, as some immediately preceding values are often sufficient, it cannot be guaranteed that all necessary values are contained in the sample. However, as shown in the motivating scenario, unexpected behavior may occur in this category.

The discussion of the three categories of data imputation transformations shows that state-of-the-art approaches only deal with two of them. The more common data imputation transformations belong to the third category and cannot be used for interactive data preprocessing so far. To enable interactive data preprocessing with these data imputation transformations as well, it must be ensured that a semantic exploration of the data is completed before applying transformations of this category. Since this exploration cannot be done by an algorithm, the domain expert has to be involved.

In this paper, we introduce DATA-IMP, a novel approach to address the aforementioned issues. The main contributions are:

- We show how DATA-IMP allows domain experts to interactively define semantically related data to enable column references required for data imputation.
- We demonstrate how this serves as a basis for the proper specification of data transformations allowing experts to leverage their domain knowledge while interactively performing data imputation transformations even on large-scale datasets.
- We evaluate DATA-IMP through a user study as well as a comprehensive comparison with non-interactive techniques for data imputation. The comparison reveals that our approach is able to outperform even the best of these techniques.

The remainder of this paper is structured as follows: In Sect. 2, we present related work. In Sect. 3, we introduce DATA-IMP, our novel approach to perform data imputation transformations in an interactive manner even on large-scale datasets. We evaluate DATA-IMP by comparison to state-of-the-art approaches in Sect. 4 and conclude this work in Sect. 5.

2   Related Work

A typical approach to integrate domain experts into analysis processes is the use of spreadsheets or tools with spreadsheet-like interfaces. However, in many cases these are not suitable for today's data volumes. This results in significant challenges, like an unresponsive user interface or long-running computations, which impede the analyst [21]. One approach to cope with large amounts of data in spreadsheets and bypass at least the unresponsiveness or freezing of spreadsheet interfaces is to split the computation into two parts: Only the current viewport is calculated instantaneously, while unperceived areas are processed in the background [3]. Outdated cells are shaded to empower the domain expert to perceive the current calculation state. This provides the feeling of high responsiveness to the domain expert, but the required calculation time remains the same.

Table 1. Data imputation categories and potential issues when applying them to a sample.

	Expected behavior
Data Imputation w/o reference	✓
Data Imputation with row reference	✓
Data Imputation with column reference	✗

However, the volumes of data available today are just too large for human perception [15]. The most common approach to reduce data volumes to a manageable size is the use of sampling algorithms. These algorithms are commonly categorized as probability sampling and non-probability sampling [20]. In probability sampling, each case of the population has an equal and known chance of being part of the sample. The most common approach in this category is Simple Random Sampling. In non-probability sampling, cases from the population are selected on the basis of a subjective decision, i. e., some cases have no chance of being included in the sample, while others have a higher chance. However, the choice of a suitable algorithm is highly dependent on the domain and the data. Hence, semantic relationships between data have to be defined by a domain expert.

In the Big Data area, sampling is used in various ways. In many cases, the goal is to obtain an initial, approximate result as quickly as possible. For example, ApproxHadoop [12] tries to approximate a MapReduce program using only some blocks of the HDFS file system and discards individual tasks of the program at random or requires the user to specify a less accurate version of the code to be executed. IncApprox [16] uses sampling to get an incrementally updated result on streaming data. In other approaches, a sample is used to clean a small part of the data and use it to either estimate the result for the entire dataset (SampleClean [17]) or train a model which is applied to the entire dataset (Active-Clean [18]). But these approaches provide an extrapolation rather than an exact and reliable result. Furthermore, none offers a fine-granular feedback loop, but to leverage domain knowledge, it is necessary to put the human into the loop.

Furthermore, sampling does not solve one important issue with spreadsheets: the enormous vulnerability to errors due to the complexity of formulas and references between columns or cells. If these errors occur when preprocessing data, they may lead to unintended results with tremendous consequences [10]. To avoid this, modern interactive tools mostly rely on the familiar spreadsheet interface while trying to make the specification of transformations on the data less error-prone. For this purpose, the programming-by-demonstration [6] approach is commonly used. Here, the domain expert provides one concrete example of a transformation on a sample. The tool derives appropriate rules, which can subsequently be applied to other cells, columns, or original datasets. Typical examples for this approach are OpenRefine,[2] Wrangler [14] or the work of Gulwani et al. [13]. In particular, Wrangler offers features to integrate the user in the preprocessing of data. First, there is an intuitive specification of transformations through a user-friendly interface, which allows the user to proceed step by step without using formulas. Second, each transformation is shown in a trackable transformation history, allowing domain experts to adjust transformations anytime. After the preprocessing, a so-called transformation script can be exported and applied to a large-scale dataset.

These fundamental principles can also be found in popular tools, such as KNIME,[3] RapidMiner[4] or Trifacta Wrangler.[5] The latter emerged from the mentioned Wrangler research project. These tools either support the graphical specification of transformation sequences using the Pipes&Filters pattern or support programming-by-demonstration and a transformation history. Nonetheless, the two phases, specification of transformations on a sample and subsequent execution on the entire dataset, are still strictly separated. An occurring discrepancy between the perceived state in the visualized sample is only detected during execution, or even worse, not before conducting a subsequent analysis. Thus, a domain expert must revise the specified transformations and restart from scratch, which takes tremendous time on large-scale datasets and prevents interactive preprocessing of data.

In the work done by Behringer et al. [2], the strict separation between the specification and the execution of transformations is eliminated. If a transformation does not depend on any precondition, the transformation is executed immediately in the backend, while possible data quality issues are identified by an error detection and are immediately made visible to the domain expert. This allows that a) the execution does not have to be restarted repeatedly from scratch, b) the domain expert retains the advantages of sampling, while at the same time being able to assess and improve the quality of the preprocessing tasks on the entire dataset, and c) the required time is massively reduced because the

---

[2] OpenRefine: https://openrefine.org.

[3] KNIME: https://www.knime.com.

[4] RapidMiner: https://rapidminer.com.

[5] Trifacta Wrangler: https://www.trifacta.com.

execution already starts during the specification. Nonetheless, this approach is agnostic to semantic relations in the data. It does not support important preprocessing functionalities like data imputation, e. g., interpolate a missing incidents value for a month with regard to the previous and subsequent month (cf. Fig. 1).

In summary, there is currently no approach that comprehensively supports interactive preprocessing on large-scale datasets. Available tools and approaches either lack an intuitive user interface that allows domain experts to leverage their domain knowledge while specifying the necessary transformations, or they come with long iteration cycles such that the users cannot immediately evaluate the specified transformations and adjust them in an interactive manner.

3   Interactive Data Imputation with Data Blocks

In this section, we present DATA-IMP, a new approach to overcome the mentioned limitations of existing approaches and to enable transformations that are dependent on the semantic relations of data. To accomplish this, DATA-IMP allows (a) to leverage domain knowledge to interactively define semantically related data blocks containing subsets of data, (b) to use these data blocks as the foundation of samples, and c) to interactively specify transformations on these data blocks.

3.1   Intuition

Most approaches consist of the following steps: 1) generating a sample, 2) visualizing this sample for the domain expert, and 3) interactively specifying and performing transformations on this sample. Finally, the specified transformations can either be exported as scripts for future repetitions or applied to the entire dataset, and afterwards, the domain expert can continue with the analysis.

In Sect. 1.1, we discussed important issues that may occur when transformations require references to semantically adjacent cells. In particular, these issues occur for typical transformations in the context of data imputation, e. g., "fill from above" or "interpolate". For such transformations, the required semantically adjacent cells are most likely not contained in the sample. However, it is not detectable in an automated way which specific semantics underlie the dataset and how they influence the intended analysis, so this has to be specified by the domain expert. As a consequence, access to semantically adjacent cells is indispensable for domain experts working on interactive data preprocessing.

The following two terms are relevant for the further description of our approach DATA-IMP:

(User-defined) Data Blocks are subsets of rows in the entire dataset that share a common underlying semantics. More formally, the available rows R are partitioned into p subsets S_i for which holds:

$$Data\ Blocks := \{S_i \mid \forall S_i \subseteq R : \bigcap_{i=1}^{p} S_i = \emptyset \wedge p \leq |R|\}$$

Block functionality describes the opportunity to apply transformations that need to access other rows of a data block. This in particular includes data imputation transformations that are not limited to row-local value access. Such transformations with block functionality are called block transformations BF, are declared with a transformation definition t_{def} and can be applied to as many data blocks as the domain expert desires. Hereby, t_{def} could be a formula, a λ-expression or a script to describe operations on data. This results in the following function signature:

$$BF(\{S_i, ...\}, t_{def})$$

DATA-IMP is based on the assumption that domain experts can identify semantically related subsets of data in the sample dataset. Two phases are at the core of this approach.

The first phase is to partition the dataset. For this purpose, two tasks are performed recursively: (a) select a feature and (b) partition the dataset into data blocks based on distinct values or value ranges of this feature. To reduce the workload for the domain expert, the current data block definition is automatically applied to the sample after each cycle of this task, which allows a preview of the resulting data blocks. When the domain expert is satisfied with the block definition, this results in several data blocks containing semantically related data as shown in Fig. 2. These data blocks can be used as the basis for a sampling algorithm, i. e., selecting entire blocks instead of single rows for the sample. Hence, the semantically related data (as specified by the domain expert) is available in the frontend. For this reason, a transformation can access any cell in this data block, e. g., if the green cell in Fig. 2 should be imputed, all gray colored cells are accessible. After this partitioning of the dataset, all data imputation transformations with block functionality that do not rely on the order of the rows in a data block, are available. Typical examples are imputing missing values with the mean or median of the column.

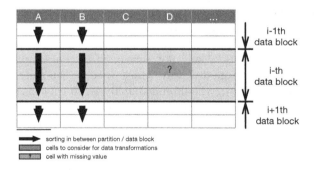

Fig. 2. Partitioning of a dataset into data blocks and cells accessible for data imputation transformations within a block.

For data imputation transformations that require the order within a data block, e. g., the mentioned *fill from above* transformation, the second phase of DATA-IMP is necessary. Hereby, the domain expert is enabled to sort the dataset as necessary, whereby the data blocks are preserved. After this sorting, the domain expert may also specify data imputation transformations that rely on the order. Furthermore, as the borders of a data block are specified, a transformation can be applied to each block independently, which prevents a behavior as shown in the motivating scenario, where values from other blocks have mistakenly been considered during transformation application and only semantically related data within each block are used. This enables the domain expert to perform data imputation transformations as expected and as perceived in the frontend on the sample.

Note that the two phases, i. e., partitioning and sorting, are also reflected in the SQL window functionality. The focus of DATA-IMP is to allow domain experts to interactively specify transformations on semantically adjacent cells without the need to provide complex statements in a language like SQL.

3.2   Walkthrough

To further illustrate DATA-IMP, we describe a representational walkthrough discussing different steps during interactive data preprocessing. DATA-IMP comprises two components: a spreadsheet-based frontend for interaction and a powerful backend responsible for computationally intensive transformations. Figure 3 illustrates the different steps and the corresponding components. In addition, we add two more steps to the conventional approaches to enable our approach: 4) generate a so-called block sampling based on data blocks and 5) a further transforming step enabling data imputation transformations with block functionality. In the following, we describe all steps in more detail:

1) Generate Row Sampling. As described before, it is necessary to draw a sample from the entire dataset before interactive preprocessing can take place. As in conventional approaches, a row-based sampling method is used in this step (Fig. 3, 1). Since, to the best of our knowledge, no sampling algorithm exists that covers every data characteristic in the sample, we use Simple Random Sampling, which gives a general overview and is usually a good choice for generic applicability. By using a sample, a domain expert only encounters a manageable subset of the data in the frontend, while a high-performance backend is responsible to process the conducted transformations on the entire dataset.

2) Feedback Loop. The obtained sample must be provided to the domain expert. For this purpose, DATA-IMP uses a feedback loop (Fig. 3, 2) as part of the user interface. This user interface presents the data in the familiar spreadsheet look and thus provides a familiar interactive environment for preprocessing data. Regarding the user interface functionality, we base the frontend of our approach on Wrangler [14] and the work done by Behringer et al. [2]. At this point in the process, we start visualizing the initial sample similar to what state-of-the-art approaches do (Fig. 3, 2a).

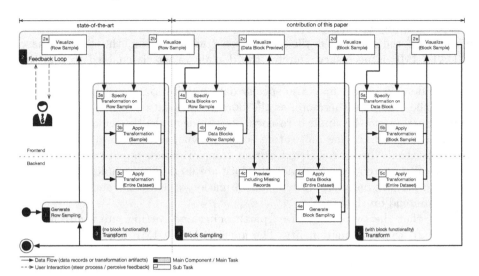

Fig. 3. Steps of DATA-IMP, the components responsible for each step, and the points of interaction for the domain expert.

3) Transform (no block functionality). After the sample has been visualized, a domain expert can specify the necessary transformations step-by-step in an interactive manner using a programming-by-demonstration approach without the need for using formulas (Fig. 3, 3a). Specified transformations are instantaneously applied to the sample in the frontend (Fig. 3, 3b) and the results are again visualized. This way, the domain expert obtains the impression of a very responsive system (Fig. 3, 2b). At the same time, the transformations are also applied to the entire dataset in the backend (Fig. 3, 3c), and in case of a conflict, i. e., an unexpected behavior not perceivable in the frontend, the domain expert is notified and is able to respond as needed in the frontend (Fig. 3, 2b). Since a single transformation rarely ensures sufficient data preprocessing, this cycle can be repeated as often as required. This phase is the last step in conventional approaches.

4) Generate Block Sampling. A domain expert requires access to other rows for data imputation transformations, which is not guaranteed in a sample. If the required values are unavailable, a differing value will be calculated for the same cell in the frontend on the sample than in the backend on the entire dataset, and a domain expert works on unreliable data. One solution is to calculate all values in the backend exclusively and to update the frontend after this calculation has been completed. This is very similar to the phase separation in state-of-the-art approaches, albeit merely for individual transformations and not for the entire preprocessing. But, this would still reduce interactivity since response times would increase tremendously. Thus, for interactive preprocessing, particularly data imputation, it must be ensured that all required rows are part of the sample and, to avoid issues of the motivating scenario (cf. Sect. 1.1), transfor-

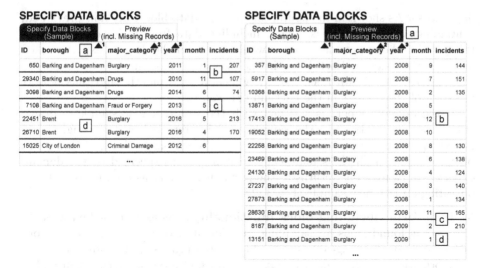

(a) Bold lines indicate the domain expert identified data blocks on the sample data.

(b) Preview of data blocks of the entire dataset used as the foundation for a sampling.

Fig. 4. The user interface of DATA-IMP.

mations must not be applied to the entire dataset unless this is the intention of the domain expert. As it is not detectable in an automated way which specific semantics underlie the dataset/analysis, this has to be specified by the domain expert. For this purpose, the domain expert identifies semantically related subsets of data (*data blocks*) on the currently visualized row sample (Fig. 3, 4a) using the approach described in Sect. 3.1. Based on the currently active block definition, this block is immediately applied to the sample (Fig. 3, 4b) and visualized to the domain expert (Fig. 3, 2c). These steps are supported by the user interface depicted in Fig. 4. In the shown example, the domain expert first sorts by *borough*, followed by *major_category*, and finally by *year* (Fig. 4a, a). Based on this sorting, semantically related data blocks are identified instantaneously and visualized by a thicker line (Fig. 4a, b). Here, once again, the reason becomes clear why a sample based on arbitrary rows is unsuitable for many data imputation transformations. In many cases, a block consists of only one representative, although it is intuitively apparent that a whole year is represented in the data. Thus, a non-existing value (Fig. 4a, c) cannot be filled reasonably based on a sample, which is why the data preprocessing cannot be continued interactively at this point. Only in one case (Fig. 4a, d) are two representatives, but this is still insufficient for any corrective treatment. However, for a domain expert, it is evident whether the block is recognized correctly and it is feasible to continue or if further adjustments are required.

After the domain expert is convinced that the block definition is correct, a preview is created (Fig. 3, 4c). The domain expert starts this step by switching to the second tab in the user interface (Fig. 4b, a) to get a preview of the resulting data blocks. As shown in the figure, the first few data blocks are now previewed, containing all of these blocks' data, including data from the backend. Hence, this preview shows how data blocks would appear if the domain expert worked on the entire dataset. Each block in the preview is most likely more extensive than before (Fig. 4b, c). Each block now contains all months and thus reflects the state of the dataset in the backend (Fig. 4a, b).

If the domain expert is satisfied with the result, a new sample is drawn (Fig. 3, 4e). In contrast to the sample used in step 3) based on single rows, this sample is now based on randomly selected data blocks. Each of these data blocks consists of all the semantically related rows as specified by the domain expert. Afterwards, one returns to the previous interface as used in step 3) now operating on this new sample (Fig. 3, 2d).

5) Transform (including block functionality). As user-defined data blocks are used as foundations for sampling, the domain expert can once again work interactively on a manageable subset of the data in this step. In addition, crucial transformations, such as data imputation transformations, which require adjacent rows, can now be specified due to the defined data blocks (Fig. 3, 5a). As described before, specified transformations are once again simultaneously applied on the sample (Fig. 3, 5b) as well as on the entire dataset (Fig. 3, 5c). To utilize such transformations, the domain expert may first sort the features unused for block selection accordingly. Note that features used to define data blocks are no longer available for further sorting, as this would either lead to no effect or require the blocks to be dissolved. In the example shown in Fig. 4b, data could further be sorted according to the attribute *month*, which subsequently allows for a data imputation transformation over the course of the year. If, for instance, a *fill from above* transformation is applied, the missing values for May, October, and December are filled with the known values from April, September, and November, respectively. However, the value for January 2009, which is also missing in our example (Fig. 4b, d), will no longer be replaced in contrast to the motivating scenario (Fig. 1), since no preceding value exists if block boundaries are taken into account. A domain expert could subsequently specify a second transformation to fill this value from known succeeding values, i. e., February.

Furthermore, to allow a large amount of freedom for this kind of transformations, domain experts should be able to choose from different scopes for a transformation: First, as outlined above, it is possible that all values in the dataset should be processed with the same transformation. That is, the same transformation is applied to *all blocks* independent of each other with respect to block boundaries. Second, a transformation can, of course, be applied to a *single block*. In this case, a transformation is applied to estimate each non-existent value only within a single data block while all of the remaining data blocks are unaffected. Third, even more detailed transformations can be applied, i. e., multiple transformations in a single block, where special characteristics of the data require different data imputation transformations. Hereby, the domain expert can also choose to apply the transformation only in the *current interval*, that is, to an arbitrary number of non-existent values between two existing values.

This enables to specify several transformations in the same block if several gaps occur in this data block.

6) Proceed/Export. It is also possible that different block definitions are needed for different kinds of transformations. For this reason, the domain expert can switch back to a row sampling at any time and specify a new block definition. If the domain expert is satisfied with the quality achieved, subsequent steps of the analysis process can be performed or the specified transformations can be exported and used for later repetition.

4   Evaluation

This section describes the evaluation of DATA-IMP. First, we conducted a user study to assess the interaction with DATA-IMP, user acceptance and achievable results. Second, we compared our results with 11 techniques for non-interactive data imputation.

4.1   User Study

In order to evaluate DATA-IMP with regard to its suitability for practicability and user acceptance, we implemented a fully working prototype with the above described functionality (cf. Sect. 3.2) using a Javascript-based frontend, components based on Python and Apache Spark and HDFS storage. The prototype supports straightforward transformations, e.g., *mean, median, fill from above/beneath, k-NN* or *moving average*.

Based on this prototype, we conducted a user study to investigate how potential users interact with DATA-IMP and how it compares to state-of-the-art approaches. Therefore, we provided several approaches to perform data imputation in our implementation. The different approaches used as the different conditions for this user study are: A_{Full}, in which the user is provided with the entire dataset but no semantically related data blocks exist, A_{Sample}, where the user works on a subset of the dataset but is not provided with block functionality and therefore has to perform data imputation on every single row as in state-of-the-art approaches and, finally, $A_{DATA-IMP}$, the presented interactive approach where the user defines the appropriate semantic-related data blocks based on available domain knowledge and can afterwards perform data imputation on these data blocks.

Participants. We recruited 12 participants (4 female, 8 male) via mailing lists and personal contacts of one of the authors. The participants were aged between 19 and 39 years ($M = 27$, $SD = 5.85$). They were either computer science or data science students or research assistants. The participants were neither rewarded for participating in this user study nor familiar with our prototype or had any knowledge of the measured variables. Furthermore, none of the participants had expert knowledge regarding data preprocessing.

Method. We conducted our study using a repeated measures design with the different approaches as the only independent variable. Each participant used the three approaches in a counterbalanced order according to the Latin Square to reduce learning effects between the conditions [9]. We used objective measures as well as subjective measures as dependent variables. As objective measures, we used the absolute error and the percentage of unprocessed cells. We collected quantitative subjective feedback through a Post-Study System Usability Questionnaire (PSSUQ) after each condition. Qualitative feedback was collected by a semi-structured interview after all conditions. Each experiment took roughly 60 min per participant and was conducted in a quiet environment.

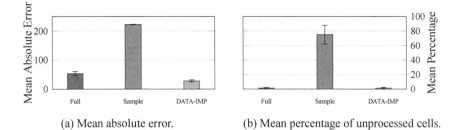

(a) Mean absolute error.   (b) Mean percentage of unprocessed cells.

Fig. 5. User study results. Lower results are better. Error bars depict the standard error.

Apparatus. We deployed a prototypical implementation of our architecture on an IBM Pure Flex cluster managed by OpenStack with 11 compute nodes and our frontend prototype on a virtual machine accessed via VNC, and each participant could keep their familiar mouse/keyboard combination. For our user study, we used the *London Crime Data* dataset[6] as ground truth. Since our evaluation requires a dataset that can be processed under all three conditions, we decided to use this rather small dataset. Note that the conditions A_{Sample} and $A_{DATA-IMP}$ would be feasible on much larger datasets, but the A_{Full} condition would not. To reduce complexity, we aggregated the dataset. The contained minor categories were summarized into their corresponding major categories to reduce the number of features, e. g., incidents of *Harassment, Common Assault, Assault with Injury* are summarized as *Violence Against the Person*. Subsequently, since this dataset does not contain empty cells, we randomly removed values. This allows us later on to compare the imputed value by the user with the correct value and thus to make statements about the results obtained. To generate the samples used in the conditions A_{Sample} and $A_{DATA-IMP}$, we used a Simple Random Sampling with a fixed seed.

Procedure. After explaining the purpose of the study and the procedure, we asked participants to perform some exemplary tasks on a training dataset with

---

[6] https://www.kaggle.com/LondonDataStore/london-crime.

COVID-19 data[7] to familiarize themselves with an interactive data preprocessing tool. These tasks included transformations on cells (renaming) and columns (sorting, combining, splitting, filling). We also gave a brief overview of other predefined transformations implemented in our prototype. To compare the different approaches, participants were asked to preprocess the dataset once under each condition in a counterbalanced order. We further requested participants to stop a preprocessing task when they were either satisfied with the achieved quality or lost motivation/confidence to accomplish the task under the current condition. We afterwards asked for subjective feedback and proceeded to the next condition. After all conditions had been processed once, we conducted a semi-structured interview.

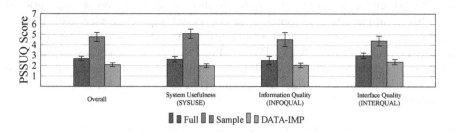

Fig. 6. Results of Post-Study System Usability Questionnaire (PSSUQ). Lower results are better. Error bars depict the standard error.

Results. We compared the conditions A_{Full}, A_{Sample} and $A_{DATA-IMP}$ regarding the absolute error and the percentage of unprocessed cells using a one-way repeated measures analysis of variance (ANOVA) to check for statistical significance. First, we analyzed the mean absolute error under each condition. Figure 5a unveils the results. A_{Full} ($M = 53.23$, $SD = 24.54$) as well as $A_{DATA-IMP}$ ($M = 28.08$, $SD = 12.57$) outperformed A_{Sample} ($M = 222.39$, $SD = 2.59$). A one-way repeated measures ANOVA revealed a significant difference between our conditions ($F(2, 22) = 486.757$, $p < .0001$). To test pairwise statistical significance between the conditions, a follow-up Bonferroni-corrected post-hoc test was performed. This test revealed that the respective pairwise differences between the conditions are statistically significant, i. e., $A_{DATA-IMP}$ is statistically the best performing condition.

Secondly, we analyzed the percentage of unprocessed cells. Figure 5b summarizes the results. It can be seen that A_{Full} ($M = 1.22$, $SD = 3.75$) and $A_{DATA-IMP}$ ($M = 1.31$, $SD = 3.72$) performed best once again, while A_{Sample} drops off strongly ($M = 75.0$, $SD = 45.22$). A one-way repeated measures ANOVA revealed a significant difference ($F(2, 22) = 32.522$, $p < .0001$) between the conditions. A follow-up Bonferroni-corrected post-hoc test proves again that A_{Sample}

---

[7] https://www.kaggle.com/antgoldbloom/covid19-data-from-john-hopkins-university.

is statistically significantly worse performing compared to the other conditions. In this case, we could not find a significant difference between A_{Full} and $A_{DATA-IMP}$. After each condition, we asked the participants to fill a Post-Study System Usability Questionnaire (PSSUQ) for subjective ratings. The detailed results for all dimensions of the PSSUQ are shown in Fig. 6. Regarding the overall score A_{Full} ($M = 2.66$, $SD = 0.73$) and $A_{DATA-IMP}$ ($M = 2.08$, $SD = 0.65$) outperformed A_{Sample} ($M = 4.74$, $SD = 1.55$). A Friedman ANOVA shows that these differences are statistically significant ($\chi^2(2) = 21.574$, $p < .001$). Furthermore, follow-up Wilcoxon tests showed significant differences between A_{Full} and A_{Sample} ($Z = -2.934$, $p < .005$), $A_{DATA-IMP}$ and A_{Sample} ($Z = -3.059$, $p < .005$), and $A_{DATA-IMP}$ and A_{Full} ($Z = -2.118$, $p < .05$).

In the concluding interviews, the majority of our participants stated that they would prefer an interactive data preprocessing tool over a conventional spreadsheet application. In particular, the possibility to specify user-defined, semantically related data blocks was highly appreciated and considered exceptionally helpful (P1, P2, P3, P4, P5, P7, P8, P9, P11, P12) as they expected to get more accurate results (P1, P3, P4, P7). Still, some participants would have preferred more support during the specification of data blocks, e. g., by a step-by-step wizard (P4, P5).

Discussion. Our comprehensive user study shows that DATA-IMP provides the same functionality on a sample that a domain expert would expect on the entire dataset. This is particularly evident when comparing the data imputations performed under the evaluated conditions. Looking at the mean absolute error, our novel approach $A_{DATA-IMP}$ is statistically significant better performing than A_{Full} and A_{Sample}. Regarding the unprocessed cells, the result is similar. A_{Full} performs slightly better than $A_{DATA-IMP}$, although both conditions are statistically significantly better than A_{Sample}. The slightly better performance of A_{Full} is caused by the separation into blocks when using $A_{DATA-IMP}$ and performed transformations are not being applied cross-block. For instance, if a *fill from above* transformation is performed and the previous values in this column are not available, this leads using A_{Full} to unprocessed cells only at the beginning of the dataset, while using $A_{DATA-IMP}$ this could occur theoretically in each block. Yet, unprocessed cells are easy to detect, thus this is only a theoretical limitation.

Finally, our participants rated our approach DATA-IMP better than state-of-the-art approaches for interactive data preprocessing. Based on our evaluation, we conclude that DATA-IMP retains the interactive functionality while additionally enabling the processing of large-scale datasets. Accordingly, our human-in-the-loop approach opens up new ways for domain experts to efficiently preprocess Big Data interactively.

4.2   Comparison to Non-interactive Data Imputation Techniques

In a further step, we evaluated how our approach DATA-IMP performs compared to non-interactive data imputation techniques.

Selection. Since many data imputation techniques and tools exist, a selection had to be made for the evaluation. To identify the most frequently used and most representative techniques, we draw on the literature reviews done by Garciarena and Santana [11] as well as Lin and Tsai [19]. Furthermore, we include DataWig [4], a framework explicitly designed for data imputation in tables and based on state-of-the-art deep learning models. In order to provide a comparison to the capabilities available to domain experts today, we looked for a data analysis tool that provides data imputation. For this reason, we also included H2O[8] as a substitute in the comparison. Overall, we have a selection of 11 techniques providing non-interactive data imputation (cf. Fig. 7).

Method. Since there is no uniform data format that each of the techniques can handle, the datasets had to be preprocessed. While H2O, DataWig, and scikit-learn work with pandas data frames, the libraries we used for the remaining techniques, impyute and missingpy, require a numpy array. Further, not all procedures can deal with categorical data, so one-hot encoding was used in order to numerically encode the dataset. If a model has to be trained for the techniques, there are two variations. Either the respective library did this itself (DataWig) or we divided the dataset into rows without missing values and rows with missing values. We used the former dataset to train the model and the latter dataset for testing. This way, classifiers like Random Forest, Naïve Bayes or k-nearest neighbor can also be used for data imputation. In the context of this paper, domain experts are the target group, and it cannot be assumed that they can adapt parameters of different techniques to suit a given task. For this reason, all of the evaluated techniques were executed with the respective default parameters for comparability. For non-deterministic techniques, e. g., Random Forest, each of these was run three times and the average result was used for the comparison. To allow a comparison with the conducted user study, the mean absolute error is once again used as a measure of performance.

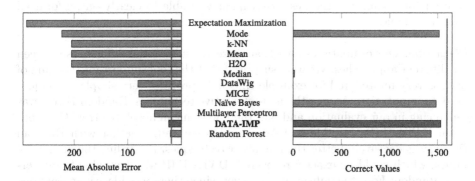

Fig. 7. DATA-IMP in comparison with non-interactive techniques. The vertical line indicates our best participant and is the best-achieved result over all techniques.

---

[8] https://www.h2o.ai/.

Results. The results in the left part of Fig. 7 show that 6 of the 11 non-interactive techniques are close to or above a mean absolute error of 200. This is not surprising for simple statistical methods such as mean, median, and mode since only a global value for the entire column is calculated and subsequently used to impute the missing values within this column. Expectation Maximization also mainly relies on the mean of the column and, in most cases, merely finds a local optimum. Similarly, H2O in its default setting uses the mean to impute missing values. Finally, k-NN estimates missing values using nearby values. However, these spatially adjacent values are not necessarily semantically adjacent, especially if individual features are not normalized. But these semantically adjacent values are important for successful data imputation. For the remaining techniques, the results are substantially closer to the original true values. Nevertheless, a further group of 4 techniques is apparent. MICE is once again based on the mean, but with additional linear regression. This leads to more accurate results, at least if linear correlations are present in the data. Next, Naïve Bayes assumes that the values of a feature are independent to the values of every other feature, which is most commonly not the case in datasets. For Multilayer Perceptron and DataWig, the underlying cause for the performance is uncertain since these techniques are black boxes and thus lack explainability. Finally, the best non-interactive technique is Random Forest, which uses many different decision trees and thus adapts well to different semantic blocks in a dataset. Our novel interactive approach DATA-IMP is close to Random Forest in terms of the mean absolute error across all participants. The green vertical line in Fig. 7 shows the error for the best participant of our user study. This indicates that DATA-IMP allows users to exploit their domain knowledge for data imputation and thus beat the best non-interactive techniques. In a further step, we evaluated the amount of correctly imputed values. The results in the right part of Fig. 7 show that most techniques could only recover very few values correctly. Only Mode, Random Forest, Naïve Bayes and our novel approach DATA-IMP show a convincing performance. Here, DATA-IMP surpasses the non-interactive techniques even on the mean, and the best participant was able to clearly outperform all other techniques.

Discussion. Our evaluation shows that there are substantial differences between the different approaches. We were surprised that the tool support for this kind of tasks is very limited and for example H2O only provides very simple techniques for data imputation. Among the non-interactive techniques, Random Forest was convincing in our evaluation and had the lowest mean absolute error. Our approach DATA-IMP was able to take second place and, together with Random Forest, was decisively better than all other techniques. Regarding the number of values, which could be exactly recovered, DATA-IMP was even able to outperform Random Forest significantly. However, since there was always at least one participant in the study who could achieve the best value across all techniques, our approach DATA-IMP can be considered the winner of the comparative evaluation.

In general, such a comparative evaluation can only be an indication for the suitability of a technique, since the results of non-interactive techniques strongly depend on the dataset characteristics [23] and due to the focus of this paper on the interactive approach. The involvement of a domain expert therefore becomes even more important, since there is just not one best technique for every use case and the explainability in many advanced techniques is not given. Both issues could be addressed if a domain expert can leverage the available domain knowledge. We therefore conclude, that our novel approach enables domain experts to exploit their domain knowledge and is able to deliver better results than achievable with non-interactive techniques.

5   Conclusion and Future Work

In this paper, we presented DATA-IMP, a novel approach for interactive data preprocessing. State-of-the-art approaches allow either high scalability with decreased interactivity or high interactivity but reduced scalability. To overcome these issues, our approach allows a domain expert to specify semantically related subsets of data, so-called data blocks in an interactive manner based on the goals of the intended analysis. We demonstrated how these data blocks could afterwards be used as foundation for sampling, allowing to perform data imputation transformations while maintaining scalability and thus, interactivity, even for large-scale datasets. In contrast to state-of-the-art approaches, our approach not only supports row-local transformations, where the result relies only on the same row, but also transformations depending on potentially all semantically adjacent cells of the data block.

In our comprehensive user study, we unveiled that DATA-IMP significantly outperforms state-of-the-art approaches in terms of accuracy. Thus, enables domain experts to exploit their domain knowledge for data preprocessing within a human-in-the-loop process and to achieve more valuable data analysis results. Furthermore, we compared DATA-IMP to 11 non-interactive techniques and showed that by involving domain experts even the best non-interactive technique was outperformed regarding accuracy. In future work, we aim to evaluate if non-interactive techniques can be improved through user-defined data blocks thus combining both approaches.

References

1. Behringer, M., Hirmer, P., Mitschang, B.: A human-centered approach for interactive data processing and analytics. In: Hammoudi, S., Śmiałek, M., Camp, O., Filipe, J. (eds.) ICEIS 2017. LNBIP, vol. 321, pp. 498–514. Springer, Cham (2018). https://doi.org/10.1007/978-3-319-93375-7_23
2. Behringer, M., Hirmer, P., Fritz, M., Mitschang, B.: Empowering domain experts to preprocess massive distributed datasets. In: Abramowicz, W., Klein, G. (eds.) BIS 2020. LNBIP, vol. 389, pp. 61–75. Springer, Cham (2020). https://doi.org/10.1007/978-3-030-53337-3_5

3. Bendre, M., et al.: Anti-freeze for large and complex spreadsheets: asynchronous formula computation. In: Proceedings of the SIGMOD 2019, pp. 1277–1294 (2019)
4. Biessmann, F., et al.: "Deep" learning for missing value imputation in tables with non-numerical data. In: Proceedings of CIKM 2018, pp. 2017–2025 (2018)
5. CrowdFlower Inc.: 2016 Data Science Report. Whitepaper (2016)
6. Cypher, A. (ed.): Watch What I Do - Programming by Demonstration (1993)
7. Endert, A., Hossain, M.S., Ramakrishnan, N., North, C., Fiaux, P., Andrews, C.: The human is the loop: new directions for visual analytics. J. Intell. Inf. Syst. **43**, 411–435 (2014)
8. Fayyad, U.M., et al.: From data mining to knowledge discovery in databases. AI Mag. **17**(3), 37–54 (1996)
9. Field, A., Hole, G.: How to Design and Report Experiments (2002)
10. Gandel, S.: Damn Excel! How the 'most important software application of all time' is ruining the world. Fortune.com, April 2013
11. Garciarena, U., Santana, R.: An extensive analysis of the interaction between missing data types, imputation methods, and supervised classifiers. Expert Syst. Appl. **89**, 52–65 (2017)
12. Goiri, I., et al.: ApproxHadoop - bringing approximations to MapReduce frameworks. ASPLOS **50**(4), 383–397 (2015)
13. Gulwani, S., et al.: Spreadsheet data manipulation using examples. Commun. ACM **55**(8), 97–105 (2012)
14. Kandel, S., Paepcke, A., Hellerstein, J., Heer, J.: Wrangler: interactive visual specification of data transformation scripts. In: Proceedings of CHI 2011, pp. 3363–3372 (2011)
15. Keim, D.A., et al.: Visual analytics: how much visualization and how much analytics? SIGKDD Explor. **11**(2), 5–8 (2010)
16. Krishnan, D.R., et al.: IncApprox: a data analytics system for incremental approximate computing. In: Proceedings of WWW 2016, pp. 1133–1144 (2016)
17. Krishnan, S., et al.: SampleClean - fast and reliable analytics on dirty data. IEEE Data Eng. Bull. **38**(3), 59–75 (2015)
18. Krishnan, S., et al.: ActiveClean: an interactive data cleaning framework for modern machine learning. In: Proceedings of SIGMOD 2016, pp. 2117–2120 (2016)
19. Lin, W.-C., Tsai, C.-F.: Missing value imputation: a review and analysis of the literature (2006–2017). Artif. Intell. Rev. **53**(2), 1487–1509 (2019)
20. Lohr, S.L.: Sampling: Design and Analysis, 2nd edn. Cengage Learning, Boston (2009)
21. Mack, K., et al.: Characterizing scalability issues in spreadsheet software using online forums. In: CHI EA 2018 (2018)
22. Shearer, C.: The CRISP-DM model: the new blueprint for data mining. J. Data Warehous. **5**(4), 13–22 (2000)
23. Thomas, T., Rajabi, E.: A systematic review of machine learning-based missing value imputation techniques. Data Technol. Appl. **55**(4), 558–585 (2021)
24. Wache, H., et al.: Ontology-based integration of information - a survey of existing approaches. In: OIS@IJCAI (2001)

Quantifying Temporal Privacy Leakage in Continuous Event Data Publishing

Majid Rafiei[1]([✉])[iD], Gamal Elkoumy[2][iD], and Wil M. P. van der Aalst[1][iD]

[1] Chair of Process and Data Science, RWTH Aachen University, Aachen, Germany
majid.rafiei@pads.rwth-aachen.de
[2] University of Tartu, Tartu, Estonia

Abstract. Process mining employs event data extracted from different types of information systems to discover and analyze actual processes. Event data often contain highly sensitive information about the people who carry out activities or the people for whom activities are performed. Therefore, privacy concerns in process mining are receiving increasing attention. To alleviate privacy-related risks, several privacy preservation techniques have been proposed. Differential privacy is one of these techniques which provides strong privacy guarantees. However, the proposed techniques presume that event data are released in only one shot, whereas business processes are continuously executed. Hence, event data are published repeatedly, resulting in additional risks. In this paper, we demonstrate that continuously released event data are not independent, and the correlation among different releases can result in privacy degradation when the same differential privacy mechanism is applied to each release. We quantify such privacy degradation in the form of temporal privacy leakages. We apply continuous event data publishing scenarios to real-life event logs to demonstrate privacy leakages.

Keywords: Privacy preservation · Differential privacy · Process mining · Privacy leakage · Event data

1 Introduction

Process mining forms a family of techniques used to analyze operational processes of organizations. These techniques use event logs extracted from information systems. An event log contains sequences of events, and each event reflects the execution of an activity with some attributes, e.g., the timestamp at which the activity was performed or the case for which the activity was performed. Some event attributes may refer to individuals, e.g., patients or customers, thus raising privacy concerns.

Data regulations, e.g., GDPR [1], limit the analysis of sensitive event logs. To circumvent such restrictions, Privacy-Preserving Process Mining (PPPM) [8]

Funded under the Excellence Strategy of the Federal Government and the Länder. We also thank the Alexander von Humboldt Stiftung for supporting our research.

M. Sellami et al. (Eds.): CoopIS 2022, LNCS 13591, pp. 75–94, 2022.
https://doi.org/10.1007/978-3-031-17834-4_5

Part (a):

	i = 1	i = 2	i = 3	...
trace₁	⟨▶,a,b,c⟩⁴	⟨▶,a,b,c,f⟩⁴	⟨▶,a,b,c,f,■⟩⁴	...
trace₂	⟨▶,d,a,b⟩²	⟨▶,d,a,b,c⟩²	⟨▶,d,a,b,c,g⟩²	...
trace₃	⟨▶,d,a,f⟩²	⟨▶,d,a,f,c⟩²	⟨▶,d,a,f,c,h⟩²	...
trace₄	⟨▶,a,b,f⟩⁴	⟨▶,a,b,f,c⟩⁴	⟨▶,a,b,f,c,■⟩⁴	...

Part (b):

	i = 1	i = 2	i = 3	...
⟨▶,a,b,c⟩	4	0	0	...
⟨▶,a,b,c,f⟩	0	4	0	...
⟨▶,a,b,c,f,■⟩	0	0	4	...
⟨▶,a,b,f⟩	4	0	0	...
⟨▶,a,b,f,c⟩	0	4	0	...
⟨▶,a,b,f,c,■⟩	0	0	4	...
⟨▶,d,a,f⟩	2	0	0	...
⟨▶,d,a,f,c⟩	0	2	0	...
⟨▶,d,a,f,c,h⟩	0	0	2	...
⟨▶,d,a,b⟩	2	0	0	...
⟨▶,d,a,b,c⟩	0	2	0	...
⟨▶,d,a,b,c,g⟩	0	0	2	...

Part (c):

	i = 1	i = 2	i = 3	...
⟨▶,a,b,c⟩	2	0	1	...
⟨▶,a,b,c,f⟩	0	3	0	...
⟨▶,a,b,c,f,■⟩	0	0	5	...
⟨▶,a,b,f⟩	3	0	0	...
⟨▶,a,b,f,c⟩	0	3	0	...
⟨▶,a,b,f,c,■⟩	0	0	1	...
⟨▶,d,a,f⟩	3	0	0	...
⟨▶,d,a,f,c⟩	1	2	0	...
⟨▶,d,a,f,c,h⟩	0	0	1	...
⟨▶,d,a,b⟩	1	0	0	...
⟨▶,d,a,b,c⟩	1	3	0	...
⟨▶,d,a,b,c,g⟩	0	1	3	...

(a) An event log containing trace variants with their frequencies, e.g., $trace_1$ happened 4 times. (b) The actual frequency of trace variants at each release point. (c) Differentially private frequency of trace variants at each release point.

Fig. 1. Continuous event data release under temporal correlations.

proposes techniques to guarantee privacy preservation, e.g., *Differential Privacy* (DP) [4] or *group-based* privacy preservation techniques, i.e., k-anonymity and its extensions [17]. DP works based on a noise injection mechanism that injects noise into published data to ensure that modifying a single user's record in the original data has a small impact on the published data. Such an impact is bounded by ϵ, so-called *privacy budget*. The smaller values of ϵ result in more noise injection and less privacy leakage.

Process mining techniques, such as *process discovery* and *conformance checking*, discover and analyze the control-flow of a process which is based on the distribution of *trace variants*, i.e., the control-flow aspect of an event log. A trace variant is a sequence of activities performed for a case. Various privacy mechanisms have been proposed to anonymize the control-flow aspect of an event log [9,11,15,17]. These approaches consider only a one-shot data release. However, business processes are continuously executed, stressing the need for Continuous Event Data Publishing (CEDP) [18]. In CEDP, events are collected up to a certain point in time or meeting a certain condition and published in the form of event logs. This publishing scenario is done continuously based on a *time-window*, e.g., daily, or a *count-window*, e.g., each new release contains one new event per trace.

CEDP may result in violating the provided privacy guarantees provided for separate releases of event logs if there are correlations among continuously released event logs. For example, consider the continuous release of the event data in Fig. 1. An organization collects its business process event data in the form of trace variants frequencies up to a release point and publishes the differentially private trace variant frequencies. Suppose that each case, e.g., a patient, contributes to only one trace variant at each release point and the trace variant of a case is the sensitive information that needs to be protected. Note that the trace variant of a case is considered sensitive information because it contains the entire sequence of activities performed for the case. For example, in the healthcare context, the activities are treatment-related, and sequences of activities can be exploited to determine the health conditions of cases, e.g., their diseases.

In order to provide an ϵ-DP guarantee, one needs to hide the participation of an individual in the released output. To this end, the output gets noisified. The amount of noise is determined by the privacy parameter ϵ and the *sensitivity* of a query. The sensitivity indicates how much uncertainty is required to hide the contribution of one individual to the query. Here, the query is the frequency of each trace variant. Since the modification of only one frequency value, i.e., the contribution of one individual, at a specific release point i in Fig. 1b affects only one trace variant, the sensitivity is set to 1. Adding noise drawn from a *Laplacian distribution* with scale $1/\epsilon$, where the sensitivity value is in the numerator, to perturb each frequency achieves ϵ-DP at each release point [5], as in Fig. 1c.

However, that may not be true with the existence of *temporal correlations*. For example, as shown in Fig. 1b, the frequency of each trace variant at release point i is not independent of the frequency of its prefix at release point $i-1$. Thus, adding Laplacian noise with scale $1/\epsilon$ at the release point $i = 3$ only achieves 3ϵ-DP, which is three times weaker than the first provided guarantee. One can interpret this situation based on *group differential privacy*, where correlated data are protected as a group [3]. Moreover, due to the nature of business processes, traces may have a particular subtrace pattern, such as "activity b always follows activity a". Such temporal correlations can be formulated as conditional probabilities to analyze their effect on the provided privacy guarantees by DP mechanisms [2].

In this paper, we adapt the approach introduced in [2]. In [2], the authors assume that probability matrices explaining the correlations between different releases are given. However, we exploit some characteristics of CEDP to obtain such probabilities. We show that different event data publishing scenarios can affect the correlations and the privacy leakage results. We also investigate the effect of specific event log characteristics on the correlations and privacy leakages. Our proposal utilizes a transition system to model traces in the form of states at each point of release. Particularly, we focus on a full-history transition system, so-called prefix automaton, where each state represents a prefix of a trace from the start point until the state. We utilize such a transition system to obtain conditional probabilities between states (traces) at each release point.

The paper is structured as follows. Section 2 discusses related work. Section 3 introduces basic notations and formal definitions. Section 4 demonstrates our approach to quantify temporal privacy leakage in CEDP. In Sect. 5, we provide experiments based on real-life public event logs. Section 6 concludes the paper and discusses some limitations of the approach.

2   Related Work

A plethora of studies has been conducted to provide privacy for process mining. In [8], the authors studied the requirements and challenges of providing privacy-preserving process mining. Several studies applied differential privacy to publish event logs. Mannhardt et al. [15] applied differential privacy to anonymize queries over event logs. PRIPEL [10] applies differential privacy to anonymize timestamps of event logs. SaCoFa [11] integrates differential privacy with event log semantics to anonymize the control flow of event logs. In [9], the authors applied differential privacy to event logs in order to prevent singling out individuals using the prefixes/suffixes of their traces. However, all of the above mechanisms assume one-shot data publishing.

Dwork et al. first studied differential privacy under continual observation, and they presented user-level [7] and event level [6] privacy. Several studies have investigated applying differential privacy in continuous data publishing. Kellaris et al. [14] studied the problem of infinite sequences. Fan et al. [12] studied differential privacy with a real-time publishing setting. Cao et al. [2] quantified the risk of using differential privacy under temporal correlation to release continuous location data. A framework for quantifying risk when publishing only one event log for process mining has been studied in [16]. To the best of our knowledge, no study has presented a risk quantification for differential privacy in continuous event data publishing. Although, in [18], the authors have elaborated possible attacks against continuous anonymized event data publishing, that work focuses on group-based privacy preservation techniques.

3   Preliminaries

In this section, we provide formal definitions for *event logs, transition systems,* and *differential privacy,* which will be used to explain the approach.

3.1   Event Log

For a given set A, A^* is the set of all finite sequences over A, and $\mathcal{B}(A)$ is the set of all multisets over the set A. A finite sequence over A of length n is a mapping $\sigma \in \{1, ..., n\} \to A$, represented as $\sigma = \langle a_1, a_2, ..., a_n \rangle$ where $a_i = \sigma(i)$ for any $1 \leq i \leq n$. $|\sigma|$ denotes the length of the sequence. Given A and B as two multisets, $A \uplus B$ is the sum over multisets, e.g., $[a^2, b^3] \uplus [b^2, c^2] = [a^2, b^5, c^2]$. A multiset set A can be represented as a set of tuples $\{(a, A(a)) | a \in A\}$ where $A(a)$ is the frequency of $a \in A$. For $\sigma_1, \sigma_2 \in A^*$, $\sigma_1 \sqsubseteq \sigma_2$ if σ_1 is a subsequence of σ_2, e.g., $\langle z, x, a, b \rangle \sqsubseteq \langle z, x, a, b, b, c, a, b, c, x \rangle$.

Definition 1 (Event). *An event is a tuple $e = (c, a, t)$, where $c \in \mathcal{C}$ is the case identifier, $a \in \mathcal{A}$ is the activity associated with the event e, and $t \in \mathcal{T}$ is the timestamp of the event e. We call $\xi = \mathcal{C} \times \mathcal{A} \times \mathcal{T}$ the universe of events. Given an event $e = (c, a, t) \in \xi$, $\pi_{case}(e) = c$, $\pi_{act}(e) = a$, and $\pi_{time}(e) = t$.*

Note that ▶ and ■ are artificial start and end activities included in $\mathcal{A}$, i.e., $\{▶, ■\} \subset \mathcal{A}$. We assume that the case identifiers are dummy identifiers referring to individuals such as patients, workers, customers, etc. These identifiers cannot be exploited to directly re-identify individuals.

Definition 2 (Trace, Trace Variant). *Let ξ be the universe of events. A trace $\sigma = \langle e_1, e_2, ..., e_n \rangle$ in an event log is a sequence of events, s.t., for each $e_i, e_j \in \sigma$, $1 \leq i < j \leq n$: $\pi_{case}(e_i) = \pi_{case}(e_j)$, and $\pi_{time}(e_i) \leq \pi_{time}(e_j)$. A trace variant is a trace where all the events are projected on the activity attribute, i.e., $\sigma \in \mathcal{A}^*$.*

Definition 3 (Event Log). *An event log L is a set of case identifiers and their corresponding trace variants, i.e., $L \subseteq C \times A^*$. If $(c_1, \sigma_1),(c_2, \sigma_2) \in L$ and $c_1 = c_2$, then $\sigma_1 = \sigma_2$. $\tilde{L} = [\sigma \mid (c, \sigma) \in L]$ is the multiset representation of traces in L, i.e., $\tilde{L} \in \mathcal{B}(A^*)$. Given $(c, \sigma) \in L$, $\pi_{case}((c, \sigma)) = c$ and $\pi_{trace}((c, \sigma)) = \sigma$.*

For instance, $L_1 = [(c_1, \langle \blacktriangleright, a, b, c, f, \blacksquare \rangle), (c_2, \langle \blacktriangleright, a, b, f, c, \blacksquare \rangle), (c_3, \langle \blacktriangleright, d, a, b, c, g \rangle), (c_4, \langle \blacktriangleright, d, a, f, c, h \rangle)]$ is an event log with artificial start activities for all the traces, and artificial end activities for the *complete traces*, i.e., the traces of c_1 and c_2. The traces of c_3 and c_4 are called *partial traces*, i.e., traces that have not yet reached the end activity. Note that our definition of an event log represent the control-flow perspective that is the focus of this work. In general, events of an event log may contain more attributes, e.g., *resources*, who perform activities.

3.2   Transition System

In this paper, we aim to quantify the privacy degradation in CEDP due to the correlations among event logs in different release points. To this end, we need to adopt an event log representation that helps to study these correlations. We consider a full-history transition system, so-called prefix automaton, as the event log representation. A transition system is one of the most basic process modeling notations which consists of states and transitions. States are represented by circles having unique labels, and transitions are represented by directed arcs with activity labels. Each transition connects two states. Figure 2 shows a transition system for the event log L_1. The labels of states are specified by a state representation function, which is defined as follows.

Definition 4 (State). *Given $\sigma \in A^*$ as a trace and $0 \leq k \leq |\sigma|$ as a number, which indicates the number of events of σ that have occurred, state (σ, k) is a function that produces a state.*

We define $state_{hd}()$ as the state representation functions describing the current state by the history of the case, i.e., given $\sigma = \langle a_1, a_2, ..., a_n \rangle$ as a trace of length n, $state_{hd}(\sigma, k) = \langle a_1, a_2, ..., a_k \rangle$.

Definition 5 (Event Log Representation). *Let $L \subseteq C \times A^*$ be an event log and state() be a state representation function. $TS_{L, state()} = (S, A, T)$ is a transition system that represents L based on state() where:*

- $S = \{state(\sigma, k) \mid (c, \sigma) \in L \land 0 \leq k \leq |\sigma|\}$ *is the state space;*
- $A = \{\sigma(k) \mid (c, \sigma) \in L \land 1 \leq k \leq |\sigma|\}$ *is the set of activities;*
- $T = [(state(\sigma, k), \sigma(k+1), state(\sigma, k+1)) \mid (c, \sigma) \in L \land 0 \leq k < |\sigma|]$ *is the multiset of transitions;*
- $S^{start} = \{state(\sigma, 0) \mid (c, \sigma) \in L\}$ *is the set of start states; and*
- $S^{end} = \{state(\sigma, |\sigma|) \mid (c, \sigma) \in L \land \sigma(|\sigma|) = \blacksquare\}$ *is the set of end states.*

Using $state_{hd}()$ as a state representation function, one can create a transition system where states represent prefixes. Consider $L_1 = [(c_1, \langle \blacktriangleright, a, b, c, f, \blacksquare \rangle), (c_2,$

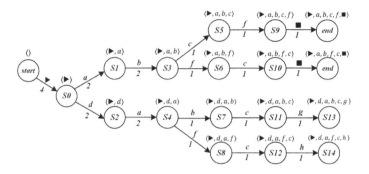

Fig. 2. The history transition system of the event log L_1. The circles represent states, and the arcs represent transitions with activity names as their labels. The numbers below arcs show the frequency of the corresponding transition.

$\langle \blacktriangleright, a, b, f, c, \blacksquare \rangle), (c_3, \langle \blacktriangleright, d, a, b, c, g \rangle), (c_4, \langle \blacktriangleright, d, a, f, c, h \rangle)]$ as an event log where c_1 and c_2 have complete traces, and c_3 and c_4 have partial traces. Figure 2 shows the history transition system, obtained by considering $state_{hd}()$ as the state representation function for the event log L_1. A history transition system can be converted to a probabilistic model to show the correlation between states as conditional probabilities. We utilize such representation of an event log to quantify the correlations between traces. Then, such correlations are used to quantify temporal privacy leakages of a DP mechanism in CEDP.

3.3 Differential Privacy

Differential privacy provides a formal definition of data privacy. The main idea of differential privacy is to randomize the data in such a way that an observer seeing the randomized output cannot tell if a specific individual's information was used in the computation [5]. Considering the distribution of trace variants as our sensitive event data, ϵ-DP can be defined as follows.

Definition 6 (ϵ-DP). *Let L_1 and L_2 be two neighbouring event logs that differ only in a single entry, e.g., $\tilde{L}_2 = \tilde{L}_1 \uplus [\sigma]$, for any $\sigma \in \mathcal{A}^*$, and let $\epsilon \in \mathbb{R}_{>0}$ be the privacy parameter. A randomized mechanism $\mathcal{M}:\mathcal{B}(\mathcal{A}^*) \to \mathcal{B}(\mathcal{A}^*)$ provides ϵ-DP if for any $(\sigma, f) \in \mathcal{A}^* \times \mathbb{N}_{>0}$ and for all $\tilde{L}' \in rng(\mathcal{M})$:*

$$log \frac{Pr((\sigma, f) \in \tilde{L}' \mid \mathcal{M}(\tilde{L}_1))}{Pr((\sigma, f) \in \tilde{L}' \mid \mathcal{M}(\tilde{L}_2))} \le e^\epsilon$$

The parameter ϵ is called the *privacy budget* and represents the degree of privacy. The smaller the privacy budget, the stronger the privacy guarantees. A real-valued query q can be made differentially private by using a *Laplace mechanism* where the noise is drawn from a *Laplacian distribution* with scale $\Delta q/\epsilon$. Δq is called the sensitivity of the query q. Intuitively, Δq denotes the amount of uncertainty that one needs to incorporate into the output to hide

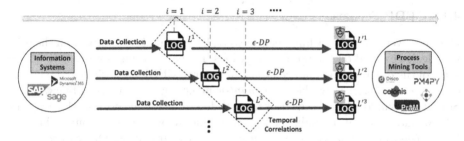

Fig. 3. The general overview of continuous event data publishing in process mining.

the contribution of single occurrences at the ϵ-DP level. In our context, q is the frequency of a trace variant. Since one individual, i.e., a case, contributes to only one trace, the sensitivity is $\Delta q = 1$ [11,15]. If an individual can appear in more than one trace, the sensitivity needs to be accordingly increased assuming the same value for privacy parameter ϵ [5].

4 Continuous Event Data Publishing

Continuous data publishing can generally be classified into three main categories: *incremental, decremental,* and *dynamic* [13]. In incremental continuous data publishing, the raw data are cumulatively collected up to a release point, and they cannot be updated or deleted after the collection phase. In decremental continuous data publishing, the previously collected raw data can only be deleted in the later releases. Dynamic data publishing assumes that new raw data can be added to the previously collected data, and the previously collected data can be updated or deleted. In the context of process mining, the events generated by an information system are cumulatively collected, and they are not updated or deleted after generation, i.e., the continuous event data publishing is *incremental.* Figure 3 shows the general overview of continuous event data publishing using an ϵ-DP mechanism in process mining. Events recorded by information systems are collected up to a release point i, then ϵ-DP mechanisms are applied to provide privacy guarantees for each event log L^i.

The incremental nature of CEDP can be considered as the main reason of temporal correlations among event logs that need to be published at different release points. For example, the complete traces in an event log L^i appear in all the next releases $L^{i+1}, L^{i+2}, \cdots$. Moreover, each trace σ in an event log L^i has a prefix in all the previous releases $L^j, L^{j+1}, \cdots, L^{i-1}$, s.t., $j < i$ and L^j is the event log where the process of the case having the trace σ started. As these examples show, temporal correlations can be categorized into two main categories: *forward* and *backward*. Given L^i as an event log at release point i, the former considers temporal correlations between L^i and its next releases, and the latter concerns temporal correlations between L^i and its previous releases.

4.1   CEDP Scenarios

Different event data publishing scenarios can have a significant impact on the privacy leakage based on temporal correlations. In the following, we briefly explain some of the different possible scenarios. In general, CEDP scenarios can be based on a *time-window*, e.g., weekly, or a *count-window*, e.g., the number of new cases. Since time-window-based scenarios are not deterministic in terms of the amount of new data that can be published in each window, we focus on count-window-based scenarios to quantify the potential privacy degradation. One can consider different count-window-based scenarios. For example, an event log is released when there exist x new cases compared to the previous release, or when there exist x new events per trace, or when there exist up to x new events per trace, etc. We classify the count-window-based scenarios into two main types: *certain* and *uncertain*. The former specifies an exact number, e.g., x new events per trace. The latter specifies a bound, e.g., up to x events per trace. This classification allows us to assess the effects of certain and uncertain CEDP scenarios on temporal privacy leakages.

Since events are the smallest units of event logs, to propose a generic approach, we consider the following certain and uncertain scenarios: (S1) an event log is released when there exist exactly x new events per trace compared to the previous release, and (S2) an event log is released when there exist up to x new events per trace compared to the previous release. In practice, such bounds can be specified to keep the process mining findings updated. Note that in both scenarios, events can belong to a new case or an existing one. In Subsect. 4.4, we demonstrate how to use transition systems to quantify the forward and backward privacy leakages considering these scenarios.

4.2   Notation Summary

For the sake of simplicity, we assume that the number of releases is λ, which does not need to be exactly specified. For a given event log L, $C_L \subset \mathcal{C}$ and $A_L \subset \mathcal{A}$ are considered as the finite set of dummy case identifiers and the set of activities that can appear in different releases of L, respectively. L^i denotes an event log that needs to be released at point $i \in [1, \lambda]$. L^i contains cases and their current states describing *full history*, i.e., traces. $\sigma_c^i \in \tilde{L}^i$ is the state of a case c at the release point i. Note that according to Definition 3, each case can only have one trace in an event log.

We consider $\mathcal{M}^i$ as the DP mechanism, which is applied to $\tilde{L}^i$ to randomize the count of trace variants. $rng(\mathcal{M}^i)$ denotes the set of all possible outputs that $\mathcal{M}^i$ can produce. For simplicity, $\mathcal{M}^i$ is considered to be the same DP mechanism, e.g., a Laplace mechanism, but maybe with different privacy budgets at each $i \in [1, \lambda]$. $\tilde{L}'^i$ in $rng(\mathcal{M}^i)$ denotes a differentially private output at release point i. In the following, we first demonstrate the potential privacy loss of $\mathcal{M}^i$ for a single release of event log at release point i. Then, we quantify the privacy leakage in the context of continuous releases when i varies from 1 to λ.

4.3   Privacy Leakage of a Single Release

Consider an adversary whose target is to identify the state of a case $c \in C_L$ at release point $i \in [1, \lambda]$. We assume that such an adversary has the knowledge of all the states at the given release point except the state of the target case c.

Definition 7 (Adversary without Temporal Correlations - $Ad^{L_c^i}$). *Let L^i be an event log that needs to be released at the point i and $\sigma_c^i \in \tilde{L}^i$ be the state of case c at the point i. $Ad^{L_c^i}$ denotes an adversary whose target is to identify σ_c^i. $L_c^i = \{(c', \sigma) \in L^i | c \neq c'\}$ is the background knowledge of such an adversary.*

$Ad^{L_c^i}$ observes $\tilde{L}'^i \in rng(\mathcal{M}^i)$ and tries to distinguish case c's state. The privacy leakage of the DP mechanism $\mathcal{M}^i$ can be formulated as follows, where $\sigma_c^i, \sigma_c'^i \in A_L^*$ are two different possible traces for the state of case c.

$$PL(Ad^{L_c^i}, \mathcal{M}^i) := \sup_{\tilde{L}'^i, \sigma_c^i, \sigma_c'^i} \log \frac{Pr(\tilde{L}'^i \mid \tilde{L}_c^i \uplus \sigma_c^i)}{Pr(\tilde{L}'^i \mid \tilde{L}_c^i \uplus \sigma_c'^i)} \tag{1}$$

$$PL(\mathcal{M}^i) := \max_{c \in C_L} PL(Ad^{L_c^i}, \mathcal{M}^i) \tag{2}$$

Equation (2) is another formal representation of differential privacy that formulates the privacy budget as the supremum of privacy leakage, i.e., considering ϵ as the privacy budget, $PL(\mathcal{M}^i) = \epsilon$.

4.4   Privacy Leakage of Continuous Releases

We exploit a full-history transition system to calculate probabilities of visiting states and to generate *forward* and *backward* temporal correlations describing the probabilities for transitions between states. We obtain a transition system form the last collected event log that needs to be published.

Definition 8 (State Probability). *Let $TS_{L, state_{hd}()} = (S, A, T)$ be a history transition system based on an event log L, the probability of visiting a state $s \in S$ is as follows: $Pr(s) = |T'|/|L|$ where $T' = [(s_1, a, s_2) \in T | s_2 = s]$.*

For instance, in Fig. 2, $Pr(S3) = 2/4$. In the following, we define forward and backward temporal correlations based on scenarios S1 and S2 (see Subsect. 4.1). Note that to simplify the notation, we abbreviate $\langle a_1, a_2, ..., a_n \rangle$ as $\langle \rangle_n$, and a sequence of event logs that need to be released, i.e., $L^1, L^2, ..., L^\lambda$, as $L^{1..\lambda}$.

Definition 9 (Forward Temporal Correlations - FTC). *Let $TS_{L, state_{hd}()} = (S, A, T)$ be a transition system based on an event log L. The forward temporal correlations are calculated based on the correlations between adjacent states. Given $s_1, s_2 \in S$ as two adjacent states, $Pr(s_2 = \langle \rangle_n | s_1 = \langle \rangle_{n-1}) = \frac{|T''|}{|T'|}$ where $T' = [(s, a, s') \in T \mid s = s_1]$ and $T'' = [(s, a, s') \in T \mid s = s_1 \wedge s' = s_2]$.*

- *The certain scenario with $x \in \mathbb{N}_{>0}$ new events:*
  Given $s_1 \in S \backslash S^{end}$, for all $s_2 \in S$, s.t., $s_1 \sqsubset s_2$, and $|s_2| - |s_1| = x$: $Pr(s_2 = \langle\rangle_n|s_1 = \langle\rangle_{n-x}) = \prod_{j=0}^{x-1} Pr(s'_2 = \langle\rangle_{n-j}|s'_1 = \langle\rangle_{n-(j+1)})$. Otherwise, $Pr(s_2|s_1) = 0$. If $s_1 \in S^{end}$, $Pr(s_2 = s_1|s_1) = 1$.
- *The uncertain scenario with up to $x \in \mathbb{N}_{>0}$ new events:*
  Given $s_1 \in S \backslash S^{end}$, let fd_{s_1} be the distance of the furthest state s_2 from s_1, s.t., $s_1 \sqsubset s_2$. $fm_{s_1}^x = min(x, fd_{s_1})$ is considered as the maximal forward move on the transition system starting from s_1. For all $s_2 \in S$, s.t., $s_1 \sqsubset s_2$, and for all $y \in [1, min(x, |s_2| - |s_1|)]$: $Pr(s_2 = \langle\rangle_n|s_1 = \langle\rangle_{n-y}) = 1/(fm_{s_1}^x + 1) \times \prod_{j=0}^{y-1} Pr(s'_2 = \langle\rangle_{n-j}|s'_1 = \langle\rangle_{n-(j+1)})$, and for $y = 0$: $Pr(s_2 = \langle\rangle_n|s_1 = \langle\rangle_{n-y}) = 1/(fm_{s_1}^x + 1)$. Otherwise, $Pr(s_2|s_1) = 0$. If $s_1 \in S^{end}$, $Pr(s_2 = s_1|s_1) = 1$.

For instance, in Fig. 2, given the certain scenario with $x = 2$, we only consider the states that their distance from a given state is 2. If the given state is $S1$, $Pr(S5|S1) = 1/2$ and $Pr(S6|S1) = 1/2$. Other probabilities given $S1$ are considered to be zero. However, given the uncertain scenario with $x = 2$, we explore all the states within the maximal distance 2. $fd_{S1} = 4$ and $fm_{S1}^x = min(2, 4)$. Thus, $Pr(S5|S1) = 1/3 \times 1/2$, $Pr(S6|S1) = 1/3 \times 1/2$, $Pr(S3|S1) = 1/3 \times 1$, and $Pr(S1|S1) = 1/3$. Other probabilities given $S1$ are considered to be zero. Note that in the uncertain scenario, we consider an equal chance for a case to stay in the same state, or move forward up to maximal x states. This is the reason for the division by $fm_{s_1}^x + 1$.

Definition 10 (Backward Temporal Correlations - BTC). *Let $TS_{L,state_{hd}()} = (S, A, T)$ be a transition system based on an event log L. The backward temporal correlations can be obtained using Bayesian inference based on FTC.*

- *The certain scenario with $x \in \mathbb{N}_{>0}$ new events:*
  Given $s_2 \in S$, for all $s_1 \in S$, s.t., $s_1 \sqsubset s_2$, and $|s_2| - |s_1| = x$: $Pr(s_1 = \langle\rangle_{n-x}|s_2 = \langle\rangle_n) = Pr(s_1=\langle\rangle_{n-x}) \times Pr(s_2=\langle\rangle_n|s_1=\langle\rangle_{n-x})/Pr(s_2=\langle\rangle_n)$. Otherwise, $Pr(s_1|s_2) = 0$.
- *The uncertain scenario with up to $x \in \mathbb{N}_{>0}$ new events:*
  Given $s_2 \in S$, let bd_{s_2} be the distance of the furthest state s_1 from s_2, s.t., $s_1 \sqsubset s_2$, and let $bm_{s_2}^x = min(x, bd_{s_2})$ be the maximal backward move on the transition system starting from s_2. For all $s_1 \in S$, s.t., $s_1 \sqsubset s_2$, and for all $y \in [1, min(x, |s_2| - |s_1|)]$: $Pr(s_1 = \langle\rangle_{n-y}|s_2 = \langle\rangle_n) = 1/(bm_{s_2}^x + 1) \times Pr(s_1=\langle\rangle_{n-x}) \times Pr(s_2=\langle\rangle_n|s_1=\langle\rangle_{n-x})/Pr(s_2=\langle\rangle_n)$, and for $y = 0$: $Pr(s_1 = \langle\rangle_{n-y}|s_2 = \langle\rangle_n) = 1/(bm_{s_2}^x + 1)$. Otherwise, $Pr(s_1|s_2) = 0$.

For instance, in Fig. 2, given the certain scenario with $x = 2$, $Pr(S1|S5) = \frac{2/4 \times 1/2}{1/4}$, and given the uncertain scenario with $x = 2$, $Pr(S1|S5) = 1/3 \times \frac{2/4 \times 1/2}{1/4}$. In the uncertain scenario, the previous state of a case can be the current state or any state within the maximal x distance, and this is the reason for the division by $bm_{s_2}^x + 1$. Note that we incrementally update the transition system based on the last collected event log. Thus, the knowledge regarding correlations is gained based on all the available data up to the last release point.

Definition 11 (Adversary with Temporal Correlations - $Ad^{L_c^{1..\lambda}}$). *Let $L^{1..\lambda}$ be the sequence of event logs that need to be released. We denote $Ad^{L_c^{1..\lambda}}$ as an adversary who has knowledge of all case's states in the entire releases range from 1 to λ except the state of the victim case $c \in C_L$. The background knowledge of such an adversary is $L_c^{1..\lambda} = \bigcup_{i \in [1,\lambda]} L_c^i$ as well as the knowledge of temporal correlations. $Ad_F^{L_c^{1..\lambda}}$ $(Ad_B^{L_c^{1..\lambda}})$ denotes such an adversary with only forward (backward) temporal correlations.*

Given $c \in C_L$, $Ad^{L_c^{1..\lambda}}$ observes the differentially private outputs $\tilde{L}'^1, \tilde{L}'^2, \dots, \tilde{L}'^\lambda$ of the DP mechanism $\mathcal{M}^i$ applied to $\tilde{L}^i$ at each release point $i \in [1,\lambda]$ and attempts to identify the state of the case c.

Definition 12 (Temporal Privacy Leakage - TPL). *Let $Ad^{L_c^{1..\lambda}}$ be an adversary with the knowledge of temporal correlations, $\mathcal{M}^i$ be a DP mechanism that is applied to each event log $\tilde{L}^i$, $i \in [1,\lambda]$, and $\tilde{L}'^i \in rng(\mathcal{M}^i)$ be the corresponding differentially private release at each release point. Considering $\sigma_c^i, \sigma_c'^i \in A_L^*$ as two different possible states for case $c \in C_L$, temporal privacy leakage of $\mathcal{M}^i$ w.r.t. $Ad^{L_c^{1..\lambda}}$ is defined as follows:*

$$TPL(Ad^{L_c^{1..\lambda}}, \mathcal{M}^i) := \sup_{\tilde{L}'^1,\dots,\tilde{L}'^\lambda, \sigma_c^i, \sigma_c'^i} log \frac{Pr(\tilde{L}'^1,\dots,\tilde{L}'^\lambda \mid \tilde{L}_c^i \uplus \sigma_c^i)}{Pr(\tilde{L}'^1,\dots,\tilde{L}'^\lambda \mid \tilde{L}_c^i \uplus \sigma_c'^i)} \quad (3)$$

$$TPL(\mathcal{M}^i) := \max_{c \in C_L} TPL(Ad^{L_c^{1..\lambda}}, \mathcal{M}^i) \quad (4)$$

The above-defined temporal privacy leakage can be broken down into backward and forward privacy leakages, as defined in Definition 13 and Definition 14.

Definition 13 (Backward Privacy Leakage - BPL). *Backward privacy leakage of $\mathcal{M}^i$, $i \in [1,\lambda]$, w.r.t. $Ad_B^{L_c^{1..\lambda}}$ is defined as follows:*

$$BPL(Ad_B^{L_c^{1..\lambda}}, \mathcal{M}^i) := \sup_{\tilde{L}'^1,\dots,\tilde{L}'^i, \sigma_c^i, \sigma_c'^i} log \frac{Pr(\tilde{L}'^1,\dots,\tilde{L}'^i \mid \tilde{L}_c^i \uplus \sigma_c^i)}{Pr(\tilde{L}'^1,\dots,\tilde{L}'^i \mid \tilde{L}_c^i \uplus \sigma_c'^i)} \quad (5)$$

$$BPL(\mathcal{M}^i) := \max_{c \in C_L} BPL(Ad_B^{L_c^{1..\lambda}}, \mathcal{M}^i) \quad (6)$$

Definition 14 (Forward Privacy Leakage - FPL). *Forward privacy leakage of $\mathcal{M}^i$, $i \in [1,\lambda]$, w.r.t. $Ad_F^{L_c^{1..\lambda}}$ is defined as follows:*

$$FPL(Ad_F^{L_c^{1..\lambda}}, \mathcal{M}^i) := \sup_{\tilde{L}'^i,\dots,\tilde{L}'^\lambda, \sigma_c^i, \sigma_c'^i} log \frac{Pr(\tilde{L}'^i,\dots,\tilde{L}'^\lambda \mid \tilde{L}_c^i \uplus \sigma_c^i)}{Pr(\tilde{L}'^i,\dots,\tilde{L}'^\lambda \mid \tilde{L}_c^i \uplus \sigma_c'^i)} \quad (7)$$

$$FPL(\mathcal{M}^i) := \max_{c \in C_L} FPL(Ad_F^{L_c^{1..\lambda}}, \mathcal{M}^i) \quad (8)$$

From Eqs. (4), (6), and (8), we can conclude Eq. (9), which shows that to quantify the temporal privacy leakage, we need to analyze BPL and FPL. We subtract $PL(\mathcal{M}^i)$ because it is included in both BPL and FPL.

$$TPL(\mathcal{M}^i) = BPL(\mathcal{M}^i) + FPL(\mathcal{M}^i) - PL(\mathcal{M}^i) \tag{9}$$

Equations (5) and (7) can be expanded based on Bayesian theorem to calculate backward and forward privacy leakages.

Quantifying BPL. As shown in [2], using Bayesian theorem, $BPL(Ad_B^{L_c^{1..\lambda}}, \mathcal{M}^i)$ can be simplified as Eq. (10) (cf. Theorem 2 and Eq. (12) in [2]). Since CEDP is incremental, the trace of a case at release point $i-1$ cannot be longer than its trace at release point i. Thus, $A_\sigma^{\leq} = \{\sigma' \in A_L^* \mid |\sigma'| \leq |\sigma|\}$ is the domain of all possible previous steps.

$$BPL(Ad_B^{L_c^{1..\lambda}}, \mathcal{M}^i) = \sup_{\substack{\tilde{L}'^1,\dots,\tilde{L}'^{i-1} \\ \sigma_c^i, \sigma'^i_c}} \log \frac{\sum_{\sigma_c^{i-1} \in A_{\sigma_c^i}^{\leq}} Pr(\tilde{L}'^1,\dots,\tilde{L}'^{i-1} \mid \tilde{L}_c^{i-1} \uplus \sigma_c^{i-1}) Pr(\sigma_c^{i-1} \mid \sigma_c^i)}{\underbrace{\sum_{\sigma'^{i-1}_c \in A_{\sigma'^i_c}^{\leq}} Pr(\tilde{L}'^1,\dots,\tilde{L}'^{i-1} \mid \tilde{L}_c^{i-1} \uplus \sigma'^{i-1}_c)}_{(a)} \underbrace{Pr(\sigma'^{i-1}_c \mid \sigma'^i_c)}_{(b)}}$$

$$+ \sup_{\tilde{L}'^i, \sigma_c^i, \sigma'^i_c} \log \underbrace{\frac{Pr(\tilde{L}'^i \mid \tilde{L}_c^i \uplus \sigma_c^i)}{Pr(\tilde{L}'^i \mid \tilde{L}_c^i \uplus \sigma'^i_c)}}_{(c)} \tag{10}$$

In Eq. (10), the part annotated with (a) refers to BPL at point $i-1$, (b) refers to the backward conditional probabilities for the case c given its state at release point i, and (c) is the privacy leakage of single release at point i without considering temporal correlations. Based on Eq. (10), if $i=1$, then $BPL(Ad_B^{L_c}, \mathcal{M}^1) = PL(Ad^{L_c}, \mathcal{M}^1)$, and if $i>1$, $BPL(Ad_B^{L_c^{1..\lambda}}, \mathcal{M}^i)$ is as follows, where $AL_B(.)$ is a function to calculate the accumulated BPL.

$$BPL(Ad_B^{L_c^{1..\lambda}}, \mathcal{M}^i) = AL_B(BPL(Ad_B^{L_c^{1..\lambda}}, \mathcal{M}^{i-1})) + PL(Ad^{L_c^i}, \mathcal{M}^i) \tag{11}$$

Equation (11) shows that BPL can be calculated recursively and may accumulate over time. According to Definition 10, and considering the certain scenario of event data publishing, the backward temporal correlation between states of a case is always on an extreme side, i.e., given σ_c^i as the state of a case $c \in C_L$ at the release point $i \in [1, \lambda]$, there exists a state for the case c at release point $i-x$, σ_c^{i-x}, s.t., $\sigma_c^{i-x} \sqsubset \sigma_c^i$, thus $Pr(\sigma_c^{i-x} \mid \sigma_c^i) = 1$. Consequently, considering $i=2$, $BPL(Ad_B^{L_c^{1..\lambda}}, \mathcal{M}^2)$ is calculated as follows:

$$BPL(Ad_B^{L_c^{1..\lambda}}, \mathcal{M}^2) = \sup_{\tilde{L}'^1, \sigma_c^1, \sigma'^1_c} \log \frac{Pr(\tilde{L}'^1 \mid \tilde{L}_c^1 \uplus \sigma_c^1)}{Pr(\tilde{L}'^1 \mid \tilde{L}_c^1 \uplus \sigma'^1_c)} + \sup_{\tilde{L}'^2, \sigma_c^2, \sigma'^2_c} \log \frac{Pr(\tilde{L}'^2 \mid \tilde{L}_c^2 \uplus \sigma_c^2)}{Pr(\tilde{L}'^2 \mid \tilde{L}_c^2 \uplus \sigma'^2_c)}$$

$$= PL(Ad^{L_c^1}, \mathcal{M}^1) + PL(Ad^{L_c^2}, \mathcal{M}^2)$$

If we consider ϵ as the privacy budget of the mechanism $\mathcal{M}^i$, i.e., for any $i \in [1, \lambda]$, $max_{c \in C_L} PL(Ad^{L_c^i}, \mathcal{M}^i) = \epsilon$. Then, $BPL(Ad_B^{L^{1..\lambda}_c}, \mathcal{M}^2) = 2\epsilon$. Consequently, $BPL(Ad_B^{L^{1..\lambda}_c}, \mathcal{M}^3) = 3\epsilon$, $BPL(Ad_B^{L^{1..\lambda}_c}, \mathcal{M}^4) = 4\epsilon$, etc. Hence, BPL for CEDP considering the certain scenario is expected to linearly increase. We investigate this observation in our experiments.

Quantifying FPL. Similar to the backward privacy leakage, the equation of the forward privacy leakage, i.e., Eq. (7), can also be simplified as Eq. (12) (cf. Theorem 2 and Eq. (14) in [2]). Since continuous event data publishing is incremental, the trace of a case at release point $i + 1$ cannot be shorter than its trace at release point i. Thus, $A_\sigma^\geq = \{\sigma' \in A_L^* \mid |\sigma| \leq |\sigma'|\}$.

$$FPL(Ad_F^{L^{1..\lambda}_c}, \mathcal{M}^i) = \sup_{\substack{\tilde{L}'^{i+1}, \ldots, \tilde{L}'^{\lambda} \\ \sigma_c^i, \sigma'^i_c}} log \frac{\sum_{\sigma_c^{i+1} \in A_{\sigma_c^i}^\geq} Pr(\tilde{L}'^{i+1}, \ldots, \tilde{L}'^{\lambda} \mid \tilde{L}_c^{i+1} \uplus \sigma_c^{i+1}) Pr(\sigma_c^{i+1} \mid \sigma_c^i)}{\underbrace{\sum_{\sigma'^{i+1}_c \in A_{\sigma'^i_c}^\geq} Pr(\tilde{L}'^{i+1}, \ldots, \tilde{L}'^{\lambda} \mid \tilde{L}_c^{i+1} \uplus \sigma'^{i+1}_c)}_{(a)} \underbrace{Pr(\sigma'^{i+1}_c \mid \sigma'^i_c)}_{(b)}}$$

$$+ \sup_{\tilde{L}'^i, \sigma_c^i, \sigma'^i_c} log \frac{Pr(\tilde{L}'^i \mid \tilde{L}_c^i \uplus \sigma_c^i)}{Pr(\tilde{L}'^i \mid \tilde{L}_c^i \uplus \sigma'^i_c)} \tag{12}$$
$$\underbrace{}_{(c)}$$

In Eq. (12), the part annotated with (a) refers to FPL at release point $i + 1$, (b) refers to the forward conditional probabilities for the case c given its state at point i, and (c) is the privacy leakage of single release at point i without considering temporal correlations. Similar to Eq. (10), in Eq. (12), if $i = 1$, then $FPL(Ad_F^{L^{1..\lambda}_c}, \mathcal{M}^1) = PL(Ad^{L_c^1}, \mathcal{M}^1)$, and if $i > 1$, $FPL(Ad_F^{L^{1..\lambda}_c}, \mathcal{M}^i)$ is as follows, where $AL_F(.)$ is a function to calculate the accumulated forward privacy leakage.

$$FPL(Ad_F^{L^{1..\lambda}_c}, \mathcal{M}^i) = AL_F(FPL(Ad_F^{L^{1..\lambda}_c}, \mathcal{M}^{i+1})) + PL(Ad^{L_c^i}, \mathcal{M}^i) \tag{13}$$

Equation (13) shows that FPL can also be recursively calculated and may accumulate over time. Since event data publishing is incremental, the complete traces remain the same in all the next releases. Thus, FPL in CEDP can be on an extreme side whenever there exist complete traces in the previous releases. Moreover, based on Eq. (12), we assume FPL in CEDP depends on the variation of traces in an event log. For instance, considering the certain scenario, if an event log only contains one trace variant, FPL can be on an extreme side because the next state of a new case is certainly known based on the previously recorded states. Hence, FPL is expected to linearly increase. We investigate the effect of the *trace uniqueness* ratio on FPL in our experiments.

Calculating Accumulative Privacy Leakage. Cao et al. [2] show that the accumulative privacy leakages can be formulated as an optimization problem where the objective function is a ratio of two linear functions and the constraints are linear equations. Since we rely on transition systems to obtain temporal correlations, the knowledge of temporal correlations is bounded to the traces in the state space of the transition system. For the traces that are not included in the state space, we consider the worst-case w.r.t. the knowledge of correlations, i.e., no correlation. We assume that adapting the optimization problem from [2], is a straightforward process. Thus, we avoid including it here. Nevertheless, we provided the adapted optimization problem and a short explanation regarding the *computational complexity* of our approach as supplementary material in our GitLab repository.[1]

5   Experiments

The aims of the experiments are as follows: (1) Investigating the effect of temporal correlations among event logs on the provided privacy guarantees, (2) Exploring the effect of different CEDP scenarios on temporal correlations and privacy leakages, and (3) Exploring the impact of trace uniqueness in event logs on temporal privacy leakages. We have implemented a Python script to conduct the experiments. The source code is available on GitLab[2] and as a Python package[3] that can be installed using *pip* commands. Table 1 shows the general statistics of the real-life public event logs that we employed for our experiments. The *trace uniqueness* shows the rate of unique traces, i.e., $^{\#Variants}/_{\#Traces}$. These event logs cover a wide range w.r.t. the trace uniqueness.

Table 1. General statistics of the event logs used in the experiments.

Event log	#Events	#Unique activities	#Traces	#Variants	Trace uniqueness
Sepsis	15214	16	1050	846	80%
BPIC-2013	65533	4	7554	1511	20%
BPIC-2012-App	60849	10	13087	17	0.12%

To simulate CEDP, we need to specify the initial release and a sequence of event logs that are considered to be continuously published. Thus, we need a *split-point* that splits an event log into two parts; *initial* and *continuous*. One can partition an event log into initial and continuous parts in a variety of ways,

---

[1] https://github.com/m4jidRafiei/QDP_CEDP/tree/main/supplementary.

[2] https://github.com/m4jidRafiei/QDP_CEDP.

[3] https://pypi.org/project/pm-cedp-qdp/.

e.g., having an initial log that contains all the cases, or having an initial log that contains $x\%$ of cases or events, and so on. We consider the percentage of events included in the initial part as a criteria for splitting an event log. We split Sepsis and BPIC-2012-App into two parts such that the initial part contains roughly 50% of events so that there is enough data to obtain reliable knowledge regarding the correlations. However, BPIC-2013 is partitioned in such a way that the initial part contains roughly 35% of events so that there exist no complete trace, yet, at the same time, there is enough data to discover a transition system and obtain the probabilities.[4] Table 2 shows general statistics of the event logs partitions after being partitioned. Note that incomplete (partial) traces are the same in both partitions.

The initial part is published as the first release. Then, each future release is generated w.r.t. the scenarios S1 and S2 (see Subsect. 4.1). In both scenarios, the window size, i.e., the number of new events per trace in a future release, varies from 1 to 4. Note that to simulate scenario S2, a random integer within the window size is generated to determine the number of new events. For each scenario, we continue the publishing process for up to 5 releases or until there are no incomplete traces to publish.

Figures 4 and 5 show the privacy leakages for different releases of the event logs based on the CEDP scenarios S1 and S2, respectively. We consider $\epsilon = 0.01$ as the privacy budget of a differential privacy mechanism $\mathcal{M}$ that is applied to each release. Thus, for the first release $FPL = BPL = TPL = 0.01$. Recall that $TPL = FPL + BPL - \epsilon$. Note that the implementation details of such a mechanism that does not consider correlations among different releases will not impact our experiments. In the following, we explain the results for each scenario.

Table 2. General statistics of the initial and continuous parts of event logs used in the experiments.

Event log	Parts	#Events	#Complete traces	#Incomplete traces
Sepsis	Initial	7290	442	84
	Continuous	7924	524	84
BPIC-2013	Initial	21705	0	2271
	Continuous	43828	5283	2271
BPIC-2012-App	Initial	29227	5849	690
	Continuous	31622	6548	690

---

[4] Note that experiments can be extended considering different partitioning scenarios and focusing on different log characteristics.

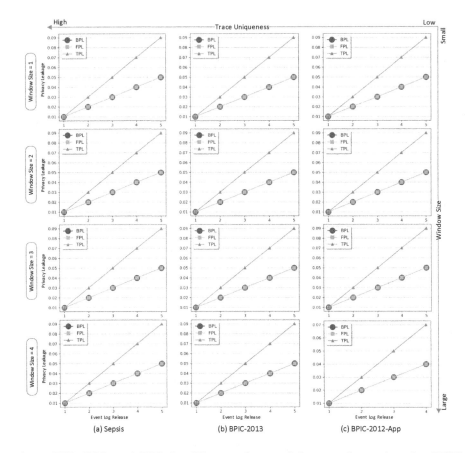

Fig. 4. FPL, BPL, and TPL for different releases of the event logs, when the CEDP scenario is S1, window size varies from 1 to 4, and $\epsilon = 0.01$. The window size indicates the number of new events per trace in a future release.

Scenario S1: The first observation is that the results are the same for all the event logs. The only different plot is at the bottom right with less number of releases because there exists no incomplete trace for BPIC-2012-App after the 4th release. Since the previous states are certain, for each state there is one state with $BTC = 1$. Thus, the correlations are strong, and BPL linearly increases for all the event logs. The same results can be seen for FPL due to different reasons. In Sepsis and BPIC-2012-App, FPL linearly increases because initial releases of these event logs contain complete traces that remain unchanged in all the next releases. Thus, there are strong correlations among those traces in all the releases. Moreover, for the most of the incomplete states (traces) there exist certain states in future releases. For example, in the second release of Sepsis, almost 78% of the incomplete states have a certain state when window size is 2. We see the same trend in BPIC-2013 although there exist no complete trace in its initial release. This is because of two reasons: (1) there are complete traces that

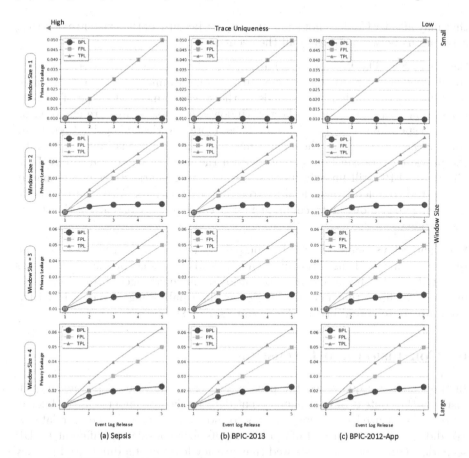

Fig. 5. FPL, BPL, and TPL for different releases of the event logs, when the CEDP scenario is S2, window size varies from 1 to 4, and $\epsilon = 0.01$. The window size indicates the maximum number of new events per trace in a future release.

appear in the second release, which is used to discover the updated transition system, and (2) BPIC-2013 contains a few distinct activities that leads to strong correlations between states. In BPIC-2013, there exist only 4 unique activities, and 86% of variants contain only two activities "Accepted" and "Queued". That leads to a situation where for many states in the corresponding transition system there exists only one possible next state that results in strong correlations.

When the window size is increased, one may expect to see lower forward correlations between states. Particularly, for the event logs with a high trace uniqueness. However, due to more complete traces that appear by increasing the window size, FPL does not decrease. We continued releasing Sepsis event logs considering 4 and 8 as window sizes until there was no more incomplete traces. According to the results, FPL never decreased.[5] Moreover, the trace uniqueness

---

[5] https://github.com/m4jidRafiei/QDP_CEDP/tree/main/more_exp.

that may affect FPL does not show any impact because of the existence of strong correlations between states in all the event logs.

Scenario S2: The first observation is that all the event logs follow the same trend based on the window size. One can see a logarithmic increase for BPL based on the window size that corresponds to the so-called moderate type of correlations. That is because for the larger window sizes more states are explored on the corresponding transition system. Thus, more knowledge is gained regarding correlations. However, at the same time, more uncertainty is imposed because the previous state can be any state within the window size distance (see Definition 10). FPL still linearly increases, similar to scenario S1, which is mainly due to the complete traces leading to strong correlations. Also, the results do not change based on the trace uniqueness because of the existence of the strong correlations.

Scenario S1 vs Scenario S2: By comparing the two CEDP scenarios, one can see that scenario S1, as a certain scenario, leads to higher privacy leakages, as expected. That is because certain scenarios result in stronger correlations. This observation shows that not revealing exact data publishing scenarios in CEDP can mitigate temporal privacy leakages to some extent.

6   Conclusion and Discussion

In this paper, we quantified the privacy leakage of differential privacy mechanisms in the context of continuous event data publishing under temporal correlations. We utilized transition systems to model and quantify the correlations. We did experiments on real-life public events logs considering different CEDP scenarios. Our experiments showed that privacy leakage of a differential privacy mechanism may increase over time. In the following, we discuss some design choices, possible next steps, and limitations that need to be taken into account.

The concept of state, which is defined based on a state representation function, provides a general way to quantify correlations w.r.t. sensitive data. For instance, if one considers the set of activities in a trace as sensitive data rather than the sequence, and the corresponding differential privacy mechanism aims to protect the set of activities in traces. Then, our approach can be adapted to quantify the corresponding temporal privacy leakage by changing the state representation function, s.t., each state represents the set of activities in a trace.

The incrementally updated transition system based on the last collected event log may not be reliable for calculating forward temporal correlations if it contains only a few states. To gain more reliable knowledge regarding the correlations, one can consider a minimum number of cases reflecting a specific correlation. One can also apply more conditions, such as only considering the correlations obtained based on complete traces.

We only considered the control-flow aspect of event logs, while in reality the events recorded by information systems often contain more attributes. Each event attribute in a trace can be used to create a new correlation model or to alter an existing one. Depending on the attributes present in published event logs, one may need to analyze the corresponding correlations to examine possible privacy leakages. Overall, this work highlights the necessity of designing differential privacy mechanisms that consider temporal correlations when event data are continuously published.

References

1. GDPR. http://data.europa.eu/eli/reg/2016/679/oj. Accessed 15 May 2021
2. Cao, Y., Yoshikawa, M., Xiao, Y., Xiong, L.: Quantifying differential privacy in continuous data release under temporal correlations. IEEE Trans. Knowl. Data Eng. **31**(7), 1281–1295 (2019)
3. Chen, R., Fung, B.C.M., Yu, P.S., Desai, B.C.: Correlated network data publication via differential privacy. VLDB J. **23**(4), 653–676 (2013). https://doi.org/10.1007/s00778-013-0344-8
4. Dwork, C.: Differential privacy. In: Bugliesi, M., Preneel, B., Sassone, V., Wegener, I. (eds.) ICALP 2006. LNCS, vol. 4052, pp. 1–12. Springer, Heidelberg (2006). https://doi.org/10.1007/11787006_1
5. Dwork, C.: Differential privacy: a survey of results. In: Theory and Applications of Models of Computation. In: 5th International Conference, TAMC 2008 (2008)
6. Dwork, C.: Differential privacy in new settings. In: SODA. SIAM (2010)
7. Dwork, C., Naor, M., Pitassi, T., Rothblum, G.N.: Differential privacy under continual observation. In: STOC, pp. 715–724. ACM (2010)
8. Elkoumy, G., et al.: Privacy and confidentiality in process mining: Threats and research challenges. ACM Trans. Manag. Inf. Syst. **13**(1), 11:1–11:17 (2022)
9. Elkoumy, G., Pankova, A., Dumas, M.: Mine me but don't single me out: Differentially private event logs for process mining. In: ICPM, pp. 80–87. IEEE (2021)
10. Fahrenkrog-Petersen, S.A., van der Aa, H., Weidlich, M.: PRIPEL: Privacy-preserving event log publishing including contextual information. In: Fahland, D., Ghidini, C., Becker, J., Dumas, M. (eds.) BPM 2020. LNCS, vol. 12168, pp. 111–128. Springer, Cham (2020). https://doi.org/10.1007/978-3-030-58666-9_7
11. Fahrenkrog-Petersen, S.A., Kabierski, M., Rösel, F., van der Aa, H., Weidlich, M.: SaCoFa: Semantics-aware control-flow anonymization for process mining, In: ICPM, pp. 72–79. IEEE (2021)
12. Fan, L., Xiong, L., Sunderam, V.S.: FAST: differentially private real-time aggregate monitor with filtering and adaptive sampling. In: SIGMOD Conference, pp. 1065–1068. ACM (2013)
13. Fung, B.C., Wang, K., Fu, A.W.C., Philip, S.Y.: Introduction to privacy-preserving data publishing: Concepts and techniques. Chapman and Hall/CRC (2010)
14. Kellaris, G., Papadopoulos, S., Xiao, X., Papadias, D.: Differentially private event sequences over infinite streams. Proc. VLDB Endow. **7**(12), 1155–1166 (2014)
15. Mannhardt, F., Koschmider, A., Baracaldo, N., Weidlich, M., Michael, J.: Privacy-preserving process mining-differential privacy for event logs. Bus. Inf. Syst. Eng. **61**(5), 595–614 (2019)

16. Rafiei, M., van der Aalst, W.M.P.: Towards quantifying privacy in process mining. In: Leemans, S., Leopold, H. (eds.) ICPM 2020. LNBIP, vol. 406, pp. 385–397. Springer, Cham (2021). https://doi.org/10.1007/978-3-030-72693-5_29

17. Rafiei, M., van der Aalst, W.M.P.: Group-based privacy preservation techniques for process mining. Data Knowl. Eng. **134**, 101908 (2021). https://doi.org/10.1016/j.datak.2021.101908

18. Rafiei, M., van der Aalst, W.M.P.: Privacy-preserving continuous event data publishing. In: Polyvyanyy, A., Wynn, M.T., Van Looy, A., Reichert, M. (eds.) BPM 2021. LNBIP, vol. 427, pp. 178–194. Springer, Cham (2021). https://doi.org/10.1007/978-3-030-85440-9_11

Dynamic Forest for Learning from Data Streams with Varying Feature Spaces

Christian Schreckenberger[1]([✉]), Christian Bartelt[1], and Heiner Stuckenschmidt[2]

[1] Institute for Enterprise Systems, University of Mannheim, Mannheim, Germany
{schreckenberger,bartelt}@es.uni-mannheim.de
[2] Data and Web Science Group, University of Mannheim, Mannheim, Germany
heiner@informatik.uni-mannheim.de

Abstract. In this paper, we propose a new ensemble method, which is called Dynamic Forest, for learning from data streams with varying feature spaces. Unlike traditional online learning where the feature space is static, in varying feature spaces, new features may emerge while others may vanish. This leads to several problems for which state-of-the-art online random forest algorithms are not equipped. We benchmark our proposed method against the state-of-the-art method $OLVF$ on data streams with varying feature spaces and against $OLVF$ and OL_{SF} on trapezoidal data streams. These trapezoidal data streams can be considered as a sub-problem of varying feature spaces, where the only characteristic is that new features emerge over time. Our proposed approach dynamically learns and relearns decision stumps while applying a dynamic weighting strategy for the decision stumps. Furthermore, it employs a dynamic strategy for adding and removing weak learners. The proposed method is empirically evaluated by replicating the benchmark of the $OLVF$ algorithm with nine UCI Machine Learning Repository datasets and one real-world dataset. In the experiments, we can show that Dynamic Forest proves to be a good addition to the current state-of-the-art for learning from data streams with varying feature spaces.

Keywords: Online learning · Data streams · Varying feature spaces · Ensemble learning · Random forest

1 Introduction

The ability to handle more and more data has led to an ever-increasing amount of available data, which in turn brought the demand to process and handle this data on the fly. Online learning is a class of machine learning algorithms aiming to solve this problem, hereby training instances are processed sequentially, and a model is learned on the fly. This is opposed to offline learning, where a fixed set of instances and features are given, and the learning algorithm derives a model based on this fixed input. An array of various online learning algorithms has been studied [1,11,18] and also been applied in a broad range of applications [14,17],

ⓒ The Author(s), under exclusive license to Springer Nature Switzerland AG 2022
M. Sellami et al. (Eds.): CoopIS 2022, LNCS 13591, pp. 95–111, 2022.
https://doi.org/10.1007/978-3-031-17834-4_6

where the instance space grows continuously. However, the assumption of online learning is that the feature space remains fixed, and only the instance space is continuously growing, which does not hold in all applications. For example, in a crowd-sensing scenario, new sensors will be added over time if users join the sensing effort, while others may vanish due to users leaving the crowd-sensing platform or sensors breaking. Other good examples of the dynamics of feature spaces are social networks, where the information provided by each user can differ significantly, and textual data, where new or different words may be used in the documents, while others may not be used. This problem, where the feature space may grow, due to new features that emerge or shrink, because of vanishing features was introduced as *varying feature spaces* by [2].

In this paper, we present Dynamic Forest (*DynFo*), which is a learning algorithm that is able to deal with varying feature spaces by dynamically learning and relearning decision stumps, as well as dynamically weighing these decision stumps according to their performance. The state-of-the-art algorithms for varying feature spaces and trapezoidal data streams focus on linear models [2,21]; however, this is not always applicable or the best choice in every scenario. As there are no ensemble methods solving the problems of varying feature spaces and trapezoidal data streams, we provide an addition to the solution space for learning from data streams with varying feature spaces. The contributions of this paper are as follows:

– A new learning algorithm for data streams with varying feature spaces, Dynamic Forest, is proposed.
– Dynamic Forest is empirically evaluated against the state-of-the-art algorithm for varying feature spaces, Online Learning from Varying Feature Spaces (*OLVF*) on the benchmark established by *OLVF* [2].
– We show that Dynamic Forest outperforms the state-of-the-art in most cases.

2   Related Work

Based on the outlined characteristics of the data that we are addressing with our proposed approach, we relate our work to online learning and learning in varying feature spaces. Furthermore, our approach itself can be related to online random forests. In the following, we will present each field and explain the shortcomings.

2.1   Online Learning

In online learning, a given learning algorithm tries to infer a model from sequentially arriving instances to be able to make predictions in the future. In this setting, the feature space is known beforehand and remains constant over time. Online learning algorithms are generally applied when the data arrives from streams, or the data volume is too high to load everything into the main memory at once [7,19]. While many online learning algorithms have been developed [4,16], they can be distinguished into two groups, i.e., first-order online learning algorithms and second-order online learning algorithms [21]. In the first group, first-order information is used for the update. Well-known examples are the Perceptron [15] algorithm and Online Gradient Descent [23]. The latter group aims to make use of the underlying structure between features [19]. However, traditional online learning methods are not able to learn from varying feature spaces, since they assume a feature space that remains fixed in size.

2.2 Learning from Varying Feature Streams

Initial ideas that the feature space is not fixed in size were described by [6]. While they had some other constraints and requirements to the data streams, e.g., a context needs to be provided, in their approach that makes it infeasible to compare to them, they outlined the properties of a feature space that changes over time. These ideas were then succeeded by [20,21], who restricted themselves to the problem of trapezoidal data streams, which is an ever-increasing instance and feature space, which means no features vanish. Hereby, the current training instance either has the same feature space as the previous instance or it has additional features. They proposed the OL_{SF} algorithm that follows a passive-aggressive update strategy, which only updates the classifier if the prediction is wrong and includes an update step if new features arrived.

Feature evolvable streams, as introduced by [8], focus on features emerging as well as vanishing. However, they assume that the feature space evolves sequentially. This means that after a new feature emerged, there exists a period where both the new and the old features are present before the old feature eventually vanishes. [2] described the downside of this assumption that if there is no overlap of the old and the new feature space, the proposed projection step fails. The same holds for the approach of [22], which also focuses on feature evolvable streams. In [13] every new and changed feature space is mapped to the first seen feature space, which leads to the problem that the approach is heavily dependent on the first seen feature space.

Based on these shortcomings and assumptions, the problem of varying feature spaces was established by [2], where features may vanish or emerge over time with no assumption on the overlap. As a result of this, they proposed $OLVF$, where the current instance and the classifier learned so far are projected onto their shared feature subspace. Based on this subspace, the algorithm makes a prediction and suffers a loss. The classifier will then be updated according to the loss with an empirical risk minimization principle with adaptive constraints. The constraints are reweighed based on the confidence of the classifier and the instance's projection. After each learned instance, the algorithm applies a sparsity step to decrease its size. However, the evaluation has shown that the algorithm has to make a trade-off between the classifier size and the accuracy of it. This is where our proposed approach ties in and provides an additional alternative to the solution space.

2.3   Online Random Forests

The initial idea of random forests was introduced by [3]. However, in this first approach for random forests, the focus was on offline learning. More recently, ideas for online learning were published. In [10], the Mondrian forests algorithm is proposed. In this algorithm, multiple Mondrian decision trees are generated based on the Mondrian Process, to form a forest. Due to the use of the Mondrian Process, the generation of the Mondrian decision trees is random. However, while this approach works in an online setting it is not applicable in data streams with varying feature spaces as there is no strategy on how to predict with trees, if a feature a Mondrian decision tree randomly split upon is missing or update the tree with an emerged feature. Another approach called Adaptive Random Forests is proposed by [5]. In their work, they make use of Hoeffding trees, which can naturally learn in an online setting. They propose a strategy to update the forest, especially when concept drifts occur. While concept drift is also a highly relevant problem for data streams, it is not in the scope of this work. However, there is no strategy to deal with emerging or vanishing features, e.g., how to predict with a Hoeffding tree that split on a vanishing feature, making them also inapplicable to data streams with varying feature spaces. To the best of our knowledge, no online random forest algorithms have been proposed that take the intricacies of varying feature spaces into account. Therefore, we want to close this gap with the proposed method of Dynamic Forest.

3   Dynamic Forest

The main idea of Dynamic Forest is increasing the weights of good performing weak learners, in our case decision stumps, and keeping them in the ensemble, while decreasing the weight of weak learners dynamically that perform not sufficiently good, which then leads to relearning the weak learners or the removal of them. This is substantially different from the known online random forest methods because they generally only focus on updating the weights of either the weak classifiers in the ensemble or the individual instances, to focus more on misclassified instances and not on the composition of the ensemble.

In this section, we first introduce the preliminaries and the notation, then we proceed to explain the main parts of the algorithm as well as the ideas and motivations for them. First, we will describe how the learning process works with regard to the weak learner used, the update strategy, and the adaptation of weak learners. Finally, we present how to predict with the presented algorithm.

3.1   Preliminaries

As of [2], a feature space that keeps changing on each instance of a data stream can be referred to as a varying feature space. The input for the learning algorithm consists of a pair (x_t, y_t), where $t = 1, 2, ..., T$. The vector $x_t \in \mathbb{R}^{x_t}$ represents the values of the available features $F(x_t)$ at time t and y_t contains the class label $c_i \in \mathcal{C}$ at step t.

Table 1. Overview of input parameters for Algorithm 1.

Parameter	Description
α	Impact on weight update
β	Probability to keep weak learner in ensemble
δ	Fraction of features to consider (bagging parameter)
ϵ	Penalty if split of decision stump is not in the current instance
γ	Threshold for error rate
M	Number of learners in the ensemble
N	Buffer size of instances
θ_1, θ_2	Bounds for the update strategy

The notation $\mathcal{L}$ is used to refer to the ensemble of all weak learners used in the algorithm. In our algorithm, we use decision stumps as weak learners. For each weak learner $\mathcal{L}_i \in \mathcal{L}$, we have a corresponding weight of $w_i \in w$ and an accepted feature space of $F_i \subseteq F_t$, where F_t are all the features seen so far by the algorithm at step t, hence $F_t = \mathbb{R}^{x_1} \cup .. \cup \mathbb{R}^{x_t}$. The accepted feature space can be considered as bagging, as it accepts a subset of the total feature space seen so far for each weak learner. As decision stumps only make one split, we denote the feature chosen for this split of a decision stump $\mathcal{L}_i$ as $\mathcal{L}_i^{split}$.

3.2 Learning with Dynamic Forest

In Algorithm 1, the steps for learning with Dynamic Forest are shown. In the following, we will give an introduction to the parameters and subsequently a high level explanation of the steps in the algorithm, on which we will elaborate in more detail in the subsequent sections.

We have a large amount of parameters (Table 1), enabling the proposed algorithm to be adapted to a lot of scenarios. The parameters α and ϵ are used for the weight update strategy, i.e. updating the weights of each weak learner of the ensemble. The parameters β, γ, as wells as θ_1 and θ_2 are used for the balancing of the amount of weak learners used and relearning of those, i.e. increasing and decreasing the amount of classifiers used and replacing some if needed. The initial amount of weak learners the ensemble starts with is determined by M. The parameter N defines the instance buffer size and δ serves as a bagging parameter, by determining the fraction of randomly selected features to consider for each weak learner and hence also forcing a diverse ensemble.

At first, we receive an instance x_t with the feature space of the corresponding time step t. We use this instance to fill the instance buffer, which is bound by the specified size N. Then we proceed to initialize or update F_i for every weak learner $\mathcal{L}_i$ with respect to the δ parameter. Subsequently, we use the current instance x_t to predict and check the learning algorithm's current performance. If the error rate in the window is higher than the threshold γ, we add a new weak learner to the ensemble and update γ. In the next step, we check if the split decision of every weak learner $\mathcal{L}_i^{split}$ is contained in the feature space of the current instance $F(x_t)$, given that this is not the case, we apply a penalty ϵ to the respective weight of the learner w_i. This is then followed by updating every weak learner's weights, where $\mathcal{L}_i^{split}$ is contained in the feature space of the current instance x_t. Based on the updated weights, it is then checked for each weight, if the weight is in the top θ_2-quantile of all weights, and if this is the case, we keep the respective weak learner in the ensemble. If the weight of a weak learner is between the threshold θ_1 and the θ_2-quantile of the total weights, there is a chance of β to keep the weak learner as well, otherwise we relearn it. So in other terms, there is a $1 - \beta$ chance that we relearn the weak learner on the current instance buffer. If the weak learner is below the θ_1 threshold with respect to its weight, we drop it entirely from the current ensemble. So in general the steps in line seven and eight, as well as line 17 help us grow or shrink the ensemble according to the performance of the ensemble and the performance of each individual weak learner. Thus making the ensemble dynamic and appropriate for a varying feature space.

Algorithm 1. Learning with DYNAMIC FOREST

1: Initialize weights $w_i = 1, i \in M$
2: Initialize weak learners $\mathcal{L}_i, i \in M$
3: **for** $t = 1, 2, ...T$ **do**
4:     receive instance $x_t \in \mathbb{R}^{x_t}$ and fill buffer
5:     initialize or update $F_i \subseteq F_t$ according to δ and x_t
6:     predict with x_t and add result to window
7:     calculate error-rate based on results of window
8:     **if** error-rate $> \gamma$ **then**
9:         initialize new $\mathcal{L}_i$ and update γ
10:    **end if**
11:    apply penalty ϵ for each $\mathcal{L}_i \in \mathcal{L}$ where $\mathcal{L}_i^{split} \notin F(x_t)$
12:    update weights for each $\mathcal{L}_i \in \mathcal{L}$ where $\mathcal{L}_i^{split} \in F(x_t)$
13:    **if** $quantile_{\theta_2}(w) \leq w_i$ **then**
14:        keep $\mathcal{L}_i$ in $\mathcal{L}$
15:    **else if** $\theta_1 \leq w_i < quantile_{\theta_2}(w)$ **then**
16:        select with a chance of $1 - \beta$ to relearn $\mathcal{L}_i$
17:    **else**
18:        drop $\mathcal{L}_i$ from $\mathcal{L}$
19:    **end if**
20: **end for**

Weak Learners. The first design decision that had to be made was on how to train the weak learners and which kind of weak learner to chose that will later form the base of the ensemble. Our decision hereby fell on decision stumps [9]. Decision stumps are decision trees with a maximum depth of one. Hence, only one attribute with a respective splitting point will be used as the weak learner. This has the advantage that it is straightforward if it is possible to use the decision stump and when it is not possible, i.e., we can only use the respective decision stump when the split decision is present in the instance space. However, as we are in an online learning setting, there is the problem that decision stumps can not naturally deal with streaming data. Therefore, we decided to use a small instance buffer, which works as a reservoir to learn the decision stumps. Once learned, the decision stumps provide a stable and consistent prediction throughout the time they are being used. Each instance that arrives at the Dynamic Forest algorithm is put into the instance buffer. The instance buffer follows a first-in-first-out strategy, this means that we keep the last N instances of the data stream. This should also help adapt to concept drift, as our weak learners are constantly learned from recent instances, which is triggered when decision stumps become bad in the ensemble. When a weak learner, i.e., a decision stump, is initialized, we also initialize and later update which features are accepted by this weak learner according to the δ parameter and the features that have been seen so far. This serves as bagging, which depending on the value used, will lead to a more diverse ensemble.

In Dynamic Forest, we start with a specified amount of weak learners M; each weak learner is referenced by $\mathcal{L}_i$ where $i = 1, ..., M$. Each weak learner is always learned on the current instance buffer. In the beginning, this means that the weak learner should be relearned more often, and when the ensemble starts to settle, we can relearn less frequently unless there are changes in the feature space impacting the performance.

Weight Updates. The weight updates are performed in line eleven and twelve of Algorithm 1 respectively. In the following, we will first discuss the penalty and then elaborate on the weight update strategy.

As described, we keep a weight w_i for every weak learner in our ensemble, which is initialized with a value of one. There is no upper bound on the weight of a weak learner in the ensemble. So given the case that a weak learner made a split on a very rare feature, this weak learner would never get replaced based on the proposed update strategy, as this strategy only updates those weak learners that could make a prediction for the current instance. In consequence, this means that we need to apply some penalty to the weight of this weak learner so that in the case of it providing no benefit, it will eventually get replaced by another decision stump. This is done by subtracting a constant ϵ from the weight of that weak learner as shown in Eq. 1, if the split of the weak learner is not in the feature space of x_t, i.e. $\mathcal{L}_i^{split} \notin F(x_t)$.

$$w_i = w_i - \epsilon \tag{1}$$

The following function of $I(y_t, \hat{y}_t)$ in Eq. 2 is used to indicate if a prediction made by a weak learner was correct or not. If the weak learner's prediction was correct, the function will return a one, otherwise it will return a zero.

$$I(y_t, \hat{y}_t) = \begin{cases} 1 & \text{if } y_t = \hat{y}_t \\ 0 & \text{otherwise} \end{cases} \tag{2}$$

The indicator function can then be used to update the weights based on Eq. 3. This equation updates a weight with respect to α by multiplying 2α with the indicator function and adding the current weight w_i to it. This is then divided by $\alpha + w_i$. As it was previously mentioned, the weight for each weak learner is initialized with one. If the prediction of the weak learner is correct, it will increase, otherwise decrease. If the weight of a weak learner is below one, it increases faster and decreases slower, while a weight that is above one increases slower and decreases faster for correct and wrong predictions, respectively.

$$w_i = \frac{I(y_{i,t}, \hat{y}_t) * 2\alpha + w_i}{1 + \alpha} \tag{3}$$

By increasing the weight of the weak learners with correct predictions and decreasing the weight for weak learners with wrong predictions, we can ensure that good weak learners remain in the ensemble and bad weak learners get dropped. Due to the update mechanism, the weights will increase slower the higher the current weight of a weak learner is and vice versa. This bounding of the weights leads to good weak learners being able to be replaced faster with the proposed algorithm, if they are starting to become bad, i.e., their individual performance deteriorates.

Adaption of Weak Learners. The last part of the learning strategy of Dynamic Forest is the dynamic adaption of the amount of decision stumps used as weak learners, i.e., adding or deleting weak learners.

As varying feature spaces are highly dynamic, there is a need to increase the amount of weak learners if unknown or new features arise and the previous amount of weak learners is not sufficiently large enough to deal with the feature space at hand. Therefore, we added a mechanism to track the error rate over a sliding window. If the error rate surpasses the threshold γ, we add a new weak learner to the ensemble and also update γ according to the error rate. This step should detect if the performance plummets based on experienced performance so far, and then introduce further weak learners if they are needed.

On the other hand, we have a strategy in place to relearn as well as drop weak learners that are performing poorly. Hereby, we make use of two bounds defined as the parameters θ_1 and θ_2, where the value range is between zero and one. For each weak learner, we check if their weight is bigger than the quantile of all the weights bound by θ_2; if this is the case, the weak learner is in the top bracket of the weak learners, and therefore we keep it in the ensemble. However, if the weight is between the described quantile bound of θ_2 and the threshold of θ_1, there is a probability of *beta* that we keep it as well, or in other words, there is a probability of $1 - \beta$ that we relearn the respective weak learner. If we happen to relearn the weak learner, we reset the respective weight of it to one. If a weak learner's weight is below the θ_1 threshold, then we drop this weak learner completely and do not relearn a new one instead. The reason to use a variable bound to check for the good performing weak learners and a hard set threshold for the bad performing weak learners is that it delivered more consistent results.

So the general idea of this approach is that the good decision stumps are kept in the ensemble, while the mediocre decision stumps are relearned by chance, and the worst decision stumps are dropped; hence the feature space that was chosen by the bagging parameter δ for this weak learner is dropped as well and if the performance plummets based on this decision, we get the chance to add new weak learners to the ensemble in accordance to line eight to ten of the learning algorithm.

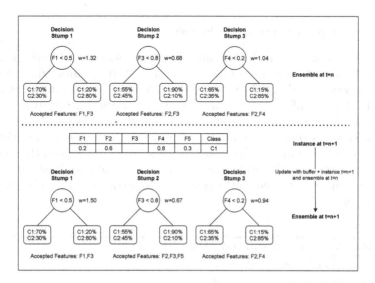

Fig. 1. Example of weight updates and accepted feature space, based on a new data instance at $t = n + 1$.

Example. In Fig. 1 an example of the algorithm is shown. In this example, we have a small ensemble with three decision stumps, which we will abbreviate with DS1, DS2, DS3. We assume that we have observed four features $(F1, F2, F3, F4)$ at $t = n$. DS1 splits on F1 at the value of 0.5, DS2 splits on F3 at the value of 0.8, and DS3 splits on F4 at the value of 0.2. Furthermore, each decision stump has *accepted features*, which are determined by the δ parameter. In the next step t = n + 1, we receive a new instance, which contains a new feature $F5$ but also missed the feature $F3$. We then use the new instance and the buffer of previously seen instances (not depicted) and update the ensemble of $t = n$. According to the algorithm, the first step is to update the feature space for each weak learner. In our example, $F5$ is added to DS2 as a potential feature to learn from. We then use the given γ to check if we need to add a new learner, which is not the case in this example. Following the algorithm leads us to apply the penalty of ϵ to each weak learner, where a split is done on a feature that is not present in the current feature space. Assuming that $\epsilon = 0.01$, we reduce the weight of D2 accordingly. As the other two weak learners' splits are present in the feature space, we do not apply this penalty to DS1 and DS3. However, we update the weights according to Eq. 3, assuming that $\alpha = 0.1$ that results in a new increased weight of 1.5 for DS1, as it makes a correct prediction on the current instance, and a new decreased weight of 0.94 for DS3. In the last step, we would then determine if we keep, relearn or drop a weak learner from the ensemble according to the θ_1, θ_2 parameter. While it is not depicted, in this case, DS1 would most likely be kept in the ensemble, while DS2 depending on the threshold would probably either be relearned or dropped, and DS3 would be relearned with regard to β.

3.3   Predicting with Dynamic Forest

The steps for predicting with Dynamic Forest are shown in Algorithm 2. The input for the algorithm is an instance x. We first start by initializing an empty array w_c, where $c_i \in C$, we then iterate over all weak learners in the ensemble. If the split decision of the weak learner $\mathcal{L}_i$ is not in the feature space of x, we omit this weak learner and continue with the next weak learner. Given that a weak learner has a split on one of those features present in x, we use the weak learner to predict the probabilities for the classes p_c. Then we add the weight of the weak learner times the probability for a class to the initialized class weight array. Based on the gathered statistics in w_c, the prediction is the class with the maximum weight.

Algorithm 2. Predicting with DYNAMIC FOREST

Input: x instance to predict class for
1: Initialize class weights $w_c = (0, .., 0) \in C$
2: **for all** $\mathcal{L}_i \in \mathcal{L}$ **do**
3:     **if** $\mathcal{L}_i^{split} \notin F(x_t)$ **then**
4:         continue
5:     **end if**
6:     predict probabilities for classes p_c with $\mathcal{L}_i(x)$
7:     add $p_c * w_i$ to class weights
8: **end for**
9: return $\mathrm{argmax}_{c_i} \, w_c$

---

4   Evaluation

In the following, we will present the empirical evaluation of the Dynamic Forest algorithm by showing the impact of the parameters on the algorithm on one exemplary dataset, as well as the performance in three different scenarios. The three scenarios were proposed to evaluate the state-of-the-art algorithm $OLVF$ by [2]:

- The first scenario is a simulation of varying feature spaces, by randomly removing a fraction of the data.

- The second scenario is a simulation of trapezoidal data streams, which can be considered to be a sub problem of varying feature spaces [21], where new features emerge but none of the existing features vanish.
- The third scenario is an experiment on a real-life dataset of varying feature spaces.

We replicate the evaluation settings as they are given by the benchmark [2]. In each scenario, we receive an instance, use it to make a prediction to measure the accuracy of the learning algorithms and then feed it to the learning algorithms. For the first and second scenario, nine UCI Machine Learning repository datasets[1] were used. For the real-life dataset, the benchmark makes use of the *imdb* movie review dataset, which was introduced by [12].

In the first scenario, we benchmark our approach against the $OLVF$ algorithm, and in the second and third scenario we benchmark ourselves additionally against the OL_{SF} algorithm, as it was done in the $OLVF$ benchmark. The characteristics, in terms of features and instances for each dataset, are shown in Table 2. Similar to the benchmark from $OLVF$, we determine the best set of parameters in a single run and then repeat the experiments for each UCI dataset 20 times and report the score as the mean error over these 20 runs with the respective standard deviation. For the OL_{SF} and $OLVF$ we use the parameters as they were presented in [2].

Table 2. The datasets used for evaluation with their respective features and samples.

Dataset	#Samples	#Features	Dataset	#Samples	#Features
wpbc	198	34	svmguide3	1,234	21
ionosphere	351	35	spambase	4,601	57
wdbc	569	31	magic04	19,020	10
wbc	699	10	imdb	25,000	7500
german	1,000	24	a8a	32,561	123

4.1 Impact of Parameters

The first part of our evaluation are experiments on the impact of the parameters. We hereby evaluate the impact of the parameters α, β, and δ. While the choice of the other parameters still has an impact on the final result, it is hard to evaluate them in a structured manner. The impact of the parameters is shown on the *german* dataset by simulating varying feature spaces with a removal ratio of 0.25. We report on the relearning operations, which are counted every time we reach line 16 of Algorithm 1 and the error for the respective values of the inspected parameter. The relearning can be considered the most expensive operation in our proposed algorithm and should therefore be minimized while managing the trade-off with the errors.

---

[1] https://archive.ics.uci.edu/ml/index.php.

Weight Impacts of Alpha. The α parameter impacts the weight updates for the respective weak classifiers. In the experiments with different values of α it showed that for a lower α value of 0.1, we have less relearns than for a high α value of 1.0. However, while the change in the number of relearns is consistent, the impact is relatively small. For the lowest α value, we had 1494 relearning operations, while we had 1323 operations for the highest α value. In terms of performance, it shows that a lower α value is beneficial over a higher α value.

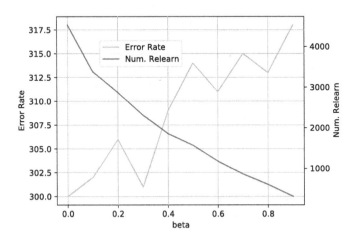

Fig. 2. Influence of the value of β on the total errors and the number of relearns on the *german* dataset with a removal ratio of 0.25.

Relearning with Beta. The parameter β is the probability of keeping a weak learner despite not being in the top bracket of the weights. The impact of β on the error rate and the amount of relearning operations for a simulated varying feature space with a removal ratio of 0.25 is shown in Fig. 2. It can be seen that with an increasing value for β, the error number increases as well. However, the additional performance comes at the cost of roughly 4000 relearns for a low β value, which can be decreased to about 500 relearns for a β value of 0.9. Further experiments have shown that the impact of β for higher removal ratios, i.e., varying feature spaces that have a higher sparsity, is not as significant as for the presented removal ratio of 0.25. Therefore, depending on the sparsity, we recommend a lower β value for dense data streams and a higher β value for sparser data streams. Setting β to one means no relearning operations are performed; the algorithm's dynamic would then only come from the dropping and the addition of new learners based on γ and θ_2.

Feature Diversity for Delta. The δ parameter determines the accepted feature space for a weak learner. Hence, it serves as a bagging parameter. We evaluated the parameter δ with respect to the feature diversity it introduces as well as the relearns it forces. We could observe that with an increasing value for δ, the number of relearns grows. While the impact is not as big as it is for β, it increased from 1271 to 2389 for $\delta = 0.1$ and $\delta = 1.0$ respectively. While for $\delta = 0.1$, all features of the dataset were used in the final ensemble, for $\delta = 1.0$, only a small subset of four features were actually used in the final ensemble. This means that δ can be considered to impact the feature diversity of the model. Considering that in varying feature spaces, not every feature is always present at a given time step, it is desirable to increase the diversity with a rather low value for δ. The actual value that should be used depends on the expected feature space, which is usually not known beforehand in the setting of varying feature spaces.

4.2   Experiment with Varying Feature Spaces

For the simulation of varying feature spaces, we replicate the experiment setup of [2]. Hereby, varying feature spaces are simulated by randomly removing features for each instance in a given dataset. This is done for removing ratios (Rem.) of 0.25, 0.5, and 0.75. The results are shown in Table 3. With regard to the parameters, we followed the example of [2] as well, who performed a grid search. For the N values, i.e. the buffer size, we used for all datasets, except the *magic04* and the *a8a* dataset, a value of ten percent of the instances to avoid learning from the whole dataset towards the end of the simulated data stream, as some datasets are rather small. The N values for the *magic04* and the *a8a* dataset were both set to 500, which is less than ten percent of the instances. The two bounding parameters theta were set to $\theta_1 = 0.05$, and $\theta_2 = 0.75$, while the rest of the parameters were determined from a random grid search.

Table 3. Average number of errors made by $OLVF$ and $DynFo$ on simulated data streams with varying feature spaces on the nine UCI ML Repository datasets with removing ratios (Rem.) of 0.25, 0.5, and 0.75.

	german		ionosphere		spambase	
Rem	$OLVF$	$DynFo$	$OLVF$	$DynFo$	$OLVF$	$DynFo$
0.25	333.4 ± 9.7	$\mathbf{302.0 \pm 3.6}$	77.2 ± 7.1	$\mathbf{67.1 \pm 5.2}$	$\mathbf{659.8 \pm 14.5}$	885.4 ± 61.4
0.5	350.9 ± 7.8	$\mathbf{307.1 \pm 7.3}$	79.5 ± 7.4	$\mathbf{75.9 \pm 5.6}$	$\mathbf{864 \pm 20.6}$	939.6 ± 36.1
0.75	365 ± 3.6	$\mathbf{325.5 \pm 17.2}$	$\mathbf{79.7 \pm 5.9}$	102.9 ± 7.2	1375 ± 21.5	$\mathbf{1120.8 \pm 30.6}$
	magic04		svmguide3		wbc	
Rem.	$OLVF$	$DynFo$	$OLVF$	$DynFo$	$OLVF$	$DynFo$
0.25	6152.4 ± 54.7	$\mathbf{5229.6 \pm 90.7}$	346 ± 11.6	$\mathbf{286.1 \pm 8.9}$	$\mathbf{25.3 \pm 1.4}$	42.5 ± 5.6
0.5	6775 ± 27.4	$\mathbf{5295.2 \pm 80.5}$	367.2 ± 11.9	$\mathbf{295.7 \pm 11.3}$	60.6 ± 5.3	53.6 ± 6.6
0.75	7136 ± 2.7	$\mathbf{5674.7 \pm 55.9}$	371 ± 11.7	$\mathbf{322.1 \pm 22.3}$	123.1 ± 3.6	$\mathbf{92.8 \pm 9.0}$
	wpbc		wdbc		a8a	
Rem.	$OLVF$	$DynFo$	$OLVF$	$DynFo$	$OLVF$	$DynFo$
0.25	88.5 ± 5.8	$\mathbf{55.4 \pm 4.2}$	$\mathbf{40.8 \pm 3.5}$	50.6 ± 4.7	8993.8 ± 40.3	$\mathbf{7834.4 \pm 14.3}$
0.5	90.2 ± 5.1	$\mathbf{60.6, \pm 6.7}$	55.2 ± 5.4	$\mathbf{55.1 \pm 4.9}$	9585.8 ± 53.8	$\mathbf{7805.15 \pm 22.3}$
0.75	107.7 ± 7.7	$\mathbf{71.2 \pm 7.2}$	202.85 ± 7.5	$\mathbf{78.0 \pm 7.0}$	12453 ± 74.4	$\mathbf{7709.6 \pm 58.9}$

In 22 out of the 27 recorded experiments for simulating varying feature spaces, we outperform the state-of-the-art algorithm $OLVF$. We checked for statistical significance with a two-sided t-test and found the results for $DynFo$ to be significantly better than $OLVF$ with $p < 0.05$ on the *german, magic04, svmguide3,* and *wpbc* dataset, as well as marginal significant with $p < 0.1$ on the *a8a* dataset. On the other datasets, we reported mixed results regardless, which makes it plausible that there is no significantly better approach for them. There is no clear tendency on these nine datasets that would show if Dynamic Forest is better in a more sparse environment or a more dense environment; we have examples for both settings where $DynFo$ outperforms $OLVF$ and vice versa, and we experienced it to be dependent on the characteristics of the dataset. For example, on the *ionosphere* dataset, our approach performs better for removing ratios of 0.25 and 0.5, while the opposite can be observed on the *wbc* and the *wdbc* dataset, where $DynFo$ performs better for removing ratios of 0.5 and 0.75. Another interesting observation can be made on the *a8a* dataset, where our approach actually gains performance slightly as the removal ratio increases. Considering that the *a8a* dataset is relatively sparse with binary values, the removal of mostly zero values seems beneficial.

4.3   Experiment with Trapezoidal Data Streams

As a secondary evaluation case, we also benchmark Dynamic Forest against OL_{SF} and $OLVF$ on trapezoidal data streams. We again follow the evaluation setup of [2]. Where trapezoidal data streams are simulated by splitting the dataset into ten chunks, where for each chunk, the feature space is increased. For each chunk, the feature space increases by ten percent, meaning that in the first chunk, we will have ten percent of the features, in the second chunk 20%, and so forth. For Dynamic Forest we again used a random grid search, while we fixed the values for the θ_1, θ_2, and N parameter according to the experiment for varying feature spaces. The results are shown in Table 4.

In this experiment, $DynFo$ outperforms $OLVF$ and OL_{SF} on six of the nine UCI datasets. It performs worse than the state-of-the-art algorithms on the *ionosphere, wbc,* and *spambase* dataset. All three of them are datasets on which we also had not a perfect performance, in the sense that for at least one of the three removing ratios we performed worse, compared to $OLVF$, in the experiment for varying feature spaces. This again indicates that the data's underlying structure is influential to the algorithms, and an addition to the solution space is beneficial.

Table 4. Average number of errors made by OL_{SF}, $OLVF$, and $DynFo$ in the simulated trapezoidal data streams on the nine UCI ML Repository datasets, and on the *imdb* dataset, which represents the real-world dataset for varying feature spaces.

Algo.	german	ionosphere	magic04	svmguide3	wpbc
OL_{SF}	369.0 ± 10.9	85.3 ± 5.8	6109.5 ± 62.1	379.8 ± 26.0	84.8 ± 5.4
$OLVF$	356.3 ± 9.1	$\mathbf{58.3 \pm 3.4}$	6408.5 ± 78.0	438.3 ± 31.8	88.1 ± 11.0
$DynFo$	$\mathbf{303.1 \pm 12.2}$	70.6 ± 5.1	$\mathbf{5242.6 \pm 68.4}$	$\mathbf{303.1 \pm 21.6}$	$\mathbf{53.5 \pm 5.6}$
Algo.	wdbc	spambase	wbc	a8a	imdb
OL_{SF}	125.5 ± 10.1	$\mathbf{977.6 \pm 47.4}$	37.9 ± 9.1	10356.4 ± 140.1	11761.5 ± 48.1
$OLVF$	74.4 ± 10.5	1163.5 ± 14.9	$\mathbf{31.6 \pm 2.2}$	11522.3 ± 119.6	9804.2 ± 65.9
$DynFo$	$\mathbf{70.2 \pm 5.2}$	108.0 ± 44.5	50.2 ± 6.4	$\mathbf{7852.6 \pm 10.2}$	$\mathbf{8535.6 \pm 584.9}$

4.4 Experiment with Real-World Varying Feature Spaces

In the *imdb* Movie Reviews dataset, the task is to perform sentiment analysis, i.e., if they have a positive or negative sentiment, for movie reviews. Each movie review has a feature space on its own, hence if we feed the dataset row by row to the learning algorithms, we have a data stream with a varying feature space and apply $OLVF$ and $DynFo$ to it. Furthermore, the problem can also be considered as a trapezoidal data stream, where we assume that non-existing features are missing. For the evaluation, we used the parameters as they were reported by [2]. However, in this experiment, we had to make assumptions on which kind of data they have used, as the original dataset has over 90,000 features, and they reported it as only having 7,500 with no explanation on how to choose these 7,500 features, we decided to use the most frequent 7,500 features. These features may not be the ones that have the most predictive power, as they contain stopwords and other low-impact words, but in this case, it made the most sense. Despite choosing the most frequent features, the one with the most occurrences, still only has a total of 672 occurrences to put it into perspective. For our approach we used grid search to determine the best parameters, while fixing $N = 1000$, which resulted in the following: $\alpha = 0.5$, $\beta = 0.3$, $\delta = 0.01$, $\epsilon = 0.001$, $\gamma = 0.7$, $\theta_1 = 0.05$, $\theta_2 = 0.6$ and $M = 1000$.

The results of the average number of wrong predictions for the *imdb* dataset are shown in Table 4. Hereby, we can see that the $DynFo$ outperforms the two baselines by making roughly 1265 fewer errors on average than $OLVF$. However, it has to be noted that for this particular dataset, we have a higher standard deviation in the results, while the other two approaches seemed to perform more consistently on this dataset. We explain this by the extreme sparsity of the features. If certain values for a predictive feature are highly spread over the dataset, then there are fewer instances that fall into the range of the instance buffer at once. Therefore, we might miss this split on a feature, as the gain for splitting on this feature is not as high as it could be. The experiment has furthermore shown that for a higher β value, the standard deviation, as well as the performance, decreases, while still beating the state-of-the-art.

5   Conclusion

In this paper, we presented Dynamic Forest, an online random forest approach to deal with varying feature spaces in data streams, where each new arriving instance can be different from the ones seen before. Dynamic Forest relies on dynamically learning and relearning, weighting, and dropping of weak learners in the ensemble during the learning process and then using the weak learners' probability predictions and the learned weights for the final prediction. Our work was evaluated on nine UCI Machine Learning repository datasets for varying feature spaces as well as trapezoidal data streams and one real-world dataset for varying feature spaces. We could show that we outperform the state-of-the-art algorithms in a significant majority of the cases. However, the performance also seemed to be impacted by the respective dataset characteristics, such as the number of instances, feature space size, and sparsity of values.

Acknowledgments. This research was supported by the Federal Ministry for Housing, Urban Development and Building (Grant No. 13622847). We would also like to thank the reviewers for their valuable remarks.

References

1. Agarwal, S., Saradhi, V.V., Karnick, H.: Kernel-based online machine learning and support vector reduction. Neurocomputing **71**(7–9), 1230–1237 (2008)
2. Beyazit, E., Alagurajah, J., Wu, X.: Online learning from data streams with varying feature spaces. In: Proceedings of the AAAI Conference on Artificial Intelligence, vol. 33, pp. 3232–3239 (2019)
3. Breiman, L.: Random forests. Mach. Learn. **45**(1), 5–32 (2001)
4. Domingos, P., Hulten, G.: Mining high-speed data streams. In: ACM SIGKDD International Conference on Knowledge Discovery and Data Mining, pp. 71–80 (2000)
5. Gomes, H.M., et al.: Adaptive random forests for evolving data stream classification. Mach. Learn., 1469–1495 (2017). https://doi.org/10.1007/s10994-017-5642-8
6. Gomes, J.B., Gaber, M.M., Sousa, P.A., Menasalvas, E.: Mining recurring concepts in a dynamic feature space. IEEE Trans. Neural Netw. Learn. Syst. **25**(1), 95–110 (2013)
7. Hoi, S.C., Wang, J., Zhao, P.: LIBOL: a library for online learning algorithms. J. Mach. Learn. Res. **15**(1), 495–499 (2014)
8. Hou, B.J., Zhang, L., Zhou, Z.H.: Learning with feature evolvable streams. In: Advances in Neural Information Processing Systems, pp. 1417–1427 (2017)
9. Iba, W., Langley, P.: Induction of one-level decision trees. In: Machine Learning Proceedings 1992, pp. 233–240. Elsevier (1992)
10. Lakshminarayanan, B., Roy, D.M., Teh, Y.W.: Mondrian forests: efficient online random forests. In: Advances in Neural Information Processing Systems, vol. 27 (2014)
11. Leite, D., Costa, P., Gomide, F.: Evolving granular neural networks from fuzzy data streams. Neural Netw. **38**, 1–16 (2013)
12. Maas, A., Daly, R.E., Pham, P.T., Huang, D., Ng, A.Y., Potts, C.: Learning word vectors for sentiment analysis. In: Proceedings 49th Annual Meeting of the Association for Computational Linguistics, pp. 142–150 (2011)

13. Masud, M.M., et al.: Classification and adaptive novel class detection of feature-evolving data streams. IEEE Trans. Knowl. Data Eng. **25**(7), 1484–1497 (2012)
14. Pardo, J., Zamora-Martínez, F., Botella-Rocamora, P.: Online learning algorithm for time series forecasting suitable for low cost wireless sensor networks nodes. Sensors **15**(4), 9277–9304 (2015)
15. Rosenblatt, F.: The perceptron: a probabilistic model for information storage and organization in the brain. Psychol. Rev. **65**(6), 386 (1958)
16. Roughgarden, T., Schrijvers, O.: Online prediction with selfish experts. In: Inh: Advances in Neural Information Processing Systems, pp. 1300–1310 (2017)
17. Shi, Q., Abdel-Aty, M.: Big data applications in real-time traffic operation and safety monitoring and improvement on urban expressways. Transp. Res. Part C Emerging Technol. **58**, 380–394 (2015)
18. Yu, H., Neely, M., Wei, X.: Online convex optimization with stochastic constraints. In: Advances in Neural Information Processing Systems, pp. 1428–1438 (2017)
19. Zhang, P., Zhou, C., Wang, P., Gao, B.J., Zhu, X., Guo, L.: E-tree: an efficient indexing structure for ensemble models on data streams. IEEE Trans. Knowl. Data Eng. **27**(2), 461–474 (2014)
20. Zhang, Q., Zhang, P., Long, G., Ding, W., Zhang, C., Wu, X.: Towards mining trapezoidal data streams. In: IEEE International Conference on Data Mining, pp. 1111–1116 (2015)
21. Zhang, Q., Zhang, P., Long, G., Ding, W., Zhang, C., Wu, X.: Online learning from trapezoidal data streams. IEEE Trans. Knowl. Data Eng. **28**(10), 2709–2723 (2016)
22. Zhang, Z.Y., Zhao, P., Jiang, Y., Zhou, Z.H.: Learning with feature and distribution evolvable streams. In: International Conference on Machine Learning, pp. 11317–11327. PMLR (2020)
23. Zinkevich, M.: Online convex programming and generalized infinitesimal gradient ascent. In: International Conference on Machine Learning, pp. 928–936 (2003)

Enabling Multi-process Discovery
on Graph Databases

Ali Nour Eldin[1,2(✉)], Nour Assy[1], Meriana Kobeissi[1,3], Jonathan Baudot[2],
and Walid Gaaloul[1]

[1] Telecom SudParis, Institut Polytechnique de Paris, Paris, France
{ali.nour_eldin,nour_assy,meriana.kobeissi,walid.gaaloul}@telecom-sudparis.eu
[2] Bonitasoft, Grenoble, France
{jonathan.baudot,ali.nour-eldin}@bonitasoft.com
[3] Faculty of Sciences, Lebanese University, Beirut, Lebanon

Abstract. With the abundance of event data, the challenge of enabling
process discovery in the large has attracted the community attention.
Several works addressed the problem by performing process discovery
directly on relational databases, instead of the traditional file based
computations. Preliminary results show that moving (parts of) process
discovery to the database engine outperforms file based computations.
However, all existing works consider the traditional storage of event data
which assumes that a clear and predefined process instance notion exists,
and that events are correlated to one process instance. In this work, we
go two steps further. First, we address the problem of process discovery on *object-centric event data* which allows several process instance
notions to be flexibly defined. We refer to it as *multi-process discovery* Second, motivated by the intrinsic nature of process discovery that
searches for relationships in event data, we address the question of *how
graph-based storage of object-centric event data improves the performance
of multi-process discovery?* We propose in-database process discovery
operators based on labeled property graphs. We use Neo4j as a DBMS
and Cypher as a query language. We compare different discovery strategies that involve graph and relational databases. Our results show that
process discovery in graph databases outperform existing approaches.

Keywords: Object-centric · Process mining · Process discovery ·
Property graph · Cypher language

1 Introduction

Process mining techniques [2] seek to extract information from event data that
can help organizations improve their business processes. Such data include the
events that are produced as result of the execution of activities within a process.
An event records the name of the activity that was executed, its timestamp and
additional data such as the objects that were affected by the executed activity.

© The Author(s), under exclusive license to Springer Nature Switzerland AG 2022
M. Sellami et al. (Eds.): CoopIS 2022, LNCS 13591, pp. 112–130, 2022.
https://doi.org/10.1007/978-3-031-17834-4_7

Process discovery [5] is one of the most prominent process mining techniques. It allows to automatically discover a process model that explains the behavior observed in the data. The process model is typically represented in petri nets [18], but other formats as also possible (e.g. BPMN [6]). Process discovery is traditionally applied on *event logs* which are usually obtained by querying a database and storing the data in a file. However, as the volume of data increases, this approach faces a scalability issue, in terms of time and memory efficiency. The computation may become time consuming and the size of the file may not fit the computer's memory which requires event data to be partitioned [9].

Several works addressed this problem by moving the heavy parts of process discovery to the database engine, namely relational database, where event data often reside (e.g. [7,17]). This approach has not only revealed scalable, but also solved the burden of repeatedly extracting and moving copies of the data to the analysts' environment where the processing power of the database cannot be used anymore. However, these promising results are constrained by the event data schema assumed by existing works and its implication on the required queries. In fact, all existing approaches are based on the traditional assumption that events are related to a single predefined *case notion*. A case notion defines a process instance and can be seen as the identifier of a process execution. Fixing the case notion implies a simplified event data schema that does not require writing queries with many JOIN operations which are known to be expensive.

Assuming that event data is stored w.r.t. a fixed case notion is unrealistic in practice [3]. In fact, event data is multidimensional in nature since process instances can be defined from multiple perspectives. For instance, one may look at the process from the order perspective (i.e. each order defines a process instance), from the customer perspective, or from both the order and customer perspective (i.e. each combination of order and customer defines a process instance).

In this work, we relax this assumption by considering object-centric event data (OCED) [3,11]. OCED does not require a fixed case notion and allows event data to be stored in a multi-dimensional way which is closer to the reality. We study the problem of enabling in-database process discovery on OCED (referred to as multi-process discovery) stored in graph databases. Our choice is motivated by the intrinsic nature of i) event data which is naturally interconnected and ii) process discovery algorithms which search for data relationships. In addition, we compare different strategies involving graph and relational databases using real life event logs with varying characteristics. Our evaluation shows that in-graph database discovery outperforms relational and traditional file-based computations. Our contributions can be summarized as follow:

1. We propose to store OCED in labeled property graphs [4]. Compared to [8], we do not require to explicitly store the case notions in nodes. Instead, we store data in its most natural format, i.e. without any reference to an explicit case notion.
2. We propose two different strategies to enable multi-process discovery on labeled property graphs using Cypher language[1]. Our operators allow to con-

---

[1] https://neo4j.com/developer/cypher/.

struct a Directly-Follows Graph (DFG) which is the intermediary structure required by most process discovery techniques.

3. We compare the performance, in terms of execution time and memory consumption, of our proposed strategies with existing relational-based and file-based process discovery. To the best of our knowledge, this is the first work that studies and compares the performance of multi-process discovery in graph databases.

The remainder of this paper is organized as follows. In Sect. 2, we discuss the existing works related to our contribution. In Sect. 3, we define some concepts related to the graph based storage of object-centric data and to the query language Cypher. In Sect. 4, we present our in-database operators for process discovery. In Sect. 5, we discuss and evaluate different strategies for process discovery using graph and relational databases before concluding in Sect. 6.

2   Related Work

Process discovery is one of the most studied process mining techniques. A plethora of discovery techniques have been proposed in the literature (e.g. [1,10,13,19]). The majority of them take an event log in the XES[2] format as input. The XES standard groups events under a single case notion which corresponds to a well defined view on the process. For instance, in a hiring process, one may look at the process from the candidate perspective (corresponds to a case notion) or from the hiring personnel perspective (another possible case notion). In our work, we relax this assumption by addressing the problem of process discovery on OCED [3] which allow different case notions to be flexibly defined. Additionally, existing approaches necessitate the storage of event data in a file, which causes scalability issues in terms of time and memory efficiency [9].

To address the scalability problem, some approaches proposed to move parts of process discovery to the database engine, namely relational database [7,16,17]. The data is stored in a format close to XES. These approaches rely on the development of SQL queries to correlate events and create the so-called directly-follows relations required by process discovery. The correlation of events require to query relationships using JOIN operators which are know to be expensive in relational querying. However, since these approaches assume that events are correlated to pre-defined case notions, the number of required JOIN operators is naturally reduced in the queries. This however may not hold anymore when storing object-centric event data.

Recent approaches have started to investigate the suitability of graph-based storage of event data. S. Esser and D. Fahland in [8] propose a data model in which multi-dimensional event data are stored in a labeled property graph and queried using the Cypher language. The proposed model allows to store different case notions but requires that events are explicitly correlated to every possible case notion. This means that dedicated nodes and relations need to be added to

---

[2] https://xes-standard.org/.

encode such information which adds overhead to the graph model and makes its maintenance complicated. In addition, the proposed model is not fully compliant with the Object-Centric Event Log (OCEL) standard [11] since OCEL does not require to explicitly encode every possible case notion. In our work, we also use labeled property graphs. However, following OCEL, we do not require to explicitly encode case notions; we simply store event data in terms of events and the affected objects.

A. Jalali [12] investigated the efficiency of graph databases, namely Neo4j queried with Cypher, for process discovery which is closely related to ours. However, this paper stores the data following the XES format while in our work we follow an object-centric approach and store OCED. In addition, this work evaluates only the time efficiency compared to a file based computation. In our work, we evaluate the time and memory efficiency and we compare different strategies involving relational database and file based computations.

3 Preliminaries

This section details i) the graph data model we used to store event data based on labeled property graphs (Sect. 3.1) and ii) an overview of the Cypher language which is used to query labeled property graphs (Sect. 3.2).

3.1 Graph-Based Storage of Object Centric Event Data

We propose to store OCED in labeled property graphs following Object Centric Event Log [11], a recently proposed standard for storing object-centric event data that does not require a predefined case notion. A labeled property graph is a directed multigraph with labeled nodes and relationships. Properties that correspond to key-value pairs of attributes can be assigned to each node/relation. Definition 1 provides a formal definition of a labeled property graph.

We assume that L is a set of labels (for nodes and edges), P is a set of property names, V is a set of atomic values. For a set S, we denote by S^+ the set of all subsets of S excluding the empty set.

Definition 1 (Labeled Property Graph). *A labeled property graph is a tuple $G = (N, R, \gamma, \lambda, \rho, \sigma)$ where:*

- *N is a set of nodes;*
- *R is the set of relations;*
- *$\gamma : R \mapsto N \times N$ is a total function that associates each relation to a pair of nodes. For a relation $r \in R$, we denote by $\gamma(r).start$ the start node and $\gamma(r).end$ the end node of r;*
- *$\lambda : (N \cup R) \mapsto L$ is a partial function that associates a node/relation with a label from L;*
- *$\rho : (N \cup R) \mapsto P^+$ is a partial function that associates nodes/relations with properties;*

– $\sigma : (N \cup R) \times P \mapsto V$ *is a partial function that associates for each node/relation property a value from* V.

The OCEL standard defines event data in terms of events and objects. Events correspond to executed activities. They have as mandatory attributes the activity name and the timestamp. Objects correspond to artifacts manipulated by activities. They have as mandatory attributes the object type. Figure 1 shows the metamodel of the corresponding event property graph. An example of its instantiation with event data from a hiring process is shown in Fig. 2.

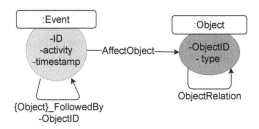

Fig. 1. Event property graph metamodel based on OCEL standard

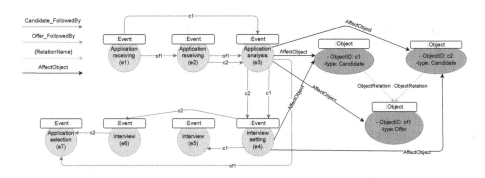

Fig. 2. An excerpt of an event property graph related to a hiring process. For readability, some relations are excluded. The event names are shown in the event nodes with the identifiers between brackets. Only the ObjectID is shown on the {Object}_FollowedBy relations differentiated by the edge's color

Two node types (i.e. labels) are defined in the event property graph: i) Event which refers to the occurrence of an activity and ii) Object which refers to artifact objects modified by activities. An event has the following mandatory properties: a unique identifier ID, an activity name which refers to the executed activity and a timestamp. Objects have a unique identifier ObjectID and an object type as mandatory properties. The AffectObject relation indicates that the occurrence of an activity within an event affects the corresponding object.

Compared to OCEL, we store two additional relations: {Object}_FollowedBy and ObjectRelation. The {Object}_FollowedBy relation allows to model the temporal order between events from the perspective of a single object type. The term {Object} is a placeholder and is replaced by an actual object type when the metamodel is instantiated. For example, in Fig. 2, the blue relations are labeled with Offer_FollowedBy, while the red relations are labeled with Candidate_FollowedBy. {Object}_FollowedBy relations have the property ObjectID which refers to a specific object. For instance, the Candidate_FollowedBy relations in Fig. 2 may refer to candidates "c1" or "c2". Object nodes can be associated through the relation ObjectRelation[3] (akin to foreign keys in relational databases). In our example in Fig. 2, a candidate can apply to a job offer. This information is encoded in the relationship created between c1 and of1 and between c2 and of1.

3.2 Cypher Language

To query the property graph, we use the Cypher language, a widely used declarative graph query language. Each Cypher query is made up of (Clause, Patterns) pairs. A **Clause** specifies the type of operation to be used. A **Pattern** specifies the inputs that must be provided to these clauses. Cypher queries are made up of the following main clauses: *MATCH-WHERE-WITH-RETURN*.

- **MATCH**: allows for the selection of sub-graphs with the same predefined structure of nodes and relations.
- **WHERE:** limits the chosen sub-graph by imposing restrictions on node/edge labels and attributes.
- **WITH:** enables query sections to be chained together, allowing results from one to be used as beginning points or criteria in the next. It comes after the WHERE clause and is used to specify new variables within the query.
- **RETURN:** is used to specify the query's output, which can be any graph element (e.g., node/edge or property values) as well as sub-graphs or any declared variables inside the query.

A simple example of a Cypher query applied on the labeled property graph in Fig. 2 is shown in Listing 1.1.

```
1 MATCH (ev:Event)-[:AffectObject]->(ob:Object)
2 WHERE ob.ObjectID = "c1"
3 RETURN ev
```

Listing 1.1. Example of cypher query

The *MATCH* clause retrieves all sub-graphs consisting of :Event nodes connected to Object nodes through the relation AffectObject. The *WHERE* clause filters the matched sub-graphs and keeps only those whose Object node has the ObjectID equal to "c1." The *RETURN* clause returns the Event nodes of the matched sub-graphs which are the nodes of e1, e3, e5 and e4.

---

[3] Additional properties such as the relation name can be added to ObjectRelation.

4   In-graph Database Operators for Multi-process Discovery

This section details our in-graph database operators for enabling multi-process discovery on labeled property graphs. In Sects. 4.1 and 4.2, we present the main ingredients of our approach in terms of the directly-follows graph (DFG) which is the approach output and the different possible definitions of case notions in OCED. In Sect. 4.3, we discuss different approaches for constructing a DFG.

4.1   Directly-Follows Graph

The majority of process discovery techniques build an intermediary data structure called *directly follows graph* (DFG), from which a process model can be easily inferred. Roughly speaking, a DFG shows how activities follow each other in terms of the so-called *directly-follows relations*. For example, the Inductive Miner [14] uses the DFG to extract a process model. Other algorithms like α-algorithm [15] construct the directly-follows relations before deriving the model.

The construction of the DFG requires to scan the entire dataset in order to correlate events and create the directly-follows relations between activities. Therefore, it is considered as the heaviest part of a process discovery technique. In this work, we propose to move the computation of the DFG to the graph database engine. A DFG can be formally defined as a labeled property graph where nodes are labeled with Activity, and relations connecting nodes are labeled with directly-follows abbreviated as DF. A node has an activity name as a mandatory property and an optional property indicating whether it is a start or end node of the graph. Nodes (and relations) can have additional properties that can be inferred from the data such as frequency which indicates the number of times the corresponding activity (relation) is observed in the event data.

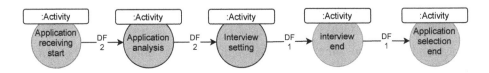

Fig. 3. An example of a DFG extracted from the event property graph in Fig. 2

An example of a DFG that was extracted from the event data in Fig. 2 is shown in Fig. 3. This DFG shows the activities performed when looking at the process from the Candidate perspective. The process starts by receiving the candidate's application (Application receiving with the property start). The application is then analyzed (Application analysis). Afterwards, an interview is scheduled (interview setting) and is realized (interview). For some candidates, the process terminates (indicated by the end property) or continued by selecting the candidate's application (Application selection). The relations have the frequency property. For example, the relation (Application receiving, Application analysis) has a frequency equal to 2 which means that Application receiving was directly followed by Application analysis two times in the event data.

4.2   Case Notion in OCED

Before discovering a DFG, one has to decide the way events should be correlated which is defined by specifying a *case notion* and deriving the corresponding *traces*. Given an event property graph, case notions can be defined in terms of Object types. For instance, in Fig. 2, Candidate and Offer can be defined as case notions. The DFG in Fig. 3 is discovered according to the case notion Candidate. Case notions can be also composite, akin to composite primary keys, e.g. {Candidate, Offer}. Therefore, the set of all possible case notions is defined as the powerset of object types in the event data as given in Definition 2.

Definition 2 (Single and Composite Case notion). *Let $G = (N, R, \gamma, \lambda, \sigma)$ be an event property graph, and $\mathcal{O}^T$ be the nonempty set of object types in G. The set of all possible case notions in G is defined as $\mathcal{C} = \mathcal{P}(\mathcal{O}^T) \setminus \emptyset$. A case notion $C \in \mathcal{C}$ can be single, i.e. $|C| = 1$ or composite, i.e. $|C| > 1$.*

Given an event property graph G and a case notion $C \in \mathcal{C}$, traces are created by correlating events w.r.t. to the {Object}_FollowedBy relation. A trace contains the sequence of events executed within one process instance identified by a *case identifier*. A case identifier is defined based on object identifiers (ObjectID). For example, given the event property graph in Fig. 2 and the case notion C ={Candidate}, two case identifiers can be defined: c1 and c2. Figure 4 shows the two traces with the Candidate_FollowedBy relation corresponding to c1 and c2. In the remainder, we refer to a trace as a sequence of events using the following notation $t = <e_1, \ldots, e_n>$.

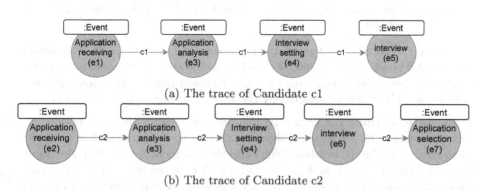

(a) The trace of Candidate c1

(b) The trace of Candidate c2

Fig. 4. The traces of different case identifiers of the case notion {Candidate}

When a single case notion is selected (as in the above example), deriving the case identifiers and their traces is straightforward. However, with composite case notions, we need to define the valid case identifiers. For instance, given the case notion C ={Candidate, Offer}, one can define the following possible case identifiers (c1,of1) and (c2,of1). To identify valid case identifiers, we rely on the relation ObjectRelation between objects in the event property graph. This relation is similar to foreign keys in relational databases and allows to define object instances that are associated. By looking at the event property graph in Fig. 2, we can conclude that (c1,of1) and (c2,of1) are valid case identifiers since Object c1 is connected to Object of1 and Object c2 to Object of1.

Definition 3 (Valid Case Identifier). *Let $G = (N, R, \gamma, \lambda, \sigma)$ be an event property graph and $C = \{o_1^T, \ldots, o_n^T \mid n \geq 1\} \in \mathcal{C}$ be a case notion. A case identifier of C, denoted as id_C, is defined as $id_C = (o_1, \ldots, o_n)$ such that $\forall 1 \leq i \leq n$, $o_i \in N$ and $\lambda(o_i) = Object$ and $\sigma(o_i, type) = O_i^T$. In case of composite case notion, id_C is a valid case identifier iff $\forall 1 \leq i, j \leq n$, $\exists r \in R$ such that $\gamma(r) = (o_i, o_j)$. We denote by ID_C the set of all valid case identifiers of C.*

Once valid case identifiers are defined, we need to derive the corresponding traces. As already explained, traces are derived based on {Object}_FollowedBy relations. In case of a single case notion, deriving traces for different case identifiers is straightforward as shown in Fig. 4. Formally, given an event property graph and a single case notion, a trace is defined as given below.

Definition 4 (Trace for single case notion). *Let $G = (N, R, \gamma, \lambda, \sigma)$ be an event property graph, $C = \{o^T\} \in \mathcal{C}$ be a single case notion and $id_C \in ID_C$ be a case identifier. The trace of id_C is defined as $t = <e_1, \ldots, e_n>$ such that $\forall 1 \leq i \leq n-1$, $e_i \in N$:*

1. *$\exists r \in R$: $\gamma(r) = (e_i, e_{i+1})$ and $\lambda(r) = \{o^T\}\_FollowedBy$ and $\sigma(r, ObjectID) = id_C$;*
2. *$\nexists r_m, r_n \in R$: $\gamma(r_m).end = e_1$ and $\lambda(r_m) = \{o^T\}\_FollowedBy$ and $\sigma(r_m, ObjectID) = id_C$ and $\gamma(r_n).start = e_n$ and $\lambda(r_n) = \{o^T\}\_FollowedBy$ and $\sigma(r_n, ObjectID) = id_C$.*

However, since our event property graph stores only the {Object}_FollowedBy relations for single object types, we need to define the way we define traces for composite case notions. To do so, we define two operators: *trace union* and *trace intersection* which can be selected by the user according to his/her preference.

Trace Intersection: For each case identifier of a composite case notion, we derive the traces for each single object according to Definition 4. For example, given the case notion {Candidate, Offer} and the case identifier (c2,of1), the traces $t_{c2} = <e2, e3, e4, e6, e7>$ and $t_{of1} = <e1, e2, e3, e7>$ can be derived. The trace intersection consists of generating a trace where only common events appear. In our example, the trace intersection results in $t = <e2, e3, e7>$ which corresponds to the trace of the case identifier (c2,of1). Figure 5a shows a visual representation of the resulting trace.

Trace Union: The trace union consists of merging the traces into one trace that contains all the events. The events in the resulting trace are ordered according to the timestamp[4] in the event property graph. Taking our previous example of the case identifier (c2,of1), the union of traces generates the trace $t = <e2, e3, e4, e6, e7>$. By inspecting the result, we can see that this trace contains the event Application receiving (e1) which corresponds to the application of1 of candidate c1 rather than candidate c2 as assumed by the case identifier (c2,of1). Therefore, we post-process the result to remove all events that affect an object whose id is different from the one in the case identifier. The post-processing step on our example removes the event e1 since it affects the object id c1 which is different from c2. The result is visually shown in Fig. 5b.

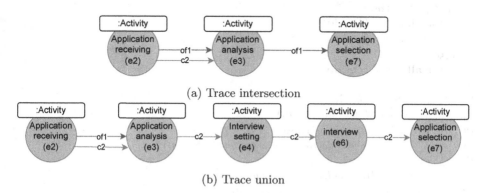

(a) Trace intersection

(b) Trace union

Fig. 5. Visual representation of trace intersection and union for (c2,of1)

4.3   DFG Construction

In this section, we present two different approaches for building a DFG from event property graphs using Cypher queries.

Approach 1 - Trace-Based: This approach requires that the set of traces are *pre-computed* and are then *merged* using the Merge feature of Cypher to construct the DFG. Therefore, given an event property graph and a selected case notion, we need first to derive all case identifiers and their corresponding traces as explained in the previous section. To compute traces, we take advantage of path querying in Cypher. For example, the Cypher query (e1:Event)-[:Candidate_FollowedBy*]->(e2:Event) queries all paths of events with the Candidate_FollowedBy relation between them by adding the '*' operator.

Algorithm 1 shows the high level steps required to construct a DFG using the trace-based approach. It takes as input the event property graph, the case notion, and the desired operator (intersection or union) for composite case notions. The algorithm starts by calculating all valid case identifiers (Line 3). A variable is declared to store all the computed traces (Line 4). For single case notion, the set of traces are derived for each case identifier following Definition 4 (Lines 5–7). For multi-case notion (Lines 8–16), for each case identifier, we iterate over

---

[4] We assume that events are totally ordered. In case this assumption is violated, we choose a random order.

each object and get the corresponding trace (Lines 10–12). The traces are then merged into one trace using the intersection or the union operator (Lines 13–16). The resulting trace is added to the list of traces.

Algorithm 1. Trace-based approach for DFG construction

1: **Input:** event property graph G, case notion C, Operator Op
2: **Output:** Directly follows graph DFG
3: $ID_C = get\_case\_identifiers(G, C)$
4: $Array\_Traces = []$
5: **if** $|C| == 1$ **then**
6:    **for all** $id_C \in ID_C$ **do**
7:       $Array\_Traces.add(get\_trace(G, id_C))$
8: **else**
9:    **for all** $id_C \in ID_C$ **do**
10:       $traces = []$
11:       **for all** $o \in id_C$ **do**
12:          $traces.add(get\_trace(G, o))$
13:       **if** $Op == intersection$ **then**
14:          $Array\_Traces.add(trace\_intersection(G, traces))$
15:       **else**
16:          $Array\_Traces.add(trace\_union(G, traces))$
17: $DFG = DFG\_merge(Array\_Traces, \text{'activity'})$

Once all traces are computed, they are merged to construct the DFG (Line 17). The DFG_merge function consists of merging the traces based on the activity property of events[5]. The algorithm has been translated to Cypher queries[6]. The get_traces is written using the path querying feature of Cypher. The intersection and union operators are defined using the Awesome Procedures On Cypher (APOC) library The DF_merge function is written with the help of the Merge clause in Cypher. For example, Listing 1.2 shows the Cypher query of the get_traces function. The first block of the query searches for the start and end events of each case identifier which are required as per Definition 4 (lines 1–3). Then, the WITH clause (Line 4) allows to use the results (start and end events) in the second query block which retrieves the trace of each case identifier using the path querying feature (Lines 5–6).

```
1 MATCH (eStart:Event)-[:AffectObject]->(:Object{Type:"Candidate",ObjectID:
     caseIdentifier}),(eEnd:Event)-[:AffectObject]->(:Object{Type:"Candidate",
     ObjectID:caseIdentifier})
2 WHERE NOT EXISTS((:Event)-[:Candidate_FollowedBy{ObjectID:caseIdentifier}]->(
     eStart))
```

---

[5] The merging can be performed on other events' properties. This concept is known as *classifier* in process mining.

[6] Available at: https://github.com/Noureldin-Ali/GraphProcessDiscovery.

```
3 AND NOT EXISTS((eEnd)-[:Candidate_FollowedBy{ObjectID:caseIdentifier}]->(:
       Event))
4 WITH caseIdentifier,eStart,eEnd
5 MATCH path = (eStart)-[:Candidate_FollowedBy*{ObjectID:caseIdentifier}]->(eEnd
       )
6 WITH NODES(path) AS trace,caseIdentifier
```

Listing 1.2. Cypher query for computing the traces of the case notion Candidate

As an example, given the case notion {Candidate}, the case identifiers are c1 and c2. The traces of the case identifiers are shown in Fig. 4. By merging these two traces based on activity names, we obtain the DFG in Fig. 3. The calculation of the frequency information is not shown in the algorithm but is available in the Cypher queries.

Approach 2 - On-the-Fly. In this second approach, we do not precompute the traces as we did in the trace-based approach. Instead, for each case identifier, we traverse the event property graph following the {Object}_FollowedBy relations and we incrementally construct the DFG by adding the associated activities. Listing 1.3 shows the corresponding Cypher query for a single case notion (e.g. {Candidate}). The **Match** clause searches for all pairs of events that are connected through the Candidate_FollowedBy relation. The **Merge** clauses create and add the activities' names of the matched events as activity nodes connected by a DF relation in the DFG.

```
1 MATCH (e1:Event)-[:Candidate_FollowedBy]->(e2:Event)
2 MERGE (a1 : DFG{activityName : e1.activity})
3 MERGE (a2 : DFG{activityName : e2.activity})
4 MERGE (a1)-[DF]->(a2)\label{1st:onspsthespsfly}
```

Listing 1.3. Cypher query for on the fly construction of DFG

The pseudo-code for constructing a DFG using the on-the-fly approach is shown in Algorithm 2. The algorithm takes as input the event property graph and the case notion[7]. Similarly to the trace-based approach, the algorithm starts by computing all valid case identifiers (Line 1). A variable is defined to store all derived pairs of events (Line 2). For single case notions, we simply get all pairs of events connected by an {Object}_FollowedBy relation, where Object refers to the object type in the case notion C (Lines 5–6). For composite case notions (line 7–13), for each object id of each case identifier (Lines 9–10), we retrieve the pairs of events connected through an {Object}_FollowedBy whose id is equal to the object id. We add an additional constraint that keeps only the pairs whose events affect all the objects of the id_C (Lines 11–12). This ensures that the intersection operator defined over traces is correctly performed. Once all pairs of events are computed, they are merged to create the DFG (Line 13).

---

[7] For composite case notions, the on-the-fly approach works only with the intersection operator. The union operator requires ordering events and therefore pre-computing the traces.

Algorithm 2. On-the-fly approach for DFG construction

1: **Input:** event property graph G, case notion C
2: **Output:** Directly follows graph DFG
3: $ID_C = get\_case\_identifiers(G, C)$
4: $Array\_Pairs\_Events = []$
5: **if** $|C| == 1$ **then**
6:    $Array\_Pairs\_Events = get\_pair\_events(G, relation = \{C\}\_FollowedBy)$
7: **else**
8:    **for all** $id_C \in ID_C$ **do**
9:       $Pair\_Events = []$
10:       **for all** $o \in id_C$ **do**
11:          $Pairs\_Events = get\_pair\_events(G, relation = \{o^T\}\_FollowedBy, id = o, affect = id_C)$
12:       $Array\_Pairs\_Events.add(Pairs\_Events)$
13: $DFG = DFG\_merge(Array\_Pairs\_Events, 'activity')$

---

5 Evaluation

In this section, we present the results of the comparative experiments we conducted to evaluate the approach in terms of time and memory efficiency. We used real life event logs from BPI 2012 to 2017[8]. The characteristics of the event logs are presented in Table 1.

Table 1. Characteristics of the used event logs. For BPI 2017, the number of cases, activities and traces for each object type is reported

Datasets	Cases	Event	Activity	Trace length		
				Min	Mean	Max
BPI 2012	13087	262200	36	3	20	175
BPI 2013	7554	65533	13	1	9	123
BPI 2014	46616	466737	39	10	10	178
BPI 2015	1156	59083	285	5	51	154
BPI 2017	31509	561671	26	8	18	61
	42995		15	3	6	21

The BPI event logs are stored in XES format. We manually identified object types in each event log and the relations between them. We identified one object type for the BPI 2012–2015 and two object types for BPI 2017. We then wrote a script to populate an event property graph for each BPI log. All materials including the script, the dump files, the Cypher queries and the obtained results are publicly available[9].

---

[8] https://www.tf-pm.org/resources/xes-standard/about-xes/event-logs.
[9] https://github.com/Noureldin-Ali/GraphProcessDiscovery.

5.1 Experiment Description

We compared our two approaches referred to as GDB (trace-based and on the fly) presented in Sect. 4 with relational (RDB) and file based computations.

For the first GDB approach (i.e. trace-based), we investigated the use of indexes to accelerate the path querying. We relied on Database Hits to discover the main performance bottlenecks and identify the properties on which the index could be defined. As a result, we added a composite index on the properties type and ObjectID of the node Object. We name this third approach as "trace-based+index" and report its performance as well in the experiments.

For the RDB, we compared our approaches with the most recent one presented in [7]. This work assumes that activities are correlated to only one case notion. For the file based computations, we use the pm4py library[10] to construct a DFG from an XES file. It is worthnoting that Neo4j is based on optimized java while pm4py on python. The comparison is therefore not fair. However, since pm4py is widely used, and for completeness, we report its efficiency as well.

5.2 Test Environment

Our GDB approach is implemented in Neo4j 4.3.1. The RDB is built in Microsoft SQL server 2019. The file based approach is executed in process mining for python (pm4py 2.2.9).

We considered two configurations for our experiments. In the first configuration, we measured the efficiency of the different approaches in terms of time and memory consumption. We used an HP laptop, powered by Intel Core i7 (7th Gen) processor, coupled with 16 GB of RAM and 1 TB HDD storage, and running on Windows 10 Home Basic operating system. In the second configuration, we compared the performance of the different approaches by altering the CPU (from 0.5 GHz to 2 GHz) and RAM (from 2 GB to 8 GB). We containerized and performed the experiments with Docker[11]. Docker is a Platform as a Service (PaaS) platform for creating, executing, and managing containers. It gives control over the resources (RAM and CPU) that each container has access to.

For all approaches, we report the measures for executing the approach from end to end. For relational and graph databases, this includes the time to retrieve data from the hard disk and to get the results[12]. In our approach, we generate a DFG that is visualized inside the graph database. In RDB, the result is a table that includes only the directly-follows relations. In PM4PY, we include the time spent to load the data and to visualize the DFG.

5.3 Results

Time Efficiency. Table 2 reports the time performance (in seconds) of the different approaches on the BPI datasets. All queries involved a one case notion.

---

[10] https://pm4py.fit.fraunhofer.de/.

[11] https://www.docker.com/.

[12] In [7], the authors exclude the time to retrieve data from the hard disk.

This table shows that, overall, our second approach (on the fly) outperforms all other approaches (including relational database RDB and PM4PY) in all the five datasets. The trace-based approach without index is clearly time consuming because all traces need to be precomputed before constructing the DFG. When adding an index, the performance has largely improved, but still did not outperform the on the fly approach.

Table 2. Time performance in seconds of different approaches. *indicates that the time does not include the visualization because of the high number of activities

Datasets	GDB			RDB	PM4PY
	Trace-based	Trace-based+index	On the fly		
BPI2012	109	1.9	**0.35**	22	19.51
BPI2013	35	0.45	**0.1**	3	6.57
BPI2014	>10 min	3.2	**0.6**	22	236.77
BPI2015	1.3	0.75	**0.16**	19	4.7*
BPI2017	>10 min	4.2	**1.2**	74	56.97

Table 3 shows the time performance of our approach when a composite case notion is defined. We did not include existing works since they do not support the querying of object-centric event data. We report only the results on BPI2017 since it is the only dataset that contains two object types. The results show that for composite case notion, the trace-based approach with index outperforms the two other approaches in orders of magnitude. The poor performance of the on the fly approach can be explained by the fact that it requires to compute the intersection and union repeatedly which is time consuming. Whereas in single case notion, these two operators are not applicable. The trace-based approach without index has also a poor performance. This can be explained by the fact that path querying in graph databases is in general costly unless the start and/or end of the path are known. Using indexes, we accelerated the search for these start and end nodes in our queries.

In the second configuration, we measured the time performance by varying the CPU from 0.5 GHZ to 2 GHZ and the RAM from 2 GB to 8 GB. Figure 6 shows the results of the GDB (on the fly), RDB and PM4PY on different datasets[13]. The plots show that the performance of our GDB based approach is stable across all datasets against the CPU and RAM variations. The performance of the RDB and PM4PY based approaches are mainly affected by the CPU.

---

[13] Because of space constraints, we do not show all results. All remaining results are available at: https://github.com/Noureldin-Ali/GraphProcessDiscovery.

Table 3. Time performance in seconds of our proposed approaches with multi-case notion (Intersection and Union operators)

Datasets	Operator	GDB		
		On the fly	Trace-based	Trace-based+index
BPI2017	Intersection	>10 min	>10 min	**10**
	Union	Undefined	>10 min	**19**

Table 4. Memory consumption in MB of GDB vs RDB approaches

Datasets	GDB			RDB
	Trace-based	Trace-based+index	On the fly	
BPI2012	**27.68**	28.74	28.74	1138.8
BPI2013	**9.56**	**9.56**	11.28	1150.3
BPI2014	**30.39**	**30.39**	**30.39**	1049.21
BPI2017	**17.84**	**17.84**	**17.84**	1060.17

Memory Efficiency. Table 4 shows the memory consumption (in MB) of the GDB vs RDB approaches on the different datasets. The results clearly show that our GDB based approaches consume less memory resources than RDB. The memory consumption of all the three GDB approaches is roughly the same.

5.4 Threats to Validity

The evaluation results presented in this section suggest that graph database technologies are a promising solution for enabling process mining in the large. In addition, they provide a flexible storage of event data as it has been shown with our object-centric metamodel.

In our evaluation, we focused on the efficiency of the analysis and querying aspect since our aim is to demonstrate the scalability gain for process discovery in particular. We did not evaluate the efficiency of the creation, update and delete in the CRUD operations which could be costly in graph databases. In particular, the creation operation may be the most important since event data may, in practice, be stored in relational databases and need to be moved to the graph database environment. This limitation can be mitigated by scheduling the creation operations using batch incremental loading outside of peak hours.

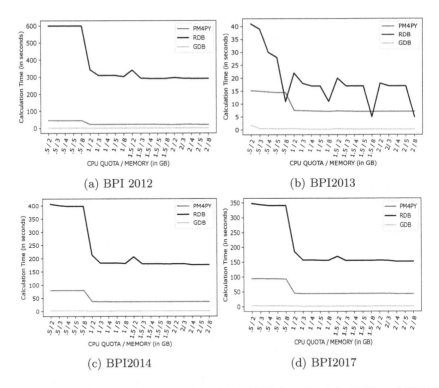

Fig. 6. Time performance (in seconds) of the GDB (on the fly), RDB and PM4PY approaches on different datasets when varying CPU (in GHZ) and RAM (in GB)

6   Conclusion

In this paper, we proposed in-database operators for discovering DFGs from object-centric event data stored in labeled property graphs. We used Neo4j as DBMS and Cypher as query language. We compared our approach in terms of time and memory consumption with existing works using relational databases and file based computations. The results show that in-graph process discovery outperforms existing approaches.

The performance results obtained in this paper are promising and open the door for enabling process mining in the large on graph databases. In our future works, we plan to perform an in-depth study of the scalability of in-graph database process discovery. We also aim at extending our operators so that we can generate and store process models (e.g. in petri nets or BPMN) as labelled property graphs.

References

1. van der Aalst, W.M.P.: Decomposing Petri nets for process mining: a generic approach. Distrib. Parallel Databases **31**(4), 471–507 (2013)
2. van der Aalst, W.M.P.: Process Mining - Data Science in Action, 2nd edn. Springer (2016). https://doi.org/10.1007/978-3-662-49851-4
3. Aalst, W.M.P.: Object-centric process mining: dealing with divergence and convergence in event data. In: Ölveczky, P.C., Salaün, G. (eds.) SEFM 2019. LNCS, vol. 11724, pp. 3–25. Springer, Cham (2019). https://doi.org/10.1007/978-3-030-30446-1_1
4. Angles, R.: The property graph database model. In: Proceedings of the 12th Alberto Mendelzon International Workshop on Foundations of Data Management, vol. 2100 (2018)
5. Augusto, A., et al.: Automated discovery of process models from event logs: review and benchmark. IEEE Trans. Knowl. Data Eng. **31**(4), 686–705 (2019)
6. Chinosi, M., Trombetta, A.: BPMN: an introduction to the standard. Comput. Stand. Interfaces **34**(1), 124–134 (2012)
7. Dijkman, R., Gao, J., Syamsiyah, A., van Dongen, B., Grefen, P., ter Hofstede, A.: Enabling efficient process mining on large data sets: realizing an in-database process mining operator. Distrib. Parallel Databases **38**(1), 227–253 (2019). https://doi.org/10.1007/s10619-019-07270-1
8. Esser, S., Fahland, D.: Multi-dimensional event data in graph databases. J. Data Semant. **10**(1–2), 109–141 (2021)
9. Evermann, J.: Scalable process discovery using map-reduce. IEEE Trans. Serv. Comput. **9**(3), 469–481 (2016)
10. Evermann, J., Assadipour, G.: Big data meets process mining: implementing the alpha algorithm with map-reduce. In: Symposium on Applied Computing, SAC, 2014, pp. 1414–1416. ACM (2014)
11. Ghahfarokhi, A.F., Park, G., Berti, A., van der Aalst, W.M.P.: OCEL: a standard for object-centric event logs. In: Bellatreche, L., et al. (eds.) ADBIS 2021. CCIS, vol. 1450, pp. 169–175. Springer, Cham (2021). https://doi.org/10.1007/978-3-030-85082-1_16
12. Jalali, A.: Graph-based process mining. In: Leemans, S., Leopold, H. (eds.) ICPM 2020. LNBIP, vol. 406, pp. 273–285. Springer, Cham (2021). https://doi.org/10.1007/978-3-030-72693-5_21
13. Leemans, S.J.J., Fahland, D., van der Aalst, W.M.P.: Discovering block-structured process models from event logs containing infrequent behaviour. In: Lohmann, N., Song, M., Wohed, P. (eds.) BPM 2013. LNBIP, vol. 171, pp. 66–78. Springer, Cham (2014). https://doi.org/10.1007/978-3-319-06257-0_6
14. Leemans, S.J.J., Fahland, D., van der Aalst, W.M.P.: Scalable process discovery and conformance checking. Softw. Syst. Model. **17**(2), 599–631 (2016). https://doi.org/10.1007/s10270-016-0545-x
15. Li, J., Liu, D., Yang, B.: Process mining: extending α - algorithm to mine duplicate tasks in process logs. In: Chang, K.C.-C., et al. (eds.) APWeb/WAIM -2007. LNCS, vol. 4537, pp. 396–407. Springer, Heidelberg (2007). https://doi.org/10.1007/978-3-540-72909-9_43
16. Schönig, S., Rogge-Solti, A., Cabanillas, C., Jablonski, S., Mendling, J.: Efficient and customisable declarative process mining with SQL. In: Nurcan, S., Soffer, P., Bajec, M., Eder, J. (eds.) CAiSE 2016. LNCS, vol. 9694, pp. 290–305. Springer, Cham (2016). https://doi.org/10.1007/978-3-319-39696-5_18

17. Syamsiyah, A., van Dongen, B.F., van der Aalst, W.M.P.: DB-XES: enabling process discovery in the large. In: Ceravolo, P., Guetl, C., Rinderle-Ma, S. (eds.) SIMPDA 2016. LNBIP, vol. 307, pp. 53–77. Springer, Cham (2018). https://doi.org/10.1007/978-3-319-74161-1_4

18. Weber, M., Kindler, E.: The Petri Net Markup Language. In: Ehrig, H., Reisig, W., Rozenberg, G., Weber, H. (eds.) Petri Net Technology for Communication-Based Systems. LNCS, vol. 2472, pp. 124–144. Springer, Heidelberg (2003). https://doi.org/10.1007/978-3-540-40022-6_7

19. Weijters, A., Aalst, W., Medeiros, A.: Process mining with the heuristics miner-algorithm. BETA Working Paper Series, WP 166 (2006)

Collaborative Patterns for Workflows with Collaborative Robots

Stefan Samhaber and Maria Leitner[✉]

University of Vienna, Faculty of Computer Science,
Research Group Workflow Systems and Technology, Vienna, Austria
{stefan.samhaber,maria.leitner}@univie.ac.at

Abstract. Collaborative work environments have gained more attention in manufacturing in recent years, in particular with the development of collaborative robots (cobots), a special type of industrial robot that is built for the safe interaction between humans and robots. Recent advances have shown that there are several collaboration scenarios between humans and robots, such as, synchronized, cooperation, collaboration and coexistence. So far, most literature focuses only on the collaboration between one human and one robot. However, literature also predicts that there will be more collaboration scenarios with one or many humans collaborating with one or many robots. Furthermore, literature on collaboration scenarios often focuses only on a generic process perspective and does not detail tasks nor other aspects. In this paper, we aim to address these gaps by investigating collaboration scenarios for one to many and many to many relations between robots and humans in workflows. First, we formalize the collaboration pattern and its types (synchronized, cooperation, collaboration and coexistence). Our approach allows for the specification of time-based, spatial and functional constraints at task level in collaborative work environments. Second, we demonstrate our findings with a proof-of-concept implementation that consists of a workflow system, a cobot simulation and a communication and data platform. Third, we evaluate our model with altogether seven use cases (e.g., spot taping). The results show that the patterns can be applied for the specification of collaboration scenarios in modern, process-oriented work environments. For future work, we would like to investigate questions on process modeling and visualization of collaborative patterns.

Keywords: Business processes · Collaborative robots · Cobots · Patterns · Workflow systems

1 Introduction

Over the last few years, the manufacturing industry has and will continue to change significantly, as consumer markets move from mass-produced goods towards increasingly high customized products and mass customization [4]. A growing number of product variants combined with shorter product life cycles

ⓒ The Author(s), under exclusive license to Springer Nature Switzerland AG 2022
M. Sellami et al. (Eds.): CoopIS 2022, LNCS 13591, pp. 131–148, 2022.
https://doi.org/10.1007/978-3-031-17834-4_8

and the demand for shorter lead times are leading to an increasingly complex manufacturing landscape [23]. In order to keep up with the ever-changing consumers' demands, there is a need for an adaptive, flexible and cost-efficient production environment.

Even with industrial automation (e.g., industrial robots), a lot of tasks are still performed by manual labor, as humans are excellent in dealing with uncertainties and variability coming from mass customization [11,31]. Humans, however, are limited by their physical abilities and cannot compete with robots in various aspects like speed, repeatability, strength, etc., which results in reduced efficiency and quality [11]. The combination of the complementary strengths of humans and robots [10,18] would provide all means to deal with the aforementioned challenges of modern manufacturing in the Industry 4.0 era. One approach to achieve this is to use a new generation of robots, the so-called *collaborative robots* (cobots) [23]. Cobots are a special type of conventional industrial robots. They are usually smaller and much lighter than their counterparts, and are specifically designed to directly interact with humans, which builds a core part of their functionality [18]. This is well reflected in their overall appearance. To prevent injuries like cuts, cobots usually do not have open sharp edges. Recent research shows that cobots are utilized in workflows (e.g., [13,30,39]).

Current research on cobot shows that there are different collaboration patterns (synchronized, cooperation, collaboration and coexistence) that focus on different collaboration scenarios between humans and robots (e.g., [11,26]). However, state of the art neither specifies nor provides types of collaboration patterns that can be utilized in workflows. They integrate a high level process without further specification of tasks or control flow aspects. Hence, further task level aspects are often missing. However, this is very important for process execution and monitoring and would be highly important for workflows with cobots. Furthermore, all patterns are only specified for one human collaborating with one robot (and vice versa). However, current literature (e.g., [9,28,33]) shows that there are already some use cases where *one or more* humans and *one or more* robots are working together.

In this paper, we will investigate the collaboration patterns for workflows with cobots. In particular, we contribute a formal specification of collaborative patterns for business processes and for all four pattern types (synchronized, cooperation, collaboration and coexistence). We demonstrate the applicability of our approach with a proof-of-concept implementation using the workflow management system (WfMS) Bonita and the URSim offline simulator of two or more cobots (see Sect. 4). Furthermore, we evaluate our findings with the implementation of seven use cases. Our proposed approach enables a process-oriented collaboration between humans and robots in modern work environments. It provides a first specification of collaboration types which can be used to secure workflows with cobots. Hence, our findings can support manufacturers who are aiming at building production processes between one or more humans and one or more robots. Furthermore, process modeling and execution engineers can leverage this work to design and monitor collaboration scenarios. Researchers may be able to further increase the interoperability between cobots and WfMS in human-robot collaboration (HRC). For future work, we aim to investigate how to further visualize and model the collaboration patterns in workflows and how to enact and monitor constraints (e.g., function and space).

The rest of the paper is structured as follows: Sect. 2 introduces related work on collaborative robots and human-robot collaboration research. Section 3 specifies the collaborative patterns for workflows with cobots. Furthermore, Sect. 4 outlines the architecture and proof-of-concept implementation. Section 5 summarizes the main results of the successful applicability of seven use cases. Section 6 summarizes discussion points for future work, and Sect. 7 concludes the paper.

2   Background

This section summarizes related work on cobots and collaboration scenarios.

2.1   Collaborative Robots

Cobots are a special type of conventional industrial robots focusing on the interaction with humans. Due to their light weight, small space requirements and easy programming, cobots are relatively easy to deploy. As they can take over repetitive tasks from humans, they can boost productivity and quality [35]. A lot of the potentially partially automatable tasks can only be considered for task automation due to the cobots' ability to work alongside humans. Cobots are also rather flexible. They can be easily re-deployed from one task to another.

Cobot Activities are considered fundamental functionalities and abilities of cobots. By using and chaining them together, tasks resulting from different use cases can be fulfilled. A few of these example activities are described below:

- *Positioning* is a basic functionality of robots in general, which they can perform with extremely high precision, speed and repeatability (e.g., [16,34]).
- *Gripping* is an essential mechanism, as it enables the cobot to manipulate things in its surroundings in a controlled way. Robotic manipulators can be equipped with end-effectors, including various types of grippers (e.g., [29]).
- *Motion synchronization* is the ability to synchronize to other motions, which is useful in different kinds of tasks. A requirement could be for example to move in tandem with another cobot or follow the motions of a human [6].
- *Object recognition* is used whenever a task requires dealing with objects in non-standard positions and orientation. This is usually performed by additional camera systems that can be stationary but also attached onto the cobot's arm [35].
- *Hand guiding* is a mode where a cobot can be moved manually by a human. This makes complex and interactive collaboration possible [11].
- *Collision detection/avoidance* is especially important in highly collaborative scenarios. Different methods exist to deal with the uncertainty a human introduces to the workspace, such as safety-rated monitored stop, speed and separation monitoring, power and force limiting [2,11].

Cobots are increasingly utilized with WfMS. For example in [13], a pick and place use case has been implemented that uses a WfMS to implement an assembly workflow. Furthermore, [30] outlines a similar approach using a WfMS to model the workflow of cobots. An adaptive, process-aware production system is described in [39]. We could not find any literature on types of collaboration patterns for workflows with cobots.

2.2   Collaboration Scenarios

In a literature review [11,15,18,19,25,26,37,38], we identified several collaboration scenarios, although the authors used sometimes a different terminology for similar concepts. In the approach of [26], the variants are distinguished by temporal and spatial separation and are called *synchronized, cooperation, collaboration* and *coexistence*. We will further use this classification in our paper. Furthermore, we successfully verified the four patterns with 14 identified use cases from industry and research to ensure a high applicability. Figure 1 shows an approach to describe such collaboration categories.

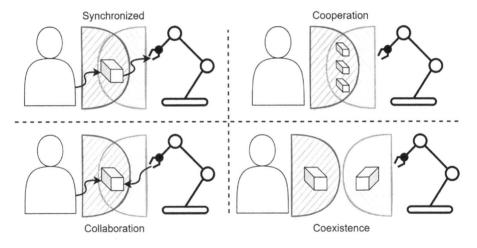

Fig. 1. Types of collaboration between humans and cobots based on [24,26] (own representation).

Synchronized cases have an operator and cobot work in the same workspace, but at different times [24]. Both perform their manufacturing tasks on the same workpiece. As these processes are time-dependent, the output of one working step acts as an input for another work step. Cobot and operator each have different tasks to accomplish, but most of the time, the cobot is set up to take over tedious tasks to improve the working conditions for the worker [11]. Such a use case is shown in [5], where a human inserts screws in holes from one side of a plate and then a cobot tightens bolts onto them from the other side.

Cooperation describes an environment where an operator and a cobot perform separate processes on the same workpiece concurrently [11, 25]. Although they are independent of each other in terms of time and tasks, the cobot still needs to respect the worker's space. To ensure this, the cobot has to be spatially aware of the workers and their task requirements [11]. The ability to act concurrently on one workpiece improves productivity and space utilization [11, 25]. In [25] human and cobot work in cooperation for the configuration of a welding station, which allows the human and cobot to perform some process steps concurrently.

Collaboration builds the highest level of collaborative behavior between a worker and a cobot. As described in [11], both worker and cobot work interactively towards the same process on the same workpiece. Their actions depend on each other. That is, one cannot perform its task without the help of the other. To successfully provide appropriate assistance, the cobot needs to understand the worker's intentions and the task requirements. Examples of this category are the joint movement of a load carried by a cobot and guided by a human [22], and a collaborative assembly task, where human and cobot complement each other while working together on an assembly process [9].

Coexistence is a scenario where both human and robot are working mostly independently of each other, but have a shared environment. This shared environment is often without any fences or guards. Other than that, both actors work independently on separate workpieces and individual manufacturing processes [11] and generally do not interact with each other [24]. To achieve the required safety levels, the cobot's intrinsic safety elements are utilized. Additionally, to further enhance safety, external hardware and software safety elements can be added. With the help of these features, the cobot is aware of the workers and acts accordingly to ensure their safety [11, 25]. Classical examples for coexistence are machine tending tasks, where the cobot picks parts from some sort of feeder configuration and places them into a fixed location in a machine, which enables the human worker to operate on larger batches of parts and handle multiple machines alone [35].

The literature showed that the collaboration patterns are mainly described on an abstract process level and only consider the collaboration between a single operator and cobot. Most HRC related literature also focuses on 1:1 scenarios as well, despite the fact that others mention cases with multiple actors (humans/cobots). Hence, we consider the possibility of multiple human and robotic actors in the following sections. Furthermore, the collaboration patterns are discussed at the abstraction level of tasks within processes rather than processes themselves. So far, literature has not formalized collaboration scenarios for workflows with cobots.

2.3   Process Constraints

Constraints have become a powerful tool to enforce and monitor compliance in business processes (e.g., [17]). Examples can be found for instance for time constraints [8,20] and instance-spanning constraints [12,21] in business processes. Please refer to Sect. 6 for a discussion on future investigations.

3   Collaborative Patterns for Workflows

This section specifies patterns of collaboration scenarios between human and robotic process actors. First, the main elements of collaborative patterns are described and a formal definition for collaboration patterns is proposed. Subsequently, using the proposed definition, formal requirements for each of the patterns *synchronized, cooperation, collaboration and coexistence* are defined.

3.1   Basics

In the following, the basic elements of the definition are described.

A **Collaborative Pattern** (CP) describes a collaborative working environment where humans and cobots may interact. The main elements of a collaborative pattern are a process, actors, a workpiece type, and constraints. This approach of a formal definition focuses on the general architecture of such environments and on the different kinds of constraints between actors and their tasks within a process.

A **Process** consists of tasks and summarizes the (automated) workflow within a collaborative working environment (see [1]). A process comprises multiple tasks, where each of them is executed by one process actor and has a distinct beginning and end. This approach uses Petri nets [1] as a representation of processes. The transition elements of the Petri net are used to denote the tasks of the process. Tasks describe a simple action of an actor (e.g., push a button, move to a position). Each task is performed by exactly one process actor.

An **Actor** is an individual and can either be a human, called operator, or a cobot. In HRC, at least one human actor, as well as one cobot, are part of a collaborative environment.

A **Workpiece type** is a category of workpiece. In our approach, we assume that workpieces are inputs or outputs of the processes or parts of the process (e.g., tasks).

Constraints are used to model dependencies between tasks within a process in a collaborative pattern. Here, tasks of different process actors are principally independent. Hence, their execution order is undefined, and they might also be executed in parallel. This may change as soon as constraints are added. Each task can be constrained by other actors' tasks. These constraints can be of three types (time, space, functional), leading to different behavior in the task flow:

- A **time-based constraint** defines where the output of one task is needed as the input of another task. The resulting effect on two tasks of different actors is that it clearly defines the order in which they are executed.
- A **spatial constraint** arises when the order of multiple actors' tasks is of no importance, hence they are not time-dependent, but the actors need to access the same working area to perform these tasks.

- The **functional constraint** describes the relation between interactive tasks across actors that rely on each other in order to be executed successfully. This type is usually present in highly collaborative environments, where different actors work interactively together to achieve a common goal. Tasks that are connected by this type of constraint have to be executed together. In this sense, they are performed in parallel, with the difference that one cannot be completed without the other. To give a simple example: a gesture task like thumbs up, performed by an operator, needs to have a matching counterpart, for example, a gesture recognition task on the side of a cobot.

With the definition of these basic entities, the collaborative pattern can be specified.

3.2   Definition: Collaborative Pattern

Hence, let the definition of a collaborative pattern *CP* be a *7-tuple (N, A, w, actassign, wpassign, tperformer, constr) where*

- *N is a Petri net* [1] *(P, T, F), depicting a business process, where*
  - *P is a finite set of places*
  - *T is a finite set of transitions, that denotes tasks of a process, such that* $P \cap T = \emptyset$
  - $F \subseteq (P \times T) \cup (T \times P)$ *is a set of directed arcs*
- $A = C \cup O$ *is a finite set of actors, such that* $|A| \geq 1$, *where*
  - *C is a finite set of cobots*
  - *O is a finite set of operators*
  - *such that* $C \cap O = \emptyset$
- *w is a workpiece type*
- *actassign* $\in A \rightarrow \{N\}$ *is a total surjective function, assigning all actors to the process, with*
  - *domain:* $dom(actassign) = A$
  - *range:* $rng(actassign) = \{N\}$
- *wpassign* $\in \{w\} \rightarrow \{N\}$ *is a total surjective function, assigning the workpiece type to the process*
- *tperformer* $\in T \twoheadrightarrow A$ *is a partial surjective function, assigning transitions to actors, with*
  - $dom(tperformer) \subseteq T$
  - $rng(tperformer) = A$
- *constr* $\in T \times T \twoheadrightarrow \{time, space, func\} : (t_a, t_b) \mapsto constr(t_a, t_b)$ *is a partial function denoting the type of constraint between two transitions (tasks), such that*
  - $dom(constr) \subseteq T \times T$
  - $rng(constr) \subseteq \{time, space, func\}$
  - $(t_a, t_b) \in dom(constr) : t_a \neq t_b$ *the constrained tasks are different*
  - $(t_a, t_b) \in dom(constr) : tperformer(t_a) \neq tperformer(t_b)$ *the constrained tasks have different task performers*

- {*time, space, func*} *denote the type of constraint (e.g., timely (time), spatially (space), and functionally (func) constrained).*
  * *timely constrained:* $constr(t_a, t_b) = time \implies t_b$ *is timely constrained by* t_a, *i.e.,* t_b *must be executed after* t_a
  * *spatially constrained:* $constr(t_a, t_b) = space \implies t_a$ *and* t_b *are spatially constrained, i.e., the order of execution is undefined and potentially concurrent, and task interruptions due to space limitations are possible*
  * *functionally constrained:* $constr(t_a, t_b) = func \implies t_a$ *and* t_b *are functionally constrained, i.e.,* t_a *and* t_b *must be executed together to complete the operation*

In the following, four types of the collaborative patterns (see Sect. 2.2) are described using this definition. Each of them starts with a brief description, followed by the formal requirements of the pattern.

3.3   Collaborative Pattern: Synchronized

Synchronized use cases typically share a few key features. Actors perform their tasks in a shared workspace on the same workpiece type. An important characteristic is that these tasks are time-constrained, which implies two things. First, the constrained tasks are executed at different times, and second, one of them requires the output of the corresponding task in order to be executed. Therefore, time constraints are a characterization of the synchronized pattern. A synchronized collaborative pattern CP_{synch} is specified as:

$$CP_{synch} = (N_i, A_i, w_i, actassign_i, wpassign_i, tperformer_i, constr_i) \text{ with}$$

- $|C_i| \geq 1 \ \land \ |O_i| \geq 1$ there is at least one cobot and at least one operator
- $\forall constr_{i_m} \in constr_i : constr_{i_m}(t_{i_j}, t_{i_k}) = time$ all constraints between transitions are time constraints

3.4   Collaborative Pattern: Cooperation

Cooperative scenarios are, in a certain way, similar to synchronized ones, as the actors perform their work on the same type of workpiece. The key difference is, that these steps are not timely but spatially constrained. That is, the order in which they are performed does not matter. These use cases aim to execute tasks concurrently, thus, increasing efficiency and productivity. The fact that actors may need to operate in each other's workspace simultaneously demands for additional requirements, especially regarding safety aspects. As a result, the cobots need to have mechanisms to be aware of other actors and protect them. This is especially important when human actors are involved. Furthermore, there is also usually less interaction between actors than in synchronized cases, if any at all. A cooperative collaborative pattern CP_{coop} is defined as:

$$CP_{coop} = (N_i, A_i, w_i, actassign_i, wpassign_i, tperformer_i, constr_i) \text{ with}$$

- $|C_i| \geq 1 \ \land \ |O_i| \geq 1$ there is at least one cobot and at least one operator
- $\forall constr_{i_m} \in constr_i : constr_{i_m}(t_{i_j}, t_{i_k}) = space$ all constraints between transitions are space constraints

3.5   Collaborative Pattern: Collaboration

Collaborative cases are designed with interactive behavior in mind. The actors are working together to achieve a common goal. Parts of their actions are functionally dependent on some tasks of other actors. That is, those tasks rely on each other to be executed successfully. This type of scenario represents the most comprehensive type of collaboration. In theory, the cobot should act instinctively, based on the behavior of human actors, e.g., repositioning of the axes to make it easier for the operator to access certain locations when approaching them, or monitoring the environment to anticipate and avoid collisions, and re-plan trajectories [7,14]. A collaborative pattern CP_{coll} is specified as:

$$CP_{coll} = (N_i, A_i, w_i, actassign_i, wpassign_i, tperformer_i, constr_i) \text{ with}$$

- $|C_i| \geq 1 \ \wedge \ |O_i| \geq 1$ there is at least one cobot and at least one operator
- $\forall constr_{i_m} \in constr_i : constr_{i_m}(t_{i_j}, t_{i_k}) = func$ all constraints between transitions are functional constraints

3.6   Collaborative Pattern: Coexistence

The coexistence collaborative pattern specifies individual actors that work independently of each other. This signifies that they are working on different types of workpieces and execute independent processes that are performed on those workpiece types. A coexistent collaborative pattern CP_{coex} is defined as:

$$CP_{coex} = \{CP_1, \ldots, CP_n\} = \{(N_1, A_1, w_1, actassign_1, wpassign_1, \\ tperformer_1, constr_1), \ldots, (N_n, A_n, w_n, actassign_n, wpassign_n, tperformer_n, \\ constr_n)\} \text{ with}$$

- $\forall CP_j, CP_k \in CP_{coex} : CP_j \neq CP_k \implies CP_j \cap CP_k = \emptyset$ all CP_j, CP_k in CP_{coex} are pairwise disjoint
- $\forall CP_i \in CP_{coex} : |A_i| = 1$ there is exactly one actor in every CP_i in CP_{coex}
- $\left| \bigcup_{i=1}^{n} C_i \right| \geq 1$ there is at least one cobot in all C_i in CP_{coex}
- $\left| \bigcup_{i=1}^{n} O_i \right| \geq 1$ there is at least one operator in all O_i in CP_{coex}
- $\forall CP_i \in CP_{coex} : constr_i = \emptyset$ there are no constraints in every CP_i in CP_{coex}

4   Implementation

This section summarizes the architecture and the proof-of-concept implementation of the collaborative patterns.

4.1   Architecture

Figure 2 outlines the selected architecture. There are three major components: a Workflow Management System (WfMS), a cobot simulation and an Open Platform Communications Unified Architecture (OPC UA) server and client. The figure shows that at least two instances of virtual machines (VM) must be deployed. One of them contains the WfMS and the OPC UA client implementation. The other one consists of the simulation of the cobot and also the OPC UA server implementation. In case more cobots are needed for a use case, the second VM can be cloned. With just minor adjustments, the additional cobot simulation is ready to be used.

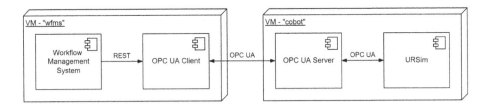

Fig. 2. Architecture.

4.2   Proof-of-Concept

For this implementation, we selected the following components as they were freely accessible with an academic license.

- Bonita is an open source WfMS and is used for business process automation and optimization [3].
- We used the simulation tool URSim from Universal Robots [36] for the cobot simulation. URSim offers a 3D simulation of the cobot and supports OPC UA for external communication.
- The communication between WfMS and Cobot simulation is done via OPC UA. It is a platform independent interoperability standard for data exchange in industrial automation and other industries [27]. The OPC UA client from a library called *opcua-smart*[1] is instantiated in a middleware.

Figure 3 shows a screenshot of the proof-of-concept implementation executing the use case "spot taping" (see Sect. 5.1).

5   Use Case Evaluation

For evaluation, we instantiated and implemented seven exemplary use cases based on the four collaboration pattern types synchronized, cooperation, collaboration and coexistence. For each, we provided a specification and an implementation using the setup described in Sect. 4. Due to space limitations, this

---

[1] https://github.com/etm/opcua-smart (visited on June 8, 2022).

Fig. 3. Implementation of use case "spot taping". User tasks can be performed in the Bonita User Application on the left. The two cobots on the right (left cobot - top, right cobot - bottom) are waiting for a handshake initiated by Bonita.

section gives only a brief overview of one use case called "spot taping". In total, seven use cases[2] were successfully implemented: (1) spot taping (synchronized), (2) extended spot taping (synchronized), (3) quality inspection (cooperation), (4) polishing (cooperation), (5) fixture (collaboration), (6) collaborative assembly (collaboration) and (7) pick & place (coexistence).

5.1   Use Case: Spot Taping

Collaborative Work Environment. The spot taping process modeled in this section is a simplified variation of a use case described in [28]. The goal is to improve the current process for spot taping wire harnesses, which was performed manually, by adding robotic arms that collaborate with the human worker. As shown in Fig. 4, a custom work cell was developed in [28]. The human worker sits in front of a desk, where two working areas are mounted on a linear axis. The linear axis has two defined positions. One where the left working area is in front of the worker, and one where the other area is in front of the worker. The operator has two foot pedals that can be operated to send a signal indicating that the linear axis can be moved to the left or to the right.

On both sides of the worker, a cobot is placed (see Fig. 4). These cobots perform the spot taping of the wire harnesses. In each production cycle, two wire harnesses are processed. One on each of the two working areas. When the linear axis is positioned on the left side, the left cobot has access to its working

---

[2] See a full set of use cases including the full BPMN diagram of the use case spot taping at https://tinyurl.com/yskk989s.

area, while the worker prepares things on the right working area. Once both are finished, the axis can move to the right, and the worker performs tasks on the left working area, while the right cobot has access to the right working area. A more detailed description of the sequence is shown in the diagram in Fig. 5.

Fig. 4. Design of the spot taping work space described in [28] (own representation and created in Microsoft Paint3D).

Modeling and Enactment. Figure 6 shows the beginning of the process model of the spot taping use case. The full version can be downloaded via the aforementioned report. The first sub process *Preparation and Startup* in the figure summarizes the mandatory starting procedure of the work environment (e.g., *Check process settings, Load Program, Start both cobots* or *Power on*).

After the start-up, Fig. 6 shows the first steps of a production cycle in the spot taping process. The process model outlines the same course of action as defined in Fig. 5. At first, the operator has to perform two tasks: (1) the preparation of the left workspace for the first spot taping (see *"put first part of wires in place [...]"*) and (2) operating the left foot pedal. Subsequently, the linear axis moves to the left. Now the operator and the left cobot can work on their tasks simultaneously (parallel gateway *"P4 open"* opens two paths). The operator repeats his two previous tasks, with the difference that this time the tasks are performed for the right workspace and the right foot pedal must be pushed. In the meantime, the left cobot performs the first spot taping on the left workspace. As soon as both actors finished their respective tasks, the two paths are joined by the closing parallel gateway *"P4 close"*, and the linear axis can move back to the right. We can see in Fig. 6 that we have solved the time-based constraints in this use case with the control flow of the workflow. We will further elaborate this approach in Sect. 6. The proof-of-concept implementation of the use case is shown in Fig. 3.

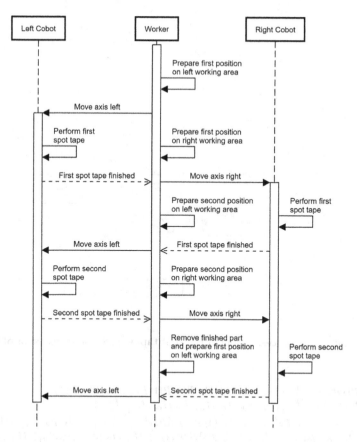

Fig. 5. Sequence diagram of the spot taping process described in [28] (own representation).

Specification. In this section, we specify a simplified version of the spot taping use case based on the synchronized collaboration pattern defined in Sect. 3.3. In general, two work steps have to be performed on each workpiece. These steps $(t_{c_{1_1}}, t_{c_{1_2}}, t_{c_{2_1}}, t_{c_{2_2}})$ are done by the two cobots (see Fig. 4). Prior to performing those work steps, the workpieces have to be prepared. This is done manually by the operator $(t_{o_1}, t_{o_2}, t_{o_3}, t_{o_4})$. Once the parts are finished, the operator removes them (t_{o_5}, t_{o_6}).

The tasks have to be performed in a specific order, i.e., they are time-constrained. Operator o starts with t_{o_1}. After that, cobot c_1 can perform $t_{c_{1_1}}$. This relation is modeled with a time constraint $((t_{o_1}, t_{c_{1_1}}), time)$. In the meantime, t_{o_2} can be performed, and after that $t_{c_{2_1}}$. Once $t_{c_{1_1}}$ is finished, the operator can start with t_{o_3}. This is systematically repeated towards the end of the process, and is reflected in the function *constr* of the formalization below.

Let the synchronized collaborative pattern be defined by
$$CP_{spot} = (N, A, w, actassign, wpassign, tperformer, constr) \text{ with}$$

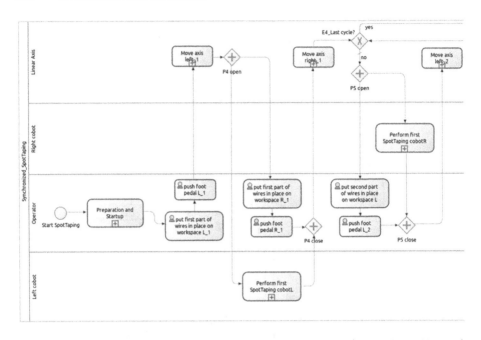

Fig. 6. Section of the process model of the spot taping use case (screenshot of Bonita).

- $P = \{p_1, p_2, p_3, p_4, p_5, p_6, p_7, p_8, p_9, p_{10}, p_{11}, p_{12}, p_{13}, p_{14}, p_{15}\}$
- $T = \{t_1, t_2, t_{c_{1_1}}, t_{c_{1_2}}, t_{o_1}, t_{o_2}, t_{o_3}, t_{o_4}, t_{o_5}, t_{o_6}, t_{c_{2_1}}, t_{c_{2_2}}\}$
- $F = \{(p_1, t_1), (t_1, p_2), (t_1, p_5), (t_1, p_{12}), (p_2, t_{c_{1_1}}), (t_{c_{1_1}}, p_3), (p_3, t_{c_{1_2}}), (t_{c_{1_2}}, p_4),$
  $(p_5, t_{o_1}), (t_{o_1}, p_6), (p_6, t_{o_2}), (t_{o_2}, p_7), (p_7, t_{o_3}), (t_{o_3}, p_8), \quad (p_8, t_{o_4}), (t_{o_4}, p_9), (p_9,$
  $t_{o_5}), \quad (t_{o_5}, p_{10}), (p_{10}, t_{o_6}), \quad (t_{o_6}, p_{11}), (p_{12}, t_{c_{2_1}}), \quad (t_{c_{2_1}}, p_{13}), (p_{13}, t_{c_{2_2}}), \quad (t_{c_{2_2}},$
  $p_{14}), (p_4, t_2), (p_{11}, t_2), (p_{14}, t_2), (t_2, p_{15})\}$
- $C = \{c_1, c_2\}, \quad O = \{o\}$
- $actassign = \{(c_1, N), (o, N), (c_2, N)\}, \quad wpassign = \{(w, N)\}$
- $tperformer \quad = \quad \{(t_{c_{1_1}}, c_1), (t_{c_{1_2}}, c_1), (t_{o_1}, o), (t_{o_2}, o), (t_{o_3}, o), (t_{o_4}, o), (t_{o_5}, o),$
  $(t_{o_6}, o), (t_{c_{2_1}}, c_2), (t_{c_{2_2}}, c_2)\}$
- $constr = \{((t_{o_1}, t_{c_{1_1}}), time), ((t_{c_{1_1}}, t_{o_3}), time), ((t_{o_3}, t_{c_{1_2}}), time), ((t_{c_{1_2}}, t_{o_5}),$
  $time), \quad ((t_{o_2}, t_{c_{2_1}}), time), \quad ((t_{c_{2_1}}, t_{o_4}), time), \quad ((t_{o_4}, t_{c_{2_2}}), time), \quad ((t_{c_{2_2}}, t_{o_6}),$
  $time)\}$

Figure 7 visualizes the Petri net for the use case spot taping. The constraints, highlighted in green, are <u>only</u> outlined for visualization purposes.

In summary, we specified the synchronized collaborative pattern and implemented the pattern using a proof-of-concept implementation for the use case spot taping. With the evaluation of seven use cases, we demonstrated its applicability in collaborative process-oriented work environments.

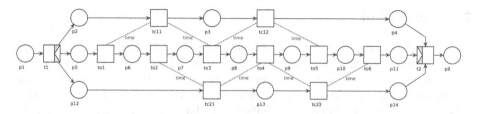

Fig. 7. Petri net N of the Spot taping use case. The time constraints of the pattern are highlighted with green dashed lines only for visualization purposes.

6   Discussion

During our work, we came across several discussion points that we would like to discuss and investigate for future work. First of all, we presented four patterns that are derived based on literature (see Sect. 2.2). We do not assume that this is an exhaustive list, and future research might extend or adapt the collaborative patterns. Furthermore, robot-to-robot collaboration scenarios were out of the scope of this paper as we focused only on HRC. However, all patterns are designed to integrate multiple robots.

As mentioned before, process constraints are a powerful tool and there are many examples how to enable the constraints for collaborative environments. For this paper, the investigation of current approaches (e.g., [20,32]) and how they can enact the presented collaborative patterns not investigated due to space limitations and will be part of future work.

At first sight, the time-based constraints seem to be very close to the control flow specification of workflows. This is only true if the relevant tasks are very close in the process (e.g., task A directly follows task B). However, in case of larger production processes where the tasks might not follow directly and might even be on different process branches, a more general approach is needed. Therefore, we decided to define the time-based constraint as a more general approach.

Furthermore, the authors could not fully validate the space constraint. A collaborative work environment requires a setup and design that is following the constraints and safety policies. However, in the proof-of-concept implementation, we could only simulate the constraints (e.g., using the coordinates). Hence, we aim to investigate more questions related to how to measure and enforce space constraints in workflows.

In our use case evaluation, we aimed also to extend and increase the actors in order to identify potential challenges. For example, we extended the use case spot taping with an additional human actor, which resulted in a total number of two humans and two robots. We identified several challenges that concern the complexity of process modeling. For example, the challenges of space and overlapping elements in large process models. For future work, we aim to investigate how these process modeling and visualization challenges can be mitigated for collaborative work environments.

7 Conclusion

The aim of this paper was to investigate collaboration patterns in workflows for collaborative robots in modern production environments. The review showed four collaboration scenarios (i.e. synchronized, cooperation, collaboration and coexistence) that can be identified during the interaction between humans and robots. These four scenarios were defined as collaborative patterns. This definition also takes the possibility of multiple process actors and business processes and tasks into account. Each of the four pattern types has been specified. Furthermore, we implemented a proof-of-concept with the cobot simulation URSim and the WfMS Bonita and demonstrated the applicability of our approach and the four identified collaborative patterns. We successfully evaluated our findings with seven use cases applying various collaborative pattern types. We contribute to the understanding of collaborative workflows with cobots and provide a first specification and implementation of four collaboration scenarios.

For future work, we aim to further investigate process modeling and visualization of collaborative patterns. During the exploration of different visualization approaches, it became apparent, that once a certain level of detail should be depicted, i.e., process instance level including multiple actors, a number of potential problems regarding the design of modeling notations arise. Therefore, developing a visualization of the proposed formal definition would be a highly interesting topic for future research.

References

1. van der Aalst, W.: Process Mining: Discovery, Conformance and Enhancement of Business Processes. Springer, Germany (2011). https://doi.org/10.1007/978-3-642-19345-3
2. Bi, Z., Luo, C., Miao, Z., Zhang, B., Zhang, W., Wang, L.: Safety assurance mechanisms of collaborative robotic systems in manufacturing. Robot. Comput. Integr. Manuf. **67**, 102022 (2021)
3. Bonitasoft, S.A.: Bonita Documentation. https://documentation.bonitasoft.com/bonita/2021.2/. Accessed 10 Feb 2021
4. Buerkle, A., Eaton, W., Lohse, N., Bamber, T., Ferreira, P.: EEG based arm movement intention recognition towards enhanced safety in symbiotic human-robot collaboration. Robot. Comput. Integr. Manuf. **70**, 102137 (2021)
5. Cherubini, A., Passama, R., Fraisse, P., Crosnier, A.: A unified multimodal control framework for human-robot interaction. Robot. Auton. Syst. **70**, 106–115 (2015)
6. Chua, Y., Tee, K.P., Yan, R.: Human-robot motion synchronization using reactive and predictive controllers. In: 2010 IEEE International Conference on Robotics and Biomimetics, pp. 223–228 (12 2010)
7. Dumonteil, G., Manfredi, G., Devy, M., Confetti, A., Sidobre, D.: Reactive planning on a collaborative robot for industrial applications. In: 2015 12th International Conference on Informatics in Control, Automation and Robotics (ICINCO), vol. 02, pp. 450–457 (2015)
8. Eder, J., Panagos, E., Rabinovich, M.: Time constraints in workflow systems. In: Jarke, M., Oberweis, A. (eds.) CAiSE 1999. LNCS, vol. 1626, pp. 286–300. Springer, Heidelberg (1999). https://doi.org/10.1007/3-540-48738-7_22

9. El Makrini, I., Merckaert, K., Lefeber, D., Vanderborght, B.: Design of a collaborative architecture for human-robot assembly tasks. In: 2017 IEEE/RSJ International
Conference on Intelligent Robots and Systems (IROS), pp. 1624–1629 (2017)
10. El Makrini, I., et al.: Design and investigation of social robotic coworkers in facto-
ries, pp. 1–2. IEEE (2017)
11. El Zaatari, S., Marei, M., Li, W., Usman, Z.: Cobot programming for collaborative
industrial tasks: an overview. Robot. Auton. Syst. **116**, 162–180 (2019)
12. Fdhila, W., Gall, M., Rinderle-Ma, S., Mangler, J., Indiono, C.: Classification and
formalization of instance-spanning constraints in process-driven applications. In:
La Rosa, M., Loos, P., Pastor, O. (eds.) BPM 2016. LNCS, vol. 9850, pp. 348–364.
Springer, Cham (2016). https://doi.org/10.1007/978-3-319-45348-4_20
13. Froschauer, R., Lindorfer, R.: Workflow-based programming of human-robot interaction for collaborative assembly stations. In: Proceedings of ARW & OAGM
Workshop 2019, pp. 85–90 (2019)
14. Hermann, A., Mauch, F., Fischnaller, K., Klemm, S., Roennau, A., Dillmann,
R.: Anticipate your surroundings: predictive collision detection between dynamic
obstacles and planned robot trajectories on the GPU. In: 2015 European Conference on Mobile Robots (ECMR), pp. 1–8 (2015)
15. International Federation of Robotics: Demystifying collaborative industrial robots.
Frankfurt, Germany (2018). https://ifr.org/papers/demystifying-collaborative-
industrial-robots-updated-version. Accessed 12 June 2022
16. Jiang, Y., Yu, L., Jia, H., Zhao, H., Xia, H.: Absolute positioning accuracy improvement in an industrial robot. Sensors **20**(16), 4354 (2020)
17. Knuplesch, D., Reichert, M., Pryss, R., Fdhila, W., Rinderle-Ma, S.: Ensuring
compliance of distributed and collaborative workflows. In: 9th IEEE International
Conference on Collaborative Computing, pp. 133–142 (2013)
18. Kopp, T., Baumgartner, M., Kinkel, S.: Success factors for introducing industrial human-robot interaction in practice: an empirically driven framework. Int.
J. Adv. Manuf. Technol. **112**(3), 685–704 (2020). https://doi.org/10.1007/s00170-
020-06398-0
19. Krüger, J., Lien, T., Verl, A.: Cooperation of human and machines in assembly
lines. CIRP Ann. **58**(2), 628–646 (2009)
20. Kumar, A., Sabbella, S.R., Barton, R.R.: Managing controlled violation of temporal process constraints. In: Motahari-Nezhad, H.R., Recker, J., Weidlich, M. (eds.)
BPM 2015. LNCS, vol. 9253, pp. 280–296. Springer, Cham (2015). https://doi.
org/10.1007/978-3-319-23063-4_20
21. Leitner, M., Mangler, J., Rinderle-Ma, S.: Definition and enactment of instance-
spanning process constraints. In: Wang, X.S., Cruz, I., Delis, A., Huang, G. (eds.)
WISE 2012. LNCS, vol. 7651, pp. 652–658. Springer, Heidelberg (2012). https://
doi.org/10.1007/978-3-642-35063-4_49
22. Lichiardopol, S., van de Wouw, N., Nijmeijer, H.: Control scheme for human-robot
co-manipulation of uncertain, time-varying loads. In: 2009 American Control Conference, pp. 1485–1490 (2009). https://doi.org/10.1109/ACC.2009.5160062
23. Malik, A.A., Brem, A.: Digital twins for collaborative robots: a case study in
human-robot interaction. Robot. Comput. Integr. Manuf. **68**, 102092 (2021).
https://doi.org/10.1016/j.rcim.2020.102092
24. Matheson, E., Minto, R., Zampieri, E.G.G., Faccio, M., Rosati, G.: Human-robot
collaboration in manufacturing applications: a review. Robotics **8**(4), 100 (2019).
https://doi.org/10.3390/robotics8040100

25. Müller, R., Vette, M., Geenen, A.: Skill-based dynamic task allocation in human-robot-cooperation with the example of welding application. Procedia Manuf. **11**, 13–21 (2017). https://doi.org/10.1016/j.promfg.2017.07.113. 27th International Conference on Flexible Automation and Intelligent Manufacturing, FAIM2017, 27–30 June 2017, Modena, Italy

26. Müller, R., Vette, M., Mailahn, O.: Process-oriented task assignment for assembly processes with human-robot interaction. Procedia CIRP **44**, 210–215 (2016). https://doi.org/10.1016/j.procir.2016.02.080. 6th CIRP Conference on Assembly Technologies and Systems (CATS)

27. OPC Foundation: What is OPC?. https://opcfoundation.org/about/what-is-opc/. Accessed 23 Nov 2021

28. Román Ibáñez, V., Pujol, F., García Ortega, S., Sanz Perpiñán, J.: Collaborative robotics in wire harnesses spot taping process. Comput. Ind. **125**, 103370 (2021). https://doi.org/10.1016/j.compind.2020.103370

29. Samadikhoshkho, Z., Zareinia, K., Janabi-Sharifi, F.: A brief review on robotic grippers classifications. In: 2019 IEEE Canadian Conference of Electrical and Computer Engineering (CCECE), pp. 1–4 (2019). https://doi.org/10.1109/CCECE.2019.8861780

30. Schmidbauer, C., Hader, B., Schlund, S.: Evaluation of a digital worker assistance system to enable adaptive task sharing between humans and Cobots in manufacturing. Procedia CIRP **104**, 38–43 (2021)

31. Schneider, G., Wendl, M., Kucek, S., Leitner, M.: A training concept based on a digital twin for a wafer transportation system. In: 2021 IEEE 23rd Conference on Business Informatics (CBI), vol. 02, pp. 20–28 (2021)

32. Steinau, S., Andrews, K., Reichert, M.: Modeling process interactions with coordination processes. In: Panetto, H., Debruyne, C., Proper, H.A., Ardagna, C.A., Roman, D., Meersman, R. (eds.) OTM 2018. LNCS, vol. 11229, pp. 21–39. Springer, Cham (2018). https://doi.org/10.1007/978-3-030-02610-3_2

33. The Robot Report Staff: Scoliobot aims to improve spinal surgery accuracy. https://www.therobotreport.com/scoliobot-spinal-surgery-accuracy/. Accessed 13 Apr 2021

34. Tlach, V., Cisar, M., Kuric, I., Zajacko, I.: Determination of the industrial robot positioning performance. In: MATEC Web of Conferences, vol. 137 (2017)

35. Universal Robots A/S: An introduction to common collaborative robot applications. https://info.universal-robots.com/hubfs/Enablers/White%20papers/Common%20Cobot%20%20Applications.pdf. Accessed 15 Nov 2021

36. Universal Robots A/S: Offline simulator - e-series - ur sim for linux 5.11.5. https://www.universal-robots.com/download/software-e-series/simulator-linux/offline-simulator-e-series-ur-sim-for-linux-5115/. Accessed 16 Nov 2021

37. Wang, L., et al.: Symbiotic human-robot collaborative assembly. CIRP Ann. **68**(2), 701–726 (2019)

38. Wang, X.V., Kemény, Z., Váncza, J., Wang, L.: Human-robot collaborative assembly in cyber-physical production: classification framework and implementation. CIRP Ann. **66**(1), 5–8 (2017)

39. Weichhart, G., et al.: An adaptive system-of-systems approach for resilient manufacturing. e & i Elektrotechnik und Informationstechnik **138**(6), 341–348 (2021)

PK-Graph: Partitioned k^2-Trees
to Enable Compact and Dynamic Graphs
in Spark GraphX

Bruno Morais, Miguel E. Coimbra$^{(\boxtimes)}$ (iD), and Luís Veiga (iD)

INESC-ID/IST, Universidade de Lisboa, R. Alves Redol 9, Lisbon, Portugal
{bruno.c.morais,miguel.e.coimbra}@tecnico.ulisboa.pt,
luis.veiga@inesc-id.pt
https://www.inesc-id.pt/research-areas/distributed-parallel-and-secure-systems/

Abstract. Graphs are becoming increasingly larger, with datasets having millions of vertices and billions (or even trillions) of edges. As a result, the ability to fit the entire graph into the main memory of a single machine faces challenges in common hardware, even more so in edge/IoT-like devices (i.e., more energy efficient but also more resource constrained). Reading the graph from secondary storage may pose in itself significant overhead, negatively impacting query performance and storage requirements. It thus becomes relevant to explore techniques to optimize the storage of graphs, specially in memory, in a way that circumvents space limitations, while avoiding compromising the performance of processing.

We observe that current graph storage systems manage the graph representation by storing graphs in an uncompressed format, either: i) in a shared architecture which leads to a higher space overhead and the inability to represent the graph entirely in main memory, or ii) in a distributed architecture, where the graph dataset is partitioned over a cluster of machines with each one storing in main memory only a fragment (shard) of the (uncompressed) graph. We present PK-Graph, our proposal which extends a distributed graph processing system, highly used in academia and industry (`Spark GraphX`), in order to deploy the use of a compressed graph representation, with added support for dynamic updatable graphs (not currently supported in `GraphX`). Our experimental results show that PK-Graph can achieve up to 50% lower graph memory usage, while maintaining competitive performance in executing typical graph operations used in common applications.

Keywords: Graph representation · Graph databases · Graph processing systems · Optimization · Compression

1 Introduction

Graphs are now more relevant than ever and their importance will continue to expand [38], as well continuing to grow in size, having millions of vertices and billions (or even trillions) of edges in some cases [9,15], stimulating the need for

© The Author(s), under exclusive license to Springer Nature Switzerland AG 2022
M. Sellami et al. (Eds.): CoopIS 2022, LNCS 13591, pp. 149–167, 2022.
https://doi.org/10.1007/978-3-031-17834-4_9

novel and more efficient storage and representation solutions due to increasing space requirements. Fitting an entire graph in the main memory of a single multiprocessor machine becomes challenging if the graph is very large. This may lead to a significant overhead by having to read the graph from secondary storage. Thus, it is relevant to try to minimize the storage requirements of the graph, for efficiency and viability, without degrading access time and ideally even improving it. Current solutions store graphs in uncompressed format [16, 18, 19, 22, 24, 39, 42, 44]. By using a lossless graph compression technique, it is possible to store the graph in a compressed format that can reside in the main memory of a single resource-rich machine [6, 28, 43], achieving equal or better performance when accessing the graph, thus motivating the employment of compression techniques in graph storage.

A relevant use-case when working with graph-based data is the ability to modify it as a dynamic graph, where it is possible to add or remove vertices and edges. For this use-case, using basic compression techniques would require converting the graph to an uncompressed format before modifying it, which would imply limitations in required storage and obtained speed. Popular graph algorithms, such as *PageRank* [31], mutate attributes stored in the vertices and edges of graphs as part of their logic. As a consequence, the ability to use compressed graph representations which support graph-changing operations without having to decompress becomes very important.

Existing solutions focus on partitioning graphs based on their edges to achieve better work distribution among computing nodes [24, 44]. This leads to edges being assigned to unique partitions and vertices, while being replicated throughout various partitions. In a worst-case scenario, a vertex needs to be replicated throughout all partitions. This approach is used because the number of edges is typically much higher than the number of vertices, leading to smaller storage requirements when replicating vertices. We focus on addressing several shortcomings that current solutions present, such as: *i)* not being able to store large graphs completely in main memory, requiring access to secondary storage which is much slower; *ii)* storing graphs in an uncompressed format, potentially leading to higher resource consumption and comparatively worse processing performance than compressed representations; *iii)* immutable graphs that do not support removing or adding vertices/edges, requiring the entire graph to be reconstructed when adding new elements.

Herein we present our design, implementation and evaluation of PK-GRAPH, an extension to the storage component of the **Spark GraphX** distributed graph processing system, incorporating the k^2-tree lossless compressed graph representation to improve space-efficiency. Our solution was designed with the goal of achieving performance within the same order of magnitude of the uncompressed version of the system and with the goal of supporting dynamic graphs, with mutation of attributes and addition/removal of graph elements. This paper is structured as follows. Section 2 addresses relevant state-of-the-art in graph processing systems, graph databases, and optimized graph representations. In Sect. 3 we present the architecture of PK-GRAPH. Section 4 describes the evaluation methodology and the results obtained for our implementation. Section 5 concludes by summarizing our findings and mentioning future vectors of research.

2   Related Work

Distributed Graph Processing Systems. They focus on scalable iteration of potentially large input graphs in order to execute algorithms over them. Their approach consists in partitioning the graph throughout a cluster of processors, where each processor stores only a fraction of the total graph in main memory. They maintain serialized graph formats in secondary storage, at penalty, and only if the graph is too large. These systems do not typically require fine-grained access to the vertices and/or edges of the graph and instead iterate all elements of the graph or a subset of them.

Apache Spark [20] and Apache Flink [45] are known examples of generic distributed processing systems, based on dataflow programming. Although they are generic, graph-specific libraries have been built over them, such as GraphX [44] on Spark and Gelly on Flink. There are also systems designed with an *ab initio* architectural focus on graph processing such as Apache Giraph [42], implementing a vertex-centric approach known as *think-like-a-vertex* (TLAV), where a user-defined function is applied in the context of each vertex. This model first debuted in Google Pregel [26]. Other approaches exist regarding the unit of computation when expressing graph-processing logic. The computational unit may also be the edge, in which case the system is said to be edge-centric, known as *think-like-an-edge* (TLEV). This approach was popularized with the X-Stream [37] and Chaos [36] graph processing systems (they are no longer maintained or developed). Other approaches exist, such as defining the unit of computation as a part of the graph, but they are outside this scope.

In terms of dynamism, systems such as Spark and Flink typically only allow for applying changes to the graph (updating attributes or adding/removing vertices/edges), by transforming an existing graph into a new one [3]. This a functional programming aspect of the dataflow-based computation of these systems, and even if the systems provide primitives to reuse or cache data between dataflow jobs to keep changing and using a graph, that does not necessarily lead to an improvement in these sequences of graph changes [10]. In the literature there are other efficient graph processing systems such as GraphBolt [27], PowerLyra [8] and GraphTau [17], among others. While presenting innovative distributed graph processing techniques, as far as we know they typically do not have an active development community or were tailor-made for specific experiments.

Graph Databases. Graph database systems are akin to typical relational databases, but have specialized formats to efficiently store graphs. These systems also focus on fine-grained access to the vertices and edges of a graph, allowing for complex queries to be made while not necessarily needing to traverse the entire graph for each query. As such, the storage of the graph is made to be very space efficient but also to allow for very low latency when performing queries. Throughout these databases we find graph storage location approaches such as: storing in the file system, potentially a distributed one like HDFS [41] or S3 [32]; in key-value stores, where the vertices and edges are stored by mapping their identifier to their attributes, or in NoSQL databases adapted to store graph data.

The database can also be distributed, with the graph stored across multiple machines, or centralized, with the entire graph stored in a single machine. In some cases, where specialized hardware is available, centralized systems may have similar or even better performance than distributed ones (such as `Ringo` [33] and `Mosaic` [25]). An example of a relevant graph database is `Neo4j` [16], a *native* graph database platform used to store, query, analyze and manage highly connected data expressed in the property graph model. It provides its own query language `Cypher` [14], with data stored on disk as linked lists of fixed-size records. Properties are stored as a linked list of property records, each holding a key and value and pointing to the next property.

Compact Graph Representations. Compressed graph representations are employed to reduce the computational space complexity of graphs, lowering their storage requirements and enabling their processing with hardware that is less powerful. In the context of this work, we focus on computational representations that are directly compatible with or enabling components of the property graph model [2], which allows for attributes to be held in the elements of the graph. Depending on the relationship between the representation design and its implementation, it is possible to store element attributes in a compressed form together with the rest of the graph structure. There are factors that influence the design of a representation. Whether the graph is directed or undirected has an influence on the representation. If the graph is directed, then twice the number of edges (of an equivalent undirected graph) would be necessary, as each undirected edge may be represented with two edges with opposing directions (between the same two vertices). For example, another factor influencing the representation is tied to the potential need of representing more than one edge between the same two vertices (multi-graph) or not (simple graph). In the context of dynamism, if compressed graph representations allow mutating graphs, they are also known as compact representations.

Some of the most well-known compressed representations are the `WebGraph` [5] framework and the k^2-tree [6]). The `WebGraph` [5] framework uses mathematical analysis and information theory [30] to represent the graph (in a lossless way) with lower complexity (using traits such as vertex ordering [4]). `WebGraph` enabled the exploration of many graph datasets, enabling researchers to analyze them and obtain statistics using files with smaller sizes. It is implemented in `Java` and does not support mutating the graph, which limits the scope of its applicability.

Some more recent work in compressed graph representations includes `g-Sum` [34], a graph summarization approach for large social networks that minimizes the *Reconstruction Error (RE)* of the representation, allowing for a more accurate summarization and improving its usefulness. Another recent work [21] presents `MoSSo`, an algorithm for incremental lossless graph summarization. This work provides a novel approach in the efficient and lossless summarization of fully dynamic graphs. However, this representation is not suitable for distributed processing systems like `Spark GraphX` since the graph would need to be partitioned throughout various executors. Furthermore, the summarization is not intended to allow for the iteration of all edges/vertices of the graph, instead it focuses on specifically handling the processing of individual changes to the underlying graph.

Hornet [7] is a data structure for efficient computation of dynamic sparse graphs and matrices using GPUs. It is platform-independent and implements its own memory allocation operation instead of standard function calls. The implementation uses an internal data manager which makes use of block arrays to store adjacency lists, a bit tree for finding and reclaiming empty memory blocks and B^+ trees to manage them. It was evaluated using an NVIDIA Tesla GPU and experiments targeted the update rates it supports, algorithms such as breadth-first search (BFS) and sparse matrix-vector multiplication. While a relevant mark in the literature, it is GPU-focused.

Another recent example is the k^2-tree [6], an optimized compressed graph representation that takes advantage of sparse adjacency matrices by recursively decomposing them. Figure 1 shows one such tree. The tree represents the structure of the graph's adjacency matrix, where each node in the tree is represented by a single bit: 1 for internal nodes and 0 for leaf nodes, except in the last level where all nodes are leaves and represent the bit values in the adjacency matrix. Different implementations (C/C++) of the k^2-tree exist, and although the original one did not support graph mutability, more recent implementations allow the graph to be mutated, either by directly using dynamic bit vectors (which suffers a performance bottleneck on compressed dynamic indexing [29,30]), or more recently, by using techniques to provide dynamic behavior on underlying static collections [11], achieving competitive performance compared to other implementations [12].

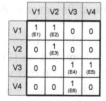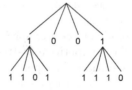

Fig. 1. Adjacency matrix and corresponding k^2-tree.

3   PK-GRAPH: Architecture

While many graph processing systems are available, many were released solely to assess and validate specific scientific ideas. From our analysis of graph processing systems, we find value in attributes such as the pace of development of the systems as well as active communities with which it is possible to engage to discuss ideas or troubleshoot development challenges that are found. While Flink and Spark are prime candidates with these attributes, Spark was chosen to implement our contribution, as its design implementation already has some concern for some form of data reuse (such as its cache() operator).

In Spark, data storage is handled by its Resilient Distributed Dataset (RDD) construct. It represents an immutable collection of elements which may

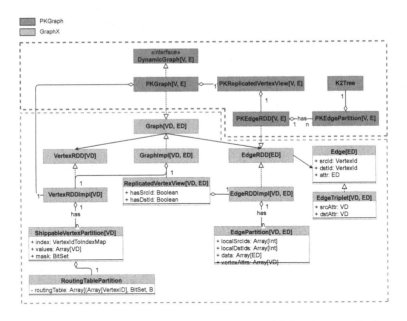

Fig. 2. Overview of PK-GRAPH architecture. (Color figure online)

undergo transformations (e.g. `map()`, `filter()`) defined in the functional programming paradigm, and they can be processed in distributed fashion by splitting elements into various partitions and having different machines in the cluster process different partitions.

Our solution extends **Spark**'s **GraphX** graph library to make use of a recent dynamic, compact and competitive k^2-tree implementation [11,12], allowing for a compressed representation of property graphs in main memory. PK-GRAPH is built into a **JAR** file which must be coupled with **GraphX**'s own **JAR** in order to use it. **GraphX** provides an abstraction over graphs, containing views of: *a)* vertices; *b)* edges; *c)* edge triplets which correspond to the union of an edge with its corresponding source and destination vertices. All views are partitioned according to user criteria (with default strategies also offered). **GraphX** implements this abstraction by replicating the vertices in the edge partitions, thus efficiently performing a join between an edge and its corresponding vertices. This abstraction is static and does not allow the addition/removal of vertices/edges. It is possible to update the attributes of either vertices or edges, but because **Spark**'s **RDD** is immutable, updating the graph becomes a challenge (within the same dataflow job). Our solution provides the same three views while maintaining a compressed and fully dynamic representation of the graph, capable of adding new edges or vertices as well as updating their attributes.

3.1   Overall Architecture

Figure 2 shows a diagram of the architecture overview of our system and how it integrates with the GraphX platform. The main classes of the GraphX implementation are shown in blue and the main classes of our system are in green. The Graph class provides an interface for all basic graph operations, primitives used to implement graph algorithms and access to the underlying vertex and edge RDDs. All graph operations are executed in a lazy and distributed fashion, by propagating them throughout a cluster of computing nodes and aggregating the result in the driver program. Figure 3 shows an example of how a graph operation can be distributed throughout a cluster.

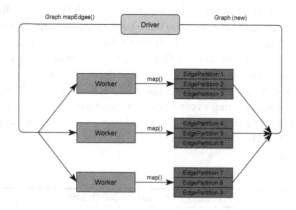

Fig. 3. Distributed graph work in a cluster.

Vertices: Representation. The VertexRDD class provides an interface for vertex-specific RDDs, containing operations to iterate and transform the underlying vertices of the graph. The VertexRDDImpl contains the default GraphX implementation of the VertexRDD class. Our solution incorporates the k^2-tree data structure to optimize operation on edges, with the vertex functionality of PK-Graph remaining unchanged from what GraphX provides.

The vertex partitions (where the actual vertices are stored) are implemented by the ShippableVertexPartition that keeps them in a format ready to be *shipped* to their corresponding edge partitions. Each vertex partition keeps track of the routing information for each of its vertices, later to be used to determine to which edge partition the vertices are shipped. The mask bitset keeps track of all active vertices in the partition. The vertex operations of a partition are only applied to the active vertices. To access the vertices of a partition, all set bits in the mask are iterated, retrieving the corresponding vertex identifier and attribute (see Algorithm 3.1).

Algorithm 3.1. Iterating the vertices of a given partition.

---

procedure ITERATE_VERTICES(partition)
   $i \leftarrow partition.mask.nextSetBit()$
   while $i >= 0$ **do**
      $vertexId \leftarrow partition.index[i]$
      $attr \leftarrow partition.values[i]$
      output $Vertex(vertexId, attr)$
      $i \leftarrow partition.mask.nextSetBit()$

Edges: Representation. The `EdgeRDD` class provides an interface for edge-specific RDDs and contains operations to iterate and transform the underlying edges of the graph. Our solution extends this abstraction with the `PKEdgeRDD` class, providing a specific implementation of the edge partitions (`PKEdgePartition`) using the compressed k^2-tree data structure to store the edges of the graph (`K2Tree`). The edge partitions are stored in the `PKEdgePartition` class, which provides operations to iterate and transform the underlying edges. The actual edges are stored in the `K2Tree` class, which implements the k^2-tree compressed data structure. In our modified edge partitioning, every operation in the edge partition creates a new instance with copies of the previous data and any modifications applied. This is done in order to offer the same expected semantics of `GraphX` when changing the elements of an RDD.

Algorithm 3.2. Iterating the edges of a given partition.

---

procedure ITERATE_EDGES(partition)
   $iterator \leftarrow tree\_iterator(k^h, 0, 0, -1)$ ▷ k^h is the size of the global adjacency
matrix
   $i \leftarrow 0$
   while $iterator.hasNext()$ **do**
      $(localSrc, localDst) \leftarrow iterator.next()$
      $srcId \leftarrow partition.local2Global[localSrc]$
      $dstId \leftarrow partitino.local2Global[localDst]$
      $attr \leftarrow partition.edgeAttrs[i]$
      output $Edge(srcId, dstId, attr)$
      $i \leftarrow i + 1$

procedure TREE_ITERATOR(size, line, col, pos)
   if $x \geq |T|$ **then**   ▷ leaf node
      if $L[pos - |T|] = 1$ **then output** (line, col)
   else   ▷ internal node
      if pos = -1 **or** T[pos] = 1 **then**
         $y \leftarrow rank(T, pos) \cdot k^2$ ▷ k^2-tree *rank* operation to find child node
         for $i = 0..k^2 - 1$ **do**
            $tree\_iterator(size/k, line \cdot (size/k) + i/k, col \cdot (size/k) + i \bmod k, y + i)$

The dynamic operations (**addEdges** and **removeEdges**) can add or remove edges from the partition. Although they are dynamic operations, the edge partition does not need to be mutable, since a new instance of the `PKEdgePartition` class is returned as a result of these operations.

As stated previously, the edge partition uses a k^2-tree compressed data structure to store the edges of the graph. This data structure is capable of representing the edges of a graph in a very space-efficient format. Our architecture only requires that the implementation of this structure provides a method to access and iterate its edges. This will require iterating the k^2-tree in a depth-first fashion and calculating the line and column in the adjacency matrix of each edge. Each line and column will correspond to local vertex identifiers, which then will need to be efficiently mapped to global identifiers, as well as determining for each edge its corresponding attribute. Algorithm 3.2 shows an example in pseudo-code of a possible implementation to access the edges of an edge partition by iterating its corresponding k^2-tree.

In a similar fashion to the `GraphX` system, our solution also uses a simple wrapper over an edge RDD, provided by the `PKReplicatedVertexView` to handle the shipping of vertices to the underlying edge partitions. This class stores the underlying `PKEdgeRDD` instance and keeps track of whether the view includes the attributes of both the source and destination vertices or if these are only partially shipped, since in some cases these may be unnecessary.

Dataflow Operations. The `GraphX` API offers dataflow operators to manipulate the graph. We list the most relevant ones here.

The **updateVertices** operation receives an iterator referencing cached vertices in the partition that should be updated with new attributes. The **reverse** operation reverses all edges in the partition by switching the source vertices with the destination vertices. This operation is directly used by the graph abstraction to perform its own **reverse** operation. The **map** operation applies a user function to all edges stored in the partition. The **filter** operation filters both the vertices of an edge and the actual edge according to the user defined predicates. The **innerJoin** operation performs an inner join between two edge partitions. The **aggregateMessages** operation is the primitive used to implement all popular graph algorithms. It implements a `Pregel`-like messaging system to exchange messages between the vertices of a graph. Each vertex is capable of sending a message through an edge to another vertex. These messages are then aggregated and merged at each vertex and collected after all messages have been sent.

The `GraphX` computing model also has the ability to maintain only some vertices in an active state, with only the active vertices able to receive messages. Active vertex information is stored in each edge partition and the non-active vertices are skipped when aggregating messages. The activeness requirements can then be specified as a parameter of the **aggregateMessages** function.

3.2 Dynamism

The `DynamicGraph` interface exposes various functions to both add and remove vertices and edges from a graph. However, since the underlying `Spark RDDs` are immutable, some partitions of the graph will need to be rebuilt, or at the very least a new copy of them will need to be made. This does not necessarily mean that the entire graph will need to be rebuilt, only the partitions which we are transforming. Thus, adding or removing both vertices and edges will require determining the partitions affected, and only transforming these.

The **addVertices** and **addEdges** functions add new vertices and edges, respectively, to the graph, returning a new graph instance in the process. The **removeVertices** and **removeEdges** functions remove the given vertices and edges from the graph, also returning a new graph instance in the process. Both of these functions work very similarly to applying a filter over the graph, with the slight optimization that only either the vertices or the edges of a graph are affected, instead of always having to filter both. All dynamic functions receive RDD instances as parameters to allow for these operations to be distributed throughout a computing cluster. We note that the impact of PK-GRAPH and the k^2-tree data structure is focused only on the **addEdges** and **removeEdges** functions.

3.3 Partitioning

Because `GraphX` processes the graph data in a distributed fashion, our solution will also need to address the problem of how to partition the graph to allow for spatial and computational efficiency. The input graph is represented by two RDDs provided by the user, one representing the vertices and another representing the edges (similar to the `GraphX` implementation). For the case of edges, our solution will interpret them as an edge adjacency matrix that will be partitioned using a 2D partitioning scheme [1] that splits the adjacency matrix into several sub-matrices of equal size, each assigned to a unique partition.

In case the number of partitions is not a perfect square, the last column will have a different number of rows than the others. One problem with this distribution is that it leads to poor work balance since, given a sparse adjacency matrix, some partitions will have many more edges than others. To overcome this, we shuffle the vertex locations in order to evenly distribute them through all partitions.

Like `GraphX`'s implementation, our solution will also replicate the vertices in the edge partitions to provide an efficient way to join the edges with their respective vertices. Using this distribution we guarantee that any vertex is replicated at most $2 \times \sqrt{|P|}$ times, where $|P|$ is the number of partitions of the adjacency matrix, since any vertex is represented by a line and a corresponding column in the matrix, and every line and column intersect at most $\sqrt{|P|}$ partitions.

The described partitioning scheme is applied by default, with no configuration required for the edges. It is also possible for the programmer to specify a different partitioning scheme by using the already existing interface provided by `Spark`. For the vertices, we would default to the partitioning scheme supplied by the user or, if no scheme was provided, default to a uniform partitioning strategy such as the one based on the hash of each vertex. In cases where the graph becomes unbalanced, the user can repartition the underlying vertex and edge RDDs to either increase or decrease the number of partitions, using `Spark`'s **repartition** function. Increasing the number of partitions implies shuffling, which will incur a significant overhead due to network communication between workers. However, when decreasing the number of partitions, it is possible to avoid a shuffling phase by using Spark's **coalesce** function.

The GraphX platform already offers several partition strategies such as: **EdgePartition2D**, this is the strategy described earlier and implements a strategy that divides the adjacency matrix of the graph into several blocks, as well as shuffling the vertices of the graph to provide a more balanced work distribution; **EdgePartition1D**, which groups together edges with the same source vertex; **RandomVertexCut**, which distributes the edges based on the hash code of both the source and destination vertex identifiers; **CanonicalRandomVertexCut**, the same strategy as the **RandomVertexCut** but also taking in consideration the direction of the edge when performing the hash. Our solution also introduces a new partition strategy, represented by the **PKGridPartitionStrategy** class. This strategy is similar to **EdgePartition2D** of GraphX. The main difference between the strategies is that the vertices will not be shuffled, in order not to change the data locality of the edges, thus providing a more space-efficient representation of the entire graph in some cases, at the cost of worse workload distribution in the cluster.

4   Evaluation

To evaluate the implementation of our solution, we performed various benchmarks in a cluster of computing nodes, each node corresponding to a Spark worker that keeps part of the total graph in main memory. We submitted several graph processing jobs to the cluster, executing some basic graph operations and some of the more popular graph algorithms, using relevant graph datasets and analyzing the gains (penalties) our solution has in terms of compression storage improvements and processing performance.

The cluster was prepared using the AWS EMR service [13], which enables the easy setup of a cluster of Spark workers. The cluster uses a single master node and various worker nodes.

The actual number of employed workers varies throughout each test. Each machine in the cluster has a 4-core processor with 16 GB of available main memory, in order to represent typical cost-efficient cloud-provider servers. Note that in edge cloud scenarios, servers would normally include more resource-constrained machines [40] that would make memory efficiency a much more pressing issue.

The Spark jobs are submitted from a driver program in a remote machine and the datasets are retrieved from AWS S3 buckets to be used in the jobs executed in the cluster.

Datasets. The datasets used in the evaluation of our implementation are from the Network Repository [35] and the Stanford Large Network Dataset Collection (SNAP) [23]. The datasets chosen for the benchmarks are the following:

- YouTube Growth (3M vertices, 12.2M edges)

- EU (2005) (863K vertices, 19M edges)
- Indochina (2004) (7M vertices, 194M edges)
- UK (2002) (18M vertices, 298M edges)

Memory Overhead. Our benchmarks show that the memory overhead of the data structure of the graph remains the same independently of the number of processors. This is due to the fact that the number of used partitions chosen by Spark, based on the size of the file where the dataset was read from, remains the same.

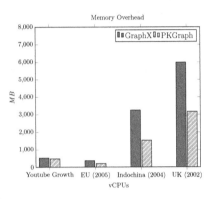

Fig. 4. Results of the memory overhead for each dataset.

Figure 4 shows the results of the memory usage of the entire graph for all datasets. The results show that our solution has significantly less memory overhead than the GraphX implementation. When testing the memory usage of the entire graph, comparing to the GraphX implementation, results range from a reduction of 30% to 50% (roughly 1.50 to two-fold more memory efficient) of 60% to 70% (roughly three-fold more memory efficient). This is in part due to the partitioning of the graph and its nature. The best performance is observed on the web graphs, since these have much higher edge clustering when compared to other types of graphs. Furthermore, the number of processors has no significant impact

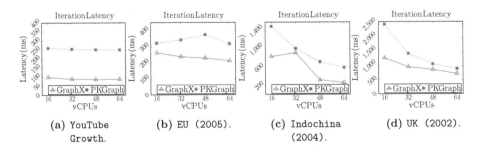

Fig. 5. Iteration latency and vCPU counts for chosen datasets (PK-GRAPH: $k = 8$).

on the graph size in memory. Regarding memory efficiency of edges specifically, it improves three fold (30%, of initially used).

Workload Latencies. The workloads presented in this subsection compare the latency between PK-Graph and GraphX for different graph algorithms. Latency is defined as the total time the system takes to execute graph processing jobs.

Basic Iteration. This workload iterates all edges of the graph and applies a user function to each edge (for evaluation, this function simply multiplies the edge's integer value by a constant). The obtained results are shown in Figs. 5a, 5b, 5c and 5d. As observed with the previous tests, as the number of processors increases, the iteration latency decreases. As the GraphX implementation is more efficient at traversing all edges in an edge partition, it achieves a lower latency compared to PK-Graph, even when using a k value that optimizes processing performance. In terms of iteration latency, overall our implementation is between 15% to 40% slower than the GraphX implementation, depending on the type of graph, obtaining better results for web graphs when compared to social network graphs.

PageRank. For the *PageRank* algorithm, we observe similar patterns to the basic iteration test, with PK-Graph's latency approaching that of GraphX with higher vCPU counts on the Indochina (2004) and UK (2002) datasets. The latency results for *PageRank* are depicted in Figs. 6a, 6b, 6c and 6d. For larger graphs, as the number of available processors increases, the latency of the graph operation decreases.

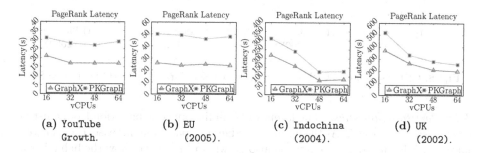

(a) YouTube Growth.

(b) EU (2005).

(c) Indochina (2004).

(d) UK (2002).

Fig. 6. *PageRank* latency and vCPU counts for chosen datasets (PK-Graph: $k = 8$).

Triangle Count. This workload executes an algorithm to count triangles, which is typically used in social network analysis to detect communities and measure clustering coefficients. It is an algorithm which has less latency than PageRank. *Triangle Count* latency results are presented in Figs. 7a, 7b, 7c and 7d. For this algorithm, the relationship between latency and number of vCPUs exhibited behavior similar to PageRank, with datasets Indochina (2004) and UK (2002) seeing a smaller latency gap between PK-Graph and GraphX when executing with a higher number of vCPUs.

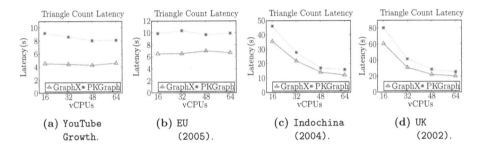

Fig. 7. *Triangle Count* latency and vCPU counts for chosen datasets (PK-GRAPH: $k = 8$).

CPU Usage Results. They are presented in Figs. 8a, 8b, 8c and 8d. For this metric, we compare the total run time of `Spark` executors to their total CPU time for each dataset, showing the percentage of the total run time spent on the processor. PK-GRAPH achieves a higher CPU usage as the iteration algorithms used by our solution are heavier.

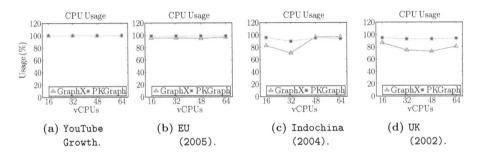

Fig. 8. CPU usage and vCPU counts for the chosen datasets (PK-GRAPH: $k = 8$).

Edge Partition Statistics. The latency of building an edge partition from a list of edges is shown in Fig. 9. As the number of edges in a partition increase, the incurred latency while building the partition also grows. In Fig. 10 we show the behavior of iteration latency as the number of edges increases. The higher the value of parameter k in the k^2-tree, the better the iterator performance due to the smaller height of the tree.

Analysis and Discussion. Overall, while considering the detailed evaluation of our implementation, our solution provides a significant reduction in memory usage, i.e. between 40% and 50% depending on the k value used for the k^2-tree, the type of graph and the partitioning strategy employed. As we are using a k^2-tree as the compressed data structure, the sparser the adjacency matrix of the graph is, the better the compression achieved. This enables the employment of comparatively less capable devices, such as in those deployed in community micro clouds

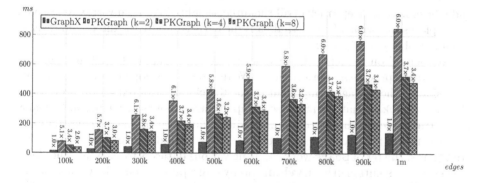

Fig. 9. Edge partition build latency compared to partition size.

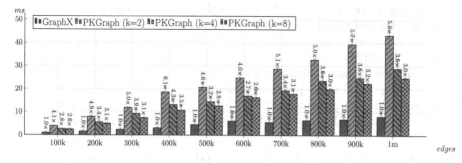

Fig. 10. Edge partition iteration latency compared to number of edges.

(i.e., in edge cloud and IoT-like scenarios), as well as those low-cost made available by cloud providers (i.e., spot instances and virtual machines tailored to microservices and serverless computing).

Our implementation also provides competitive processing performance when compared to the GraphX implementation, specially considering that this current GraphX approach focuses mainly on having the best possible processing performance by keeping all edges in an array with no application of compression techniques. The performance penalty of PK-GRAPH decreases in inverse relation with the complexity of workload algorithm and the size of the dataset. Nonetheless, while requiring less memory (the resource harder to share across time between workloads), results show that at times PK-GRAPH incurs a higher CPU usage than GraphX, due to the increased graph processing complexity over the compact data structure, as our iteration algorithms are more demanding on it.

5   Conclusion

We improve upon GraphX's implementation, using a k^2-tree, a data structure that efficiently represents binary relations between two vertices. GraphX's implementation uses two arrays to store the local source and destination vertex identifiers and a hash map to keep track of all the direct neighbors of each vertex. Our solution replaces this with a k^2-tree that can efficiently compute the direct and reverse neighbors of any local vertex.

We focused on reducing the memory usage of graphs while still maintaining a competitive processing performance. We designed, developed and evaluated an extension to the storage component of the GraphX distributed graph processing library of Spark so that the processed graph is made more space-efficient by using the k^2-tree lossless compressed representation, while also aiming to achieve similar performance to the uncompressed version. We evaluated the performance of PK-GRAPH in a cluster of Spark workers, using various datasets to showcase the effectiveness of our solution in both web and non-web graphs, as well as how our solution scales as the size of the graph and the number of available processors increase. Our experimental results highlight that our solution offers a significant reduction in memory usage of graphs, specially for web graphs, while achieving competitive processing performance when compared to the GraphX implementation. PK-GRAPH demonstrates an innovative combination of data representation and processing techniques for distributed processing systems while decreasing space complexity, resulting in a middleware which enables execution in resource-constrained scenarios, with application on less powerful machines and spot-type virtual instances. For the different iteration workloads, the latency difference between GraphX and PK-GRAPH tended to decrease with bigger datasets and higher number of vCPUs.

Future Work. We envision the integration of the k^2-tree data structure on other processing systems such as Flink, as well as exploring the possibility of integrating other schemes such as the WebGraph [5] representation. Orthogonal to this, it would be relevant to expand evaluated datasets to include more diverse real-world graphs and to evaluate further ideas with datasets of greater size. Evaluating our contribution with other algorithms and also comparing with other similar works will be relevant.

Acknowledgements. This work was supported by national funds through FCT, Fundação para a Ciência e a Tecnologia, under projects UIDB/50021/2020 and PTDC/EEI-COM/30644/2017.

References

1. Álvarez-García, S., Brisaboa, N.R., Gómez-Pantoja, C., Marin, M.: Distributed query processing on compressed graphs using K2-trees. In: Kurland, O., Lewenstein, M., Porat, E. (eds.) SPIRE 2013. LNCS, vol. 8214, pp. 298–310. Springer, Cham (2013). https://doi.org/10.1007/978-3-319-02432-5_32
2. Angles, R.: The Property Graph Database Model (2018). http://ceur-ws.org/Vol-2100/paper26.pdf. Accessed 24 Apr 2020
3. Besta, M., Fischer, M., Kalavri, V., Kapralov, M., Hoefler, T.: Practice of streaming and dynamic graphs: concepts, models, systems, and parallelism. CoRR abs/1912.12740 (2019). http://arxiv.org/abs/1912.12740

4. Boldi, P., Vigna, S.: The WebGraph framework II: codes for the World-wide Web. In: 2004 Data Compression Conference (DCC 2004), 23–25 March 2004, Snowbird, UT, USA, p. 528. IEEE Computer Society (2004). https://doi.org/10.1109/DCC.2004.1281504

5. Boldi, P., Vigna, S.: The WebGraph framework I: Compression techniques. In: Feldman, S.I., Uretsky, M., Najork, M., Wills, C.E. (eds.) Proceedings of the 13th International Conference on World Wide Web, WWW 2004, New York, NY, USA, 17–20 May 2004, pp. 595–602. ACM, New York, NY, USA (2004). https://doi.org/10.1145/988672.988752

6. Brisaboa, N.R., Ladra, S., Navarro, G.: k^2-trees for compact web graph representation. In: Karlgren, J., Tarhio, J., Hyyrö, H. (eds.) SPIRE 2009. LNCS, vol. 5721, pp. 18–30. Springer, Heidelberg (2009). https://doi.org/10.1007/978-3-642-03784-9_3

7. Busato, F., Green, O., Bombieri, N., Bader, D.A.: Hornet: an efficient data structure for dynamic sparse graphs and matrices on GPUs. In: 2018 IEEE High Performance Extreme Computing Conference (HPEC), pp. 1–7. IEEE (2018)

8. Chen, R., Shi, J., Chen, Y., Zang, B., Guan, H., Chen, H.: PowerLyra: differentiated graph computation and partitioning on skewed graphs. ACM Trans. Parallel Comput. (TOPC) 5(3), 1–39 (2019)

9. Ching, A., Edunov, S., Kabiljo, M., Logothetis, D., Muthukrishnan, S.: One trillion edges: graph processing at Facebook-scale. Proc. VLDB Endow. 8(12), 1804–1815 (2015)

10. Coimbra, M.E., Esteves, S., Francisco, A.P., Veiga, L.: VeilGraph: incremental graph stream processing. J. Big Data 9(1), 1–29 (2022)

11. Coimbra, M.E., Francisco, A.P., Russo, L.M.S., de Bernardo, G., Ladra, S., Navarro, G.: On dynamic succinct graph representations. In: Data Compression Conference (DCC), p. 10. IEEE, January 2020. https://sigport.org/documents/dynamic-succinct-graph-representations

12. Coimbra, M.E., et al.: A practical succinct dynamic graph representation. Inf. Comput. 285, 104862 (2021)

13. Deyhim, P.: Best practices for amazon EMR. Technical report, Amazon Web Services Inc. (2013)

14. Francis, N., et al.: Cypher: an evolving query language for property graphs. In: Proceedings of the 2018 International Conference on Management of Data, pp. 1433–1445 (2018)

15. Gabielkov, M., Legout, A.: The complete picture of the twitter social graph. In: Proceedings of the 2012 ACM Conference on CoNEXT Student Workshop, pp. 19–20 (2012)

16. Guia, J., Soares, V.G., Bernardino, J.: Graph databases: Neo4j analysis. In: ICEIS (1), pp. 351–356 (2017)

17. Iyer, A.P., Li, L.E., Das, T., Stoica, I.: Time-evolving graph processing at scale. In: Proceedings of the Fourth International Workshop on Graph Data Management Experiences and Systems, pp. 1–6 (2016)

18. Kaepke, M., Zukunft, O.: A comparative evaluation of big data frameworks for graph processing. In: 2018 4th International Conference on Big Data Innovations and Applications (Innovate-Data), pp. 30–37. IEEE (2018)

19. Kang, U., Tong, H., Sun, J., Lin, C.Y., Faloutsos, C.: GBASE: an efficient analysis platform for large graphs. VLDB J. 21(5), 637–650 (2012)

20. Katsifodimos, A., Schelter, S.: Apache Flink: stream analytics at scale. In: 2016 IEEE International Conference on Cloud Engineering Workshop, IC2E Workshops, Berlin, Germany, 4–8 April 2016, p. 193. IEEE Computer Society (2016). https://doi.org/10.1109/IC2EW.2016.56

21. Ko, J., Kook, Y., Shin, K.: Incremental lossless graph summarization. In: Proceedings of the 26th ACM SIGKDD International Conference on Knowledge Discovery & Data Mining, pp. 317–327 (2020)

22. Kyrola, A., Blelloch, G., Guestrin, C.: GraphChi: large-scale graph computation on just a {PC}. In: Presented as Part of the 10th {USENIX} Symposium on Operating Systems Design and Implementation ({OSDI} 2012), pp. 31–46 (2012)

23. Leskovec, J., Krevl, A.: SNAP Datasets: Stanford large network dataset collection. http://snap.stanford.edu/data, June 2014

24. Low, Y., Gonzalez, J.E., Kyrola, A., Bickson, D., Guestrin, C.E., Hellerstein, J.: GraphLab: a new framework for parallel machine learning. arXiv preprint arXiv:1408.2041 (2014)

25. Maass, S., Min, C., Kashyap, S., Kang, W., Kumar, M., Kim, T.: Mosaic: processing a trillion-edge graph on a single machine. In: Proceedings of the Twelfth European Conference on Computer Systems, pp. 527–543, EuroSys 2017. ACM, New York, NY, USA (2017). https://doi.org/10.1145/3064176.3064191

26. Malewicz, G., et al.: Pregel: a system for large-scale graph processing. In: Proceedings of the 2010 ACM SIGMOD International Conference on Management of Data, SIGMOD 2010, pp. 135–146. ACM, New York, NY, USA (2010). https://doi.org/10.1145/1807167.1807184

27. Mariappan, M., Vora, K.: GraphBolt: dependency-driven synchronous processing of streaming graphs. In: Proceedings of the Fourteenth EuroSys Conference 2019, EuroSys 2019, pp. 25:1–25:16. ACM, New York, NY, USA (2019). https://doi.org/10.1145/3302424.3303974

28. Martínez-Bazan, N., Águila-Lorente, M.Á., Muntés-Mulero, V., Dominguez-Sal, D., Gómez-Villamor, S., Larriba-Pey, J.L.: Efficient graph management based on bitmap indices. In: Proceedings of the 16th International Database Engineering & Applications Sysmposium, pp. 110–119 (2012)

29. Munro, J.I., Nekrich, Y., Vitter, J.S.: Dynamic data structures for document collections and graphs. In: ACM Symposium on Principles of Database Systems (PODS), pp. 277–289 (2015)

30. Navarro, G.: Compact Data Structures: A Practical Approach. Cambridge University Press, Cambridge (2016)

31. Page, L., Brin, S., Motwani, R., Winograd, T.: The PageRank citation ranking: bringing order to the web. Technical report 1999-66, Stanford InfoLab (1999). http://ilpubs.stanford.edu:8090/422/

32. Palankar, M.R., Iamnitchi, A., Ripeanu, M., Garfinkel, S.: Amazon S3 for science grids: a viable solution? In: Proceedings of the 2008 International Workshop on Data-Aware Distributed Computing, pp. 55–64 (2008)

33. Perez, Y., et al.: Ringo: interactive graph analytics on big-memory machines. In: Proceedings of the 2015 ACM SIGMOD International Conference on Management of Data, SIGMOD 2015. ACM, New York, NY, USA (2015). https://doi.org/10.1145/2723372.2735369

34. ur Rehman, S., Nawaz, A., Ali, T., Amin, N.: g-Sum: a graph summarization approach for a single large social network (2021)

35. Rossi, R.A., Ahmed, N.K.: The network data repository with interactive graph analytics and visualization. In: AAAI (2015). http://networkrepository.com

36. Roy, A., Bindschaedler, L., Malicevic, J., Zwaenepoel, W.: Chaos: scale-out graph processing from secondary storage. In: Proceedings of the 25th Symposium on Operating Systems Principles, SOSP 2015, pp. 410–424. ACM, New York, NY, USA (2015). https://doi.org/10.1145/2815400.2815408

37. Roy, A., Mihailovic, I., Zwaenepoel, W.: X-Stream: edge-centric graph processing using streaming partitions. In: Proceedings of the Twenty-Fourth ACM Symposium on Operating Systems Principles, SOSP 2013, , pp. 472–488. ACM, New York, NY, USA (2013). https://doi.org/10.1145/2517349.2522740

38. Sakr, S., et al.: The future is big graphs: a community view on graph processing systems. Commun. ACM **64**(9), 62–71 (2021). https://doi.org/10.1145/3434642

39. Salihoglu, S., Widom, J.: GPS: a graph processing system. In: Proceedings of the 25th International Conference on Scientific and Statistical Database Management, pp. 1–12 (2013)

40. Selimi, M., Cerdà Alabern, L., Freitag, F., Veiga, L., Sathiaseelan, A., Crowcroft, J.: A lightweight service placement approach for community network micro-clouds. J. Grid Comput. **17**(1), 169–189 (2019)

41. Shvachko, K., Kuang, H., Radia, S., Chansler, R.: The Hadoop distributed file system. In: 2010 IEEE 26th Symposium on Mass Storage Systems and Technologies (MSST), pp. 1–10, May 2010. https://doi.org/10.1109/MSST.2010.5496972

42. Tian, Y., Balmin, A., Corsten, S.A., Tatikonda, S., McPherson, J.: From "Think Like a Vertex" to "Think Like a Graph". Proc. VLDB Endow. **7**(3), 193–204 (2013). https://doi.org/10.14778/2732232.2732238

43. Wheatman, B., Xu, H.: Packed compressed sparse row: a dynamic graph representation. In: 2018 IEEE High Performance Extreme Computing Conference (HPEC), pp. 1–7. IEEE (2018)

44. Xin, R.S., Gonzalez, J.E., Franklin, M.J., Stoica, I.: GraphX: a resilient distributed graph system on spark. In: First International Workshop on Graph Data Management Experiences and Systems, GRADES 2013, pp. 2:1–2:6. ACM, New York, NY, USA (2013). https://doi.org/10.1145/2484425.2484427

45. Zaharia, M., et al.: Apache Spark: a unified engine for big data processing. Commun. ACM **59**(11), 56–65 (2016). https://doi.org/10.1145/2934664

A Distributed Architecture for Privacy-Preserving Optimization Using Genetic Algorithms and Multi-party Computation

Christoph G. Schuetz[1]([✉])[ID], Thomas Lorünser[2][ID], Samuel Jaburek[1],
Kevin Schuetz[1], Florian Wohner[2], Roman Karl[2], and Eduard Gringinger[3][ID]

[1] Institute of Business Informatics – Data and Knowledge Engineering,
Johannes Kepler University Linz, Linz, Austria
`{schuetz,jaburek,kschuetz}@dke.uni-linz.ac.at`
[2] AIT Austrian Institute of Technology, Vienna, Austria
`{Thomas.Loruenser,Florian.Wohner,Roman.Karl}@ait.ac.at`
[3] Frequentis AG, Vienna, Austria
`eduard.gringinger@frequentis.com`

Abstract. In many industries, competitors are required to cooperate in order to conduct optimizations, e.g., to solve an assignment problem. For example, in air traffic flow management (ATFM), flight prioritization in case of temporarily reduced capacity of the air traffic network is an instance of the assignment problem. Participants, however, are typically reluctant to share sensitive information regarding their preferences for the optimization, which renders conventional approaches to optimization inadequate. This paper proposes a method for combining genetic algorithms with multi-party computation (MPC) as the basis for building a platform for optimizing the assignment of resources to different agents under the assumption of an honest-but-curious platform provider; the method is illustrated on the ATFM use case. In the proposed method a genetic algorithm iteratively generates a population of candidate solutions to the assignment problem while a Privacy Engine component evaluates the population in each iteration step. The participants' private inputs are kept from competitors and not even the platform provider knows those inputs, receiving only encrypted input which is processed by MPC nodes in a way that preserves the secrecy of the inputs.

Keywords: Security · Evolutionary optimization · Assignment problem · Air traffic flow management

1 Introduction

Solving optimization problems often requires inputs from different parties, which do not necessarily want to disclose those inputs, neither to each other nor to a trusted third party. In that case, the optimization should be carried out

© The Author(s), under exclusive license to Springer Nature Switzerland AG 2022
M. Sellami et al. (Eds.): CoopIS 2022, LNCS 13591, pp. 168–185, 2022.
https://doi.org/10.1007/978-3-031-17834-4_10

using methods for *privacy-preserving computation*, e.g., multi-party computation, which typically come with a considerable performance overhead, rendering such methods impractical in many real-world settings where time is an issue. In this context, the term "privacy" is synonymous with "secrecy" and "confidentiality", referring to the goal of "keeping information secret from all but those who are authorized to see it" [12, p. 3].

In this paper we present an architecture for privacy-preserving computation of solutions to optimization problems by combining multi-party computation (MPC) with evolutionary optimization algorithms. The proposed architecture is useful in time-critical settings where a solution to an optimization problem is required in a relatively short amount of time, which privacy-preserving implementations of deterministic optimization algorithms cannot achieve. We specifically consider the assignment problem, although the proposed architecture could also be potentially employed for solving other types of optimization problems.

In the proposed architecture, an evolutionary optimization algorithm—in this paper, a genetic algorithm—iteratively looks for candidate solutions to an optimization problem. The fitness values for the candidate solutions are obtained using MPC. The evolutionary optimization algorithm receives only limited information about the fitness of a population to protect the confidentiality of the participants' inputs. Our experiments show that even with limited information regarding the fitness of candidate solutions, genetic algorithms can find good solutions in a considerably shorter time than privacy-preserving implementations of deterministic optimization algorithms, e.g., MPC implementations of the Hungarian method; we refer to an online appendix [16] for detailed experimental results, including links to datasets and source code of the implementation.

Although the architecture is applicable to optimization problems in many domains, the presented use case in this paper is flight prioritization in air traffic flow management, where privacy-preserving implementations of deterministic optimization algorithms would not find a result in time. Flight prioritization is an assignment problem: Multiple airlines would like to find an optimal assignment of flights to slots in situations of temporarily reduced capacity in the air traffic network. Since airlines are reluctant to share preferences regarding the slot assignment, which may reveal confidential information about an airline's cost structure, the optimization must keep the inputs hidden from an honest-but-curious provider of an optimization platform.

The remainder of the paper is organized as follows. In Sect. 2 we present background information, including a review of related work. In Sect. 3 we give an overview of the proposed architecture. In Sect. 4 we present the Heuristic Optimizer component of the proposed architecture. In Sect. 5 we present the Privacy Engine component. In Sect. 6 we state our conclusions.

2 Background

In the following, we first present the flight prioritization problem in air traffic flow management (ATFM) before introducing background information on multi-party computation and genetic algorithms. We also review related work.

2.1   Use Case: Flight Prioritization

When airports are at full capacity small disruptions, e.g., bad weather, lead to flight delays, causing costs for airlines. To minimize delay costs in such situations, airlines have to prioritize individual flights [1] since costs are dependent on the flight and severity of the delay. Some flights can be pushed back even further whereas for other flights, additional delay will be more costly. To maximize cost savings, flights must be prioritized across airlines, which is inherently difficult since airlines are reluctant to disclose business secrets [13], e.g., flight-specific delay costs. Flight prioritization is time-critical since the situation is constantly evolving and for a new flight list to take effect, airlines, airport, and the Network Manager must accept the flight list. In the SlotMachine project[1], we determined with experts from EUROCONTROL and Swiss International Air Lines that an optimization algorithm should finish within two to three minutes.

Flight prioritization in ATFM can be considered an *assignment problem* [15]. The optimization problem is to find a mapping between two sets of objects – flights and slots – either minimizing overall costs or maximizing overall utility given a cost or a utility matrix, respectively. A cost matrix and a utility matrix specify the costs or the utility, respectively, of each slot for each flight. If the goal is to minimize costs or maximize the utility of the assignment, the problem is a single-objective assignment problem. The problem is unbalanced if the number of elements differs between the mapped sets; in the flight prioritization problem there are possibly more slots than flights. A well-known algorithm for the assignment problem is the Hungarian method [9].

In the SlotMachine project we are currently developing a platform that will allow multiple airlines to prioritize flights in cases of reduced capacity in the air traffic network. We determined that airlines often cannot precisely quantify the monetary utility (or costs) of different ATFM slots. Therefore, we propose to allow airspace users to capture preferences in terms of the following *margins* and a priority for each flight, which are translated into weight maps (utility matrix), expressing the utility of each available slot for each flight.

- **Time wished**. The flight should be assigned a slot close to that time.
- **Time not before**. The flight should not be assigned a slot before that time.
- **Time not after**. The flight should not be assigned a slot after that time.
- **Priority**. A numeric value that indicates the priority of the flight.

2.2   Multi-party Computation

Privacy-preserving computation enables parties to evaluate a function on their private inputs in an oblivious way, such that no individual party learns any information beyond the function result and what can be deduced from the result. Multi-party computation (MPC) [2] can be considered the most practical approach for generic computation on encrypted data. In principle, any (computable)

---

[1] http://slotmachine.frequentis.com/.

function can be computed in an MPC system. In practice, however, MPC protocols introduce an overhead of several orders of magnitude compared to regular computation that is not privacy-preserving.

Regarding performance and scalability it is important to note that in an MPC setting, common operations do not behave in the same way as in regular computation. In an (arithmetic) multi-party setting, some common operations, e.g., comparing two numbers, have a considerable overhead while others, e.g., addition, have almost no overhead. The cost of operations is measured in communication rounds, with addition on the one end of the spectrum requiring none, and comparison operations on the other end requiring multiple communication rounds. To achieve optimal performance, it is essential to perform as many operations as possible in a single communication round.

We picked different variations of the Hungarian method for solving the assignment problem and implemented MPC versions of the algorithm using the MPyC framework[2]. None of the variations of the Hungarian method are particularly MPC-friendly. Our measurements [11] show that even under favorable network conditions, MPC implementations of the Hungarian method will not finish within an acceptable timespan for flight prioritization in ATFM.

2.3   Genetic Algorithms

A genetic algorithm is a kind of evolutionary, population-based algorithm inspired by natural selection in biology [17]. A genetic algorithm iteratively improves a population of candidate solutions to an optimization problem over multiple generations. An individual of a population is referred to as phenotype and is characterized by the genotype, which consists of chromosomes, i.e., a collection of genes, and is the actual representation of the solution; an individual of a population is a candidate solution to the optimization problem. Through recombination (or crossover) and mutation of genotypes, new candidate solutions are created. Finding the appropriate genotype representation for a problem, e.g., in binary form, is arguably the most challenging task when using genetic algorithms. The other task is to find the appropriate fitness function that allows to evaluate the solutions for an optimization problem. Further important design decisions are the choice of selectors (which select individuals for recombination and survival), the choice of alterers for recombination and mutation, and finding an initial population from which to start. Existing frameworks, e.g., Jenetics[3], facilitate the development of genetic algorithms.

2.4   Related Work

Funke and Kerschbaum [5] propose an approach for a privacy-preserving genetic algorithm based on additive-homomorphic encryption, running entirely in the encrypted domain, which significantly limits the functionality given the employed

---

[2] https://github.com/lschoe/mpyc.
[3] https://jenetics.io/.

encryption primitive. The genetic algorithm is purely mutation-based and does not support recombination. The genetic algorithm works well for the considered problem but the results cannot be transferred to the assignment problem or any other optimization problem, unlike our proposed architecture.

Golle [7] and Franklin et al. [4] provide privacy-preserving implementations of Gale and Shapley's matching algorithm [6], based on mix networks and homomorphic encryption, considering a weak (passive) adversary model only. Doerner et al. [3] provide an MPC-based implementation of the matching algorithm, scaling to multiple thousands of input values. A provably secure and scalable implementation [14] is based on garbled circuits. A privacy-preserving version of the Hungarian method based on homomorphic encryption [19] has been proposed, but only the theoretical complexity of the protocol was analyzed, and no performance data are available.

3   System Overview

The proposed architecture (Fig. 1) consists of the local systems of the participants in an optimization run, an optimization platform, and a number of MPC nodes performing the privacy-preserving computations. The participants' local systems host user interfaces and possibly rule-based systems to capture the participants' preferences; those systems also encode/encrypt the preferences. The platform's components conducting the actual optimization are the *Heuristic Optimizer* (see Sect. 4) and the *Privacy Engine* (see Sect. 5). The Privacy Engine employs MPC nodes, which are external to the platform, e.g., hosted by the participants. A controller component coordinates the interactions between the participants' local systems, the Heuristic Optimizer, and the Privacy Engine. Hence, the controller initiates an optimization run, collects the preferences from the participants, and initializes the Privacy Engine with the collected preferences, thereby ensuring that the Heuristic Optimizer and the Privacy Engine can communicate properly when actually conducting the optimization.

In the SlotMachine project we currently develop a system based on the proposed architecture that will allow multiple airspace users (airlines) to participate in optimization runs. To work in practice the platform must also include a market mechanism that allows for actual slot swaps for flights and compensation of airspace users giving up favorable slots. Furthermore, the Network Manager, who is responsible for the functioning of the air traffic network, also communicates with the optimization platform, providing information regarding the situations of reduced capacity and accepting/rejecting optimized flight lists. The SlotMachine system also employs a blockchain that serves as a tamper-proof audit trail, which should increase the participants' trust in the fairness of the system. Furthermore, the blockchain could be the basis for a credit-based market mechanism.

4   Heuristic Optimizer

In this section we first present the implementation of the Heuristic Optimizer before discussing experimental results.

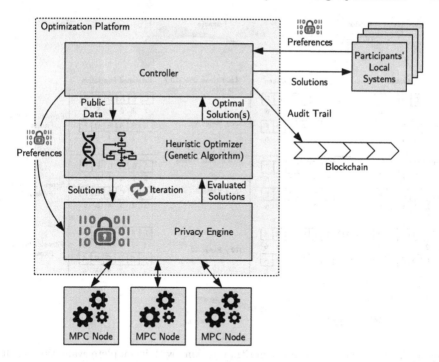

Fig. 1. Distributed architecture for privacy-preserving optimization

4.1 Implementation

We implemented the Heuristic Optimizer using the Jenetics framework for running a genetic algorithm with configurable parameters to search for candidate solutions to the assignment problem. The Jenetics framework already provides a suitable encoding as well as implementations of operators for the assignment problem [18, p. 59]. The *naive approach* to privacy-preserving optimization in the proposed architecture has the Heuristic Optimizer receive the fitness value (possibly with added noise) for each individual in the population. In that case, however, an honest-but-curious platform provider could deduce information regarding the confidential preferences submitted by the participants (see Sect. 5.2); the individual weights are not sufficiently protected from an attacker.

To avoid leaking information regarding the participants' preferences, we investigate different methods to obfuscate the precise fitness of candidate solutions, which results in the genetic algorithm receiving limited information regarding the fitness of a population. Figure 2 illustrates the principle of running a genetic algorithm with such limited information. Hence, the result of the evaluation that is disclosed to the Heuristic Optimizer is either a (variant of) ranked list of candidate solutions or a classification of candidate solutions according to their fitness, along with information whether the best solution found in a generation improves the previously best found solution, e.g., by disclosing the maximum fitness in the population. The Heuristic Optimizer then estimates the

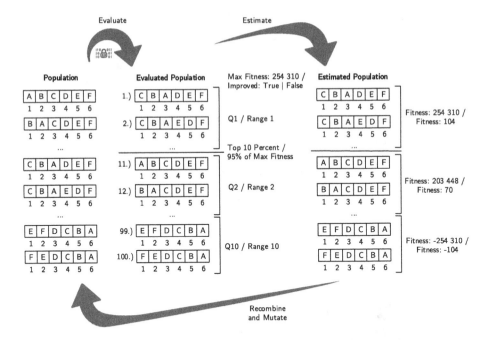

Fig. 2. Illustration of the genetic algorithm working with incomplete evaluation results and estimated fitness values

fitness value of individuals using a configurable estimation function. The fitness estimates are the basis for recombination and mutation of the solutions, which produce the next generation of the population. In particular, we consider the following methods to obfuscate the precise fitness.

1. **Order.** The individuals in a population are ordered from best to worst according to their fitness value. The Heuristic Optimizer receives the precise order of the solutions.
2. **Order quantiles.** The individuals are ordered from best to worst according to fitness value but the precise order remains unknown to the Heuristic Optimizer, which receives only the quantile of each individual.
3. **Top individuals.** The top individuals are distinguished from the other individuals, which is the only information regarding fitness known to the Heuristic Optimizer; precise order remains unknown.
4. **Fitness range.** The individuals of a population are collected into buckets, each bucket comprising the individuals within a certain fitness range. The total number of buckets and the bucket of each individual are revealed, precise order and actual ranges remain unknown.
5. **Above threshold.** The individuals above a certain threshold, expressed as a percentage of the maximum fitness within a population, are distinguished, which becomes known to the Heuristic Optimizer. The precise order of individuals remains unknown to the Heuristic Optimizer.

The methods *order*, *order quantiles*, and *top individuals* essentially require the Privacy Engine to order the individuals in a population. The Privacy Engine, however, cannot parallelize the privacy-preserving computation following these methods, which may be a problem in time-critical settings. The methods *fitness range* and *above threshold* facilitate parallel privacy-preserving computation within the Privacy Engine. Those methods essentially require the Privacy Engine to classify the individuals into multiple classes based on the fitness.

To obtain fitness values for individuals, quantiles, and fitness ranges, the Heuristic Optimizer may employ different estimators. Each estimator takes a maximum value and an estimated minimum value as input while returning a given number of fitness values using a distribution function between the maximum and the minimum fitness. In the current implementation, the minimum value of a population is estimated to be $minFitness = maxFitness - (2 \times maxFitness)$. The distribution function could be a linear, sigmoid, or logarithmic curve fitted between maximum and estimated minimum fitness.

We also investigated the use of variants of the proposed obfuscation methods where the maximum fitness remains hidden from the Heuristic Optimizer, further strengthening the protection of confidential inputs. Hence, the Privacy Engine reveals only whether the best candidate solution in the current population was an improvement with respect to the best candidate solution found so far. The best solution may or may not be revealed to the Heuristic Optimizer. Revealing the best solution is not critical from the perspective of keeping the privacy if the fitness value is not disclosed. Initially, the Heuristic Optimizer assigns a fitness value equal to the number of individuals in the population, e.g., 100, to the best solution, best order quantile, top individuals, best fitness range, or the individuals with a fitness above a certain fitness threshold. The Heuristic Optimizer remembers that fitness value as the maximum fitness value so far. If a population contains a better solution than the best previously found solution, the Heuristic Optimizer increments the maximum fitness value so far. In case the precise order is known, the rank becomes the fitness, except for the best individual of the current population, which is assigned the maximum fitness value so far. If only order quantiles, fitness ranges, or top individuals are known, fitness values are estimated. If the best individual of the population is known, only that individual is assigned the maximum fitness value so far while other solutions in the best quantile, best fitness range, top individuals, or individuals above a certain threshold are assigned a fitness equal to the number of individuals in the population.

4.2 Performance Evaluation

We use flight prioritization in ATFM as the use case which we base our experiments upon. We ran the experiments on an OpenVZ virtual machine on a physical machine with an Intel Xeon CPU E5-2640 v4 with 2.40 GHz. The virtual machine had 4 GB of main memory and could use up to 40 cores of the physical CPU. The operating system of the virtual machine was CentOS Linux 7. We used OpenJDK 16 for running the Heuristic Optimizer.

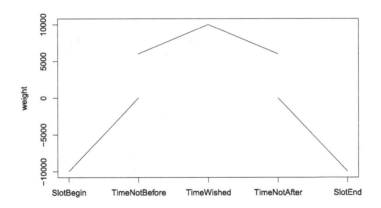

Fig. 3. Example conversion of margins into weights

We first generated synthetic datasets (Cases 1–27) with preferences for 100 flights in various scenarios regarding the concentration of the flights' wished time slots, the margin widths, and priorities; we refer to the appendix [16] for details regarding the characteristics of the datasets. We used what we refer to as broad (100 min), normal (60 min), and narrow (20 min) margin widths, i.e., difference between time not after and time not before; the wider the margins, the easier the optimization. We used what we refer to as even, moderate, and extreme concentrations of the times wished by flights; the more evenly spread out the wished times for flights, the easier the optimization. We also varied priorities, from even priorities, where every flight has the same priority, to higher priorities being put on the flights in the middle or the fringes, respectively, of the timeline. The priorities serve as a multiplier for the weights derived from the time wished and the margins. Figure 3 illustrates the derivation of the slot weights (utility matrix) for a flight: For the slot closest to the wished time of a flight, the weight is highest (normally 10 000, possibly multiplied by the flight's priority), with a linear decrease between the time not before and the time not after, and a steep drop in the weights assigned to slots outside those margins.

Concerning the configuration of the genetic algorithm, we used a tournament selector with a tournament size of ten individuals for selecting the survivors of a population, with generally 30% of the population surviving. We used a tournament selector with a tournament size of ten individuals for selecting individuals for recombination, and partially matched crossover to actually recombine the selected individuals, with a crossover probability of 90%. We used a swap mutator with a 15% probability of mutation for generating new candidate solutions. Furthermore, we experimented with population sizes of 500 individuals and 100 individuals, respectively. We ran experiments with and without elimination of duplicate individuals in each generation.

We refer to the appendix [16] for a detailed presentation of the results. We note that for the easy scenarios among Cases 1–27—those cases with even distribution of flights' wished times and/or wider margins given by the participants—

the genetic algorithm quickly finds the optimal solution or a solution very close to the optimum (>95% of the fitness of the optimal solution). For more complex scenarios, where optimizations are hardly possible due to high concentration of wished times on a few slots and/or narrow margins submitted by the participants, the genetic algorithm requires more generations—we stopped at 500 generations—to find a solution that achieves about 80–90% of the fitness of the optimal solution found by the Hungarian method.

We ran more experiments with additional randomly generated synthetic datasets, ten of which with 100 flights (Cases 28–37) and another ten with 150 flights (Cases 38–47), using specific probabilities for margin widths and concentration of wished times that are described in the appendix [16]. In those datasets, margin widths are generally smaller than 70 min but there are also wider margins. Furthermore, flights generally have unique wished times, although it may also occur that the same time is wished by two or three flights, occasionally more. We obtained these probabilities from preliminary smaller datasets manually annotated by experts from Swiss International Air Lines in the course of the SlotMachine project. Real-world datasets will look slightly different, though, because the datasets we received did not take into account all operational constraints, which would result in wider margins becoming even less frequent, with margin widths usually lower than an hour.

Figure 4 shows results of selected experiments using the Cases 28–47, running the genetic algorithm with elimination of duplicates in the population but without revealing actual fitness values. In the experiments with a population size of 100 individuals, we investigated a variant of the obfuscation methods where the best solution of the population is also disclosed to the genetic algorithm, but again without revealing actual fitness values. We refer to the appendix [16] for more experimental results and additional information. In particular, we experimented with more variants of the obfuscation methods than shown in Fig. 4, using different numbers of frequency-range buckets, different numbers of order quantiles, different thresholds, different percentages of top individuals, and different estimators, respectively. We note that with a population size of 100 individuals and a problem size of 100 flights (Cases 28–37), the fitness of the best solution found after 1 500 generations typically achieves about 90% of the optimal solution found by the Hungarian method. For the larger problem size with 150 flights (Cases 38–47), more generations would be required to achieve similar results. We also note that a larger population size typically needs fewer generations to achieve solutions of similar quality, but the privacy-preserving evaluation over larger populations also takes longer (see Sect. 5).

We found out that some obfuscation methods are too restrictive regarding the information revealed to the genetic algorithm. We note that revealing the order or only the order quantiles does not make a great difference in terms of performance. The choice of fitness estimator did not impact the performance when the order or the order quantiles are revealed. We looked at the differences in performance when using five, seven, or ten quantiles; the number of quantiles seems not have a great impact on the performance. When revealing the frequency-range buckets,

Ten order quantiles with linear estimator

	Population 500 500 generations			Population 100 1500 generations		
Case	avg	min	max	avg	min	max
28	97%	95%	97%	95%	93%	97%
29	94%	92%	96%	90%	88%	92%
30	92%	91%	94%	90%	86%	94%
31	91%	89%	92%	89%	83%	91%
32	94%	92%	96%	90%	87%	92%
33	93%	91%	94%	90%	88%	92%
34	93%	91%	95%	90%	89%	91%
35	93%	90%	94%	91%	89%	94%
36	94%	93%	96%	92%	90%	94%
37	94%	91%	96%	91%	89%	92%
38	84%	82%	87%	82%	79%	84%
39	85%	84%	86%	80%	78%	82%
40	86%	84%	88%	84%	82%	86%
41	86%	83%	87%	83%	79%	86%
42	84%	81%	85%	82%	78%	85%
43	85%	82%	87%	81%	80%	83%
44	85%	82%	86%	80%	78%	83%
45	86%	81%	88%	83%	81%	84%
46	84%	83%	85%	82%	80%	85%
47	86%	85%	87%	83%	81%	86%

Twenty frequency ranges with linear estimator

	Population 500 500 generations			Population 100 1500 generations		
Case	avg	min	max	avg	min	max
28	84%	82%	87%	91%	88%	95%
29	83%	81%	85%	87%	85%	89%
30	78%	76%	79%	87%	82%	90%
31	79%	77%	82%	87%	84%	88%
32	82%	80%	83%	90%	88%	93%
33	84%	81%	87%	88%	86%	89%
34	82%	80%	86%	88%	82%	92%
35	81%	79%	84%	86%	84%	89%
36	82%	80%	83%	89%	86%	93%
37	80%	78%	83%	88%	85%	91%
38	72%	68%	74%	77%	73%	79%
39	73%	71%	74%	75%	71%	80%
40	70%	66%	75%	77%	77%	79%
41	74%	69%	77%	78%	73%	82%
42	73%	70%	75%	78%	77%	79%
43	74%	71%	76%	78%	77%	79%
44	71%	69%	76%	77%	75%	78%
45	74%	70%	76%	77%	75%	78%
46	74%	72%	78%	76%	74%	79%
47	75%	74%	77%	80%	79%	81%

Individuals above 95% threshold

	Population 500 500 generations			Population 100 1500 generations		
Case	avg	min	max	avg	min	max
28	84%	82%	86%	93%	91%	95%
29	82%	79%	86%	91%	90%	93%
30	82%	79%	86%	91%	86%	93%
31	79%	73%	82%	90%	86%	92%
32	83%	80%	86%	90%	89%	92%
33	81%	79%	83%	90%	86%	92%
34	81%	79%	81%	90%	89%	91%
35	82%	78%	85%	90%	88%	92%
36	82%	79%	86%	91%	89%	92%
37	79%	76%	82%	90%	87%	92%
38	71%	70%	74%	80%	78%	80%
39	72%	68%	76%	79%	76%	81%
40	73%	71%	75%	81%	80%	83%
41	75%	72%	77%	81%	77%	84%
42	73%	71%	75%	80%	78%	82%
43	74%	68%	79%	81%	80%	83%
44	74%	70%	78%	79%	79%	80%
45	73%	69%	75%	80%	79%	83%
46	72%	69%	74%	80%	79%	82%
47	75%	74%	76%	83%	80%	86%

Fig. 4. Average, minimum, and maximum fitness of best solutions found over five runs of the genetic algorithm, using different obfuscation methods for fitness, shown as percentage of fitness of the optimal solution found by Hungarian method

more buckets led to better results. Using only five fitness-range buckets resulted in considerably lower performance than seven buckets, using seven buckets in considerably lower performance than ten buckets. The difference in performance between using ten fitness-range buckets and twenty fitness-range buckets was less pronounced. When revealing only the individuals above a certain threshold, the higher the threshold the better the performance. For example, it takes the genetic algorithm longer to find results of a certain fitness when revealing only individuals with at least 70% of the current population's best individual's fitness compared to a threshold of 90% of the best individual's fitness.

5   Privacy Engine

In this section we first describe the implementation of the Privacy Engine and discuss performance of MPC computations before conducting a security analysis.

5.1   Implementation and Performance Evaluation

The Privacy Engine (PE) encapsulates the functionality for secure computation of fitness values of candidate solutions. The PE is responsible for the management and protection of confidentiality of sensitive input submitted by the participants in encrypted form while conducting computations over the inputs using MPC. The PE provides a REST interface for the Heuristic Optimizer to invoke the PE and employs MPC nodes, accessed via TCP protocol, to conduct the computations (Fig. 5). The nodes maintain separate TCP connections with each

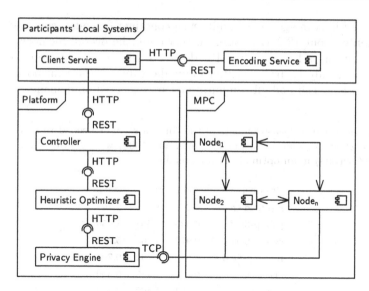

Fig. 5. Dependencies and interfaces between the participants' local systems, the platform, and the MPC nodes

other, operated and controlled by the underlying MPC framework. In addition, each participant locally runs an encoding service, which allows participants to encode/encrypt inputs before sending the inputs to the MPC nodes, preventing information leakage.

The main functionality of the PE is managing sensitive data. The PE enables the Heuristic Optimizer to compute the relative fitness of populations without revealing the underlying inputs, i.e., the submitted weights (utilities) for combinations of slots and flights. Thus, after the weight maps have been communicated to the PE, the optimizer can then invoke the PE to compute aggregates over the weights in a privacy-preserving way. If data the data is encoded and securely sent to the MPC nodes, it is guaranteed that no component of the platform has access to the sensitive input data of the participants.

The PE operates on the basis of optimization runs. An optimization run is characterized by a list of flights and a list of (time) slots as well as by the inputs (preferences) submitted by the participants. The encoding service, locally run by each participant, turns a plain-text weight map into a secret-shared form that is suitable input for the MPC nodes. The different shares are encrypted for the respective MPC nodes and sent from the participants' local systems to the PE via the platform's controller component.

The PE implementation builds on various Python libraries and integrates MPC using different frameworks. The REST interface and automatically generated online documentation is provided by FastAPI. PyInstaller is used to prepackage the code together with all necessary libraries and the Python interpreter, so that the components can be put into compact Docker containers based on the base Alpine Linux image. As a result, each container (encoder, controller, MPC node) is only about 13 MB in size. Furthermore, the overall memory footprint during execution is low since the PE do not store any data beyond optimization runs and only keeps encrypted input data during the run; no additional information is logged and all computations are executed on demand.

Table 1. Performance measurements of the time in seconds needed to sort vectors of different lengths (population size of 100, 500, and 1000) with various MPC protocols (MP-SPDZ scripts) in an optimal network setting

Protocol	100	500	1000
rep-field.sh	0.242	1.446	3.703
ps-rep-field.sh	0.535	3.568	8.656
sy-rep-field.sh	0.972	6.165	15.280
mal-rep-field.sh	0.580	3.792	10.795
atlas.sh	0.376	2.485	6.350
shamir.sh	0.184	1.163	3.077
mal-shamir.sh	0.778	5.081	12.805
sy-shamir.sh	4.489	30.130	80.043
mascot.sh	0.146	1.111	3.199
semi.sh	0.077	0.492	1.404
lowgear.sh	0.148	1.127	3.110
highgear.sh	0.151	1.118	2.955
cowgear.sh	0.155	1.137	3.041
chaigear.sh	0.149	1.122	2.997
hemi.sh	0.082	0.493	1.393
soho.sh	0.102	0.419	1.205

To estimate the overall performance achievable with the presented optimization approach, we conducted intensive benchmarking for both the sorting problem and data classification using MPC. In general we opted for a setting with three MPC nodes and support for many more input parties, which rendered two party protocols based on garbled circuits inadequate. The presented PE benchmarks were measured in a local setup on a single Intel NUC computer equipped with an Intel Core i5-8259U CPU with 2.30 GHz. We employed the MP-SPDZ framework [8], which implements multiple MPC protocols for benchmarking purposes. The protocol names refer to the respective MP-SPDZ protocol scripts[4] with default settings, e.g., *shamir.sh* refers to the honest majority protocol based on Shamir secret sharing with three nodes in the semi-honest setting. Finally, optimal network conditions were set (no delay and loss) to show the best achievable results for the given hardware platform. Performance for more diverse deployments with more delay can be estimated from the given values by adding delay time multiplied by the number of protocol rounds.

---

[4] https://github.com/data61/MP-SPDZ.

Sorting is the most important building block for the genetic algorithm running with information about the *order, order quantiles*, or *top individuals*. In those cases the population has to be sorted by fitness, which constitutes a performance bottleneck. We compared the performance of the most relevant protocols based on secret sharing for sorting populations of various sizes; Table 1 shows the results. Honest majority protocols based on replicated and Shamir secret-sharing turned out to be the best solution, which also fit our security model. Surprisingly, the online phase of dishonest majority protocols is very fast, but the computation overhead of the offline phase should not be underestimated, as can be seen by the number of triples needed for the circuit (Table 3).

Sorting is an expensive operation in MPC because of its sequential nature. Nevertheless, the achieved performance is already a major improvement compared to MPC-based Hungarian method (see [11] for detailed performance evaluation). For example, solving the flight prioritization problem for 100 flights can be expected to take up to 15 min when using an MPC-based implementation of the Hungarian method in an optimal network setting, which in the time-critical ATFM use case is not acceptable. Fitness evaluation for the genetic algorithm when conducting MPC-based sorting of a population by fitness for 1 500 generations with a population size of 100 individuals, which generally yields results achieving around 90% of the fitness of the optimal solution, takes only $1500 \times 0.077 = 115.5$ s using the semi.sh protocol (see Table 1).

From the MPC point of view, a more promising approach than sorting is classification of individuals according to fixed fitness bounds, i.e., dividing the fitness range into buckets. The main advantage of classification is that it can be done in parallel for the entire population. MPC performance is governed by communication complexity and in particular the number of rounds needed to execute a certain function, which corresponds to the multiplicative depth of the arithmetic circuit to compute. Therefore, making individual operations independent of each other, and executing the operations in parallel, reduces the multiplicative depth of the circuit and speeds up execution, especially when considering latency on the network.

In our classification experiments we determine the minimum and maximum fitness values of the population and then assign the individuals a predefined number of equally distributed buckets. The genetic algorithm running with information about the *fitness range* and *above threshold* fall into the classification category and benefit from optimized MPC processing. The corresponding performance measurements for MPC-based oblivious classification are shown in Table 2. The results of selected protocols show a significant improvement (about a factor three to five) over the sorting approach. However, with classification, the genetic algorithm generally requires more generations to achieve a similar quality of the found solution compared to sorting. Fitness evaluation for the genetic algorithm when conducting MPC-based classification of a population by fitness for 1 500 generations with a population size of 100 individuals, which generally yields results achieving about 90% of the fitness of the optimal solution, takes $1500 \times 0.017 = 25.5$ s using the semi.sh protocol (see Table 2).

Table 2. Performance measurements of the time in seconds needed for classification of 16-bit integer values into ten classes, with three different population sizes (100, 500, and 1000), using selected, optimized MPC protocols (MP-SPDZ scripts)

Protocol	100	500	1000
rep-field.sh	0.073	0.328	0.638
shamir.sh	0.074	0.329	0.680
mal-shamir.sh	0.291	1.285	2.641
mascot.sh	0.034	0.162	0.327
semi.sh	0.017	0.077	0.172
soho.sh	0.017	0.095	0.158

Table 3 shows a more detailed analysis of properties of the generated arithmetic circuits defining the MPC functions for sorting and classification. Besides substantial resource savings in terms of bits and Beaver triples, the most significant impact is on the number of rounds. Classification is particularly favorable in these regards, especially with larger vectors, where classification outperforms sorting by an order of magnitude. In general, the results also confirm the expected behavior of classification in MPC, i.e., an almost constant number of rounds independent of vector length, ideal for parallelization. The minor increase in rounds can be attributed to the max/min and bucket boundary computations, which add some rounds for larger population sizes.

Table 3. Circuit size for sort and classify, respectively, where *bits* refers to the bits needed for the computation, *triples* refers to the number of Beaver triples needed for the multiplications, and *rounds* refers to the number of communication rounds needed

	Sort			Classify		
	100	500	1000	100	500	1000
bits	157655	1037335	2558615	71078	351078	701078
triples	179462	1186694	2935686	32161	157761	314761
rounds	324	1324	3000	94	106	112

5.2 Security Analysis

The presented approach for privacy-preserving optimization of the assignment problem is based on the idea of splitting the computation into two interactive parts, one which is done obliviously on sensitive data and another part which is done in the clear. The performance advantage achieved compared to fully oblivious implementation of the Hungarian method is substantial and results from the reduction of computations done in the encrypted domain, which are time-consuming and typically slower by orders of magnitudes.

Performing certain operations in clear comes at the price of information leakage; only specific algorithms allow for this kind of partitioning. Heuristic optimization as used in our application turned out to be well suited. The challenge was to tailor the optimization algorithms in a way that they work with only minimum information to prevent attackers from compromising the private inputs (weights). Attackers having access to PE communication must not be able to recover individual weights and even for the Heuristic Optimizer the privacy property should hold. In fact, the PE only reveals relations between solutions, i.e., an ordering of solutions in the population, but no absolute quality parameter. Even with such limited information the Heuristic Optimizer is able to conduct privacy-preserving optimization with outstanding performance.

The confidentiality of inputs is governed by two facts. First, provable secure MPC protocols in the PE allow computations in a fully oblivious way. Second, the PE interface guarantees that the Heuristic Optimizer is only revealing information about the ordering of a population of correct swaps. The approach is closely related to the concept of order preserving and order revealing encryption [10], which also reveals the order between ciphertexts. In our case we do not even leak ciphertexts, which is even better. The PE serves as an oracle only revealing the ordering of swaps and, therefore, the privacy property also holds in our setting. In addition, in the case of classification, the definitive order of a population is also hidden, which further increases the difficulty for an attacker.

Interestingly, the problem of recovering weights from PE queries turns out to be impossible even if the PE is also revealing the fitness values in clear. This is due to the fact that if an attacker knows the fitness for all possible $n!$ slot permutations for a problem instance with n flights and n slots, i.e., n^2 weights, it would not be able to solve the corresponding system of equations for the weights. This is due to the special nature of the assignment problem which requires a one-to-one mapping of slot to flights and only allows for column permutations in the weight matrix. Therefore, it is important that the PE only answers correct swaps, where each flight is assigned to exactly one slot.

Table 4. Rank of equation system given by the set of all $n!$ possible swap permutations Π for given problem size n with n^2 unknown weights.

n	n^2	$n!$	$rank(\Pi)$
3	9	6	5
5	25	120	17
7	49	5040	37
9	81	362880	65

In Table 4 we show the calculated rank of the system of equations derived from querying the fitness of all possible permutations of a problem from the PE. The rank of the equation system is always smaller than the number of unknown weights (n^2). We calculated the rank for $n < 10$ and we expect this property to continue for larger n. This means that even if the PE would output individual fitness values an attacker would not be able to recover the weights directly. However, this assumption only holds if the weights are independent of each other, which is not the case in our application. Input preferences from an individual participant typically will have a certain structure, e.g., the weights of slots for flights depend on margins and priority as shown in Fig. 3, which is additional information to be used in an attack. Finally, the leakage would be input-dependent, i.e., if fitness values for two sequences that only differ in one swap are known, dependencies between weights are learned. Therefore, we are also preventing the PE from leaking the fitness values at all to achieve confidentiality according to the order-revealing security property described above.

6 Conclusions

Privacy-preserving implementations of the Hungarian method, which finds the optimal solution for assignment problems, have a considerable computational overhead. In time-critical settings, e.g., flight prioritization in air traffic flow management (ATFM), getting an optimization result of acceptable quality within a certain amount of time might be more important than finding the optimum. We introduced a distributed architecture based on genetic algorithms and multiparty computation (MPC) that allows to find solutions close to the optimum in a considerably smaller amount of time while preserving confidentiality of the submitted user inputs. Performance experiments have shown that for the flight prioritization problem in ATFM, the proposed optimization method generally finds solutions achieving about 90% of the fitness of the optimal solution found by the Hungarian method in only about one tenth to one twentieth of the time.

Acknowledgements. This work was conducted as part of the SlotMachine project. This project received funding from the SESAR Joint Undertaking under grant agreement No 890456 under the European Union's Horizon 2020 research and innovation program. The views expressed in this paper are those of the authors.

References

1. Castelli, L., Pesenti, R., Ranieri, A.: The design of a market mechanism to allocate air traffic flow management slots. Transp. Res. Part C Emerg. Technol. **19**(5), 931–943 (2011). https://doi.org/10.1016/j.trc.2010.06.003
2. Cramer, R., Damgård, I.B., Nielsen, J.B.: Secure Multiparty Computation. Cambridge University Press, Cambridge (2015)
3. Doerner, J., Evans, D., Shelat, A.: Secure stable matching at scale. In: Weippl, E.R., Katzenbeisser, S., Kruegel, C., Myers, A.C., Halevi, S. (eds.) ACM Conference on Computer and Communications Security, pp. 1602–1613 (2016)

4. Franklin, M., Gondree, M., Mohassel, P.: Improved efficiency for private stable matching. In: Abe, M. (ed.) CT-RSA 2007. LNCS, vol. 4377, pp. 163–177. Springer, Heidelberg (2006). https://doi.org/10.1007/11967668_11
5. Funke, D., Kerschbaum, F.: Privacy-preserving multi-objective evolutionary algorithms. In: Schaefer, R., Cotta, C., Kołodziej, J., Rudolph, G. (eds.) PPSN 2010. LNCS, vol. 6239, pp. 41–50. Springer, Heidelberg (2010). https://doi.org/10.1007/978-3-642-15871-1_5
6. Gale, D., Shapley, L.S.: College admissions and the stability of marriage. Am. Math. Mon. **120**(5), 386–391 (2013)
7. Golle, P.: A private stable matching algorithm. In: Di Crescenzo, G., Rubin, A. (eds.) FC 2006. LNCS, vol. 4107, pp. 65–80. Springer, Heidelberg (2006). https://doi.org/10.1007/11889663_5
8. Keller, M.: MP-SPDZ: a versatile framework for multi-party computation. In: Proceedings of the 2020 ACM SIGSAC Conference on Computer and Communications Security (2020). https://doi.org/10.1145/3372297.3417872
9. Kuhn, H.W.: The Hungarian method for the assignment problem. Naval Res. Logistics Q. **2**(1–2), 83–97 (1955)
10. Lewi, K., Wu, D.J.: Order-revealing encryption: new constructions, applications, and lower bounds. Cryptology ePrint Archive, Report 2016/612 (2016)
11. Lorünser, T., Wohner, F., Krenn, S.: A verifiable multiparty computation solver for the assignment problem and applications to air traffic management (2022). https://doi.org/10.48550/ARXIV.2205.03048
12. Menezes, A., van Oorschot, P., Vanstone, S.: Handbook of Applied Cryptography. CRC Press, New York (1997). https://doi.org/10.1201/9780429466335
13. Pilon, N., Guichard, L., Bazso, Z., Murgese, G., Carré, M.: User-driven prioritisation process (UDPP) from advanced experimental to pre-operational validation environment. J. Air Transp. Manag. **97**, 102124 (2021). https://doi.org/10.1016/j.jairtraman.2021.102124
14. Sadegh Riazi, M., Songhori, E.M., Sadeghi, A.R., Schneider, T., Koushanfar, F.: Toward practical secure stable matching. In: Proceedings on Privacy Enhancing Technologies Symposium (PoPETs), pp. 62–78 (2017)
15. Schuetz, C.G., Gringinger, E., Pilon, N., Lorünser, T.: A privacy-preserving marketplace for air traffic flow management slot configuration. In: 2021 IEEE/AIAA 40th Digital Avionics Systems Conference (DASC), pp. 1–9 (2021). https://doi.org/10.1109/DASC52595.2021.9594401
16. Schuetz, C.G., et al.: A distributed architecture for secrecy-preserving optimization using genetic algorithms and multi-party computation - Appendix. http://files.dke.uni-linz.ac.at/publications/schu22c/appendix.pdf
17. Simon, D.: Evolutionary Optimization Algorithms. Wiley, New York (2013)
18. Wilhelmstötter, F.: Jenetics library user's manual 7.1 (2022). https://jenetics.io/manual/manual-7.1.0.pdf
19. Wüller, S., Vu, M., Meyer, U., Wetzel, S.: Using secure graph algorithms for the privacy-preserving identification of optimal bartering opportunities. In: Proceedings of the 2017 Workshop on Privacy in the Electronic Society, pp. 123–132 (2017)

Data-Driven Evolution of Activity Forms in Object- and Process-Aware Information Systems

Marius Breitmayer$^{(\boxtimes)}$, Lisa Arnold , and Manfred Reichert

Institute of Databases and Information Systems, Ulm University, Ulm, Germany
{marius.breitmayer,lisa.arnold,manfred.reichert}@uni-ulm.de

Abstract. Object-aware processes enable the data-driven generation of forms based on the object behavior, which is pre-specified by the respective object lifecycle process. Each state of a lifecycle process comprises a number of object attributes that need to be set (e.g., via forms) before transitioning to the next state. When initially modeling a lifecycle process, the optimal ordering of the form fields is often unknown and only a guess of the lifecycle process modeler. As a consequence, certain form fields might be obsolete, missing, or ordered in a non-intuitive manner. Though this does not affect process executability, it decreases the usability of the automatically generated forms. Discovering respective problems, therefore, provides valuable insights into how object- and process-aware information systems can be evolved to improve their usability. This paper presents an approach for deriving improvements of object lifecycle processes by comparing the respective positions of the fields of the generated forms with the ones according to which the fields were actually filled by users during runtime. Our approach enables us to discover missing or obsolete form fields, and additionally considers the order of the fields within the generated forms. Finally, we can derive the modeling operations required to automatically restructure the internal logic of the lifecycle process states and, thus, to automatically evolve lifecycle processes and corresponding forms.

Keywords: Data-centric process management · Event log · Process improvement · Process enhancement · Generated forms

1 Introduction

Activity-centric approaches to business process management (BPM) focus on the order in which the activities of a business process shall be executed (i.e., the control-flow perspective), whereas other perspectives, such as the data required during process execution, are considered as second-class citizens [17]. Moreover, the activities of a process are usually treated as a black box by the process execution environment. As a consequence, additional efforts, such as the manual specification of the user forms implementing a human task become necessary when implementing activity-centric processes. By contrast, data-centric and -driven

© The Author(s), under exclusive license to Springer Nature Switzerland AG 2022
M. Sellami et al. (Eds.): CoopIS 2022, LNCS 13591, pp. 186–204, 2022.
https://doi.org/10.1007/978-3-031-17834-4_11

approaches to BPM (see [20] for an overview) treat data as first-class citizens by representing a business process in terms of multiple interacting objects with a particular focus on (data-driven) *object behavior* and *object interactions*. Usually, the data-driven behavior of a single object (e.g., order, invoice, or exercise) is described in terms of a *lifecycle process*, which specifies the allowed object states, the respective object transitions as well as the data required (i.e., object attributes to be set) to complete each step. In turn, this enables a white-box approach with respect to process data that allows for an increased flexibility due to declarative rules and automatically generated forms based on the respective lifecycle process logic decreasing implementation efforts. Examples of data-centric process management approaches include case handling [10], artifact-centric processes [2], and object-aware processes [15].

The automated generation of forms at runtime not only decreases implementation efforts, but also introduces challenges for lifecycle modeling. While forms are well established [7], the internal form logic is often unclear to the form modeler and implementer, respectively. In general, the order in which the fields of a form may be accessed (i.e., the logic for writing certain object attributes specified by a lifecycle state) is not always evident at lifecycle process modeling time. Moreover, end users might prefer a different sequence of filling the form fields than the one considered as being intuitive by the modeler. If the order of a generated form (i.e., the modeled sequence of writing object attributes within a state) is not intuitive for users, higher mental efforts as well as more user interactions are required and, thus, form completion times increase, while at the same time user satisfaction and effectiveness decrease [14].

In the context of data-centric and -driven process management, a lifecycle process specifies the sequence in which the various user forms as well as their form fields are displayed to users, including more complex logic (e.g., conditional form fields) as well. The order in which forms are displayed is specified by the logic between states, whereas the logic of the steps within a state determines the content of the corresponding generated form. When executing data-centric processes, event logs record about the order in which the form fields are actually filled. Thus, process mining techniques provide promising perspectives for evolving the user forms. Note that the ability to evolve user forms offers promising perspectives for evolving information systems.

The approach presented in this paper is capable of analyzing an event log, comparing it with the lifecycle process used to generate the forms, and discovering potential improvements that can be realized by adding, deleting or reordering the auto-generated forms and their corresponding fields. Moreover, the approach is able to derive the operations required to dynamically evolve the information system [4] and its lifecycle process, allowing for the auto-optimization of the generated forms at runtime.

This paper is structured as follows: Sect. 2 introduces fundamentals. Section 3 describes our proposed approach, whereas Sect. 4 elaborates on deriving corresponding positions. Section 5 describes how we identify improvements. In Sect. 6 we describe how we derive suitable improvement actions. Section 7 evaluates our approach. In Sect. 8, we relate our approach to existing approaches. Section 9 summarizes the paper and provides an outlook.

2   Backgrounds

This section introduces PHILharmonicFlows, our approach to object-centric and data-driven process management. Further, it introduces concepts for process model evolution and ad-changes used for form evolution.

2.1   PHILharmonicFlows

PHILharmonicFlows enhances the concept of data-centric and -driven process management with the concept of *objects*. In PHILharmonicFlows, each business object of the real world is represented as one object. An object, in turn, is described by its data and represented in terms of *attributes*. Its behavior is expressed by a state-based *object lifecycle process* model.

Based on PHILharmonicFlows we implemented *PHoodle*, a sophisticated data- and process-aware e-learning application, and ran it over one semester with a total of 137 users and 39890 transactions. This application includes objects such as *Lecture, Exercise, Attendance,* and *Submission.* Figure 1 depicts the lifecycle process of object *Exercise* and the auto-generated form of the corresponding state *Edit*.

Each *state* of the lifecycle process (e.g., *Edit, Published, Past Due* and *End*), in turn, may comprise several *steps* (e.g., steps *Lecture, Name, Points, Due Date* and *Exercise Files* in state *Edit*). Each of these steps refers to a write access on a specific object attribute. In other words, the steps of a lifecycle process define the attributes required to complete the state. Once all required attributes have been written, the respective state is completed, and the object may transition to its next state.

At runtime, object lifecycle processes allow for the automated and dynamic generation of forms (cf. Fig. 1 for the form of state *Edit*) based on the order set out by the lifecycle process for the steps of the respective state. Accordingly, data acquisition is based on the information modeled in lifecycle processes. The auto-generated form of state *Edit*, which is shown in Fig. 1, orders the form fields according to the internal logic of state *Edit* in the depicted lifecycle process.

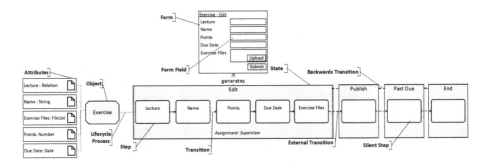

Fig. 1. Simplified exercise lifecycle process with generated form for state edit

Note that, in general, a business process not only comprises one single object, but involves multiple interacting objects such as *Submissions*, *Lectures* and *Exercises* as well as their corresponding lifecycle processes. In PHILharmonicFlows, a *data model* captures all relevant objects (including their attributes) and the semantic relations between them (including cardinality constraints) [15]. A semantic relation denotes a logical association between two objects, e.g., a relation between a *Lecture* and an *Exercise* implies that multiple exercises may be related to a single lecture.

At runtime, each object may be instantiated multiple times [4]. The lifecycle processes of different object instances are then executed concurrently. Additionally, relations between object instances instantiated enabling associations between them resulting in a relational process structure at runtime [19]. This results in novel information and intertwines the executed instances [15].

2.2 Process Model Evolution and Ad-hoc Changes

Process Model Evolution [18] and *Ad-hoc changes* [4] allow performing runtime changes to object-aware processes, including lifecycle processes and, therefore, the auto-generated forms [4]. Amongst others, corresponding changes may include the insertion, deletion and reordering of both lifecycle states and steps.

Process Model Evolution. Process model evolution is concerned with changes introduced to the process model by deploying updated process models to existing process instances [18]. In this context, *deferred process model evolution* is accompanied by the introduction of new process model versions, which may then co-exist with older model versions. Therefore, existing process instances may be executed according to the old (i.e., outdated) process model versions.

In contrast, *immediate process model evolution* tries to migrate running process model instances to the new model version, allowing for a greater flexibility at runtime. In PHILharmonicFlows, we implemented *immediate process model evolutions* [4], which additionally enable improvements of already running lifecycle process models (e.g., the insertion, deletion or reordering of the states and steps of a lifecycle process) [3]. In turn, this allows for the dynamic optimization of lifecycle processes, including the auto-generated forms, at runtime.

Ad-hoc Changes. Ad-hoc changes constitute a particular type of *immediate process model evolution,* in which a specific running process model instance becomes changed.

Ad-hoc changes allow, for example, inserting, deleting, or reordering the steps within a state of a lifecycle process instance. This, in turn, allows users to deviate from the pre-specified process model in various ways, while also reducing model complexity as not every possible execution variant needs to be modeled in advance [3]. For an in-depth introduction to ad-hoc changes, we refer interested readers to [4].

3   Proposed Approach

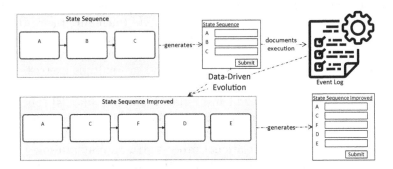

Fig. 2. Proposed approach

The goals of our approach for evolving lifecycle processes as well as their auto-generated forms are two-fold: First, we want to identify in which way lifecycle processes can be improved to minimize ad-hoc changes such as the insertion and deletion of the states and steps. Ad-hoc changes usually require some intervention from process supervisors (e.g., the approval of insertions and deletions of lifecycle states and steps). Second, we want to improve lifecycle states and, thus, the auto-generated forms, concerning the control flow logic in which the steps of a state are organized and the order in which states may become active. This allows generating more intuitive forms, that are based on actual form executions rather than on the subjective perception of a modeler during lifecycle process specification.

To identify corresponding improvements, we analyze the actual interactions users have had with the implemented system documented in an event log. Note that during these interactions, users may utilize the process flexibility enabled by PHILharmonicFlows [4], such as filling auto-generated forms in an arbitrary order or initiating ad-hoc changes (e.g., by dynamically adding or deleting form fields). We (anonymously) document these user interactions with various object instances, for example, writing attribute *Points* in state *Edit* of object instance *Exercise2*, in an event log (cf. Fig. 7). The latter is then compared with the lifecycle process model, which, in turn, enables us to automatically evolve the lifecycle processes and, thus, the forms dynamically generated during their execution.

In such an event log, one may assign a *position* to each interaction documented. We enable the comparison between modeled and actual lifecycle process behavior by assigning positions to the states as well as the steps of a lifecycle processes. This way, we may compare the position of a state or step of the model with the one recorded in the event log to discover potential improvements with respect to both the order and assignment of steps and states. We are able to detect whether steps (i.e., form fields) are filled in the pre-specified order, in the pre-specified state, and whether states or steps are added or deleted at runtime due to ad-hoc changes. Consequently, we can identify actions for evolving and improving lifecycle process models and execute them using the concepts introduced in Sect. 2.2. Our approach is illustrated in Fig. 2.

4 Position-Based Lifecycle and Event Log Representation

When comparing the lifecycle process executions captured in an event log with a given lifecycle process model, a suitable representation is required for both the event log and the lifecycle process model. This representation should enable an efficient comparison as well as the easy detection of deviations between actual behavior and the behavior captured in the lifecycle process model. In the following, we propose a *position-based approach* representing both event logs and the logic of lifecycle processes in a homogeneous way.

4.1 Lifecycle Process Step Positions

Each step is associated with two positions. The first one corresponds to its relative position within the state it belongs to (see the positions with red labels in Fig. 3), whereas the second position expresses the relative position of the corresponding state in the entire lifecycle process (see the positions with green labels in Fig. 3). Note that this distinction allows positioning lifecycle steps in relation to both the other steps of the corresponding state as well as the steps of other states.

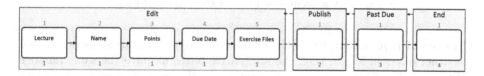

Fig. 3. Positions for lifecycle process submission (Red: Step, Green: State) (Color figure online)

As discussed in Sect. 2, lifecycle processes capture *object behavior* allowing for basic control flow patterns such as sequence and choice within and across states. While choices between states (e.g., to express that an object may transition to either state A or B) are possible, an object must not be in two states at the same time[1]. To be more precise, lifecycle processes must not contain parallel splits between states. Remember that the sequence of steps within an individual lifecycle state is utilized to auto-generate a form as well as its internal logic guiding users in filling the form fields (e.g., indicating the field to be edited next

---

[1] Note that PHILharmonicFlows allows for the concurrent processing of multiple lifecycle process instances (of same or different type) in the context of a multi-object business process. The concurrent processing is controlled by a coordination process.

after writing a specific field). Due to the high runtime flexibility of both object-aware processes and auto-generated forms, however, users need not adhere to this guidance when filling the respective forms. As soon as all mandatory attributes are set, a state may be completed independent from the order in which the form fields (i.e., steps) were actually edited. Choices within a state are represented by displaying or hiding form fields at runtime.

In the following, we present the patterns that may be used to model the behavior of a lifecycle state, the forms that can be auto-generated from these patterns, and the positions assigned to the steps of the respective state.

Sequence. If the steps of a state are organized sequentially (cf. Fig. 4), their position can be derived in a straightforward manner. To each step its position is assigned according to the order of the steps within the state (see the red numbers in Fig. 4). The form and its cursor control during form processing are organized accordingly.

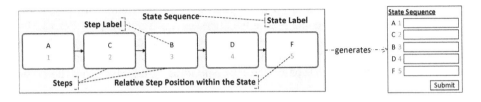

Fig. 4. A sequential state with the generated form

Choices of Equal Length. If the steps of a state are organized using a choice construct of equal length (i.e., the alternative paths all have the same number of steps, cf. Fig. 5), we derive their position by allocating the same position to multiple steps in different paths. For example, in Fig. 5, alternative steps D and B both have the same position.

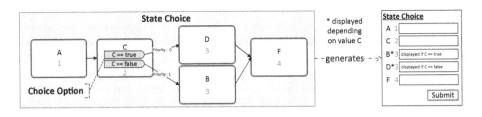

Fig. 5. A state with choice and the generated form

Choices of Different Lengths. If the steps of a state are organized using a choice construct with paths of different lengths (i.e., the alternative paths do not all comprise the same number of steps, cf. Fig. 6), the above approach must not be applied. In the lifecycle process from Fig. 6, for example, the position of the step following both alternative paths (i.e., step E in Fig. 6) depends on the path previously chosen based on the attribute value provided in the context of step B in Fig. 6. In this example, the position of step E will be 3 if the bottom path is chosen, and 6 if the top path is taken. In general, we treat each possible path of steps through the lifecycle process as an individual sequence. This enables us to properly represent positions for choice constructs of different lengths. Note that if no step joins the choice construct, each possible path through the lifecycle state is also represented as an individual sequence.

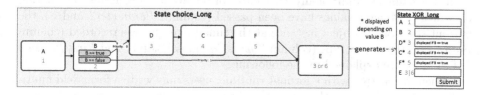

Fig. 6. A state with different length choice and the generated form

4.2   Lifecycle Process State Positions

To each state of a lifecycle process we assign a relative position as well. We can accomplish this based on the same patterns as presented in Sect. 4.1. Additionally, we assign to each step the relative position of its state as well. Consequently, to all steps of a specific lifecycle state the same number is assigned in this context. An example derived from the lifecycle process illustrated in Fig. 1 is presented in Table 1.

4.3   Leveraging Lifecycle Process Model Positions

Based on the presented patterns, to each step we can assign its relative position within its corresponding state. Moreover, to each state we can assign its relative position within the lifecycle process (cf. Table 1 for the representation of object *Exercise*). Note that the lifecycle process of object *Exercise* does not contain a choice construct, and, consequently, only pattern *sequence* is used.

Table 1. Representation of exercise lifecycle process model (derived from Fig. 1)

ObjectType	State	Step	Step position	State position
Exercise	Edit	Lecture	1	1
Exercise	Edit	Name	2	1
Exercise	Edit	Points	3	1
Exercise	Edit	Due Date	4	1
Exercise	Edit	Exercise Files	5	1
Exercise	Publish	Silent	1	2
Exercise	Past Due	Silent	1	3
Exercise	End	Silent	1	4

4.4   Event Log Positions

We now describe how we represent the position of a step regarding the actual execution of the instances of the corresponding lifecycle process. An event log generated by an object-centric and data-driven approach like PHILharmonicFlows comprises information about the execution of an object-aware process. Figure 7 depicts an extract of the event log corresponding to the execution of state *Edit* of the *Exercise* lifecycle process instance *Exercise Sheet 1*. In general, the event log records which user (column *User ID*) executes which operation (column *Method*) on which object instance (column *Instance*) at what point in time (column *Timestamp*). Additionally, each entry of the event log contains information on which parameter values have been passed (columns *Parameter1* and *2*), the current state of the object instance at the time the event was recorded (column *State*), and the object type (column *Type*). Columns *Position* and *First Position* (c.f., Fig. 7) are explained in the following.

When interacting with a form at runtime, users may write a form field multiple times, e.g., in case a value provided in a previous form field becomes changed. This behavior is then documented in the event log in terms of multiple write access events corresponding to the same form field (i.e., step). To represent the order in which the auto-generated form was actually filled at runtime, we sort the recorded events according to their timestamps and add two columns for each event log entry of an object instance. Column *Position* assigns multiple write accesses of a form field their respective positions each time. Each write access is assigned its position in the event log. Column *First Position* only reflects the order concerning first write access to a form field as only the first event log entry corresponding to a write access is documented. The difference is illustrated for step *Description* in the event log from Fig. 7. Column *Position* assigns to this step the positions 4, 6, and 7, whereas *First Position* assigns position 3 to the first access, neglecting subsequent entries. This differentiation allows customizing our approach by utilizing domain knowledge, e.g., when users change form fields regularly, *First Position* might be more suitable, whereas *Position* is able to account for, e.g., multiple interactions with a form field. Positions of states are derived in a similar way.

User ID	Instance	State	Type	Method	Parameter1	Parameter2	Timestamp	Position	First Position
employee2@uni-ulm.de	Blatt 1	Edit	Exercise	InstantiateObjectTypeAndLink	Lecture	Datenbanken	23.04.2019 09:00	1	1
employee2@uni-ulm.de	Blatt 1	Edit	Exercise	ChangeAttributeValue	Name	Blatt	23.04.2019 09:00	2	2
employee2@uni-ulm.de	Blatt 1	Edit	Exercise	ChangeAttributeValue	Name	Blatt 1	23.04.2019 09:00	3	
employee2@uni-ulm.de	Blatt 1	Edit	Exercise	ChangeAttributeValue	Description		23.04.2019 09:00	4	3
employee2@uni-ulm.de	Blatt 1	Edit	Exercise	ChangeAttributeListValue	Exercise Files	Blatt1.pdf	23.04.2019 09:00	5	4
employee2@uni-ulm.de	Blatt 1	Edit	Exercise	ChangeAttributeValue	Description	a	23.04.2019 09:00	6	
employee2@uni-ulm.de	Blatt 1	Edit	Exercise	ChangeAttributeValue	Description		23.04.2019 09:00	7	
employee2@uni-ulm.de	Blatt 1	Edit	Exercise	ChangeAttributeValue	Begin Date	25.04.2019 00:00:00	23.04.2019 09:01	8	5
employee2@uni-ulm.de	Blatt 1	Edit	Exercise	ChangeAttributeValue	Due Date	09.05.2019 00:00:00	23.04.2019 09:01	9	6
employee2@uni-ulm.de	Blatt 1	Edit	Exercise	ChangeAttributeValue	Maximum Points	25	23.04.2019 09:01	10	7
employee2@uni-ulm.de	Blatt 1	Edit	Exercise	ChangeAttributeListValue	Solution Files	Blatt1-Lsg.pdf	23.04.2019 09:03	11	8
employee1@uni-ulm.de	Blatt 1	Edit	Exercise	ChangeAttributeValue	Due Date	10.05.2019 00:00:00	08.05.2019 13:47	12	

Fig. 7. Event log positioning Phoodle excercise state edit

After grouping all event log entries by *(object) type, (object) state* and *(object) instance,* we assign positions (cf. Sect. 4) to each write access in the event log (i.e., methods *ChangeAttributeValue, ChangeAttributeListValue,* and *InstaticateObjectTypeAndLink* in Fig. 7). Note that we additionally filter the event log for the different paths of a choice construct if necessary.

We then calculate the "average position" for each step across all object instances (cf. Fig. 8). The latter correspond to the average position in which the form field is filled in by users, according to the event log. In addition, this allows ordering the fields (i.e., the lifecycle process steps) of a form (i.e., the lifecycle process states) using a ranking. Thereby, the rank of each step documents the position in which the form field was filled, whereas the rank of each state documents the position in which the form was displayed in relation to the other forms of the lifecycle process. Figure 8 depicts the positions (columns *Position Step Log* and *Position State Log*) as well as resulting ranks (columns *Rank Step Log* and *Rank State Log*) from a real-world deployment of PHoodle (cf. Sect. 7 for more details on the event log). The average position according to which, for example, step *Description* was edited is 4.6. After ranking all steps and states based on their average position in the event log, we obtain the order in which the auto-generated form fields of state *Edit* of object *Exercise* are usually filled as well as the position in which the form was displayed.

Type	State	Step	Position Step Log	Rank Step Log	Position State Log	Rank State Log
Exercise	Edit	Lecture	1,0	1	1	1
Exercise	Edit	Name	2,0	2	1	1
Exercise	Edit	Exercise Files	3,6	3	1	1
Exercise	Edit	Description	4,6	4	1	1
Exercise	Edit	Begin Date	5,6	5	1	1
Exercise	Edit	Due Date	6,2	6	1	1
Exercise	Edit	Maximum Points	6,4	7	1	1
Exercise	Edit	Solution Files	6,6	8	1	1

Fig. 8. Position and rank event log of state edit

5 Data-Driven Evolution of Forms

The following approach utilizes the positions of the states and steps in a lifecycle process as well as the positions of the corresponding entries in the event log to identify possible improvements of the lifecycle process.

In a first step, we join the two representations using an SQL-like full outer join syntax on *(object) type, (object) state,* and *step,* respectively. This enables us to compare the actual position of states and steps, as documented in the event log, with the corresponding positions according to the modeled lifecycle process.

We compare the position of a state according to the event log (cf. column *Position State Log* in Fig. 9) with the position of this state in the lifecycle process model (cf. column *Position State Model* in Fig. 9) and calculate the difference between the two. This enables us to check whether or not the order in which the forms are displayed to the users complies with the modeled order. If the two positions deviate from each other, we can determine the new position of the state. Note that for object *Exercise* (cf. Fig. 9) the order in which the forms have been displayed complied with the lifecycle process model, whereas the analysis for object *Submission* revealed that the ordering of states *Rated* and *Waiting* may be changed for the model to better comply with the actual execution recorded by the event log.

Type	State	Position State Log	Position State Model	State Difference	State Position New
Exercise	Edit	1	1	0	1
Exercise	Publish	2	2	0	2
Exercise	Past Due	3	3	0	3
Exercise	End	4	4	0	4
Submission	Edit	1	1	0	1
Submission	Submit	2	2	0	2
Submission	Waiting	4	3	1	4
Submission	Rated	3	4	-1	3
Submission	Inspected	5	5	0	5

Fig. 9. State position analysis objects exercise and submission

Furthermore, we can check whether certain steps (i.e., form fields) were never written, were written in another state (i.e., form) than pre-specified, or steps were added to a state, indicated by *NaN* values in the corresponding columns of the outer join. Step *Solution Files* in Fig. 10, for example, has not been specified in the lifecycle model as column *Step Position Model* is *NaN*, but set at (average) position 6.6 (or rank 8 respectively) in the event log. Additionally, the silent steps in states *Publish, Past Due,* and *End* have not been documented in the event log, indicated by the *NaN-values* in columns *Position Log* and *Rank Log* in Fig. 10 respectively. Note that silent steps are not recorded in the event log as no attribute is written when executing them.

Subsequently, we calculate the difference between the position recorded in the event log and the one reflected by the lifecycle model by subtracting the step position in the model from the corresponding rank in the event log (cf. column *Difference* in Fig. 10). This enables us to check which steps are placed at the correct position (i.e., column *Difference* equals 0) and which ones need to be relocated (i.e., column *Difference* does not equal 0). Steps with a difference of *NaN* are either not contained in the event log or the lifecycle model and are possible candidates for addition or deletion.

Type	State	Step	Position Log	Rank Log	Step Position Model	Step Difference	Step Position New
Exercise	Edit	Lecture	1	1	1	0	1
Exercise	Edit	Name	2	2	2	0	2
Exercise	Edit	Description	4,6	4	3	1	4
Exercise	Edit	Exercise Files	3,6	3	4	-1	3
Exercise	Edit	Begin Date	5,6	5	5	0	5
Exercise	Edit	Due Date	6,2	6	6	0	6
Exercise	Edit	Maximum Points	6,4	7	7	0	7
Exercise	Publish	Silent	NaN	NaN	1	NaN	NaN
Exercise	Past Due	Silent	NaN	NaN	1	NaN	NaN
Exercise	End	Silent	NaN	NaN	1	NaN	NaN
Exercise	Edit	Solution Files	6,6	8	NaN	NaN	8

Fig. 10. Step position analysis object exercise

6 Lifecycle Process Improvement Actions

This section introduces process improvement patterns for lifecycle processes and the improvement actions that can be derived from them. Following the patterns, we can automatically derive the modeling operations needed to evolve the corresponding process model accordingly. That means, we are able to dynamically evolve the forms during runtime using the concepts introduced in Sect. 2.2.

6.1 Correct Positions

Ideally, the states and steps are correctly positioned and the position in the lifecycle process model complies with the rank of the average position in the event log. Consequently, no actions would be required in this case as the generated form (i.e., the lifecycle state) is displayed and executed exactly according to the logic used for its generation; e.g., this applies to steps *Lecture, Name, Begin Date, Due Date,* and *Maximum Points* in Fig. 10. The steps are correctly positioned if column *Difference* equals to 0. Consequently, no improvement action is required.

6.2 Missing States and Steps

Missing states and steps can be identified based on the *NaN* values contained in the comparison depicted in Fig. 10. Certain states and steps may be missing either in the event log, if a state is never reached or a form field is never filled, or the lifecycle process model, in case a state or step is added by executing corresponding ad-hoc changes at runtime [4].

Missing states in the event log indicate that either the state has never been reached during lifecycle process execution, or it does only contain one silent step, and, therefore, no events related to that state are recorded in the event log. Note that such states are candidates for being deleted. However, as silent states are often used in the context of coordinating interacting objects, checking coordination constraints prior to the deletion becomes necessary.

If the missing state in the event log is not part of any process coordination constraint [19], it may be deleted.

Missing steps in the event log indicate that the corresponding form field has never been filled. This may be the case, for example, if steps are deleted in an ad-hoc manner or alternative paths of a choice construct have never been used. Furthermore, *silent steps* (e.g., the steps in states *Publish, Past Due,* and *End* of Fig. 1) correspond to steps in which no attribute needs to be set. To be more precise, there may be no event log entries for silent steps, as no object attributes are required. We can identify missing steps in the event log, if the step is not a silent step (i.e., column *Step* != "Silent") and columns *Position Log* or *Rank Log* contain empty values. If a step is missing in the event log, we may execute the corresponding modeling operations, i.e., the identified step and its transitions are deleted from the lifecycle process. Additionally, we reconnect the remaining steps according to the previously defined order.

Assume, for example, that step *Due Date* in state *Edit* (cf. Fig. 1) is missing in the event log, i.e., the event log does not contain any events related to this step. Step *Due Date* as well its two transitions are then deleted. Moreover, step *Points* is connected with step *Exercise Files* through a directed transition.

Missing states in the lifecycle process model indicate that an object reached a state that has not been foreseen in the lifecycle process model. This may happen if ad-hoc changes are applied to a lifecycle process at runtime, due to which a new state (and at least one corresponding step) was added to the object instance. If such dynamically defined states are recorded in the event log, they can be added to the lifecycle process at the identified position. This requires the insertion of the state, the corresponding steps, and the transitions to correctly integrate the new state into the lifecycle process model.

Suppose a new state *Pending* with attribute *Date* is added to the lifecycle of object *Exercise* between states *Edit* and *Publish* (cf. Fig. 1). This would then require the insertion of state *Pending* and attribute *Date,* the insertion of a new transition between state *Date* and the silent step in state *Publish,* and the re-linking of the existing transition from step *Exercise Files* to step *Date.*

Missing steps in the lifecycle process model indicate that steps (i.e., form fields) have been written during the execution of lifecycle process instances that were previously not specified in the lifecycle process (state). Such steps are represented in the lifecycle process part of the outer join (e.g., columns *Step Position* and *State Position* in Fig. 10). We can discover missing steps in the lifecycle process model through *NaN* values in columns *State Position* and *Step Position* (e.g., an additional form field might be required, or an attribute be written in a state other than the one foreseen in the lifecycle process model). In Fig. 10, step *Solution Files* was executed according to the event log, but is not contained in the lifecycle process and, therefore, should be added at the position suggested by the event log (cf. column *Step Position New* in Fig. 10).

As example assume, that the additional step *Solution* is required after executing step *Exercise Files* in state *Edit* (cf. Fig. 1). The needed operations are to add step *Solution,* link it to step *Exercise Files* (through an additional lifecycle transition), and re-link the existing transition from step *Exercise Files* to step *Solution*.

6.3   Auto-adjusting the Form Logic

While the previously discussed improvement actions have dealt with the addition or deletion of steps from a lifecycle process, another important aspect is to identify of the correct logic of the steps within a state (i.e., the execution order of the steps). Recall that this logic is utilized by PHILharmoniFlows to auto-generate a form with corresponding user guidance. A step executed in the context of a state might not be ideally positioned for a user filling out the form, but users may flexibly choose the order in which they actually fill in the form. The event log that records the order of the latter, therefore, contains the information "how" users interact with the form. Consequently, the actual order of the steps discovered from the event log allows re-organizing the ordering of the steps within a state. By subtracting the step position of the lifecycle process model from the rank in the event log (cf. column *Difference* in Fig. 10), we obtain the difference between the position in the event log and the position in the lifecycle process model. If this difference does not equal 0, the steps within the state are not ideally ordered, i.e., users prefer filling the form in another order. Furthermore, we can identify the new position for each step of a lifecycle process by adding columns *Difference* and *Step Position Model*.

In the comparison presented in Fig. 10, this is the case for steps *Description* and *Exercise Files*. According to the event log, the rank of the average position over all lifecycle process instances of step *Exercise Files* is 3, and 4 for step *Description* (i.e., step *Exercise Files* is executed before step *Description*), essentially switching their positions.

The modeling operations needed to implement this change are to delete the associated transitions between the states and to add new ones according to the new ordering. In the scenario described in Fig. 10, this includes the deletion of transitions between steps *Name, Description, Exercise Files*, and *Begin Date* and their re-linking by adding new transitions between steps *Name* and *Exercise Files, Exercise Files* and *Description*, and between *Description* and *Begin Date*.

7   Evaluation

To evaluate the presented approach, we applied it to an event log[2] we obtained in the context of a real-world deployment of our data- and process-aware e-learning system *PHoodle*, which we had implemented with PHILharmonicFlows. During its use, *PHoodle* replaced the established Moodle e-learning platform for a course with more than hundred students from Management Science over one semester. During this experiment we gathered the system logs from the PHILharmonicFlows process engine, including data of users (anonymized due to General

---

[2] Event log provided: https://www.researchgate.net/project/CoopIS-Phoodle-Data.

Data Protection Regulation), object instances, object states, object types, and provided attribute values, together with the corresponding timestamps (cf. Fig. 7 for an example event log). In total, the e-learning system event log consists of 39890 entries including information on 848 object instances of 9 different object types (cf. Table 2). Note that column *Number of log entries* corresponds to the number of interactions such as the setting of an attribute, including users displaying an object at a given state (e.g., a student checks the due date of an exercise). Column *Number of interactions* represents those log entries that refer to the setting of an attribute value (e.g., a supervisor provides files in step *Exercise Files* of state *Edit* - cf. Fig. 1) or to transitions between states of a lifecycle process (e.g., state *Edit* is completed and an exercise transitions to state *Publish* cf. Fig. 1).

When applying our approach to this PHoodle scenario (with First Position for lifecycle steps, cf. Sect. 4.4), we identified several potential improvements:

For object *Attendance* (cf. Fig. 11), we could derive the following improvements:

States Regarding the lifecycle process states of object *Attendance*, the comparison of event log and lifecycle process suggests moving state *Unassign Tutorial* to position 1, and state *Start* to position 2, essentially switching positions of the two states. States *Assign Tutorial* and *End* are positioned correctly.

Steps Regarding steps, the approach suggests adding steps *Lecture* (position 1) and *Person* (position 2) to state *Unassign Tutorial,* while moving the existing step *Tutorial* to position 3. Furthermore, step *Person* in state *Start* should be removed as it has never been set in the event log.

Table 2. PHoodle log statistics

Object	Number of objects	Number of log entries	Number of interactions
Person	133	290	274
Attendance	137	3233	584
Download	14	4574	152
Employee	2	14	8
Exercise	5	7323	110
Lecture	1	11741	14
Submission	498	10689	3920
Tutor	6	116	18
Tutorial	52	1910	443
Total:	848	39890	5523

For object *Exercise* (cf. Fig. 11), we propose the following improvement actions:

States The ordering of the states of object *Exercise* complies with the one recorded in the event log. Therefore, no improvement is needed.

Steps The steps corresponding to state *Edit* of object *Exercise* may be improved by switching the positions of steps *Exercise Files* and *Description* and adding the step *Solution Files* at position 8.

Object	State Analysis						Step Analysis					
	State	Log State	Model State	Difference State	Position State New	State Improvement	Step	Log Step	Model Step	Difference Step	Position Step New	Step Improvement
Attendance	Unassign Tutorial	1	2	-1	1	Move State Unassign Tutorial to position 1	Lecture	1	NaN	NaN	1	Add Step Lecture: State Unassign Tutorial, Position 1
Attendance							Person	2	NaN	NaN	2	Add Step Person: State Unassign Tutorial, Position 2
Attendance							Tutorial	3	1	2	3	Move Step Tutorial to position 3
Attendance	Start	2	1	1	2	Move State Start to position 2	Lecture	1	1	0	1	Correct
Attendance							Person	NaN	2	NaN	NaN	Remove Step Person
Attendance	Assign Tutorial	3	3	0	3	Correct	Achieved Points	1	1	0	1	Correct
Attendance	End	NaN	4	NaN	4	Correct (Silent)	Silent	NaN	1	NaN	NaN	Correct (Silent)
Exercise							Lecture	1	1	0	1	Correct
Exercise							Name	2	2	0	2	Correct
Exercise							Exercise Files	3	4	-1	3	Move Step Exercise Files to Position 3
Exercise	Edit	1	1	0	1	Correct	Description	4	3	1	4	Move Step Description to Position 4
Exercise							Begin Date	5	5	0	5	Correct
Exercise							Due Date	6	6	0	6	Correct
Exercise							Maximum Points	7	7	0	7	Correct
Exercise							Solution Files	8	NaN	NaN	8	Add Step Solution Files: State Edit, Position 8
Exercise	End	NaN	4	NaN	4	Correct (Silent)	Silent	NaN	1	NaN	NaN	Correct (Silent)
Exercise	Past Due	NaN	3	NaN	3	Correct (Silent)	Silent	NaN	1	NaN	NaN	Correct (Silent)
Exercise	Publish	NaN	2	NaN	2	Correct (Silent)	Silent	NaN	1	NaN	NaN	Correct (Silent)

Fig. 11. Excerpt of the PHoodle comparison - lifecycle process vs. Event log

We also applied the identified improvement actions to the corresponding lifecycle processes. Depending on the respective action, this either resulted in an alternative ordering of the displayed forms or forms that better comply with the actual execution through the addition, reordering or deletion of lifecycle steps. Figure 12 depicts the improvement of State *Edit* for the lifecycle process of object *Exercise* including the generated and improved forms.

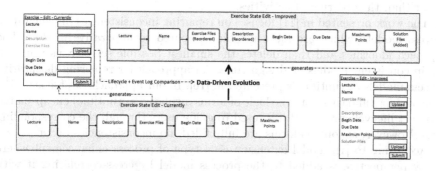

Fig. 12. Improvement of state edit for object exercise

8   Related Work

The work presented in this paper is part of two research areas: user forms in information systems and business process improvement.

User forms have already been subject to research for a long time, e.g., alignment of user form labels [12] and guidelines for usable web forms [7]. The guidelines tackle user form elements such as, for example, content, layout, input types, error handling, and the submission of user forms. However, the ordering of fields in a form is only mentioned as "keep questions in an intuitive sequence". The presented approach enables us to automatically derive such an intuitive sequence from the event log and to auto-adapt the generated forms accordingly at runtime using techniques known from process model evolution [18].

Process improvement is concerned with model repair and extension. Model repair changes a process model for it to better fit real executions, whereas extension is concerned with adding additional perspectives to a process model. Regarding model repair, [13] proposes a technique that preserves the original model structure by introducing subprocesses to the model in order to permit replaying a given event log on the repaired model. Conformance checking results are used to identify in which part of the process a subprocess needs to be added, whereas discovery algorithms mine the to-be-added subprocesses. As our approach does not follow the activity-centric paradigm (like [13] does), similarity is not a concern. Our approach changes the logic of user forms generated at runtime rather than the actual "control-flow" of the business processes. In other words, our approach improves the order and logic of forms presented to users rather than the activities to be executed. Furthermore, due to the flexible nature of forms in the context of data-driven processes, deviations (e.g., filling a form in a different order) from the modeled logic are implicitly tolerated as well.

The repair approach presented in [5] transforms BPMN process models and event logs into a Prime Event Structure (PES) to identify patterns regarding task, sequence flow, and gateway modifications. Identified discrepancies are then displayed to users on top of the model to decide on individual fixes. In contrast, our approach focuses more on the usability aspect during process execution rather than the ordering of activities.

The work presented in [11] focuses on repairing inconsistencies in declarative process models, which are more flexible compared to imperative models. The approach identifies and then deletes the smallest possible set of constraints to regain consistent models at design time. An approach for repairing declarative process models at runtime is presented in [16]. In our approach, we focus on the logic of steps (and therefore the logic of forms displayed at runtime) encapsulated in object lifecycle process states, used to guide users through the corresponding form. However, as long as forms are fully filled, no inconsistencies occur.

According to [1], model extension is "a type of process enhancement where a new perspective is added to the process model by cross-correlating it with the log.". Typically, model extension focuses on the organizational or temporal perspective. The temporal perspective [6] focuses on identifying the process fragments with extended times as interesting for process improvement actions.

In contrast, the organizational perspective [9] focuses on adding associations between roles and the execution of processes to a model.

9   Conclusions and Outlook

This paper presented an approach for automatically improving lifecycle processes based on the behavior that can be observed in an event log. We introduced various control flow patterns of lifecycle processes as well as their auto-generated form at runtime. We then characterize the steps and states of object lifecycle processes by allocating their positions. Additionally, we assign corresponding positions to the relevant log entries. The latter are then analyzed and aggregated for the event log, allowing for a representation of the average position of a step as recorded in the event log. In other words, we analyze in which order users filled in forms at runtime.

We further compare this position for each step with the modeled position. This, in turn, enables us to identify obsolete and missing steps in the lifecycle process model. Additionally, we are able to check whether the logic within lifecycle states (i.e., the user guidance when filling in forms) is ideal, or whether the user guidance can be improved by adapting the logic used to generate the form.

Additionally, we are able to derive the required modeling operations that enable PHILharmonicFlows to perform the corresponding process model evolution that implements identified improvements.

In future work we will extend the presented approach in a two-fold manner: First, we plan to combine it with conformance categories [8] and heuristics to further account for the frequency of changes to lifecycle process models. Second, we plan to use the infrequent (user-specific) behavior to individually adapt lifecycle processes based on previous executions from individual users.

Acknowledgment. This work is part of the SoftProc project, funded by the KMU Innovativ Program of the Federal Ministry of Education and Research, Germany (F.No. 01IS20027B).

References

1. van der Aalst, W.M.P.: Process Mining: Data Science in Action. Springer, Cham (2016). https://doi.org/10.1007/978-3-662-49851-4
2. van der Aalst, W.M.P., Weske, M., Grünbauer, D.: Case handling: a new paradigm for business process support. DKE **53**(2), 129–162 (2005)
3. Andrews, K., Steinau, S., Reichert, M.: A tool for supporting ad-hoc changes to object-aware processes. In: Demo Track of the 22nd International EDOC Conference (EDOC 2018), pp. 220–223. IEEE Computer Society Press, October 2018
4. Andrews, K., Steinau, S., Reichert, M.: Enabling runtime flexibility in data-centric and data-driven process execution engines. Inf. Syst. **101**, 101447 (2021)
5. Armas Cervantes, A., van Beest, N.R.T.P., La Rosa, M., Dumas, M., García-Bañuelos, L.: Interactive and incremental business process model repair. In: Panetto, H., et al. (eds.) OTM 2017. LNCS, vol. 10573, pp. 53–74. Springer, Cham (2017). https://doi.org/10.1007/978-3-319-69462-7_5

6. Ballambettu, N.P., Suresh, M.A., Bose, R.P.J.C.: Analyzing process variants to understand differences in key performance indices. In: Dubois, E., Pohl, K. (eds.) CAiSE 2017. LNCS, vol. 10253, pp. 298–313. Springer, Cham (2017). https://doi.org/10.1007/978-3-319-59536-8_19

7. Bargas-Avila, J., Brenzikofer, O., Roth, S., Tuch, A., Orsini, S., Opwis, K.: Simple but crucial user interfaces in the world wide web: introducing 20 guidelines for usable web form design. In: User Interfaces. IntechOpen, Rijeka (2010)

8. Breitmayer, M., Arnold, L., Reichert, M.: Enabling conformance checking for object lifecycle processes. In: Guizzardi, R., Ralyté, J., Franch, X. (eds.) 16th International Conference on Research Challenges in Information Science (RCIS 2022). LNBIP, vol. 446. Springer, Cham (2022). https://doi.org/10.1007/978-3-031-05760-1_8

9. Burattin, A., Sperduti, A., Veluscek, M.: Business models enhancement through discovery of roles. In: 2013 IEEE Symposium on Computational Intelligence and Data Mining (CIDM), pp. 103–110 (2013)

10. Cohn, D., Hull, R.: Business artifacts: a data-centric approach to modeling business operations and processes. IEEE Data Eng. Bull. **32**(3), 3–9 (2009)

11. Corea, C., Nagel, S., Mendling, J., Delfmann, P.: Interactive and minimal repair of declarative process models. In: Polyvyanyy, A., Wynn, M.T., Van Looy, A., Reichert, M. (eds.) BPM 2021. LNBIP, vol. 427, pp. 3–19. Springer, Cham (2021). https://doi.org/10.1007/978-3-030-85440-9_1

12. Das, S., McEwan, T., Douglas, D.: Using eye-tracking to evaluate label alignment in online forms. In: Proceedings of the 5th Nordic Conference on HCI, NordiCHI 2008, pp. 451–454. Association for Computing Machinery (2008)

13. Fahland, D., van der Aalst, W.M.P.: Model repair - aligning process models to reality. Inf. Syst. **47**, 220–243 (2015)

14. Hassenzahl, M.: User experience (UX): towards an experiential perspective on product quality. In: Proceedings of the 20th Conference on l'Interaction Homme Machine, IHM 2008, pp. 11–15. Association for Computing Machinery (2008)

15. Künzle, V., Reichert, M.: PHILharmonicFlows: towards a framework for object-aware process management. J. Softw. Maintenance Evol. Res. Pract. **23**(4), 205–244 (2011)

16. Maggi, F.M., Westergaard, M., Montali, M., van der Aalst, W.M.P.: Runtime verification of LTL-based declarative process models. In: Khurshid, S., Sen, K. (eds.) RV 2011. LNCS, vol. 7186, pp. 131–146. Springer, Heidelberg (2012). https://doi.org/10.1007/978-3-642-29860-8_11

17. Reichert, M.: Process and data: two sides of the same coin? In: Meersman, R., et al. (eds.) OTM 2012. LNCS, vol. 7565, pp. 2–19. Springer, Heidelberg (2012). https://doi.org/10.1007/978-3-642-33606-5_2

18. Reichert, M., Weber, B.: Enabling Flexibility in Process-Aware Information Systems: Challenges, Methods, Technologies. Springer, Cham (2012). https://doi.org/10.1007/978-3-642-30409-5

19. Steinau, S., Andrews, K., Reichert, M.: The relational process structure. In: Krogstie, J., Reijers, H.A. (eds.) CAiSE 2018. LNCS, vol. 10816, pp. 53–67. Springer, Cham (2018). https://doi.org/10.1007/978-3-319-91563-0_4

20. Steinau, S., Marrella, A., Andrews, K., Leotta, F., Mecella, M., Reichert, M.: DALEC: a framework for the systematic evaluation of data-centric approaches to process management software. Softw. Syst. Model. **18**(4), 2679–2716 (2019)

Automating Process Discovery Through Meta-learning

Gabriel Marques Tavares[1]([✉]) [ID], Sylvio Barbon Junior[2] [ID],
and Ernesto Damiani[3] [ID]

[1] Università degli Studi di Milano (UNIMI), Milan, Italy
`gabriel.tavares@unimi.it`
[2] Università degli Studi di Trieste (UniTS), Trieste, Italy
`sylvio.barbonjunior@units.it`
[3] Khalifa University (KUST), Abu Dhabi, UAE
`ernesto.damiani@kustar.ac.ae`

Abstract. Analyzing event logs generated during the execution of digital processes, organizations can monitor the behavior of dysfunctional or unspecified processes. For achieving the most refined results, high-quality and up-to-date process models are required. However, the selection of the proper process discovery algorithm is often addressed by human experts that can relate quality criteria, event logs behavior, and discovery techniques. Exploiting a meta-learning approach, we created a procedure that identifies the optimal discovery technique based on a user-defined balance of quality metrics. Our experiments exploited 1091 event logs representing extensive possible business process behaviors. Given a set of available algorithms, we obtained an F-score of 0.76 for recommending the discovery algorithm that maximizes quality criteria. Moreover, our method supports a more in-depth investigation of the process discovery problem by mapping log behavior and discovery techniques.

Keywords: Process discovery · Meta-learning · Model quality · Recommendation · Process mining

1 Introduction

Extracting information from event data can enhance management capabilities, revealing process deviations and improvement opportunities using techniques referred to as Process Mining (PM) [1]. One of the most active research topics in PM is Process Discovery (PD) [26]. The result of PD is a process model, which is representative of the underlying processes executions, based on the event logs recorded in organizations' information systems. PD reduces the deviations between the documented target process and the actual executed process. These deviations lead to incorrect process analyses, which, in turn, lead to little or no effective optimization measures. Nonetheless, eliciting an appropriate and up-to-date process model may require significant effort [2]. One of the key

© The Author(s), under exclusive license to Springer Nature Switzerland AG 2022
M. Sellami et al. (Eds.): CoopIS 2022, LNCS 13591, pp. 205–222, 2022.
https://doi.org/10.1007/978-3-031-17834-4_12

design choices is selecting the proper discovery algorithm among several different options [14–16, 28, 32]. Depending on the dimension to be optimized, the algorithms that offer the best performance, in terms of model quality, are different [3]. Besides, the event log characteristics also impact the model quality [3, 5]. Experiments with several different discovery algorithms showed a substantial performance complementarity since different algorithms perform best in different scenarios [5, 12]. Among the multiple quality dimensions identified, the literature has largely discussed *recall* (a.k.a. *fitness*), *precision, generalization* and *simplicity* [4]. PD algorithms are often suggested to balance these dimensions [3]. Although the analytical goal to be addressed can determine the most prominent one. For example, audit questions are best answered using a model with high recall, optimization is best performed on a model with high precision, implementation is simplified by models with high generalization, and human interpretation is eased by simple models [10]. Less attention has been devoted in the literature to studying the relationships between event log profiles, i.e., the features characterizing an event log, PD algorithms, and quality criteria.

To overcome these issues, we studied a method to *automate the selection of the optimal process discovery algorithm* given an event log. In particular, we are interested in two research questions. **RQ1**: *To which extent can process discovery algorithm selection be automated?* **RQ2**: *Which event log features are significant in selecting the best discovery algorithm?* To answer these questions, we investigate the process discovery task from an algorithm selection perspective using a Meta-learning (MtL) approach [13]. Leveraging the MtL potential, we developed a data-driven solution to recommend a suitable process discovery algorithm given an event log. Our MtL approach provides a novel tool for identifying a discovery technique that balances model quality metrics based on user preference and given a specific event log profile. Moreover, it provides a method to exhaustively compare discovery algorithms in terms of the quality metrics they optimize and to study the relationship between quality results and event log features. Our method does not prevent the use of domain-specific knowledge an expert can apply in handling the PD procedure. For example, filtering the event log or applying conformance checking results in light of organizational constraints. However, we believe connecting the event log profile to the suitable PD algorithms, is an essential pre-flight instrument our approach can provide to guide an expert. The number of source event logs and characterizing features exploited in the training of the MtL model offers a solution unparalleled in the literature and shines a light on the algorithm selection for PD.

The paper is organized as follows. Section 2 introduces concepts that support our work. Section 3 delves into the details of the proposed MtL framework, introduces the theoretical foundations required, and exposes the feature extraction step, and the materials used for experimentation. Section 4 reports the results of the experiments and presents a discussion of the relationship between the features of the event log, the discovery techniques, and the quality of the model. Section 5 discusses the related work, while Sect. 6 summarizes and concludes the paper.

2   Basic Notions

This section defines crucial concepts from PM and MtL that substantiate the development of our approach.

Definition 1 (Event, Attribute, Case, Event log). *Let Σ be the event universe, i.e., the set of all possible event identifiers. Σ^* denotes the set of all sequences over Σ. Events may have various attributes, such as timestamp, activity, resource, cost, and others. Let $\mathcal{AN}$ be the set of attribute names. For any event $e \in \Sigma$ and an attribute $A \in \mathcal{AN}$, then $\#_A(e)$ is the value of attribute A for event e. Let C be the case universe, that is, the set of all possible identifiers of a business case execution. C is the domain of an attribute $\text{CASE} \in \mathcal{AN}$. An event log L can be viewed as a set of cases $L \subseteq \Sigma^*$, where each event appears only once in the log, i.e., for any two different cases, the intersection of their events is empty.*

A model can be discovered given an event log as input. Therefore, considering the relationship between events, a process discovery technique produces a model representing the event log behavior.

Definition 2 (Process discovery [11]). *An event log L can be viewed as the multiset of traces induced by the cases in L. Formally, $\overline{L} := \{t | \exists c_i \in L, c_i(i \rightarrow n) = t(i \rightarrow n)\}$. The behavior of L can be viewed as the set of the distinct elements of $\overline{L}$, formally $\mathcal{B}(L) = support(\overline{L})$. Given a process model M, we refer to its behavior $\mathcal{B}_M$ as the multiset of traces that can be generated by its execution. A process discovery algorithm constructs a process model from an event log and can thus be seen as a function $\delta : L \rightarrow M | \mathcal{B}(L) \cong \mathcal{B}_M$.*

Therefore, the quality of the models produced can be associated with characteristics of the event log, which can potentially be mined.

Definition 3 (Event log features[22]). *Let $\mathcal{SF}$ be a set of statistical functions (e.g., mean length) and $\mathcal{RL}$ be the set of process representational levels of L (e.g., event, case, and event log). $\mathcal{PF} = \mathcal{SF} \times \mathcal{RL}$ is the set of process features, i.e., the cartesian product of functions and representational levels.*

Considering that different event logs demonstrate different behaviors, the features extracted from the logs should depict their distinctive nature. Following, discovery algorithms may produce models with varying quality depending on data characteristics. In this way, some algorithms might be favored depending on the underlying process behavior.

Definition 4 (Algorithm Selection Problem [25]). *Let $x \in \mathcal{P}$ be a problem in a problem space, let $f(x) \in \mathcal{F}$ be a function that extracts features from the problem x, let $S(f(x))$ be a function that selects the mapping between the problem space to the algorithm space $A \in \mathcal{A}$, and let $p(A, x)$ be a function that maps the performance of an algorithm to the performance measure space, i.e., $p \in \mathcal{R}^n$ where $\mathcal{R}^n$ is a n-dimensional real vector space. Then, a norm mapping is applied* on p to reduce $\mathcal{R}^n$ to a one-dimensional value that indicates the final performance of the algorithm. The goal is to determine $S(f(x))$ (the mapping of problems to algorithms) that maximizes the performance of the algorithm.

Figure 1 shows functions and their respective domains within the Algorithm Selection Problem (ASP). Given the ASP, MtL is a strategy to solve such a problem.

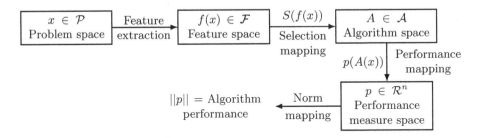

Fig. 1. Model for the Algorithm Selection Problem with features (extracted from [25]).

Definition 5 (Meta-learning [29]**).** *In traditional learning, the hypothesis space $\mathcal{H}_A$ of a learning algorithm A is fixed. Applying A to a data set described by $\mathcal{F}$ produces a hypothesis that depends on the fixed bias embedded by the learner. Let S be the space of all possible learning tasks, algorithm A can learn efficiently over a limited region R_A in S that favors the bias embedded in A. The meta-learning strategy is to learn what causes A to dominate over R_A. Therefore, meta-learning aims at mapping the relationship between the problem features and the algorithm performance.*

Moreover, the MtL problem is further divided into two parts [29]: (i) discover the properties of the task in R_A that make A suitable for such region, and (ii) discover the properties of A that contribute to dominate R_A. Hence, a solution to the MtL problem can suggest how to match algorithms and task properties, producing a guided approach to the dynamic selection of algorithms. Therefore, by applying meta-learning to the process discovery problem, we shine light on ASP for process discovery in PM.

3   Methodology

In this section, we present the procedure executed to study the applicability of MtL to the selection of process discovery algorithms. The material used in the experiments, along with the event logs and implementation, is publicly available.[1] We note that detailed instructions are given to ensure scientific reproducibility.

---

[1] https://github.com/gbrltv/process_discovery_meta_learning.

3.1   The Proposed MtL Approach

We created an MtL procedure grounded on rich PM-specific event log features (that is, mapping $f(x) \in \mathcal{F}$) for suggesting the best discovery algorithm (that is, the algorithm that maximizes $p(A(x))$). The workflow implementing our MtL approach is made up of five steps. Figure 2 presents them as follows. *Meta-Feature Extraction* is a step devoted to gathering the event log features $\mathcal{PF}$, a.k.a. meta-features according to the MtL terminology. The *Meta-Target Definition* step identifies each discovery algorithm A and ranks their dominance over R_A using quality metrics. Note that given an event log, the chosen meta-target is the technique that maximizes $p(A(x))$.

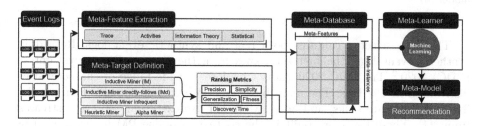

Fig. 2. Overview of the proposed MtL approach.

The *Meta-Database* step combines meta-features and meta-targets, forming the meta-instances required to train the meta-model. In the next step, a *Meta-Learner* uses machine learning to induce the meta-model based on the meta-instances. The *Meta-Model* is the outcome model able to recommend process discovery algorithms. When recommending a process discovery method for a new event log, meta-features of this new resource are extracted and forwarded to the created meta-model. The recommended discovery algorithm can be executed on the event log, generating a process model, as in Fig. 3.

3.2   Event Logs as the Problem Space

Event logs contain information about the start and completion of activities, their ordering, the resources that executed them, and the process execution to which they belong. Event logs play a significant role in our approach because they are the search space representation for creating our meta-database. Thus, we aim to build a highly heterogeneous set of logs capable of representing a wide range of possible business process behaviors. Hence, the relationship between business process characteristics and quality metrics can be better represented.

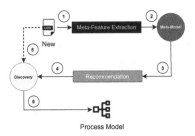

Process Model

Fig. 3. Application of our MtL approach: (1) raw event log has its features extracted, (2) features are processed using the meta-model, (3) the recommendation is outputted, (4) using the suggested algorithm, the event log is processed (5) to discover a process model (6).

The data selected contains both real and synthetic event logs. Regarding synthetic event logs, the first set comes from the Process Discovery Contest (PDC) 2020.[2] The PDC 2020 dataset explores a wide range of characteristics distributed in 192 logs. The main behaviors are dependent tasks, loops, invisible and duplicate tasks, and noise. Moreover, we extracted 750 event streams from [11]. These logs were built in the context of online PM with the goal of depicting drifting scenarios, i.e., where a change in the behavior occurs while the process is acting. The last group of synthetic logs was presented in the context of evaluating encoding capabilities in event logs [6]. The set of real-life event logs contains six logs from the Business Process Intelligence Challenges (BPIC), the environmental permit, helpdesk, and sepsis logs. The final dataset contains 1091 event logs. Their main characteristics are exposed in Table 1. As demonstrated in the table, the event logs contain a wide range of behaviors, with a diverse number of cases, events, and activities that cover a variety of patterns.

Table 1. Statistics describing our data set of event logs.

Name	#Logs	#Cases	#Events	#Activities	Trace length	#Variants
PDC 2020	192	1k	6.7k–66k	14–36	3–300	503–1k
Streams	750	100–1k	900–13.5k	15–16	2–83	22–204
Encoding	140	1k	10k–44k	22–406	1–50	383–1k
BPIC12	4	5k–13k	31k–262k	7–24	2–175	17–4.3k
BPIC13	2	1k–7k	6k-65k	4	1–123	183–1.5k
Env. permit	1	1.4k	8.5k	27	1–25	116
Helpdesk	1	4.5k	21k	14	2–15	226
Sepsis	1	1k	15k	16	3–185	841

---

[2] https://www.tf-pm.org/competitions-awards/discovery-contest.

3.3   Meta-feature Extraction

According to the Definition 4, this step maps the problem space to the feature space by extracting features from each instance of the problem, i.e., applying the function $f(x) \in \mathcal{F}$. A challenge in our approach is to correctly capture the process behavior using a representative set of descriptors. For that, we propose a large set of features that capture complementary aspects of the event log behavior. The proposed features have an extensive range of complexity, meaning that some are very simple (e.g., number of traces) while others are more complex (e.g., entropy measures). The idea of a broad set of features is to provide the meta-learner with the most information possible. The task of selecting proper meta-features to infer a model is then the following step performed by the meta-learner.

For trace level descriptors, trace lengths and variants were used as indicators of process complexity. Regarding the trace lengths, we extracted 29 descriptors: minimum, maximum, mean, median, mode, standard deviation, variance, the 25th and 75th percentile of data, interquartile range, geometric mean and standard variation, harmonic mean, coefficient of variation, entropy, and a histogram of 10 bins along with its skewness and kurtosis coefficients. Based on trace variants, we extracted additional 11 features: mean number of traces per variant, standard variation, skewness coefficient, kurtosis coefficient, the ratio of the most common variant to the number of traces, and ratios of the top 1%, 5%, 10%, 20%, 50% and 75% variants to the total number of traces. To capture the features at the activity level, we selected three groups: all activities, start activities, and end activities. For each group, we extracted a set of 12 descriptors: number of activities, minimum, maximum, mean, median, standard deviation, variance, the 25th and 75th percentile of data, interquartile range, skewness, and kurtosis coefficients.

For log level descriptors, we obtained the number of traces, unique traces, and their ratio, along with the number of events. Recently, entropy measures were proposed in the context of business processes to capture log variability and to identify whether the log is better suited to declarative or imperative mining [5]. Consequently, these metrics measure log structuredness, a very relevant descriptor of log complexity. This way, we extracted 14 entropy measures: trace, prefix, k-block difference and ratio ($k \in \{1, 3, 5\}$), global block, k-nearest neighbor ($k \in \{3, 5, 7\}$), Lempel-Ziv, and Kozachenko-Leonenko. In total, the 93 extracted features cover several complementary perspectives, such as central tendency, statistical dispersion, probability distribution shape, log structuredness, and variability, among others.

3.4   Meta-targets to be Recommended

To define the possible meta-targets, we first need to select a set of algorithms to represent the algorithm space. Considering their wide historical use in PM and the availability of reliable source code, we selected five algorithms as meta-target candidates: α-Miner (AM), Heuristic Miner (HM), Inductive Miner (IM),

Inductive Miner–infrequent (IMf), and Inductive Miner–directly-follows (IMd). All selected algorithms are suitable meta-targets in our experiment as they share the same input and output objects. They require an event log as input and express the discovered process model using the Petri net notation [20].

AM is one of the first approaches in PM that deals with concurrency. It is considered a baseline process discovery algorithm [28] as many subsequent ideas have been developed from it. Albeit AM's historical relevance, there are many known limitations such as the lack of support for loops, weakness against noise, and no consideration of frequencies [1].

To include frequencies into account, HM was introduced, applying the idea that infrequent transitions should not be represented in the model [32]. HM uses causal nets, a modeling notation that can incorporate activities and causal dependencies. A dependence measure is calculated using frequencies, and it is further used to create a dependency graph. Arcs not conforming to a threshold frequency are removed from the dependency graph. In the final step, splits and joins are introduced to represent concurrency.

The IM family of algorithms approaches the discovery problem from a divide-and-conquer perspective, recursively splitting the event log into sub-logs [14]. A crucial point of IM is that it produces a sound process model capable of replaying the entire event log. That is, perfect recall of the traces in the event log is guaranteed by the discovered model. However, due to the lack of support for duplicate or silent activities when building the process tree, IM may produce low-precision models [1]. Finally, IM is incapable of handling fixed-length repetitions and cannot handle infrequent behavior.

The basic IM algorithm is highly extendable. Thus, many variants have been proposed [15,16]. IMf incorporates the eventually-follows relation to better deal with incompleteness in event logs [15]. Moreover, IMf introduces activity and arc filters to remove infrequent behavior and produces a more precise model. As a consequence, perfect recall is not a guarantee. A drawback of both IM and IMf is the scalability due to the recursive split, which requires multi-pass analysis. IMd was proposed to overcome this problem [16]. For that, IMd performs the recursive step only on the directly-follows graph, without partitioning sub-logs. However, the non-partitioning adaptation hurts the rediscoverability property. Hence, perfect recall is not preserved. Similar to IM, IMd also cannot handle duplicate and silent activities.

3.5   Ranking Quality Criteria

The meta-database regards a suitable matching of meta-instances and meta-targets. The definition of the best choice of meta-target for a given event log is based on a ranking strategy considering several complementary perspectives, i.e., there is no unique dimension that captures the overall model quality. In this work, together with *discovery time*, we adopt the four traditional model quality metrics used in PM: *fitness*, *precision*, *generalization* and *simplicity*.

The *fitness* metric aims to measure how much behavior in the log is allowed by the model, that is, to which extent traces in the log compare to valid execution paths derived from the model [9]. It is measured by applying replay techniques that aim to compare log and model. Therefore, perfect fitness is achieved when the model can replay all the traces in the log. In this work, we adopt the fitness proposed in [7] due to its improvements in scalability and avoidance of known problems such as token flooding. Another quality dimension, *precision*, measures the extent of the behavior allowed by the model that is not observed in the log [9]. A poor precision indicates an underfitted model, i.e., it allows too many patterns not present in the event log. As the precision measures negative examples, i.e., the behavior allowed by the model but not seen in the log, and a model can potentially generate infinite behavior, the calculation is complex and often depends on approximation. In our experiment, we adopt the precision proposed in [19] because it is more efficient and granular than previous measures.

Generalization goes in the opposite direction by measuring model overfitting. Event logs present a sample of possible behavior allowed by the system, implying that there may be valid execution traces not present in the log because they were not executed yet. Process models should then describe the log behavior but also generalize it to some extent [1,9]. We adopt the computation proposed in [9] as it covers the generalization based on the usefulness of the model. *Simplicity* is the last quality dimension used in this work. The idea behind simplicity is to indicate how complex a model is [1,9]. That is, the simpler the model structure that reflects the log behavior, the better its intelligibility. We adopt the simplicity measure proposed in [30], which is based on the weighted average degree of a place/transition in the Petri net, ultimately defined by the sum of input and output arcs.

Recognizing the importance of balancing perspectives to achieve an adequate model, we propose a ranking mechanism that aggregates all dimensions. Table 2 provides an example of the ranking to identify the best discovery technique for a single event log. The log L is submitted to three discovery algorithms (A_1, A_2, A_3), then three quality metrics (Q_1, Q_2, Q_3) are extracted using the discovered model. Following, a positional rank is built for each metric considering the performance of the algorithms (R_{Q_1}, R_{Q_2}, R_{Q_3}), that is, algorithms are assigned to a position based on the comparison within them. A final rank (R) is produced by averaging the metrics ranks, i.e., the mean of $\{R_{Q_1}, R_{Q_2}, R_{Q_3}\}$. The lowest R is selected as the best discovery algorithm because it minimizes the average rank position, thus maximizing the quality criteria. In our example, $R(A_1)$ is 1.75, $R(A_2)$ is 1.5, and $R(A_3)$ is 2.75. Thus, we can conclude that A_1 is the discovery algorithm that produces the best model for log L. Therefore, when building the meta-database, A_1 is the meta-target associated with log L. Depending on the analytical goal, alternative quality metrics could be included or alternative weights could be assigned to the obtained ranks. To exemplify this possibility, in our work we consider discovery time as a quality dimension.

Table 2. Example of ranking algorithms. The final rank (R) is generated from the average rank of each quality dimension. In this example, A_1 is the recommended discovery technique for log L as it maximizes the quality metrics, i.e., produces the lowest R value.

Log	Algorithm	Q_1	Q_2	Q_3	R_{Q_1}	R_{Q_2}	R_{Q_3}	R
L	A_1	1	0.27	0.93	1	2	1	1.33
L	A_2	0.98	0.38	0.91	3	1	2	2
L	A_3	0.99	0.2	0.9	2	3	3	2.67

3.6   Meta-model

In the final step of our experiment, a machine learning algorithm, the meta-learner, is employed to induce a meta-model using the meta-database. Once the meta-model has been created, any event log can be linked to the recommended PD algorithm by extracting its meta-features and consulting the meta-model. For this experiment, we used a Random Forest [8] classifier due to its well-known stability. A holdout strategy was applied to divide the meta-database into train and test sets, using a 75%/25% split. In generating the meta-model, we performed a 30-fold cross-validation to reduce the influence of outliers. We note that the meta-database, as tabular data, represents a classification problem modeled using traditional machine learning techniques. The use of deep learning is not feasible as (i) it requires a huge amount of instances (hundreds of thousands) and (ii) the data are not sequential.

4   Results and Discussion

Figure 4a reports the discovery algorithm's average position across all event logs considering the five quality criteria. These results already confirm theoretical findings. For instance, IM's *fitness* takes the three first positions. Both IMd and IMf do not guarantee perfect fitness; still, they perform better than AM and HM. Considering that IMd does not partition sub-logs, such an important characteristic of its predecessor, the fitness result is good. Although IMf incorporates the eventually-follows relation, it performs worse than IMd from a fitness perspective. HM and AM follow with 3.1 and 4.9 average positions. AM is by far the worst-performing algorithm for fitness purposes, a problem recognized since its inception. The inability to deal with incompleteness and weakness in handling noise has a high toll on fitness performance. Another explanation for the IM family overcoming HM and AM is that IM algorithms produce a sound model, while HM and AM do not have this guarantee.

Positions change considerably when evaluating *precision*. AM becomes the algorithm with the best performance (1.4), followed by HM (1.8). IMf, IM, and IMd come next, averaging 3, 3.9, and 4.7, respectively. The IM family performs poorly in precision due to its extensive use of hidden transitions, which contributes to creating underfitting models. On the contrary, AM and HM hold superior control of the escaping edges, strengthening the precision values.

From the *generalization* perspective, IMf is the best algorithm (1.7), closely followed by AM (1.9). These algorithms excel in generating balanced models where different regions are similarly visited during trace replaying. Particularly, IMf's ability to remove infrequent behavior reflects in good generalization values. Indeed, including low-frequency traces in the model hurts the generalization capabilities. IM, IMd, and HM averaging 3, 3.6, and 4.6 are the worst-performing discovery algorithms in this dimension. *Simplicity* is an index that uniquely depends on the model and it rewards conciseness. Again, IMf is the best performing method (1.4) thanks to its cleaning procedures that remove infrequent behavior. IM and HM follow averaging 2.5 and 2.8, and IMd and AM produce the most complex models, averaging 4 and 4.2, respectively.

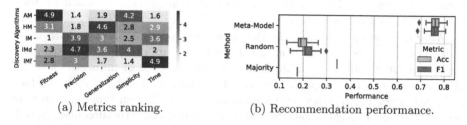

(a) Metrics ranking.   (b) Recommendation performance.

Fig. 4. a) Discovery algorithms ranked across all event logs considering each dimension. b) Our approach obtained an average accuracy of 0.76 and an F-score of 0.76. Given event log features, the method indicate the discovery algorithm that maximizes model quality. This experiment compares five discovery algorithms using five quality dimensions (fitness, precision, generalization, simplicity and time).

Time analysis tends to benefit simpler algorithms as they require fewer steps to generate a model. This explains why AM has the best time performance, averaging 1.6. IMd comes after (2) since its primary design purpose is focused on time improvement. HM, a more robust algorithm, comes third with 2.9 as the average. Lastly, IM and IMf average at 3.6 and 4.9. These two algorithms are the slowest as they demand a multi-pass recursive analysis of the log. Especially, IMf spends more time due to additional steps to remove infrequent behavior.

Following, we evaluate the meta-model's efficiency to recommend the best discovery method for a given event log. Not having other literature references, we used majority voting and random selection as baseline approaches, employed for comparison reasons. Majority voting works by indicating the class that appears most frequently in the meta-database, i.e., the algorithm that appears most frequently in the first position of the rank function (R) considering the complete meta-database. Random selection is a method that randomly chooses one of the five process discovery techniques. That is, given a meta-instance, the random selection approach arbitrarily associates it to one of the five meta-targets.

Both baselines are useful comparisons. From the machine learning perspective, majority voting is valid as it sets the minimum performance threshold. Complimentarily, the random selection approach simulates a practitioner that makes a non-guided choice of a PD algorithm.

Performance metrics are computed by comparing the ground-truth label, i.e., the best discovery algorithm and the recommended algorithm. Figure 4b presents the results for all methods, which were measured using the accuracy and F-score metrics. Our approach demonstrates a viable solution for recommending discovery algorithms with an average accuracy of 0.76 and an F-score of 0.76. The majority method has the next best accuracy (0.34), followed by the random method (0.2). Regarding F-score, random selection reaches 0.22 while majority voting stays at 0.18. The advantage of applying MtL in comparison to unintelligent approaches is clear. More importantly, the experiment confirms the relationship between event log characteristics and model quality depending on the discovery technique. Instead of simply applying the algorithm that ranks better according to the majority criterion, we can provide a guided decision based on the process behavior.

After meta-model learning, the Random Forest provides an *importance* measure to quantify the contribution of each meta-feature provided to the classification output. Figures 5a and 5b show that among the most influential features (Fig. 5a), there is a high predominance of the entropy family, namely, k-block difference, Lempel-Ziv, trace, and k-nearest neighbor. The entropy features were designed to capture log complexity and, more specifically, structuredness. Activities appear as the second most important group, with the 25th percentile ranking as the most informative feature. The activity and entropy groups are correlated as both rely on activity information. Trace variants are the last group among the top 10 most influential features with the number of unique traces. These results highlight that high-level descriptors for event logs can aid in determining the best discovery algorithm. Regarding the least influential features (Fig. 5), trace length-based features have the most appearances. These results indicate that both the number of traces and trace lengths are the worst features to describe business process behavior for the discovery problem.

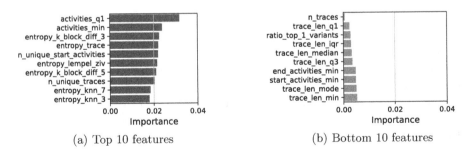

(a) Top 10 features   (b) Bottom 10 features

Fig. 5. Features relevance to induce a meta-model recommending a discovery algorithm.

4.1   Relating Problem, Feature and Algorithm Spaces

In the next experiment, we employed a leave-one-out cross-validation (LOOCV) strategy for testing the meta-model. The LOOCV approach consists of inferring a model using all instances except one, then testing the prediction in the instance excluded from training. The process is repeated for all instances. This way, a model is learned and tested $\#MI$ times, with $\#MI$ being the number of meta-instances. This analysis produced 0.78 in both accuracy and F-score. These results go in line with the previous experiment (see Fig. 4b), again confirming the method's robustness. Here we also evaluated more closely the performances related to specific meta-targets. For example, IMd was the most challenging class to identify, reaching an F-score of 0.09. This extreme performance is due to the low number of appearances as a meta-target (only 13 meta-instances were matched to IMd). Obviously, the meta-model was unable to learn the event log profiles associated with IMd, given the small set of examples to generalize. Performance changes considerably for HM and IM with 0.71 and 0.73 as F-score, respectively. HM is not an easy meta-target to recognize since it usually produces models that balance well the analyzed quality criteria. However, very rarely it maximizes the performance in one of the criteria. IM can potentially be misidentified due to its proximity to other methods from the same family. The best individual performances were reached by IMf and AM with F-scores of 0.79 and 0.86. The meta-model can more easily associate meta-instances with these methods, meaning that event log behaviors that match such algorithms were better captured by the framework.

Furthermore, we applied a dimensionality reduction technique to better visualize the meta-instances in the feature space. For that, we employed the Principal Component Analysis (PCA) algorithm [27]. Figure 6 shows the resulting feature space reduced to two dimensions. First, we note that one Principal Component (PC) explains 55.11% of data variance while the second PC explains 30.53% variance. These results indicate that most data correlations were preserved after the dimensions were reduced. Regarding class separation, we can observe that AM, IM, and IMf are the most identifiable meta-targets. This explains why in the LOOCV experiment, these three meta-targets obtained the best F-scores. AM is spread across PC1 with an evident distance from other classes. When combining PC1 and PC2, we observe that IM and IMf are also recognizable. In a particular region, several instances of different classes overlap. This behavior is due to (i) information that supports the mapping of this region was lost during the dimensionality reduction and (ii) lack of meta-features that capture additional behavior in the problem space. Figure 6 also depicts the correct and incorrect predictions in the LOOCV experiment. As the feature space shows, recommendation errors occur across the whole space, and no particular pattern was identified. Overall, the PCA analysis shows that meta-features were able to differentiate the processes' behaviors. Considering the limited dimension of the problem space, increasing the number of meta-instances and meta-features will probably lead to better class separation, hence, better recommendation performances.

Finally, we also applied a complexity analysis to complement the evaluation of class separation based on the work of Lorena et al. [17]. The Directional-vector Maximum Fisher's Discriminant Ratio (F1v) metric searches for a vector that can separate classes after instances are projected in the hyperplane. F1v is bounded by $(0, 1]$ interval with lower values indicating simpler classification problems. When applied to our meta-database, we obtain an F1v of 0.12, indicating that the classification problem (modeled using the meta-learner) is simple. The classification problem can only be simple because the $f(x) \in \mathcal{F}$ function preserves most of the behavior in the problem space when mapping instances into the feature space. In other words, our set of meta-features has a comprehensible quality. We also assessed the Ratio of Intra/Extra Class Nearest Neighbor Distance (N2) metric, which aims at capturing the shape of the decision boundary and class overlap. N2 relates the intra- and extra-class distances by comparing each instance to its closest sample from the same class and closest sample from another class. Ideally, instances from the same class should be closer between them than from instances from other classes. The N2 for our meta-database is 0.35 (optimal value is 0), indicating a simpler problem where the overall distance for different classes is higher than the overall distance to the same class. Although pointing to a simpler problem, N2 indicates that there is indeed some overlap between classes, which is corroborated by the PCA analysis (Fig. 6).

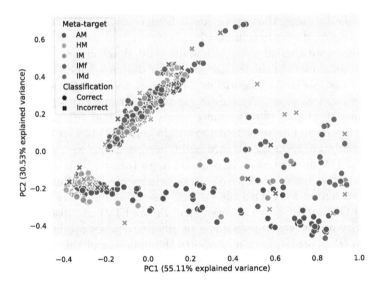

Fig. 6. Reduced feature space after applying PCA. Meta-targets have different coloring, while shapes indicate if the model correctly predicted the meta-target.

4.2   Threats to Validity

A crucial aspect of an experimental design is internal validity. Mendling et al. [18] stated that a research design is internally valid when its manipulation is causally responsible for an observed effect. Therefore, randomization is often adopted to avoid the injection of confounding factors through data selection. In our experiment, one could argue that the training dataset, although wide, may contain unidentified bias due to the unbalanced representation of some log profiles. To confute this conjecture we compared the results obtained in our first experiment, illustrated in Fig. 4b, to the results that can be obtained by resampling the dataset. In practical terms, we divided the meta-database into 10 bins considering the *activities_q1* meta-feature since it showed a considerable representational capability as the best-ranked descriptor (see Fig. 5a). Then, by randomly selecting a fixed number of samples per bin, we created a resampled meta-database, which was submitted to the same testing pipeline. Table 3 shows the accuracy and F-score performances considering the increasing size of sampled instances from each bin. As the number of selected meta-instances increases, accuracy and F-score also increase, converging to the performance obtained using the complete meta-database. This confirms the validity of our approach that, using cross-validation, was able to generalize well.

Table 3. Resampling experiment performance.

#Samples per bin	5	10	20	30	40	50
Meta-database size	42	82	148	198	246	286
Accuracy	0.54	0.6	0.67	0.7	0.72	0.72
F-score	0.49	0.56	0.64	0.68	0.71	0.71

5 Related Work

Most literature regarding the evaluation of process discovery algorithms aims to compare these techniques rather than selecting the most suitable for a given event log. In general, these frameworks create a knowledge base to support the comparison of different discovery techniques using real and synthetic event logs. An approach to recommend process discovery techniques for event logs is presented in Ribeiro et al. [24]. The authors propose a solution using a portfolio-based algorithm selection strategy to feed a recommender system. The portfolio is built using 12 log features and tested in 13 event logs. A subsequent problem was studied by Ribeiro et al. in [23] where the authors proposed a methodology based on a sensitivity analysis technique to evaluate the impact of parameter setting on process discovery algorithms. With the goal of computing model similarity among different techniques, Wang et al. [31] presented an approach based on behavioral and structural measures of process models. The information generated in the evaluation step supported the recommendation of PM algorithms. However, the need for high-quality reference models poses an important constraint to this technique. Alfonso et al. [21] constructed a knowledge base using standard model features such as control-flow patterns, invisible tasks, and infrequent behavior. The goal is to propose a group of classifiers that could associate features with predefined quality metrics the extracted models have to satisfy. However, the recommendation approach is based on model features, which are not available in scenarios where there is no gold model. On the other hand, our approach is suitable in more general scenarios since it is unsupervised, meaning it does not rely on model features (our meta-features are extracted directly from event logs).

Research developed in [24] is the most closely related to this article. The authors framed the problem from a portfolio-based selection perspective while we use MtL. We build upon this original contribution by scaling the set of log features and instances. Moreover, we rely on a single model for recommendation while the reference work builds several models, with a negative impact on computing resource consumption. Finally, we leverage the problem formalization, enabling the application of a different set of experiments to study the discovery algorithms and the discovery problem. This construction paves the way for analyzing the relationship between process behavior, discovery algorithms, and quality criteria (as seen in Sect. 4.1).

6   Conclusion

Discovering a model for an event log is a difficult task due to the many available algorithms and characteristics of business processes. This work proposes an MtL approach to map event log profiles, discovery algorithms, and quality criteria. We propose a set of 93 meta-features extracted from the event logs to capture the behavior of the process at different levels, such as activity, trace, and log. Using MtL, we show that it is possible to take advantage of the quality of the process model by automatically recommending the appropriate discovery algorithms, answering *RQ1*. The best-fitting discovery method is one that maximizes output quality based on a set of metrics. Our approach correctly assigns the best technique with 76% of accuracy in scenarios of five discovery algorithms. Overall, the method confirms the results previously discussed in the literature, but our research design provides a more rigorous evaluation of them and reveals more details on feature importance. Due to space limitations, we did not demonstrate the ability of our framework to provide information for each specific event log. However, the framework can identify the recommended algorithm for each event log and which features triggered the suggestion. Furthermore, the proposed MtL approach is highly extensible, allowing the possibility of adding more features, discovery algorithms, and quality metrics. This way, our approach paves the way for a set of experimental analyses that can further verify how generalizable is the relationship between PM tasks and event log features. For instance, we showed that entropy and activity-related features are the most important in describing log behavior for the process discovery problem, answering *RQ2*. As future work, we plan to increase *problem*, *feature*, *algorithm* and *performance spaces* to comprehend how more complex scenarios can impact MtL performance. Further, we also aim at investigating optimization techniques to increase the quality of the recommendations.

References

1. van der Aalst, W.M.P.: Process Mining: Data Science in Action, 2nd edn. Springer, Heidelberg (2016). https://doi.org/10.1007/978-3-662-49851-4
2. Van der Aalst, W.M., Rubin, V., Verbeek, H., van Dongen, B.F., Kindler, E., Günther, C.W.: Process mining: a two-step approach to balance between underfitting and overfitting. Softw. Syst. Model. **9**(1), 87 (2010). https://doi.org/10.1007/s10270-008-0106-z
3. Augusto, A., et al.: Automated discovery of process models from event logs: review and benchmark. IEEE Trans. Knowl. Data Eng. **31**(4), 686–705 (2019)
4. Augusto, A., Conforti, R., Dumas, M., La Rosa, M., Polyvyanyy, A.: Split miner: automated discovery of accurate and simple business process models from event logs. Knowl. Inf. Syst. **59**(2), 251–284 (2018). https://doi.org/10.1007/s10115-018-1214-x
5. Back, C.O., Debois, S., Slaats, T.: Entropy as a measure of log variability. J. Data Semant. **8**(2), 129–156 (2019)
6. Barbon Junior, S., Ceravolo, P., Damiani, E., Marques Tavares, G.: Evaluating trace encoding methods in process mining. In: Bowles, J., Broccia, G., Nanni, M. (eds.) DataMod 2020. LNCS, vol. 12611, pp. 174–189. Springer, Cham (2021). https://doi.org/10.1007/978-3-030-70650-0_11
7. Berti, A., van der Aalst, W.M.P.: Reviving token-based replay: increasing speed while improving diagnostics. In: van der Aalst, W.M.P., Bergenthum, R., Carmona, J. (eds.) Proceedings of the International Workshop on Algorithms Theories for the Analysis of Event Data 2019 ATAED@Petri Nets/ACSD 2019. CEUR Workshop Proceedings, vol. 2371, pp. 87–103. CEUR-WS.org (2019)
8. Breiman, L.: Random forests. Mach. Learn. **45**(1), 5–32 (2001)
9. Buijs, J.C.A.M., van Dongen, B.F., van der Aalst, W.M.P.: Quality dimensions in process discovery: the importance of fitness, precision, generalization and simplicity. Int. J. Coop. Inf. Syst. **23**(01), 1440001 (2014)
10. Buijs, J.C.A.M., van Dongen, B.F., van der Aalst, W.M.P.: On the role of fitness, precision, generalization and simplicity in process discovery. In: Meersman, R., et al. (eds.) OTM 2012. LNCS, vol. 7565, pp. 305–322. Springer, Heidelberg (2012). https://doi.org/10.1007/978-3-642-33606-5_19
11. Ceravolo, P., Tavares, G.M., Junior, S.B., Damiani, E.: Evaluation goals for online process mining: a concept drift perspective. IEEE Trans. Serv. Comput. **15**, 2473–2489 (2020)
12. De Weerdt, J., De Backer, M., Vanthienen, J., Baesens, B.: A multi-dimensional quality assessment of state-of-the-art process discovery algorithms using real-life event logs. Inf. Syst. **37**(7), 654–676 (2012)
13. He, X., Zhao, K., Chu, X.: AutoML: a survey of the state-of-the-art. Knowl.-Based Syst. **212**, 106622 (2021)
14. Leemans, S.J.J., Fahland, D., van der Aalst, W.M.P.: Discovering block-structured process models from event logs - a constructive approach. In: Colom, J.-M., Desel, J. (eds.) PETRI NETS 2013. LNCS, vol. 7927, pp. 311–329. Springer, Heidelberg (2013). https://doi.org/10.1007/978-3-642-38697-8_17
15. Leemans, S.J.J., Fahland, D., van der Aalst, W.M.P.: Discovering block-structured process models from event logs containing infrequent behaviour. In: Lohmann, N., Song, M., Wohed, P. (eds.) BPM 2013. LNBIP, vol. 171, pp. 66–78. Springer, Cham (2014). https://doi.org/10.1007/978-3-319-06257-0_6

16. Leemans, S.J.J., Fahland, D., van der Aalst, W.M.P.: Scalable process discovery with guarantees. In: Gaaloul, K., Schmidt, R., Nurcan, S., Guerreiro, S., Ma, Q. (eds.) CAISE 2015. LNBIP, vol. 214, pp. 85–101. Springer, Cham (2015). https://doi.org/10.1007/978-3-319-19237-6_6

17. Lorena, A.C., Garcia, L.P.F., Lehmann, J., Souto, M.C.P., Ho, T.K.: How complex is your classification problem? A survey on measuring classification complexity. ACM Comput. Surv. **52**(5), 1–34 (2019)

18. Mendling, J., Depaire, B., Leopold, H.: Theory and practice of algorithm engineering (2021)

19. Muñoz-Gama, J., Carmona, J.: A fresh look at precision in process conformance. In: Hull, R., Mendling, J., Tai, S. (eds.) BPM 2010. LNCS, vol. 6336, pp. 211–226. Springer, Heidelberg (2010). https://doi.org/10.1007/978-3-642-15618-2_16

20. Murata, T.: Petri nets: properties, analysis and applications. Proc. IEEE **77**(4), 541–580 (1989)

21. Pérez-Alfonso, D., Yzquierdo-Herrera, R., Lazo-Cortés, M.: Recommendation of process discovery algorithms: a classification problem. Res. Comput. Sci **61**, 33–42 (2013)

22. Pourbafrani, M., van der Aalst, W.M.P.: Extracting process features from event logs to learn coarse-grained simulation models. In: La Rosa, M., Sadiq, S., Teniente, E. (eds.) CAiSE 2021. LNCS, vol. 12751, pp. 125–140. Springer, Cham (2021). https://doi.org/10.1007/978-3-030-79382-1_8

23. Ribeiro, J., Carmona, J.: A method for assessing parameter impact on control-flow discovery algorithms, pp. 83–96. CEUR-WS.org (2015)

24. Ribeiro, J., Carmona, J., Mısır, M., Sebag, M.: A recommender system for process discovery. In: Sadiq, S., Soffer, P., Völzer, H. (eds.) BPM 2014. LNCS, vol. 8659, pp. 67–83. Springer, Cham (2014). https://doi.org/10.1007/978-3-319-10172-9_5

25. Rice, J.R.: The algorithm selection problem. In: Advances in Computers, vol. 15, pp. 65–118. Elsevier (1976)

26. dos Santos Garcia, C., et al.: Process mining techniques and applications a systematic mapping study. Expert Syst. Appl. **133**, 260–295 (2019)

27. Tipping, M.E., Bishop, C.M.: Mixtures of probabilistic principal component analyzers. Neural Comput. **11**(2), 443–482 (1999)

28. van der Aalst, W., Weijters, T., Maruster, L.: Workflow mining: discovering process models from event logs. IEEE Trans. Knowl. Data Eng. **16**(9), 1128–1142 (2004)

29. Vilalta, R., Drissi, Y.: A perspective view and survey of meta-learning. Artif. Intell. Rev. **18**(2), 77–95 (2002)

30. Vázquez-Barreiros, B., Mucientes, M., Lama, M.: ProDiGen: mining complete, precise and minimal structure process models with a genetic algorithm. Inf. Sci. **294**, 315–333 (2015)

31. Wang, J., Wong, R.K., Ding, J., Guo, Q., Wen, L.: Efficient selection of process mining algorithms. IEEE Trans. Serv. Comput. **6**(4), 484–496 (2013)

32. Weijters, A., Aalst, W., Medeiros, A.: Process mining with the heuristics miner-algorithm. BETA Working Paper Series, WP 166, Eindhoven University of Technology, Eindhoven (2006)

Random-Value Payment Tokens for On-Chain Privacy-Preserving Payments

Tiphaine Henry[1,2]([✉]), Julien Hatin[2], Léo Kazmierczak[3], Nassim Laga[2], Walid Gaaloul[1], and Emmanuel Bertin[2]

[1] Telecom SudParis, Institut Polytechnique de Paris, Paris, France
[2] Orange Labs, Paris, France
tiphaine.henry@orange.com
[3] Grenoble INP - Phelma, Grenoble, France

Abstract. Blockchain has been proposed as a trusted execution system, ensuring business process execution integrity and transparency. Smart contracts can manage the task or workflow execution and the allocation of tasks in a decentralized and reliable fashion. Nonetheless, blockchain transactions are public and accessible to their participants, and the issue of privacy is a well-known issue of blockchain systems for business process management. In the example of a service payment occurring after a sealed-bid auction, participants may not be willing to reveal the value of the accepted bid to other competitors. In this paper, we leverage smart contracts and a bank that manages per-collaboration payment tokens. The tokens are backed with fiat money with a conversion rate that is kept secret between payment partners and the bank. Hence, partners benefit from the interests of smart contracts such as autonomous programmable payment while preserving the confidentiality of the payment value. We implement this protocol in a real-world setting to demonstrate the approach's feasibility, and we carry on quantitative experiments to confirm the validity of the protocol.

Keywords: Smart-contracts · Privacy-preserving payment · Tokens

1 Introduction

Providing privacy and auditability of payment on blockchain systems has been a subject of concern in the literature since the beginning of bitcoin and cryptocurrencies [1], and most especially in the context of business process collaborations. Indeed, smart contracts can realize the binding and manage service completion for business process traceability, and automation purposes [2,3].

Such smart-contract-mediated collaborations often take place in a competitive environment where competitors agree on using the same blockchain to gain economic costs. For example, competitors may bid for a service provisioning managed by a smart contract. Hence, privacy of sensitive information is at stake and must be ensured to foster the adoption of these systems.

M. Sellami et al. (Eds.): CoopIS 2022, LNCS 13591, pp. 223–241, 2022.
https://doi.org/10.1007/978-3-031-17834-4_13

Additionally, auditability of the assignment and payment decisions are necessary to ensure trust in the system. If a claim occurs, participants must be able to rely on a tamper-proof database storing the history of services. If the blockchain ledger tamper-proof storing facility facilitates auditability by providing a trustworthy settlement log for auditing services, it goes against the imperative for privacy in competitive environments.

The need to enforce both privacy and auditability is especially salient in the case of blockchain-based payments. Indeed, a payment in cryptocurrency reveals the winning bid pricing, though the winning service provider may not wish to disclose pricing information to competitors [1]. Competitors can thus retrieve strategic positioning information or trading secrets. Hence, both auditability and privacy appear necessary at the binding and payment stages.

In the literature, ensuring privacy often implies cutting down on auditability by a third-party [4].

Among approaches focusing primarily on privacy stand private payment channels ([5–9]) though they offer limited [5] to no auditability. Mixing strategies such as in [10–13] for UTXO (Unspent transaction output) models [14], and [15] for account-based models have been proposed to anonymize transactions. Nonetheless, no focus on auditability is provided in these papers, except for [10] which proposes a retroactive auditability function that nonetheless, but provides only partial traceability of transactions.

Some approaches aim at reconciling privacy imperatives with auditability by leveraging encryption technics. In [16–18], semi homomorphic encryption and zero-knowledge proof schemes are combined to hide the transaction value, sender, and receiver identity. Following the same approach, a set of papers ([19–25]) also provide auditability functionalities. Nonetheless, zero-knowledge proofs and semi-homomorphic encryption come with computation issues. Additionally, semi-homomorphic encryption comes with complicated encryption key management.

Additionally, a middle-ground trust hypothesis considers banks as reliable proxies for payments to palliate a complex blockchain and key management setup scheme. Hence, in [26,27], banks are leveraged as trustworthy intermediates to carry on on-chain payments. Cryptography technics such as zero-knowledge proof can moreover ensure privacy [27]. Nonetheless, in both approaches, auditability is not directly addressed.

The following research question thus arises: *(RQ) How to implement a simple decentralized token payment system building on banks as trustworthy proxies that preserves privacy while offering public auditability?*

We propose a solution that uses a bank and a per-collaboration payment token linked to a random value to address this research question. Parties can use per-collaboration tokens to proceed to multiple payments while preserving the values' privacy. Token payment can be programmed to verify conditions coded in a smart contract, put into escrow, and carry partial payment. Additionally, token transactions can be audited trust-worthily by external peers as they are stored on-chain. We demonstrate our approach's feasibility through an implemented prototype and its effectiveness via experiments.

The remainder of this paper is organized as follows. Section 2 introduces key concepts about blockchain. Section 3 presents our motivating example. Then, Sect. 4 reviews related work. In Sect. 5, we describe the proposed mechanism. In Sect. 6, we validate our approach by building a prototype and carrying out experiments on the prototype. The paper concludes with Sect. 7.

2   Preliminaries

Blockchain is a decentralized peer-to-peer ledger that keeps track of transactions between users. Figure 1 illustrates the ledger: it consists into a linked list of blocks storing validated transactions. Blocks are linked together using the former block's hash, following a Merkle tree structure. Consensus algorithms such as proof-of-work, or proof-of-stake, regulate the chain's growth by verifying transactions and discarding invalid transactions. Additionally, cryptography rules ensure the pseudo-anonymity of users. Blockchain networks can be open (i.e., any user can join the network and become a transaction verifier, referred to as a miner) or permissioned (participation is limited to pre-identified users).

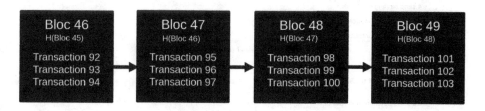

Fig. 1. Illustration of a segment of the blockchain ledger (blocks 46-49)

Smart contracts are deterministic scripts executable on a blockchain network to execute predefined functions. The smart contract, publicly stored in the ledger, autonomously runs contractual terms without calling any third party. Smart contracts are deployed in the blockchain ledger and replicated among blockchain participants: they are executed by each node of the network. If all conditions of the smart contract are verified by all nodes, then the transaction is executed and validated (i.e., appended to the chain). Functions implementing the contractual terms can be triggered by (1) pseudo-anonymous users can trigger the contract to execute functions or by (2) a triggering event such as a market price level in exchange for transaction fees. The fees are used to compensate transaction validators for computing power. As a benefit, regulators can access the history of transactions stored in blockchain logs and serves a trust basis.

Smart contracts can implement and manage blockchain tokens. These tokens can have multiple uses [28]: payment tokens, equity tokens, or cryptocurrency tokens, to name a few. With tokenization [29], tokens encapsulate sensitive data and lower risks of exposure and sensitive information leakage. The Ethereum blockchain introduces the token smart-contract standard [30]. This standard refers to the list of functionalities implemented by a smart contract for token management. Smart contracts create a new type of token by setting the total number of token supplies, the number of decimals of the token, its name, and its symbol. It also manages the tokens' first allocation from a token generator to participants while verifying the total number of token supplies limit. It keeps track of the token balance of participants and manages the transfers among participants.

3   Motivating Example

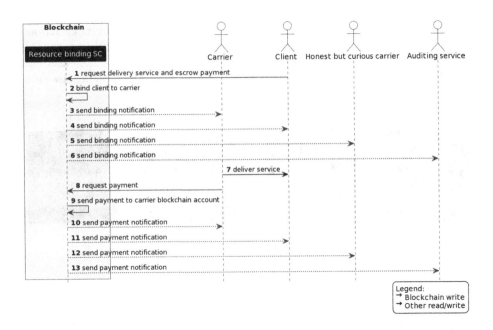

Fig. 2. Sequence diagram of a blockchain-based service payment

Figure 2 illustrates a sequence diagram for a blockchain-based delivery service, where the blockchain acts as a trustworthy and autonomous allocation service and settlement [31]. In this setting, a client requests a carrier to the resource binding smart contract for a shipment (step 1). The resource-binding smart contract compares the QoS of competitors and allocates the delivery service to one of the carriers (step 2). It sends an event notification to notify participants of the binding. Participants listening to the event will thus be notified (steps 3-6). The delivery service occurs off-chain (step 7), and the carrier requests his pay (step 8). The smart contract reallocates the service funds put in escrow to the carrier blockchain account (step 9). It sends a payment notification (e.g., under the shape of an event (steps 10-13)), the payment being recorded as a transaction in the ledger. Hence, an auditing service can access the payment transaction, e.g., assess compliance with regulation laws or ease claim resolution.

Nonetheless, the payment value is accessible to carrier competitors (step 12). For example, competitors could use this information to renegotiate contract terms with the client, which would hamper the adoption of a blockchain-based solution. Consequently, the payment should remain confidential to avoid any privacy leakage in such a competitive situation. Hence the following question arises: how to carry on a privacy-preserving payment while ensuring the auditability of the payment transactions?

4 Related Work

In permissionless blockchains, private payments can be reached using mixing services. Cryptocurrency assets are mixed, anonymizing transactions and disconnecting the sender from the receiver. For example, Dash implements a decentralized mixing service coupled with a chaining facility on bitcoin [10]. Nonetheless, Bitcoin does not provide smart contracts: programmable payments are unavailable. Additionally, auditability is computationally intensive due to using an ahead-of-time decentralized trustless mixing strategy. SilentWhispers [15] also leverages a mixing facility as payment is processed using intermediary nodes. Additionally, temporary and long-term encryption keys are used for internode payments. By so doing, transactions are not linkable, i.e., it is not possible to backtrack transactions history, thus hampering auditability. Nonetheless, the key management scheme adds complexity to the payment scheme. Finally, Monero [11] proposes a mixing technique coupled with ring signature to hide both payment issuance and value. Nonetheless, an issue arises regarding the ring signature's size, which impacts the transaction sizes directly and processing speed. Several works tried to address this limitation, such as [12] and [13] but, similarly to Bitcoin, no smart contract facility is provided in Monero.

Alongside mixing strategies, encryption and zero-knowledge proofs protocols can enforce the privacy of payments.

Zerocash [16], based on bitcoin, uses zk-SNARKs to hide the payment's sender, receiver, and amount. Users pay each other privately while corresponding anonymized transactions are stored on-chain. This method requires a trusted setup, and transaction generation is computationally expensive (two minutes are necessary to generate a transaction using zero-knowledge proof according to [13]). Several extensions to Zerocash have been proposed in the literature to add an auditability layer: [21] adds an accountability layer to audit transactions and enforce spending limits, and [22,23] propose partial anonymity for auditability using anonymity sets, coupled with El Gamal encryption and Schnorr zero-knowledge proofs. Audits can occur in a permissioned setting using verifiable public-key encryption. As a downside, the anonymity set depends on the set's size, and an encryption key management system is necessary to manage auditability. Additionally, all these solutions are based on Bitcoin, and partial payment is not provided.

Another strategy consists of hiding payment content using various semi-homomorphic schemes (Pedersen commitment, Paillier, or El Gamal algorithms) and zero-knowledge proofs [18, 24, 25, 32]. Often, Pedersen commitments encode the amount and types of assets to be transferred. Zero-knowledge proofs show the validity of a transaction once it has been processed. For example, Zerocoin [18] converts bitcoins into zero coins that offer anonymity using Pedersen commitments and zero-knowledge proofs. Additionally, the zerocoins can be reconverted into bitcoins without any origin leakage. Nonetheless, Zerocoin does not offer auditing facilities, and focuses on Bitcoin, hence does not offer smart contract facilities. MiniLedger focuses on a permissioned account-based blockchain, aiming for banks as end-users [24]. It uses Pedersen commitment and NIZK proofs to hide transaction values, senders and recipients. Each bank-to-bank collaboration, i.e., a transaction from one bank to another, uses a unique encryption key to decipher their assets privately. Additionally, storage costs is independent on the number of transactions as MiniLedger leverages pruning technics.

Nonetheless, due to Pedersen commitment schemes, off-chain systems must transmit the openings of outgoing commitments, which complexifies the design and adds a layer of trust to senders. Additionally, if one user fails to open one commitment, its account will be unusable [25]. To circumvent the Pedersen commitment issue, Pretty Good Confidentiality (PCG) [25] proposes twisted El Gamal encryption and zero-knowledge proof. They offer to display transactions and public keys on the ledger for auditability. However, it is impossible to collect amounts or provide partial payments forcibly.

Several papers use privacy-preserving payment channels [5–9]. [5] proposes token payment schemes in a private blockchain consortium. A private blockchain acts as the interoperability domain issuing tokens. The banks use private payment channels built on this master blockchain to allocate transactions. Only the transaction hash, without further transaction details, is recorded in the master blockchain to preserve privacy. Hence, only banks involved in a transaction can access the details. As a limitation, private channels complexify the information system as each bank needs to open several channels to proceed with payments with other banks. In [6,7], the Chameleon hash function guarantees that users cannot track payments under the condition that at least one intermediate payment node is honest. Nonetheless, an issue arises if intermediate nodes collude with each other. In [8], authors leverage Elliptic curve cryptography to hide transaction content. In [9], payment is processed off-blockchain in private payment channels using an untrusted intermediary. Nonetheless, in both approaches, auditability is not provided.

Another strategy uses trustworthy intermediaries to decipher encrypted payments and proceed to payments privately. In Bolt [26], the focus is set on intermediated payments carried on the Bitcoin blockchain. Privacy-preserving payment channel schemes are presented, including one leveraging trusted intermediaries. Solidus [27] offers a privacy-preserving protocol for asset transfer in intermediated bilateral transactions. Banks act as mediators or proxies to hide transaction graphs and values in this system. They do so using ORAMs (oblivious random access machines, which prevent servers from learning about data [33]) coupled with zero-knowledge proof. Nonetheless, no dedicated auditing functionality is proposed, though banks can open the content of relevant transactions upon request.

In summary, several approaches using private payment channels ([5–9]) to ensure privacy and scalability when transactions increase, but they offer little [5] to no auditability. In [16–18], semi homomorphic encryption and zero-knowledge proof schemes are combined to hide the transaction value, sender, and receiver identity. Following the same approach, a set of papers ([19–25]) also provide auditability functionalities. Nonetheless, zero-knowledge proofs and semi homomorphic encryption comes with computation issues. Additionally, semi-homomorphic encryption comes with complicated encryption key management. Mixing strategies such as in [10–13] for UTXO models, and [15] for account-based models have been proposed to anonymize transactions. Nonetheless, no focus on auditability is provided in these papers, except for [10] which proposes a retroactive auditability function. Nonetheless, this auditability facility is computationally expensive, and Dash does not offer smart contracts, hence no partial or programmable payment. In [26,27], banks are leveraged as trustworthy intermediates to carry on on-chain payments. Cryptography technics such as zero-knowledge proof in [27] ensure privacy.

This paper proposes a solution leveraging banks as trustworthy intermediaries, managing random-value payment tokens. Transactions take place on-chain and are stored in the ledger, hence offering auditability. Nonetheless, the actual payment value is not accessible on-chain, providing privacy. Using tokens avoids expensive zero-knowledge proofs computations or encryption key management.

5   The Approach

5.1   Overall Approach

Figure 3 presents the four stages composing our approach. The first stage consists of initializing the single-use payment token smart contract. The value assigned to the payment token is set randomly and provided off-chain to payment participants during this stage. The second step consists of giving payment tokens to the payment sender willing to pay the payment receiver confidentially for a service. The third stage consists of the privacy-preserving service payment using payment tokens put into escrow in the smart contract. The last step consists of the payment token smart contract settlement once the collaboration between the payment sender and the receiver terminates.

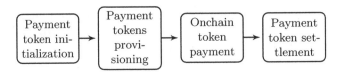

Fig. 3. Privacy-preserving smart contract payments with a bank: main stages

5.2 Payment Token Smart Contract Initialization

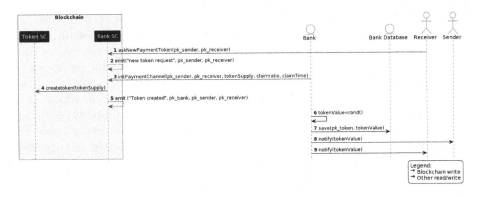

Fig. 4. Sequence diagram of the payment token smart contract initialization

Figure 4 shows the sequence diagram of the payment token initialization.

First, the payment receiver asks the smart contract manager, referred to as "Bank Contract" for a new collaboration token (Fig. 4, step 1). The transaction contains the blockchain public key of both payment sender and receiver (respectively pk_{sender} and $pk_{receiver}$), which serves as a unique identifier for keeping track of the payment history.

Bank Contract emits an event stipulating that a new payment token should be issued between the payment sender and payment receiver (Fig. 4, step 2). Participants who are listening to the smart contract (namely, the bank, the payment receiver, and the payment sender) will thus be notified of this event.

Algorithm 1 presents the structure of the payment channel C declared into the smart contract. C is defined as a struct comprising the following elements: (i) the service status (*INIT* when the channel is initialized, *DONE* when the service is done and waits to be paid, *CLAIM* if a claim occurs regarding the service delivery, and *PAYED* once payment has been fulfilled) (ii) the payment sender, the payment receiver, and the token contract blockchain addresses (iii) the token supply, i.e., the total number of tokens to generate (iv) the claim ratio used to reallocate tokens put into escrow if a claim occurs (v) the target block, that is, the delay given to the payment sender to trigger a claim using the smart contract, and (vi) the token amount, set upon a service request trigger.

Algorithm 1: Payment Channel structure

---

1 **Struct** C **contains**

    // declare participants and token addresses

2   address pk_{sender};

3   address $pk_{receiver}$;

4   address pk_{token};

    // declare payment channel parameters

5   uint tokenSupply;

6   uint claimRatio;

    // declare payment

7   serviceStatus status // { INIT, DONE, CLAIM, PAYED }

8   uint targetBlock;

9   uint tokenAmount;

Upon receiving the event asking for a payment channel creation, the bank initializes the new payment channel (Fig. 4, step 3), deploys the payment token smart contract on-chain (Fig. 4, step 4) and emits an event to confirm the creation of the token smart contract (Fig. 4, step 5). Algorithm 2 presents the initPaymentChannel function which comprises steps 3-5 of Fig. 4. The smart contract first verifies that the identity of the transaction sender corresponds to pk_{bank} (line 2). It then creates a payment channel struct (line 3) and initializes each parameter of c (lines 4-12). Service status is set to *INIT* (line 8). The target block is computed based on the claim time forwarded to the bank contract (line 9). The smart contract triggers the token contract factory to generate a new token contract (line 11): it does so by specifying the owner of the tokens (pk_{bank}), as well as the token supply. The address of the generated token contract is saved into c (line 12). The smart contract then adds c to the list of registered tokens (line 13), and notifies with an event that the token creation succeeded (line 14).

Afterwards, the bank generates a random value α that is confidentially assigned to the payment token value (Fig. 4, step 6). The payment token will be used to issue payment tokens to interested payment senders and manage payment token transactions; token smart contract payment tokens will be used as stable coins following the exchange rate 1TKN=α. Among token smart contract payment token transactions are (i) putting payment tokens into escrow when service is ongoing and (ii) allocating them to the interested participants when the service terminates.

The bank database references the random value α and the associated token smart contract payment token (Fig. 4, step 7). Afterward, the bank notifies the involved participants of the token smart contract deployment and its associated random value (Fig. 4, step 8-9).

Algorithm 2: Onchain initialisation of a new payment channel

Data: *channels* list of payment channels

1 **Function**
   initPaymentChannel($pk_{sender}, pk_{receiver}, tokenSupply, claimRatio, claimTime$):

    // VERIFY SENDER IDENTITY

2   require($msg.sender == pk_{bank}$);

    // GENERATE NEW PAYMENT TOKEN

3   C c;

4    $c.pk_{sender} \leftarrow pk_{sender}$;

5    $c.pk_{receiver} \leftarrow pk_{receiver}$;

6    $c.tokenSupply \leftarrow tokenSupply$;

7    $c.claimRatio \leftarrow claimRatio$;

8    $c.status \leftarrow serviceStatus.INIT$;

9    $c.targetBlock \leftarrow block.number + claimTime$;

10   $c.tokenAmount \leftarrow 0$;

11   $Token\ t \leftarrow new\ Token(pk_{bank}, tokenSupply)$ **// generate token contract and fetch address**

12   $c.pk_{token} \leftarrow t.pk$ **// set token address**

13   $channels.push(c)$ **// save channel**

14   emit event("token created", $pk_{bank}, pk_{sender}, pk_{receiver}$);

15 **End Function**

As a side note, participants can initiate several payment tokens: tokens will be referenced based on the public address of the token smart contract pk_{token}.

In our motivating example, we suppose $\alpha = 0.5€$. The bank deploys the token smart contract and generates a total supply of 50 payment tokens. As a side note, the total amount of tokens is set to provide enough tokens during the payment process. It is set independently by the bank in this use case, but it could be set based upon negotiation between the payment sender and the payment receiver. The bank will save the token smart contract conversion rate coin value off-chain in its database. The participants involved in the confidential transaction, here the carrier, and the logistician, are noticed off-chain of the payment token value 1TKN = 0.5€.

In this approach, payment token transactions are publicly accessible as they consist of public transactions stored on-chain. Nonetheless, their value remains confidential as it is linked to a random number by the bank. The tokens are backed with fiat money with a secret conversion rate: only the bank and participants will know the value of the tokens exchanged.

5.3   Request Payment Tokens

The next step consists into payment token issuance to the participant wishing to pay the payment receiver for a service.

First, the payment sender pays off-chain the bank in fiduciary money while specifying pk_{token}, in exchange for token smart contract payment tokens. The bank generates the conversion between the provided amount in fiduciary money and the payment token value using the payment token value stored in the bank database referenced using the token payment on-chain address pk_{token}. It obtains a quantity of n payment tokens. The bank asks the payment token to transfer these n payment tokens to the payment sender blockchain address.

In our motivating example, if we suppose the sum paid to the bank equals 10€, and $\alpha = 0.5$€, then the bank will ask the payment token smart contract to transfer 20 payment tokens to the blockchain address of the logistician.

5.4 Service Payment

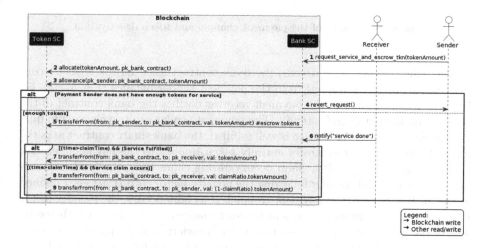

Fig. 5. Service fulfillment

Let *tokenAmount* be the token equivalent to the price of the service agreed upon by the payment receiver and the payment sender.

Figure 5 presents the sequence diagram of the service payment. Once the payment tokens are transferred (c.f. Subsect. 5.3), the payment sender launches the payment transaction request (Fig. 5, step 1). It does so by specifying the number of payment tokens *tokenAmount* to be escrowed by the smart contract. The bank smart contract will transfer these tokens to the payment receiver once the service terminates. The payment sender first authorizes the transfer of *tokenAmount* from its token balance to the bank contract balance using the allocate function (Fig. 5, step 2). The bank contract then verifies whether the payment sender has enough tokens (e.g., whether *tokenAmount* $\preceq n$) using the allowance function (Fig. 5, step 3). If there are not enough payment tokens, the transaction is reverted (Fig. 5, step 4).

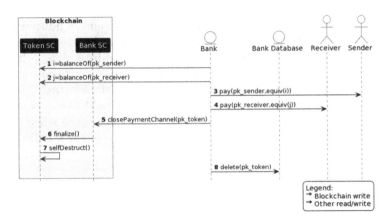

Fig. 6. Settlement of the payment channel and token deactivation

Else, the transaction proceeds: the bank contract asks the token smart contract to escrow *tokenAmount* from the payment sender balance (Fig. 5, step 5). Upon service completion, the payment receiver notifies the bank contract of the contract fulfillment (Fig. 5, step 6). The payment sender can trigger a claim during the claim time. If the service is well fulfilled, the bank smart contract asks the token smart contract to transfer entirely *tokenAmount* to the payment receiver balance (Fig. 5, step 7). If a claim occurs during claim time, the bank contract proceeds to a partial transfer following the penalty factor *claimRatio* < 1 defined at the initialization of the payment channel. If a claim occurs, the penalty factor is applied to the number of payment tokens transferred: e.g., if i = 0.4, then only 40% of the *tokenAmount* payment tokens are transferred to the payment receiver (Fig. 5, step 8). Remaining payment tokens e.g. (1-i)x = 0.6x are transferred back to the payment sender balance (Fig. 5, step 9).

As a side note, several payment token transactions can be executed between the payment receiver and the payment sender in a privacy-preserving fashion. Each payment transaction provides to auditors the transaction timestamp (when), the number of tokens exchanged (what), and the sender and receiver pseudonymous addresses (who). By so doing, a compromise is reached between full confidentiality (e.g., by losing the track of transactions between payments), and total traceability which implies revealing who completed the transaction, what amount, and when it took place.

5.5   Collaboration Settlement and Payment Tokens Deactivation

After all payment transactions have been carried on between the payment receiver and the payment sender, the bank smart contract can deactivate the payment tokens. Figure 6 presents the steps for settling the collaboration between the payment sender and the payment receiver.

The bank checks the payment token balance of the payment sender and payment receiver (Fig. 6, step 1–2). Afterward, the bank converts each payment token balance into fiduciary money, following the conversion rate α, and pays back in an off-chain channel to the payment receiver and the payment sender (Fig. 6, step 3–4). Then, the bank asks for the bank contract to close the payment channel (Fig. 6, step 5). This function triggers the token smart contract (Fig. 6, step 6) to ask it to self-destruct (Fig. 6, step 7). The remaining tokens are set to null. Finally, the bank deletes the token value from its database (Fig. 6, step 8).

6 Implementation and Evaluation

This section aims at validating our approach experimentally. We build and evaluate a privacy-preserving payment service leveraging random-value tokens.

6.1 Implementation

We implement the approach using Solidity for the smart contracts deployed on the Ethereum blockchain and Python with the web3 library for the test script.

Code of the implemented prototype is available at

https://archive.softwareheritage.org/browse/directory/
60577355b219ab188003bdaa624a31cf564f2b98/?origin_url=https://
github.com/tiphainehenry/random-value-token-payment&
revision=e2ad349e7d65c6a3dd735d48ce5a9e73ff9541c0&
snapshot=dd7f3b87913aef5990d76d4c7fc3e11998cb0a8d

Figure 7 illustrates the interaction between the actors and the contracts and between the smart contracts with themselves. The main smart contract (referred to as Bank contract) is deployed on the Ropsten network. The history of transactions related to the smart contract can be accessed at the following address 0x5F943a16Ba1Ea8E3E2FA87e8162181e3c5A6d2C0 using Etherscan (https://ropsten.etherscan.io/address/). The smart contract manages payments channels between payment senders and payment receivers. It is a trustworthy interface between payment senders, payment receivers, and the bank. The bank contract generates and interacts with a set of payment tokens defined according to the Ethereum ERC20 standard for creating tokens. Additionally, payment receivers and payment senders interact with the bank off-chain to manage fiduciary money and the random token value. These interactions are not displayed in Fig. 7 for readability.

The Bank contract interface comprises five methods. The method *initPaymentChannel* initializes a new payment channel. Then, *getPayment* gets the payment sender address, the payment receiver address, the ERC20 contract address, and the token supply of a given payment channel. *serviceDone* allows the payment receiver to signal that he provided the service. With *serviceClaim*, the payment sender can raise a claim if she is in the claiming time window. Finally, *closePaymentChannel* will close a payment channel.

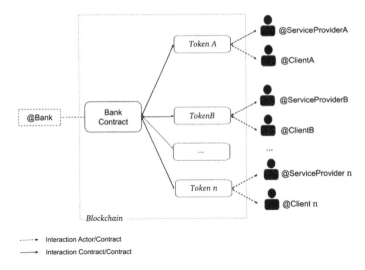

Fig. 7. Interaction Contract/Contract & Actor/Contract

Generated tokens implement the ERC20 standard, which comprises the following methods: (i) *balanceOf* gets the balance of an Ethereum address (ii) *transfer* allows the caller to transfer tokens; (iii) *approve* is used by the caller to allow an address to spend a certain amount of tokens; (iv) *transferFrom* is used by the caller to spend the tokens of a spender that allowed her to spend; and (v) *allowance* is used to get the allowance of an address to another one.

The deployment of the bank contract on the test network uses 2,353,462 gas (220$). In the following, we use April 7th, 2022 conversion rate (1ETH = 3.125$).

6.2   Evaluation

In our testing protocol, we suppose that the payment sender has paid the bank to obtain a set of unique tokens assigned to a confidential random value. We evaluate the gas consumed by the method calls required to go through the whole payment process. We repeat the experiments with 100 tokens to assess whether the number of tokens impacts gas.

Payment Token Deployment Costs

Table 1 presents the gas consumption according to the number of payment token smart contracts deployed. The deployment of the first ERC20 token uses 1,197,421 (112$). Afterward, For each new token creation (we deployed 100 ERC20 contract deployments), the gas used stays constant at 1,075,621. Hence, we only present the measurements obtained for the first five smart contracts created. The first deployment is more expensive than the others. One reason is that the bank contract must initialize the memory used for the first ERC20 contract deployment. The bank contract adds to the existing memory for the other token

Table 1. Gas measurement for the deployment of 5 payment token smart-contracts (SC). Conversion rate: 1ETH = 3.125\$ (April 7th, 2022)

	SC1	SC2	SC3	SC4	SC5
Gas	1,197,421	1,075,621	1,075,621	1,075,621	1,075,621
ETH	0.036	0.0032	0.0032	0.0032	0.0032
Estimated cost in \$	112.2	100	100	100	100

creations without any initialization. As a side note, initial bank deployment uses two times more gas than deploying a token contract. It can be explained in terms of code volume. Indeed, the bank contract has to embed the ERC20 contract to deploy a new ERC20 contract.

Payment and Settlement Stages Transaction Fees
Table 2 presents the gas consumption of the functions available in the Bank contract after the creation of one token.

Table 2. Gas measurement for the Bank Contract Methods during payment and settlement stages. Conversion rate: 1ETH = 3.125\$ (April 7th, 2022)

	Payment					Settlement
	Transfer	Approve	Request	Done	Pay	Close
Gas	51,156	44,091	47,562	43,324	57,991	37,213
ETH	0.0015	0.0013	0.0014	0.0013	0.0017	0.0011
Estimated cost in \$	4.8	4.1	4.45	4.06	5.43	3.4

Experiments for 100 token creations show that the number of payment channels created does not impact the gas required to process or settle a payment. We detail below the gas consumption for these stages. Regarding the payment stage, the payment sender can claim a dispute if she is unhappy with the service provided. There are two scenarios. Without a claim, the payment receiver receives the entire token amount, consuming 57,991 gas. Else, if the payment sender claims a dispute, tokens are distributed using a given ratio (i.e., 60% goes to the payment receiver and 40% goes to the payment sender). Claiming a dispute will consume 28,346 gas.

It is to note that the claiming ratio value does not impact the gas. The gas consumed to transfer tokens to the actors stays approximately the same at 57,908 gas. Hence, the token redistribution will consume 86,254 gas which takes 28,263 more than without claim.

Regarding the settlement stage, closing a channel (destroying the ERC20 contract and deleting the entry stored in the smart contract) requires 37,213 gas, which is 0.00111639 ETH (3.5 \$). The smart contract deletion consumes less gas than creating a new one: 37,213 gas versus 1,075,621 gas.

7   Conclusion

In this paper, we propose to leverage payment tokens assigned to a random value stored off-chain for a privacy-preserving service collaboration settlement.

A bank contract manages collaboration settlement interactions by issuing an on-demand token smart contract assigned to a random value. Hence, payment receivers and payment senders can exchange tokens and settle their services on-chain while ensuring (1) tamper-proof records of payments for auditing purposes and (2) privacy of the fiduciary payment value. One payment token smart contract can be used for multiple payments between two actors, similar to a payment channel, but carried on the main chain. Only the bank, the payment receiver, and the payment sender know the exchange rate of tokens to fiduciary money. We implement and evaluate this solution on Ethereum to demonstrate the approach's feasibility.

Banks do not need to manage accounting entries: all accounting entries are collected on-chain. The ledger keeps track in a tamper-proof fashion of the number of tokens exchanged and the blockchain pseudo-identity of the payment issuers and receivers, which can be used for auditing and claim resolution. An advantage of this approach is the easy setup as no encryption key management is necessary: only the bank manages token exchange rates. All transactions can take place using a classical token smart contract payment token.

Smart contracts offer programmable transactions enabling token escrow and programmable payments. Hence, a smart contract can directly escrow tokens during service delivery and manage claim resolution. It can enforce claim resolution, e.g., via a partial payment, during a certain agreed-upon claiming period. This service delivery and settlement history is kept on-chain and can be used in the long run to compute payment receivers' quality of service.

The main limitation of this approach could be some centralization induced by the use of the bank to manage token payment exchange rates, even if banks are often considered trusted entities. To defuses the risk of privacy leakage, several banks could be used to manage each collaboration token. Then, each bank would only have a partial knowledge of the token value. Furthermore, scalability issues may arise as we issue a new payment token value each time a new collaboration requires a confidential payment. This issue can be mitigated by using a sidechain [34] and by regrouping transactions. We should address both issues in future work.

An extension to this approach consists of implementing smart-contract-based periodic negotiations to review and update the token exchange rate. Additionally, payment senders could have the possibility to choose between public or private pricing alternatives. If public pricing occurs, then a classic payment is processed. Else, if privacy is required, a token smart contract is initialized.

References

1. Peng, L., Feng, W., Yan, Z., Li, Y., Zhou, X., Shimizu, S.: Privacy preservation in permissionless blockchain: a survey. Digital Commun. Netw. **7**(3), 295–307 (2021)
2. Weber, I., Xu, X., Riveret, R., Governatori, G., Ponomarev, A., Mendling, J.: Untrusted business process monitoring and execution using blockchain. In: La Rosa, M., Loos, P., Pastor, O. (eds.) BPM 2016. LNCS, vol. 9850, pp. 329–347. Springer, Cham (2016). https://doi.org/10.1007/978-3-319-45348-4_19
3. Henry, T., Brahem, A., Laga, N., Hatin, J., Gaaloul, W., Benatallah, B.: Trustworthy cross-organizational collaborations with hybrid on/off-chain declarative choreographies. In: Hacid, H., Kao, O., Mecella, M., Moha, N., Paik, H. (eds.) ICSOC 2021. LNCS, vol. 13121, pp. 81–96. Springer, Cham (2021). https://doi.org/10.1007/978-3-030-91431-8_6
4. Zhang, Y., Gai, K., Qiu, M., Ding, K.: Understanding privacy-preserving techniques in digital cryptocurrencies. In: Qiu, M. (ed.) ICA3PP 2020. LNCS, vol. 12454, pp. 3–18. Springer, Cham (2020). https://doi.org/10.1007/978-3-030-60248-2_1
5. Zouina, M., Outtai, B.: Towards a distributed token based payment system using blockchain technology. In: 2019 International Conference on Advanced Communication Technologies and Networking (CommNet), pp. 1–10. IEEE (2019)
6. Yu, B., Kermanshahi, S.K., Sakzad, A., Nepal, S.: Chameleon hash time-lock contract for privacy preserving payment channel networks. In: Steinfeld, R., Yuen, T.H. (eds.) ProvSec 2019. LNCS, vol. 11821, pp. 303–318. Springer, Cham (2019). https://doi.org/10.1007/978-3-030-31919-9_18
7. Malavolta, G., Moreno-Sanchez, P., Kate, A., Maffei, M., Ravi, S.: Concurrency and privacy with payment-channel networks. In: Proceedings of the 2017 ACM SIGSAC Conference on Computer and Communications Security (2017)
8. Tripathy, S., Mohanty, S.K.: MAPPCN: Multi-hop anonymous and privacy-preserving payment channel network. In: Bernhard, M., et al. (eds.) FC 2020. LNCS, vol. 12063, pp. 481–495. Springer, Cham (2020). https://doi.org/10.1007/978-3-030-54455-3_34
9. Heilman, E., Alshenibr, L., Baldimtsi, F., Scafuro, A., Goldberg, S.: Tumblebit: an untrusted bitcoin-compatible anonymous payment hub. Cryptology ePrint Archive (2016)
10. Duffield, E., Diaz, D.: Dash: A privacycentric cryptocurrency (2015)
11. Noether, S., Noether, S.: Monero is not that mysterious. Technical report (2014)
12. Sun, S.-F., Au, M.H., Liu, J.K., Yuen, T.H.: RingCT 2.0: A compact accumulator-based (linkable ring signature) protocol for blockchain cryptocurrency monero. In: Foley, S.N., Gollmann, D., Snekkenes, E. (eds.) ESORICS 2017. LNCS, vol. 10493, pp. 456–474. Springer, Cham (2017). https://doi.org/10.1007/978-3-319-66399-9_25
13. Jia, Y., et al.: Pbt: A new privacy-preserving payment protocol for blockchain transactions. IEEE Trans. Dependable Sec. Comput. **19**, 647–662 (2020)
14. Chakravarty, M.M.T., Chapman, J., MacKenzie, K., Melkonian, O., Peyton Jones, M., Wadler, P.: The extended UTXO model. In: Bernhard, M., Bracciali, A., Camp, L.J., Matsuo, S., Maurushat, A., Rønne, P.B., Sala, M. (eds.) FC 2020. LNCS, vol. 12063, pp. 525–539. Springer, Cham (2020). https://doi.org/10.1007/978-3-030-54455-3_37
15. Malavolta, G., Moreno-Sanchez, P., Kate, A., Maffei, M.: Silentwhispers: enforcing security and privacy in decentralized credit networks. Cryptology ePrint Archive (2016)

16. Sasson, E.B., et al.: Zerocash: Decentralized anonymous payments from bitcoin. In: IEEE Symposium on Security and Privacy, vol. 2014, pp. 459–474. IEEE (2014)

17. Hopwood, D., Bowe, S., Hornby, T., Wilcox, N.: Zcash protocol specification. San Francisco, CA, USA, GitHub (2016)

18. Miers, I., Garman, C., Green, M., Rubin, A.D.: Zerocoin: anonymous distributed e-cash from bitcoin. In: IEEE Symposium on Security and Privacy, vol. 2013, pp. 397–411. IEEE (2013)

19. Narula, N., Vasquez, W., Virza, M.: {zkLedger}:{Privacy-Preserving} auditing for distributed ledgers. In: 15th USENIX Symposium on Networked Systems Design and Implementation (NSDI 2018), pp. 65–80 (2018)

20. Androulaki, E., Camenisch, J., Caro, A.D., Dubovitskaya, M., Elkhiyaoui, K., Tackmann, B.: Privacy-preserving auditable token payments in a permissioned blockchain system. In: Proceedings of the 2nd ACM Conference on Advances in Financial Technologies, pp. 255–267 (2020)

21. Garman, C., Green, M., Miers, I.: Accountable privacy for decentralized anonymous payments. In: Grossklags, J., Preneel, B. (eds.) FC 2016. LNCS, vol. 9603, pp. 81–98. Springer, Heidelberg (2017). https://doi.org/10.1007/978-3-662-54970-4_5

22. Fauzi, P., Meiklejohn, S., Mercer, R., Orlandi, C.: Quisquis: a new design for anonymous cryptocurrencies. In: Galbraith, S.D., Moriai, S. (eds.) ASIACRYPT 2019. LNCS, vol. 11921, pp. 649–678. Springer, Cham (2019). https://doi.org/10.1007/978-3-030-34578-5_23

23. Bünz, B., Agrawal, S., Zamani, M., Boneh, D.: Zether: towards privacy in a smart contract world. In: Bonneau, J., Heninger, N. (eds.) FC 2020. LNCS, vol. 12059, pp. 423–443. Springer, Cham (2020). https://doi.org/10.1007/978-3-030-51280-4_23

24. Chatzigiannis, P., Baldimtsi, F.: MINILEDGER: compact-sized anonymous and auditable distributed payments. In: Bertino, E., Shulman, H., Waidner, M. (eds.) ESORICS 2021. LNCS, vol. 12972, pp. 407–429. Springer, Cham (2021). https://doi.org/10.1007/978-3-030-88418-5_20

25. Chen, Yu., Ma, X., Tang, C., Au, M.H.: PGC: decentralized confidential payment system with auditability. In: Chen, L., Li, N., Liang, K., Schneider, S. (eds.) ESORICS 2020. LNCS, vol. 12308, pp. 591–610. Springer, Cham (2020). https://doi.org/10.1007/978-3-030-58951-6_29

26. Green, M., Miers, I.: Bolt: Anonymous payment channels for decentralized currencies. In: Proceedings of the 2017 ACM SIGSAC Conference on Computer and Communications Security, pp. 473–489 (2017)

27. Cecchetti, E., Zhang, F., Ji, Y., Kosba, A., Juels, A., Shi, E.: Solidus: Confidential distributed ledger transactions via pvorm. In: Proceedings of the 2017 ACM SIGSAC Conference on Computer and Communications Security, pp. 701–717 (2017)

28. Oliveira, L., Zavolokina, L., Bauer, I., Schwabe, G.: To token or not to token: Tools for understanding blockchain tokens. In: 39th International Conference on Information Systems San Francisco (2018)

29. Scoping, S., Taskforce, T.: Information supplement: Pci dss tokenization guidelines. Standard: PCI Data Security Standard (PCI DSS) 24 (2011)

30. Victor, F., Lüders, B.K.: Measuring Ethereum-based ERC20 token networks. In: Goldberg, I., Moore, T. (eds.) FC 2019. LNCS, vol. 11598, pp. 113–129. Springer, Cham (2019). https://doi.org/10.1007/978-3-030-32101-7_8

31. Henry, T., Laga, N., Hatin, J., Beck, R., Gaaloul, W.: Hire me fairly: towards dynamic resource-binding with smart contracts. In: 2021 IEEE International Conference on Services Computing (SCC), pp. 407–412. IEEE (2021)

32. Poelstra, A., Back, A., Friedenbach, M., Maxwell, G., Wuille, P.: Confidential assets. In: Zohar, A., et al. (eds.) FC 2018. LNCS, vol. 10958, pp. 43–63. Springer, Heidelberg (2019). https://doi.org/10.1007/978-3-662-58820-8_4
33. Goodrich, M.T., Mitzenmacher, M.: Privacy-preserving access of outsourced data via oblivious RAM simulation. In: Aceto, L., Henzinger, M., Sgall, J. (eds.) ICALP 2011. LNCS, vol. 6756, pp. 576–587. Springer, Heidelberg (2011). https://doi.org/10.1007/978-3-642-22012-8_46
34. Singh, A., Click, K., Parizi, R.M., Zhang, Q., Dehghantanha, A., Choo, K.K.R.: Sidechain technologies in blockchain networks: An examination and state-of-the-art review. J. Netw. Comput. Appl. **149**, 102471 (2020)

A Data Connector Store for International Data Spaces

Danniar Reza Firdausy[1] , Patrício de Alencar Silva[1,2](✉) ,
Marten van Sinderen[1] , and Maria-Eugenia Iacob[1]

[1] University of Twente, Drienerlolaan 5, Enschede 7522 NB, The Netherlands
{d.r.firdausy,p.dealencarsilva,m.j.vansinderen,
m.e.iacob}@utwente.nl
[2] Graduate Program in Computer Science, UERN/UFERSA, Rio Grande do Norte State
University (UERN), Federal University of the Semi-Arid Region (UFERSA),
Mossoró, RN, Brazil

Abstract. The International Data Spaces Association (IDSA) has promoted the
idea of International Data Spaces as a place for companies to share data with
trust and security enforced by software and organizational competence. There has
been considerable progress in delivering corporate guidelines, technical specifications, and software components available for testing and deploying applications
to support IDS-based ecosystems, such as the IDS data connectors classified by
the Fraunhofer Institute. However, full implementation of IDS applications seems
still complex and expensive for small and medium enterprises (SMEs). A possible
strategy to deal with such an issue is to break the IDSA specification's complexity
into smaller pieces and build small IDS ecosystems formed by its core business
roles (e.g., data owners, users, and broker service providers). In this context, this
paper addresses the problem of designing an application to support the broker
service provider's role in operating in an IDS-based ecosystem. This research,
therefore, follows a Design Science approach in a three-step process. First, it
investigates problems of practical relevance elicited from the IDSA guidelines in
combination with requirements provided by representatives of the Dutch Logistics
sector. Second, it gives design to tackle the problem by combining Semantic Web,
Linked Data, and Enterprise Architecture modeling artifacts. Last, it validates
the architecture of the broker service provider's application by demonstrating its
technical feasibility, innovation, and software integration.

Keywords: Broker service provider · Enterprise architecture · International Data
Spaces · Linked data · Ontology · Semantic Web

1 Introduction

There has been a growing discussion around data sovereignty for people and companies in Europe. According to Braud et al. [1], data sovereignty means *providing data
owners with complete control over their data and digital identities*, which demands
defining who is allowed to do what in which context with the data shared by the data

M. Sellami et al. (Eds.): CoopIS 2022, LNCS 13591, pp. 242–258, 2022.
https://doi.org/10.1007/978-3-031-17834-4_14

owner. Although enforcing data sovereignty on an individual level is still a long-term goal, there has been considerable progress in the corporate instance. For instance, the International Data Spaces Association (IDSA) has delivered comprehensive organizational guidelines defining the business roles and responsibilities involved in IDS-based ecosystems [1]. From a more technical perspective, the GAIA-X project offers further guidance to build, configure and deploy the infrastructure necessary to ensure secure data transfer among companies, including specialized recommendations for cloud and network service providers to operate in an IDS-based ecosystem [2]. These representative organizations are therefore promoting research in technology to help companies and individuals (in the longer term) enforce their data sovereignty rights.

There is a "space" to enforce data sovereignty called *data space*. Initially referred to as *Industrial Data Space*, the term was recently updated to *International Data Space* (IDS) to reflect the vision of building data-sharing ecosystems crossing national boundaries [3]. According to Otto and Jarke [4], *the IDS initiative is a joint effort of various international research institutes and industrial enterprises to establish a decentralized platform for secure and trusted data sharing*. Braud et al. [1] also state that an *IDS aims to allow the building of data-driven ecosystems in which independent partners (from different sizes, ecosystems, and financial power) trust how external parties handle their data while allowing the innovative data services to be constructed cooperatively* [1]. Hence, there seems to be an association between data sovereignty and trust, which can manifest in IDS as a result of long-term successful cooperation (i.e., proven trust) or acquired competency (i.e., enforced trust). Moreover, a business ecosystem supported by organizational and technical guidelines of IDS could be called an IDS-based business ecosystem.

Proven trust takes time, and there is an urgency to attract companies to join IDS-based ecosystems. The IDS Rule Book [5] and the IDSA Reference Architecture Model (IDS RAM) [6] provide the initial guidance for that purpose. While the former describes the business roles and responsibilities of the parties willing to cooperate in an IDS-based business ecosystem, the latter specifies the technical capabilities of software components necessary to implement an IDS application to support the ecosystem. An essential software component described in both documents is the *data connector* – a software application composed of data transformation applications that can automatically enforce a company's data sovereignty requirements expressed in a machine-readable data policy [6, 7]. IDSA has paid considerable effort to deliver different types of data connectors for testing [7, 8], and there is an optimistic expectation that private companies will start offering their solutions shortly.

Although necessary, data connectors are not sufficient to implement an IDS-based application. Implementing a complete IDS ecosystem, with its organizational roles and technical mechanisms, is somewhat complex and not yet economically attractive, especially for small and medium enterprises (SMEs). Reinhold Achatz, the chairman of the IDSA board, has recently issued a call for business cases and applications to demonstrate the organizational and technical feasibility of building IDS-based business ecosystems in Europe [9]. However, in earlier work, representatives from the Dutch Logistics sector and Enterprise Integration software companies have reported that implementing even elementary viewpoints of the IDS RAM model could be considerably challenging both in the organizational and technical effort. Therefore, a possible direction to address the IDSA call for arms is to show the feasibility of the IDSA vision by parts, starting from the core business roles and software components of an IDS-based ecosystem and progressing as companies and IDS technologies become mature [10].

According to the IDSA Rule Book [5], the core business roles of an IDS-based ecosystem include *data owners*, *users*, and *broker service providers*. The latter has the responsibility to help the former to find the data resources and the suitable data connectors to send and receive data from and to the IDS ecosystem [7]. Hence, the research problem addressed in this paper is *to design an application to support the broker service provider's role in an International Data Space*. The research methodology adopted to approach this question is Design Science, as structured by Wieringa [11]. Thence, the main practical research question splits into (1) a *knowledge question* about *what architectures currently guide the design of a broker service provider application*; and (2) a *technical question* about *how a company could implement such an application*. The motivation to treat this problem is threefold. First, it is an effort to motivate companies to join IDS-based ecosystems and invest in its supporting technology. Second, it will demonstrate technological feasibility and maturity. Last, it will help identify gaps for future development to pave the IDS vision.

The execution of this research follows the Design Cycle proposed by Wieringa [11], which defines three main phases: (1) problem investigation, (2) treatment design, and (3) design validation. The first phase elicited research questions and requirements of relevance for companies and organizations interested in the development of IDS. This research has an active engagement of representatives from the Dutch Logistics sector (e.g., SUTC[1] and EMONS[2]), Enterprise Integration software companies (e.g., eMagiz[3] and CAPE Group[4]), and TNO[5] – the Dutch representative of IDSA. The requirements raised by these organizations specifically concern Enterprise Interoperability and data sovereignty issues that may hinder the adoption of the IDS vision by companies and have been published and partially addressed in earlier work [12]. The second phase focused on designing a reference architecture to guide the implementation of IDS-based ecosystems with a direct application in the Logistics sector. The first architecture model and its components have been introduced in previous work [12, 13], but the current paper opens the black box of broker service provider's infrastructure. Finally, the third phase comprehends the validation of the architecture, which is partially achieved through the application prototype described in detail in this paper.

The continuation of this paper is organized as follows. The next section discusses the role of a broker service provider in IDS, by providing an Enterprise Architecture viewpoint on its internal components and how they relate to the core business roles of an IDS-based ecosystem. Section 3 describes how the combination of Semantic Web and Linked Data technologies leveraged the internal structure of the broker service provider. Section 4 reports on the development of the prototype of a Data Connector Store – an application to help companies discover and select data connectors suitable to enforce

---

[1] https://www.sutc.nl/en_US.

[2] https://www.emons.eu/.

[3] https://www.emagiz.com/en/en-home/.

[4] https://capegroep.nl/en/.

[5] https://www.tno.nl/en/.

their data sovereignty needs. A discussion about how this work advances companion research follows in Sect. 5. Last, the paper closes with a summary of contributions, threats to validity, and research outlook.

2 The Role of a Broker Service Provider in IDS: An Enterprise Architecture Viewpoint

According to the IDS Reference Architecture Model (RAM), the *broker service provider* (hereafter referred to as BSP) is an intermediary entity that registers, publishes, and supports the search for metadata about data sources and services available in an IDS ecosystem [6]. A BSP adds value to a data space by providing services to leverage the discoverability of IDS connectors and resources offered by other participants [14]. To ensure the core functionalities of an IDS ecosystem, the International Data Spaces Association (IDSA) prescribes four essential business roles: *core participants*, *intermediary participants*, *software providers*, and *governance bodies* [6]. The BSP belongs to the second group, representing the trusted entities whose business involves managing and providing metadata to the other ecosystem participants.

It is necessary to have at least one BSP operating per business domain (e.g., the Logistics sector). Thus multiple BSPs could simultaneously serve a cross-domain application [6, 14]. According to the IDS RAM [6], a BSP may also assume other business roles, e.g., a *clearinghouse* responsible for keeping logs of all activities related to data exchange in an IDS ecosystem. However, the BSP's responsibilities are somewhat limited to supporting data users and owners with managing the metadata about a particular resource. Therefore, the direct data exchange and usage negotiation processes involving only data users and owners are not part of the responsibilities of a BSP [14].

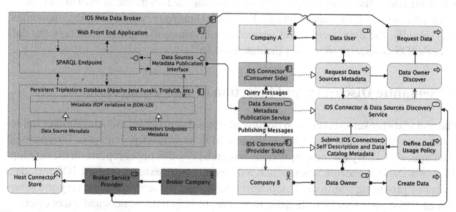

Fig. 1. Enterprise Architecture model of a broker service provider's infrastructure in an International Data Spaces Ecosystem

Figure 1 depicts an Enterprise Architecture model of a BSP, specifying how this entity interacts with other actors and components of an IDS ecosystem through an IDS metadata broker. The architecture conforms to the technical specifications of the IDS RAM and the IDS metadata broker component [6, 15]. The ArchiMate modeling language used to specify the model emphasizes the interplay between concepts in the business and application layer [16, 17]. The BSP appears orange as a business role that develops, hosts, and maintains the IDS metadata broker, which acts as a metadata repository that exposes GUIs and APIs to facilitate metadata publication services.

To carry out its metadata management responsibility, a BSP must provide an interface for data owners to publish their metadata, including descriptions of their *data connectors* and the *data catalogs* accessible through those data connectors. The metadata can be stored in the BSP's internal repository and made available for structured queries submitted by the data user. In addition to supporting the data users in retrieving the metadata of participating IDS connectors or cataloged data resources, the IDS metadata broker should also help the data owners register, activate, update, passivating, or remove metadata entries [15]. Additionally, it should provide an interface describing additional information about its functionalities and indexing services, such as supported query languages, available add-on services, and their data endpoints.

By hosting the IDS metadata broker, the BSP offers its service to the data space to support data users in finding and discovering IDS connectors and data sources provided by the data owners. Two processes must take place for this service to deliver its full potential. First, before enacting any data or metadata exchange, the data owners and users should already be in control of a certified IDS connector. Acquiring the so-called IDS-ready labels for software components is one of the requirements for business actors to participate in an IDS ecosystem after being approved on the organizational level [6, 5]. Secondly, the data owners could submit the self-description and the metadata describing the data used by their data connectors to the IDS metadata broker via the exposed interface based on a standardized protocol (e.g., REST API, OpenAPI 3.0, etc.) [8, 14, 15]. This process occurs after they create the data and define their data usage policies. Next, the data users could discover these catalogs by browsing the IDS metadata broker's metadata based on contextual information (e.g., keywords, language, usage policies, maintainer, etc.). Finally, the data users could receive the information required to access the data owner's IDS connector to request the desired data.

3   Semantic Discovery and Selection of IDS Connectors

The metadata broker specification document states that different metadata broker implementations may be developed and made available by various providers in International Data Spaces [14]. By extending previous research [13], this paper reports on the development of a Data Connector Store, which will operate as an extension of the IDS metadata broker by providing additional functionality to support the semantic discovery and selection of IDS connectors [13]. It aims, therefore, to help data owners and users discover and select the data connectors most suitable for their needs and capabilities based on information about the context in which the connectors could operate (Table 1).

The contextual information describing the IDS connectors derives from a conceptual ontology model proposed in earlier work [13]. The ontology grounded the development of the Data Connector Store proposed in this paper by providing a taxonomy of data connectors and properties that characterize their operational context. Those properties are

Table 1. Data connector's Ontology Requirements Specification Document [13]

Purpose
To describe IDS data connectors for potential participants of an IDS ecosystem

Scope
Contextual information about the business ecosystem where the data connector will operate, e.g., business domain, pricing model, and enforced data access policy

Implementation Language
The ontology is represented in OntoUML, with further translation into OWL

Intended End-Users
User 1.Business representatives of potential and existing IDS participants User 2.IT representatives of potential and current IDS participants User 3.Software and service providers who develop and supply IDS Connectors User 4.Scholars exploring the ontology's knowledge representation capabilities

Intended Uses
Use 1.Software and service providers publish their offered data connectors' metadata on the IDS Connector Store to make their data connectors discoverable Use 2.Business representatives search for IDS-compliant partners operating in the same business domain, complying with common standards, etc Use 3.IT representatives search for data connectors that match their needs and capabilities Use 4.Scholars search and import the ontology into their IDS proof-of-concept tools

Ontology Requirements

Non-Functional Requirements
NFR 1.The ontology must at least use English NFR 2.The ontology must comply, reuse and integrate with the existing IDS Ontology specified under the IDS Information Model

Functional Requirements: Competency Questions
CQ 1.*What software provider offers data connectors?* CQ 2.*Which data connectors are developed for a specific business domain?* CQ 3.*Which data connectors are complying with a particular standard?* CQ 4.*Which data connectors are offered in this pricing model?* CQ 5.*Which data connectors support these data usage agreements?* CQ 6.*Which data connectors were developed in which development framework?* CQ 7.*Which data connectors are offered in this deployment context?* CQ 8.*Which IDS actors use a particular data connector from a specific software provider?* CQ 9.*Which IDS participants operate in a particular business domain?* CQ 10.*Which IDS participants comply with a particular standard?*

Terms from Competency Questions & Frequency
Business Domain, Data usage agreement, deployment, IDS connector, participant, pricing mode, software provider, standards, technology

Objects and Terms for Answers

(continued)

Table 1. (*continued*)

Purpose
-Gatewise IDS Connector, Supplydrive IDS Connect-or, TradeCloud IDS Connector;
-Transport Logistics, Glass Manufacturing, Steel Manufacturing;
-Delete After Interval, Connector-restricted Agreement, Logging Agreement;
-Vandaglas B.V., Van Egmond Groep, Meijer Metal;
-ECI Software Solutions, Tradecloud, OTM, GS1, EDI4STEEL;
-Flat Rate, Freemium, Pay per User, Pay per Feature;
-Java, Spring Boot, JavaScript, NodeJS, VueJS, Python, On-Premise, cloud SaaS

defined to answer a list of *ontology competency questions* (CQs) related to the discovery and selection of data connectors and their respective software providers, data owners, and users. By complying with the Ontology Requirements Specification Document (ORSD) detailed in Table 1, the Data Connector Store aims to recommend data connectors that are: (1) developed by a specific service or software provider; (2) developed for a specific business domain; (3) offered in a specific pricing model; or (4) developed using a particular technology.

Figure 2 depicts an alternative ArchiMate viewpoint detailing the internal infrastructure of the Data Connector Store. It exposes the IDS connector *provisioning metadata publication service* through its *provisioning interface*, which extends the *metadata publication service* defined primarily as a standard to implement a metadata broker. This service enables software and service providers to register, update, passivate, and delete their metadata entries and the data connectors they offer.

The Data Connector Store combines Linked Data principles and Semantic Web technologies to store and provide metadata to describe data connectors and their providers. It also aims to facilitate the integration of disparate open data sources in a standardized way [18]. This design decision also relies on the IDSA technical specifications, which indicate that an IDS metadata broker should allow the discovery of data and other resources based on Linked Data principles [6, 14]. Therefore, the Data Connector Store uses the Resource Description Framework (RDF) format to describe the metadata of the data connectors and data sources by annotating them with a layer of semantics to form subject-predicate-object triples [19]. Examples of relevant triples could include: *"Company A uses data connector X"; "software provider B develops data connector Y"; "data connector X is specialized in the Transport Logistics sector";* or *"data connector Y is offered in a flat-rate pricing model"*. These knowledge representation triples could therefore support the IDS actors in discovering resources of interest based on semi-automated machine reasoning.

To store these metadata represented in RDF, the IDSA suggests the use of a triple store database (e.g., Apache Jena Fuseki, TriplyDB, etc.) or any other storage back end that fits the purpose [2, 11]. The Data Connector Store also needs to provide a SPARQL endpoint to allow data owners and users to accept and send messages that comply with the IDS Information Model (IM), as well as execute the metadata operation queries [9, 12, 13]. These IDS IM compliant messages refer to the publish message that pushes metadata into the repository and the query message that pulls metadata from it [2].

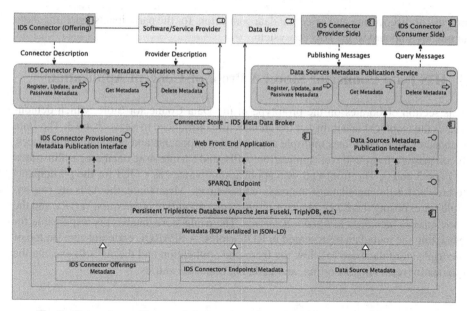

Fig. 2. Enterprise architecture infrastructure viewpoint of the Data Connector Store

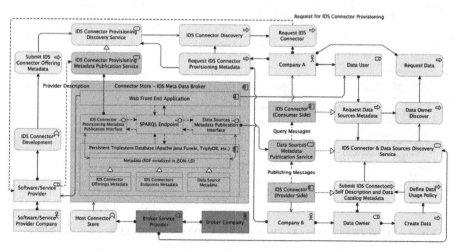

Fig. 3. Connector store ecosystem interaction viewpoint

The Data Connector Store supports the ecosystem operation illustrated in Fig. 3, according to the architecture previously depicted in Fig. 2. It helps software and service providers submit the metadata describing the data connectors they develop and offer in this ecosystem. Accordingly, the Data Connector Store allows data owners and users to find and acquire the best fit data connectors based on their contextual information and through its IDS connector provisioning service (in addition to the *data sources metadata publication service* for the essential IDS metadata broker). Its mechanism enhances the process of discovering and selecting data connectors for the participants, enabling them to quickly onboard to the IDS ecosystem.

4   IDS Data Connector Store: A Proof-of-Concept Application

This section elaborates on the prototype of the Data Connector Store, which demonstrates the technical feasibility of the architecture introduced in Sects. 2 and 3. The Data Connector Store combines multiple application components and application interfaces. It comprises a front-end web application, APIs, and a triple store database, as illustrated in Figs. 2 and 3. The front-end web application operates as a GUI for the participants to browse for the metadata of the required resources. Meanwhile, the APIs are responsible for exposing the IDS connector *provisioning metadata publication service* and the *data sources metadata publication service*. The triple store database is responsible for persisting the metadata represented in RDF triples. A SPARQL endpoint runs on top of the triple store database to allow the front-end application and the APIs to execute the queries for retrieving, inserting, and updating metadata entries.

Fig. 4. Visualization of the axioms of the IDS Connector Ontology in the Protégé tool

The first phase of the prototyping process comprised translating the conceptual ontology model proposed in earlier work [13] into an OWL serialization[6], according to the NeOn Ontology Engineering methodology [20]. This ontology serves as a knowledge base for the triple store database to structure and store the metadata instances. The Protégé tool [21] supported the design of the OWL ontology and the verification of its axioms. Accordingly, ontology individuals were created manually by referring to the

---

[6] https://raw.githubusercontent.com/danniarreza/connectorstoreontology/main/connectorstorev
7.owl.

objects and terms listed in the earlier work's Ontology Requirements Specification Document (ORSD) to reduce the development process complexity [13]. Figure 4 depicts part of the operational ontology design with the Protégé tool. Figure 5 renders a graphical visualization of the ontology with the OntoGraf Protégé plugin.

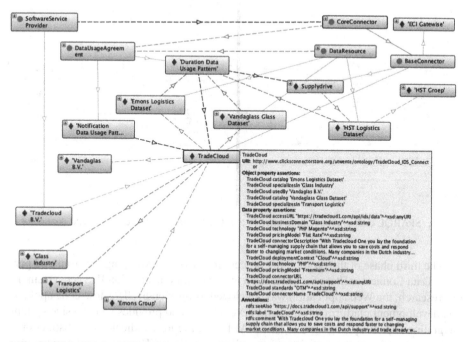

Fig. 5. Visualization of individuals of the IDS Connector Ontology in the OntoGraf plugin

In the second phase of the prototyping process, the OWL model of the IDS connector ontology was uploaded to a triple store database and made available for further querying. This research project uses a triple store associated with Platform Linked Data Netherlands (PLDN), an instance of TriplyDB [22, 23]. The triple store database accepts an ontology graph represented in the Turtle format or its equivalent (i.e., N-triples, JSON-LD, or CSV – except the default OWL or RDF/XML formats), which allows exporting the output ontology to the target format. After that, queries were formulated to retrieve metadata describing the data connectors offered by software and service providers and metadata relating to data sources provided by the data owners. Figure 6 illustrates two SPARQL queries formulated to obtain a list of data resources and descriptions of a data connector. Other SPARQL queries formulated to provide metadata for the prototype of the Data Connector Store are publicly available for external scrutiny[7].

---

[7] https://data.pldn.nl/danniar/-/queries.

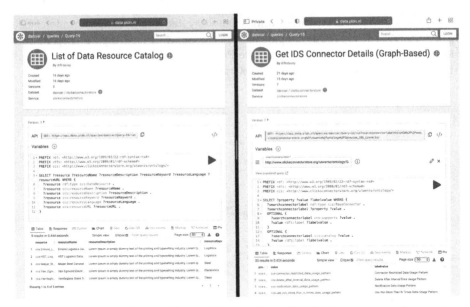

Fig. 6. SPARQL endpoint executing queries to retrieve a list of data resources and connectors

The third phase of the prototyping process focused on developing the front-end part of the Data Connector Store for interaction with the participants of an IDS ecosystem. In this research, the Web application was developed using Mendix. This low-code application development platform allows rapid development and provides an extensive system integration capability, such as via REST API [24]. Figure 7 indicates two distinct processes prescribed for the participants, as indicated in Fig. 3. The upper part of the figure shows how the Data Connector Store provides the participants with a list of data connectors and their respective descriptions. The conceptual ontology proposed in earlier work characterizes the data connectors according to their industry sector, pricing model, data catalog, supported standards, underlying technology, deployment context, and data usage policies [13]. These metadata serve as the filtering attributes to request the data connectors. The bottom part of Fig. 7 indicates a list of data sources and the details of a particular data source owned and offered by a data owner through a respective data connector. Additional metadata are also made available to further describe data sources, for instance, the usage policies constraining the data usage, data representation language, and keywords related to the data content.

Additionally, some properties describing the data connectors and sources were made available as hypertext reference (href) links. This decision aimed to maximize the advantage of following the Linked Data principles, which identifies subjects and objects with HTTP Uniform Resource Identifiers (URIs) and enables associating with one another through their URIs to leverage resource discoverability at the users' side [19, 25]. In the example illustrated in Fig. 8, when the users click on the "offered by" and "industry sector" properties from Fig. 7, they will be supplied with the details of the corresponding software and service provider and the industry sector.

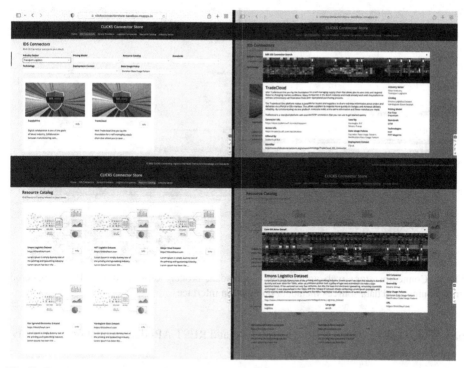

Fig. 7. Data connector store web application – request for a data connector's provisioning metadata and data sources metadata

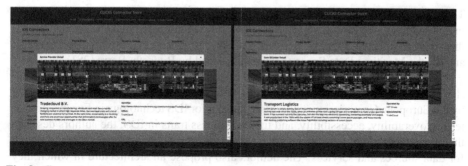

Fig. 8. Connector store web application – software and service provider and Industry sector metadata

Finally, the APIs to facilitate metadata publication services are also implemented and made available. Figure 9 depicts the documentation of the Data Connector Store's preliminary implementation of its REST APIs. Currently, three endpoints are exposed. The first one reveals the metadata broker's self-description, in which its fields refer to the attributes used by the IDS metadata broker reference implementation [8, 15]. Meanwhile, the second and the third endpoints publish the metadata that describes a particular data connector and data source, respectively. The front-end user interfacing

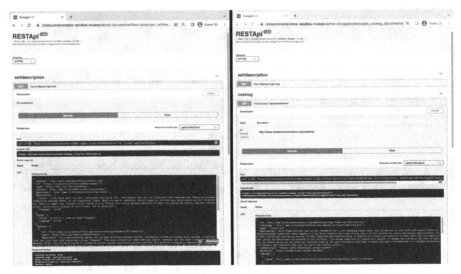

Fig. 9. Connector store web application – metadata broker self-description, IDS connector provisioning, and data sources metadata publication interface

part of the Data Connector Store's prototype and REST API documentation is publicly available for evaluation and testing[8,9,10].

5   Related Work

There are at least three companion approaches closely related to the research reported in this paper: (1) the Mobility Data Space (MobiDS) introduced by Drees et al. [26]; (2) the Smart Connected Supplier Network (SCSN) introduced by Stolwijk, Berkers [27]; and (3) the Maritime Data Space (MDS) introduced by Rødseth, Berre [28].

Drees et al. [26] proposed the MobiDS as an initiative to realize a trustworthy data-sharing ecosystem dedicated to the mobility sector, one of the nine critical sectors referred by the European Commission with a high demand for IDS technology in Europe. To foster discoverability, accessibility, and trustworthiness traits in IDS, the authors describe the implementation of a metadata broker that publishes and allows data users to search for data sources and services. The authors also propose an architecture in which they specify the interactions of the metadata broker with the other intermediary roles in an IDS ecosystem (i.e., clearinghouse, vocabulary provider, identity provider, and data apps provider). Despite the extensive description of the demonstrator (including prototypes of the intermediary services), the architecture is limited to a high-level organizational viewpoint. It does not elaborate on what kind of technologies could support the technical

---

8 https://clicksconnectorstore-sandbox.mxapps.io.

9 https://clicksconnectorstore-sandbox.mxapps.io/rest-doc/api.

10 https://github.com/danniarreza/connectorstoreontology.

implementation of its components or how to use them, which may limit its acceptance by business practitioners, developers, and scholars in exploring particular business cases. However, the architecture presented in this paper characterizes the technological components individually and how they interact with one another in alignment with the upper layer's business processes and roles. Still, the authors of MobiDS report the evaluation of its usability by highlighting use cases on a granular level (i.e., intermodal mobility, on-demand rural transport, first/last mile, and traffic management). The evaluation of the prototype's usability introduced in this paper is part of future work.

Stolwijk, Berkers [27] introduced the concept of a Smart Connected Supply Network (SCSN) as a data-sharing ecosystem for the manufacturing domain where multiple service providers are fully interconnected using IDS technology. It allows a manufacturing company to interoperate with other companies reachable in the network once they connect with one of the service providers. In an SCSN ecosystem, the service providers become the central components enacting a data space by providing manufacturing companies with IDS connectors whereby companies could exchange data. Although the authors present a high-level architecture specifying the relationships between manufacturing companies, software components, and service providers, they provide no architectural viewpoints to clarify how to realize the SCSN from a technical perspective. Their work focuses on bringing forward the projected benefits and savings learned from implementing the SCSN standard to facilitate interoperability between manufacturing companies through a simulation of three different ICT service providers.

Lastly, the Maritime Data Space (MDS) proposed by Rødseth, Berre [28] comprehends an IDS-based Maritime ecosystem aiming to tackle data ownership, access rights, and interoperability issues originating from the existing decentralized physical systems architecture and data storage. The authors propose a conceptual model for MDS, which explains its active business roles, business services, datasets, and metadata. Yet, similar to the two related approaches, their conceptual model falls short of elaborating the technical aspects of developing and implementing the proposed data space. Such a limitation may hinder technology adoption by companies interested in customizing it in their business cases.

6 Conclusion and Future Research

This paper addressed the research problem of designing an application to support the broker service provider's role in an International Data Space. Focusing on developing technology to help this role is a crucial enabler of the simplest form of an IDS-based business ecosystem, which still includes data owners' and users' roles. This work also accomplishes part of a Design Science cycle [11] started in recent work [12, 13]. The problem investigation phase combined requirements from the IDSA technical specifications [6–8] with Enterprise Interoperability and data sovereignty requirements elicited from representatives of the Dutch Logistics sector and Enterprise Integration software companies interested in joining IDS-based ecosystems shortly [12]. The primary outcome of the treatment design phase was a reference architecture to guide the implementation of IDS-based applications initially evaluated in [12] and extended in this paper with a white-box view of the components of the broker service provider. Moreover, the treatment design combined IDSA technical specifications with Semantic Web and Linked

Data technologies. The Data Connector Store represents a proof-of-concept application that partially validates the utility of the Enterprise Architecture model also described in this paper.

The main contributions of this work are threefold. First, it demonstrates the *technical feasibility* of implementing a broker service provider. As the state-of-the-art technology evolves with companies providing their data connectors and further advances in IDS infrastructure, companies, especially SMEs, are expected to become more motivated to join IDS-based ecosystems and invest in their underlying technology. Second, although not yet evaluated by end-users, the prototype of the Data Connector Store could *facilitate* the discovery and selection of data connectors for companies interested in exploring IDS ecosystems. Moreover, the architecture is customizable, including other ontologies to describe new types of data connectors and catalogs. Last, the Data Connector Store innovates the IDSA technical guidelines by combining Semantic Web and Linked Data technologies to integrate IDS technology already available for testing.

There are also some limitations threatening the validity of this work. The first one concerns the correctness of the architecture. Even though the development of this work is based on the reference architecture model and technical guidelines provided by the IDSA, a proper evaluation by an Evaluation Facility appointed by the IDSA will further guarantee its compliance with IDS specifications. The second one concerns the lack of evaluation of the prototype with end-users. Although it had a positive preliminary assessment of some of the representatives of the Dutch Logistics sector involved in this research, a direct examination by companies interested in joining an IDS-based ecosystem is necessary. That leads to the third limitation, which calls for a business case to demonstrate the prototype's utility and usability. The IDSA call for business cases is urgent [9], but companies are still skeptical about the practical benefits of investing in IDS technology. On top of this, business cases will test the prototype's performance and scalability.

There are three immediate research directions to explore from this work. The first one will comprehend the extension of the Enterprise Architecture proposed in this work with the clearinghouse role, which is essential to ensure consistency of the data transactions in an IDS-based ecosystem. Besides, it is critical to show its technical feasibility with a prototype. According to the IDSA Reference Architecture Model, a broker service provider could accumulate the clearinghouse function in a federated IDS-based ecosystem. There are also indications that the Enterprise Integration software companies involved in this research may explore their private control towers as a mechanism to realize the functionalities of a clearinghouse in IDS. The second direction is extending the Semantic Web and Linked Data functionalities used in this work to leverage the discoverability of the IDS data connectors' data applications. This work assumed that these applications were preconfigured and ensembled in a data connector for a while. However, it should be possible for companies to reuse their data transformation applications to build customizable data connectors to operate in diverse business domains. Finally, a business case involving the exchange of sensitive data among Dutch Transport Logistics partners could provide more robust evidence for the acceptance and adoption of IDS technology, at least for regional ecosystems.

Acknowledgments. This research is financially supported by the Dutch Ministry of Economic Affairs and co-financed via TKI DINALOG and NWO. The CLICKS project has granted funding for this work (grant no. 439.19.633). CLICKS is the acronym for *Connecting Logistics Interfaces, Converters, Knowledge, and Standards.* The authors thank the involved consortium partners for their support and the anonymous reviewers for their constructive feedback.

References

1. Braud, A., Fromentoux, G., Radier, B., Le Grand, O.: The road to European digital sovereignty with Gaia-X and IDSA. IEEE Netw. **35**(2), 4–5 (2021)
2. Autolitano, S., Pawlowska, A.: Europe's quest for digital sovereignty: GAIA-X as a case study. IAI Papers **21**(14), 1–22 (2021)
3. Bader, S., et al.: The international data spaces information model–an ontology for sovereign exchange of digital content. In: Bader, S., et al. (eds.) The Semantic Web – ISWC 2020. ISWC 2020. Lecture Notes in Computer Science, vol. 12507, pp. 176–192. Springer, Cham (2020). https://doi.org/10.1007/978-3-030-62466-8_12
4. Otto, B., Jarke, M.: Designing a multi-sided data platform: findings from the International Data Spaces case. Electron. Mark. **29**(4), 561–580 (2019). https://doi.org/10.1007/s12525-019-00362-x
5. IDSA: IDSA rule book version 1.0. In: Steinbuss, S. (ed.) International Data Spaces Association, Berlin (2020)
6. IDSA: IDS reference architecture model version 3.0. In: Steinbuss, S. (ed.) International Data Spaces Association, Berlin (2019)
7. IDSA: IDS Metadata Broker (2022). https://github.com/International-Data-Spaces-Association/metadata-broker-open-core. Accessed 11 June 2022
8. IDSA: IDS Metadata Broker API Reference Implementation (2020). https://app.swaggerhub.com/apis/idsa/IDS-Broker/1.3.1. Accessed 10 June 2022
9. Otto, B.: Interview with Reinhold Achatz on "data sovereignty and data ecosystems." Bus. Inf. Syst. Eng. **61**(5), 635–636 (2019)
10. Gort, E.: Developing a maturity model-based approach supporting the decision to adopt International Data Spaces. Master's thesis, University of Twente (2021)
11. Wieringa, R.J.: Design Science Methodology for Information Systems and Software Engineering. Springer, Heidelberg (2014). https://doi.org/10.1007/978-3-662-43839-8
12. Firdausy, D.R., Silva, P.D.A., van Sinderen, M., Iacob, M.-E.: Towards a reference enterprise architecture to enforce digital sovereignty in international data spaces. Paper Presented at the IEEE 24th Conference on Business Informatics (CBI), Amsterdam, The Netherlands (2022)
13. Firdausy, D., Silva, P.D.A., van Sinderen, M.J., Iacob, M.E.: Semantic discovery and selection of data connectors in international data spaces. In: Interoperability for Enterprise Systems and Applications, I-ESA 2022 (2022)
14. Bader, S., et al.: Specification: IDS meta data broker. In: Steinbuss, S. (ed.) IDSA (2020)
15. IDSA Certification Working Group: Component certification criteria catalog V2.1.2. In: International Data Spaces Association (2021)
16. Josey, A.: ArchiMate® 3.0. 1-A pocket guide. Van Haren (2017)
17. Iacob, M.E., Meertens, L.O., Jonkers, H., Quartel, D.A.C., Nieuwenhuis, L.J.M., van Sinderen, M.J.: From enterprise architecture to business models and back. Softw. Syst. Model. **13**(3), 1059–1083 (2012). https://doi.org/10.1007/s10270-012-0304-6
18. Soylu, A., et al.: Enhancing public procurement in the european union through constructing and exploiting an integrated knowledge graph. In: Pan, J.Z., et al. (eds.) ISWC 2020. LNCS, vol. 12507, pp. 430–446. Springer, Cham (2020). https://doi.org/10.1007/978-3-030-62466-8_27

19. Berners-Lee, T., Hendler, J., Lassila, O.: The semantic web. Sci. Am. **284**(5), 34–43 (2001)
20. Suárez-Figueroa, M.C., Gómez-Pérez, A., Fernández-López, M.: The NeOn methodology for ontology engineering. In: Suárez-Figueroa, M., Gómez-Pérez, A., Motta, E., Gangemi, A. (eds.) Ontology Engineering in a Networked World, pp. 9–34. Springer, Heidelberg (2012). https://doi.org/10.1007/978-3-642-24794-1_2
21. Sivakumar, R., Arivoli, P.: Ontology visualization PROTÉGÉ tools–a review. Int. J. Adv. Inf. Technol. (IJAIT) **1** (2011)
22. Kadaster B.V.: Platform Linked Data Nederland (PLDN). https://data.pldn.nl/
23. TriplyDB (2022). https://triply.cc/. Accessed 14 Apr 2022
24. Henkel, M., Stirna, J.: Pondering on the key functionality of model-driven development tools: the case of mendix. In: Forbrig, P., Günther, H. (eds.) Perspectives in Business Informatics Research. BIR 2010. Lecture Notes in Business Information Processing. Springer, Heidelberg, vol. 64, pp. 146–160 (2010). https://doi.org/10.1007/978-3-642-16101-8_12
25. Berners-Lee, T.: Linked Data (2006). https://www.w3.org/DesignIssues/LinkedData.html. Accessed 15 June 2022
26. Drees, H., Kubitza, D.O., Lipp, J., Pretzsch, S., Langdon, C.S.: Mobility data space–first implementation and business opportunities. In: ITS World Congress (2021)
27. Stolwijk, C., Berkers, F.: Scalability and agility of the smart connected supplier network approach. In: TNO (2020)
28. Rødseth, Ø.J., Berre, A.J.: From digital twin to maritime data space: transparent ownership and use of ship information. In: Proceedings of 13th International Symposium on Integrated Ship's Information Systems & Marine Traffic Engineering Conference (ISIS-MTE), pp. 1–8 (2018)

Validating Vector-Label Propagation
for Graph Embedding

Valerio Bellandi[1] (ORCID), Ernesto Damiani[1] (ORCID), Valerio Ghirimoldi[1],
Samira Maghool[1(✉)] (ORCID), and Fedra Negri[2] (ORCID)

[1] Università degli Studi di Milano (UNIMI), Milan, Italy
`{valerio.bellandi,ernesto.damiani,samira.maghool}@unimi.it`,
`valerio.ghirimoldi@studenti.unimi.it`
[2] Università degli Studi di Milano-Bicocca, Milan, Italy
`fedra.negri@unimib.it`

Abstract. Structural network analysis retrieves the holistic patterns of interactions among network instances. Due to the unprecedented growth of data availability, it is time to take advantage of Machine Learning to integrate the outcome of the structural analysis with better predictions on the upcoming states of large networks. Concerning the existing challenges of adopting methods embracing *multi-dimensional, multi-task, transparent* representations within *incremental* procedures, in our recent study, we proposed the AVPRA algorithm. It works as an embedder of both the network structure and domain-specific features making the aforementioned challenges feasible to address. In this paper, we elaborate on the validation of AVPRA by adopting it in multiple downstream Machine Learning tasks on the Twitter network of the Italian Parliament. Comparing the outcome with state-of-the-art algorithms of graph embedding, the capability of AVPRA in retaining either network structure properties or domain-specific features of the nodes is promising. In addition, the method is incremental and transparent.

Keywords: Vector-label propagation · Social network analysis · Graph embedding

1 Introduction

Network analysis comprises powerful methods to study the relationship between the elements of a network, with applications to any domain where the structure of the network can reveal interaction patterns or emerging states [10]. Most of the applied algorithms exploit graph theory to measure specific properties of the overall network, the subgraphs composing it, or the individual nodes. These measures have been successfully applied to predict the evolution of specific states of the network or its individual nodes [8]. Integrating the results of network analysis into downstream Machine Learning (ML) has become an interesting research topic due to the unprecedented growth of data availability. Leveraging ML algorithms for studying complex networks, containing large number of nodes

M. Sellami et al. (Eds.): CoopIS 2022, LNCS 13591, pp. 259–276, 2022.
https://doi.org/10.1007/978-3-031-17834-4_15

and edges with various properties, have made a huge step toward analysing and predicting the behavior of a system [34]. However, specific challenges have to be addressed to realize this integration.

The metrics from network analysis can be included in the feature space assigned to a learning procedure as any other descriptor, accounting for the structural properties of the elements of the system. Data fusion techniques offer multiple strategies to unify them with descriptors from other sources [21,25]. Nevertheless this approach suffers from the *structural determinism* of network measures i.e. results are determined by the network structure, only disregarding the role of others features characterizing individual elements in the domain [11]. For example, nodes from different communities can be represented by similar centrality values if they have similar structural relationships within the community. Thus, they may fall close in the feature space feeding a ML algorithm, even if belonging to different communities. An alternative strategy is using graph embedding algorithms to represent the network structure in low dimensional space while preserving the distances between the elements in the network [33]. These approaches generate a latent space losing a *transparent* connection to the original network space, thus, even if the distances between nodes are preserved, it is hard to explain the reasons motivating an interspace between elements. Another strategy is using graph neural networks to directly encode the network structure into the architecture of the neural network [1]. This method implies the neural network is designed to address a *specific task*. Updates in the network structure require re-initialising the neural network and the results obtained can be hardly *incrementally* integrated with results obtained in the past. Exploring a system through networks requires tools reflecting the networks features in an interpretable manner. Also, the nodes of a network often refer to dynamically changing instances. Analysing and predicting the dynamics of a network demand to measure its structural properties as well as the full picture of domain-specific features of nodes. In other words, the current methods are *structural determined* and *non transparent, task specific* and *non incremental.*

In our previous paper, addressing this matter, we proposed the agent-based Vector-label PRopagation Algorithm (AVPRA) [37] for explainable exploration through the network's feature space. Using this algorithm results in extracting the *d-dimensional* weighted vectors of features in the feature space rather than latent space, which makes them explainable. Each element of these vectors conveys information on how features formed the current status of instances in the network. In this work, we aim at verifying the applicability of AVPRA to different predictive tasks using established ML methods. More specifically, in Sect. 2 we discuss the related works, in Sect. 3 we present the AVPRA algorithm and characterize its properties, in Sect. 4 we present the experimental validation we conducted, in Sect. 5 we discuss the results achieved, and in Sect. 6 we go to the conclusion.

2   Related Works

2.1   Vector-Label Propagation

The original idea of Label Propagation was proposed in 2002, as an iterative procedure to augment data before feeding a classification task [42]. Applying this algorithm, the unlabeled nodes of the network adopt the label of the majority of nodes in their neighborhood. Considering that labels are deterministic and discrete representations of nodes' features by a single value, they are not able to picture a holistic view of the network using information from different sources. Therefore, the Vector-Label Propagation (VLP) algorithms are proposed to encode the multiple features a node could convey in a dynamic system into a vector of labels. In these algorithms, the most weighted labels or combination of all labels of the vector-labels (VL) are utilized to get the most influential features for the given node or to find out the overlapping communities it belongs to [14]. For example, to identify a list of songs to recommend to a user based on the most favored in its neighborhood.

The belonging coefficient of a label is a parameterized measurement computed aggregating the vector-labels in the neighborhood to take account of the influence a label has on the node based on how frequently it appears in the neighborhood. The aggregation procedure acquiring the neighborhood features, a.k.a *update rule*, does not necessarily follow the majority rule. A common complexity may arise when multiple labels have equal frequency hence a *random selection* should be operated. This random choice has been identified as a major source of instability, since different executions of the algorithm may result in different label assignments. To overcome this issue multiple variants of the update rule have been proposed [18,20,35,39–41], using the structural feature of nodes to reduce this type of instability. Primarily, these variants identify the most influential nodes to decide the order in which nodes are updated or the initialization of the labels in the network [2]. Overall, the VL approach helps in reducing the instability of LP algorithms as all the labels in the neighborhood can be accounted for. It also permits considering non-structural features to describe node properties in a holistic multidimensional mode.

2.2   Graph Embedding

Graph Embedding (GE) in general terms is a data preparation procedure mapping the existing information of a network as much as possible in a unified usable data format to input ML algorithms for implementing several downstream tasks. Many algorithms such as Matrix factorization-based [9,27], Random walk-based [15,29,30], and Neural network-based algorithms [16,19] are developed in order to retrieve as much as possible the properties of the network and map them in a latent space [3]. Most of these algorithms have been however criticized for adding a level of complexity to ML results [5]. The latent space they provide implies explainability issues, therefore some post-hoc interpretative analysis is needed [28].

By AVPRA, we propose to adopt a VLP algorithm as a mapping function where the belonging coefficients capture the *diffusibility* of the labels into nodes, depending on the distances from the source of the features and their frequency. To encode the diffusibility of all the features in the network, the *vector-label* includes all of them in vectors of fixed length, while the *belonging coefficient* accounts for their incidence in the node neighborhood. A big advantage of this approach is that, at the end of the propagation procedure, all the nodes of the network can be positioned in the same feature space and the output data format is suitable for implementing multiple ML tasks.

3   Methodology

We first, briefly, introduce the AVPRA algorithm characterizing the procedures it activates in exploring the space of a network and in encoding the collected information into VL.

3.1   AVPRA Model Specification

Considering the rationale behind VLP algorithms in preserving information on the features of individual nodes, we proposed an agent-based model where nodes have memory about received information from different sources and limited rationality for updating its vector label coefficients [37].

The updating rule is realized by an aggregation function unifying the received information from neighborhood. An example of such function is represented in Eq. 1. At each time step t, $b(l)$, the belonging coefficient of an element of the $\mathbf{VL}_i[l](t)$, can be updated by aggregating the k neighbors' $\mathbf{VL}_{j \in \Gamma(i)}[l](t-1)$.

$$\mathbf{VL}_i[l](t) = w_1 \mathbf{VL}_i[l](t) + w_2 \sum_{j \in \Gamma(i)} \mathbf{VL}_{j \in \Gamma(i)}[l](t-1) \qquad (1)$$

where w_1 and w_2 are the weight of current assigned labels l of node i and the weight of the neighbors $\Gamma(i)$, respectively. In a basic scenario, $w_1 = w_2 = \frac{1}{\Gamma(i)+1} = \frac{1}{k+1}$, hence, for all the common elements in $\mathbf{VL}_i$ and $\mathbf{VL}_j$ vectors, the values of the given elements l increase unconditionally and will be normalized to 1 by the inverse of the cardinality of $\Gamma(i)$. All the **VL**s get updated synchronously, to avoid conflicts in the order of update, and reflect all the changes received at the same iteration by all nodes. Following the dynamical changes of VLs, we witnessed the propagation procedure to reach the termination point, where the updated value of each element is below a certain threshold defined by the user, after a few number of iterations which is about the average path length of the network [37].

Our algorithm mechanism helps in discarding couple of instabilities caused by *random selection* and *ordering* of updates. The former is addressed by the fact that we keep all the coefficient labels up to the termination point, while the latter is addressed by averaging over a number of executions starting with different initial seeds, i.e. the nodes settled as starting points of the propagation process.

As an illustrative example of our proposal, Fig. 1 proposes a schematic network containing three agents with three initial distinct features red (R), yellow (Y) and green (G). The vector-label for agent i at time $t-1$ is as $\{R, Y, G\}_i = \{l_1, l_2, l_3\}_i$, containing the weights of all unique features. The updated vector-label at time t is created as a combination of its neighbors' vector-labels at time $t-1$, according to the update rule.

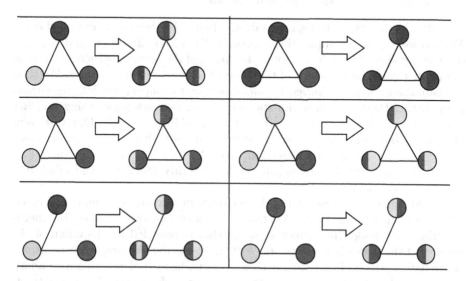

Fig. 1. The schematic view of the AVPRA algorithm implemented on a small network containing three nodes. In the first and second row, the network is fully connected and the states of nodes are depicted by colors; Red, Green, and Yellow. In each section of the picture, the initial state at time $T = t - 1$ is followed by evolved state at $T = t$ according to a propagation rule. In the third row, the connections have changed and subsequently the following state has been modified. (Color figure online)

3.2   Properties of the AVPRA Algorithm

The AVPRA algorithm is an agent-based iterative procedure where agents progress the propagation acting in response to the VLs they access in their neighborhood. To avoid conflicts in propagating the updates, all agents get updated simultaneously at each iteration. The updating rule defines the aggregation function to apply in updating VLs. To initialize the procedure, some of the agents of the network must be assigned to valued VLs but not all of them have to start with an initial valued VL. The termination of the AVPRA algorithm is achieved when the system reaches an iteration s where VLs are stationary. This implies, that the variations on the belonging coefficient of all labels must be less than a defined value p. We name p the negligibly threshold. Experimental results have shown this threshold can be achieved with a number of iterations that is close to the average path length of the network [37].

These properties of the algorithm make it *incremental*, i.e., updates in the network structure do not require re-execute the procedure but can be applied first locally and then propagated in the other nodes by a few numbers of iterations. This makes the AVPRA algorithm more ductile to integrate into downstream ML pipelines.

3.3   Validating the Representing Model

To verify the quality of the representation achieved by the vectors obtained using AVPRA we exploit a comparative approach. The idea is that high-quality graph embeddings should be able to capture key parts of the network structure [7], thus can predict common measures of the network, current or future states. We then compare the accuracy achieved by supervised and unsupervised ML algorithms in predicting these measures and states encoding network nodes using AVPRA VLs or using other state-of-the-art graph embedding methods. Our tests aim to address different relevant *analytical tasks* in network analysis, namely community and sub-community detection (Sect. 4.1 and 5.2) clustering (Sect. 4.2) link prediction (Sect. 4.3) measuring node centrality (Sect. 4.4) and label-drift detection (Sect. 4.5).

In addition to an assessment of the accuracy, our experiments underline capabilities provided by the AVPRA VLs not supported by other embedding methods. Encoding nodes into a feature space that is provided by the union of the features of the nodes in the network, AVPRA keeps *domain properties* transparent to data analysis. To let emerge these aspects, instead of adopting a standard dataset, used in research settings, we preferred to refer to a real-world dataset, where domain-related aspects can emerge.

3.4   Populite Data Set

In a collaborative study funded by the University of Milan, involving the Department of Social and Political Sciences and the Department of Computer Science, the *Populite* project has been launched. The aim is to study the behavioral patterns of Italian politicians on social media. A key aspect of this study is to depict the communities and sub-communities that the communication flow and the social network among Italian politicians on social media create. By studying the inter and intra-cohesion of these communities multiple interesting questions can be answered. Which are the political groups that interact the most, which ones are partitioned into sub-communities (i.e., intra-party factions), and to which other political groups these sub-communities are connected? Individual links can also be analyzed. Is there reciprocity between parliamentarians? Which ones are similar, based on their "neighborhood"?

Considering the Twitter social network, its API can be used to retrieve and analyze the social network and the communication flow of a set of users. This API provides the access to different resources including: *Tweets*, *Users*, *Lists*, *Trends*, *Media* and *Places*. The Political Science Department provided the list of parliamentarians, deputies and senators, and other relevant political actors in Italy. With this information in hand 41615 tweets were downloaded, in the period between January 2020 and February 2022. Information about the membership of the analyzed actors in political groups was retrieved using the open data of the Italian chamber and senate and adjusted manually for those active actors not titled of a seat in the parliament. Data were stored in a graph database to aggregate them and execute the required queries. For example, the social network of the politicians was created by using the *friendship* relation among Twitter users and extracted as the edge list matrix, to input network analysis algorithms.

4   Experimental Results

We proceed with evaluating the AVPRA outcome in implementing some downstream ML tasks exploring the Populite data set. For each task, the accuracy and execution run time are compared with some state-of-the-art algorithms, namely, Deepwalk [29], Node2vec [15], and M-NMF[38].

4.1   Community Detection

In network analysis, communities reveal the structural and functional properties of groups of nodes. Even though there is valuable literature on community detection algorithms, they mostly focus on the structural properties of the networks. In the other words, the fact that each member may be characterized by various domain-specific features toward different communities is not exploited.

In traditional approaches, the community detection task is based on the modularity maximization problem. Modularity measures the strength of division of a network into modules, i.e. strongly connected components. To address this problem, some repetitive steps take place in forming/deforming the possible partitions in the network and finding the one which results in the maximum value of modularity [6]. Among the common algorithms, the so-called *Leiden* community detection proves that the connected communities and all subsets of all partitions are locally optimally assigned [36].

Considering the Twitter connections[1] of the Italian parliament as a directed network, we take the detected communities by Leiden algorithm as ground truth labels. Leveraging these labels we run a Random Forest (RF) classifier in order to evaluate how the vectors resulting from running AVPRA or other graph embedding methods can capture the structural properties of the network similarly to the Leiden algorithm. Table 1 presents the F1 scores and the execution time for

---

[1] In particular we used the friendship relation accessible from Twitter API.

this task, comparing the AVPRA vector labels with other algorithms embedded vectors. AVPRA MW and AVPRA 10 MW are two derivatives of the AVPRA vector labels where a limited number of labels is taken into account. The former refers to the most weighted label, the latter to the ten most weighted labels. In the case of multi-class classification, some averaging metrics for F1 scores are used in the classification report. A macro-average will compute the metric independently for each class and then take the average hence treating all classes equally, whereas a micro-average will aggregate the contributions of all classes to compute the average metric. In the case of an equal number of samples for each class, macro and micro averaging will result in the same score [26]. For those algorithms with hyperparameters in the mapping function, the mean and standard deviation of F1 scores are calculated.

Table 1. The evaluation of AVPRA used for the community detection task. A RF classifier is trained on the 80% of VLs with the Leiden communities labels and tested on the 20% calculating the F1 score.

Embedding algorithms	Community detection ($mean \pm std$)		
	F1_micro	F1_macro	Execution_time(s)
AVPRA	**0.993464**	**0.993073**	3.768
AVPRA MW	0.967320	0.966128	1.879
AVPRA 10MW	0.967320	0.967105	0.627
DeepWalk	0.975163 ± 0.01164	0.97322 ± 0.01219	3.545
Node2vec	0.972222 ± 0.0119	0.971005 ± 0.1198	11.681
M-NMF	0.972549 ± 0.01503	0.971930 ± 0.0146	39.003/18.921

4.2   Clustering

Continuing the evaluation of the representation power of the AVPRA VLs, an unsupervised task is studied. In particular, we consider the capabilities of clustering techniques in grouping similar instances. A number of clusters equal to the number of partitions proposed by the Leiden community detection algorithm is formed out of the VLs by AVPRA and, embedded vectors by Deepwalk, Node2vec, and M-NMF. In the evaluation of unsupervised tasks, Normalized Mutual Information (NMI) is a measure used to evaluate network partitioning performed by community detection algorithms. The basic idea of this metric represents the amount of retrieved information from one distribution regarding the second one [23]. Spectral, Kmeans, and Agglomerative Clustering algorithms are applied to the Populite network, and the calculated NMI for each of these algorithms on embedding methods is presented in Table 2.

Table 2. The Normalized Mutual Information, comparing the clustered embedded vectors resulted by one clustering algorithm.

	NMI (*mean ± std*)		
Algorithm	Spectral clustering	Kmeans Clustering	Agglomerative Clustering
AVPRA	0.892796	0.883197	**0.882575**
DeepWalk	0.903192 ± 0.043	0.926282 ± 0.033	0.867466 ± 0.028
Node2vec	**0.926852±0.009**	**0.932014±0.011**	0.872850 ± 0.012
M-NMF	0.86433 ± 0.055	0.867234 ± 0.048	0.845866 ± 0.044

4.3 Link Prediction

The link prediction problem mainly refers to the evaluation of possible relations between two existing nodes in the network [17,22]. Often the problem is addressed using a supervised learning approach, where a model is trained based on the existing/corrupted links in the network [31]. In our experiments, we adopted a direct evaluation approach. After getting the vectors by the compared embedding algorithms, for each possible couple of nodes in the network (each possible edge), we calculate the cosine similarity of their assigned vectors in the mapping space. This way, for each node based on the maximum similarity with other nodes, we predict the presence of the edge if the similarity value is more than 0.5. After all, we evaluate the presence or absence of a predicted edge based on the true edges in the reference network. Table 3 illustrates the results achieved.

Table 3. The comparison of link prediction score using different embedding algorithms.

	Link prediction (*mean ± std*)	
Embedding algorithms	F1_micro	Execution_time(s)
AVPRA	**0.77790**	0.627
DeepWalk	0.745352 ± 0.0252	13.178
Node2vec	0.713398 ± 0.0159	11.967
M-NMF	0.741063 ± 0.0185	1.749

4.4 Centrality

Concerning the constant increasing size of network data, the calculation of some structural properties, such as node centrality, has a high computational cost. Some algorithms provide approximation solutions using sampling and calculate the single-source shortest path for a given sample of nodes [4,24]. Even though the accuracy of these algorithms is acceptable, the computational cost is still difficult to manage [12]. Motivated by this discussion, as we find the AVPRA less computationally complex in comparison to other state-of-the-art algorithms, we evaluated its capabilities in capturing the centrality of nodes.

For this purpose, using a standard SN analysis library[2], we computed the betweenness centrality of each node. Centrality measures are expressed as continuous values, some times normalized in the range $[0, 1]$, while in order to train a classifier we need discreet ground-truth labels. Witnessing the Populite heterogeneous structural characteristic, such as power-law degree centrality similar to other SNs, we propose three approaches for categorizing the nodes according to their betweenness values into different intervals:

- **approach (a):** Homogeneous intervals: the centrality values are divided by intervals of 0.05 and nodes are categorized accordingly.
- **approach (b):** Heterogeneous intervals: 100 intervals between 0.0005 and 0.05, 5 intervals between 0.05 and 0.1, $(0.1, 0.2]$, $(0.2, 0.5]$, $(0.5, 1]$.
- **approach (c):** Heterogeneous   Decreasing   intervals: $[0, x], (x, 1.5x],$ $(1.5x, 1.5 \times 1.5 \times x], \ldots$, with $x = 0.0001$.

Following the three above-mentioned approaches, we adopt the obtained categories as the ground-truth labels. An RF classifier is then trained to predict centrality categories values based on the vectors of various graph embedding algorithms. The F1 scores of each algorithm in predicting the labels of the test set are presented in Table 4 considering 80% of data set as train set and 20% test set.

Table 4. The accuracy of learning Centrality of the Populite network leveraging the VLs resulted by AVPRA for each node by a Random Forest Classifier. Using the three categorization methods defined in Sect. 4.4, the values are reported by $mean \pm std$ for AVPRA, DeepWalk, Node2Vec and M-NMF algorithms.

	Accuracy ($mean \pm std$)		
Algorithm	approach (a)	approach (b)	approach (c)
AVPRA	**0.601307**	**0.594771**	**0.555**
DeepWalk	0.4200 ± 0.051	0.5093 ± 0.033	0.3403 ± 0.063
Node2vec	0.4365 ± 0.039	0.5100 ± 0.038	0.3439 ± 0.057
M-NMF	0.3483 ± 0.052	0.4803 ± 0.030	0.2797 ± 0.042

4.5   Label-Drift Detection

In real world scenarios, both the structural properties of networks and the distribution of features in networks are constantly changing. The dynamic changes in the patterns of connections among individuals can have major impacts on the evolution of the network states and the communication flow. The VLP approach can be effective in capturing these dynamic changes as it can consider the

---

[2] https://networkx.org/.

variation of states due to diffusion and accumulation of features flowing through links. For this reason, we explored the accuracy of a prediction model based on the AVPRA VLs.

In the studied scenario a dynamic evolution of the system is due by the changes in the membership of the political groups at the Parliament that the Italian Constitution considers a fundamental right of parliamentarians. The method adopted to predict these changes is based on the idea of creating VLs for political groups which is the mean of the VLs of the members of the group. If we call this new vectors VL_p, the new group of a parliamentarian x, is the vector in VL_p most similar to VL_x, where similarity is measured by cosine distance.

To test the outcome, we consider 24 different extractions of the Populite data referring to each month in data set. For each time t, predict the new groups of all the candidates whose group changed between extraction t and $t + 1$. The calculated accuracy for each time period is presented in the Table 5, the average prediction accuracy obtained is 0.64.

Table 5. Number of changes happened in the mentioned period of time and the accuracy of prediction by our algorithm

Prediction of changing the labels		
Period	Number of changes in the political groups	Prediction accuracy
2020-01/2020-02	1	1
2020-02/2020-03	2	0.5
2020-03/2020-04	1	1
2020-04/2020-05	2	1
2020-05/2020-06	3	1
2020-06/2020-07	1	1
2020-07/2020-08	1	0
2020-08/2020-09	1	1
2020-09/2020-10	1	1
2020-10/2020-11	1	1
2020-11/2020-12	6	1
2020-12/2021-01	17	0.705882
2021-01/2021-02	4	1
2021-02/2021-03	23	0.956522
2021-03/2021-04	4	0.25
2021-04/2021-05	1	0
2021-05/2021-06	17	0.058824
2021-06/2021-07	1	0
2021-07/2021-08	2	0
2021-08/2021-09	0	–
2021-09/2021-10	2	0.5
2021-10/2021-11	0	–
2021-11/2021-12	1	0
Total period	**Mean number of drifts**	**Mean accuracy**
2020-01/2021-12	2.19047	0.641304

5   Discussion

In this section, we discuss the results we achieved and underline the capabilities of AVPRA in capturing both structural and domain-specific properties of the network.

5.1   Structural Properties of the Network

The set of experiments we conducted on a variety of network analysis tasks demonstrates the ability of AVPRA in capturing the structural properties of the network. In community detection, Sect. 4.1, our algorithm ranked first, demonstrating its ability to capture the network modularity calculated by the Leiden algorithm. In clustering, Sect. 4.2, AVPRA performs in line with other graph embedding algorithms, with variations depending on the clustering algorithm used. In link prediction, Sect. 4.3, our embedder outperforms others using a reduced execution time. AVPRA outperforms the state of the art also in measuring node centrality, Sect. 4.4, a task recognized as difficult in the literature for ML procedures while initially some neural network learning are required [13]. Finally, AVPRA is partially capable to detect label-drift detection, Sect. 4.5, a problem that is clearly influenced by a variety of factors that are endogenous to the communication network of the parliamentarians.

These results are achieved using an algorithm that is full transparent and incremental. The features composing the AVPRA vectors are directly obtained from the domain features and the addition of new features will not invalidate the previous steps of the procedure. Considering the graph embedding algorithms as the encoder of network features into a latent space, we would face difficulties in retrieving some information such as the centrality of nodes using the embedded vectors and information remains abstract and hard to interpret. Graph embedding algorithms usually create vectors of a dimension of several hundreds of latent features per node in the graph. While eigenvalue-based decomposition methods give some formal guarantees on the retained network properties, random-walk-based methods are stochastic in nature and depend heavily on hyper-parameter settings.

5.2   Domain-Specific Properties of the Network

One of the key capabilities of AVPRA is embedding the network structure directly using domain-specific features. This offers great support during the interpretation of the results. To illustrate the implications we developed an analysis of the sub-communities in the network, showing the differences between the analysis developed by AVPRA and other methods.

As we discussed in Sect. 4.1, community detection in network analysis is highly relevant in realizing the properties of members based on the community they are involved in. According to the homophily principle in social science, nodes located in one community may have more common features, in other words, nodes with similar features tend to create their communities. What is observed at the level of a network can be observed also at the level of its communities, where the members of a given community tend to form groups with a higher number of common interests or stronger affinity. Even though this important problem has been explored in the literature using different approaches and terminologies, we refer to it as sub-community detection. Getting this level of granularity reveals the complexity in the structure of the network and can offer important insight into the affinities shared by nodes in different communities.

Regarding a research question raised by Populite working group about the identification of intra-party factions, we evaluate the AVPRA output vectors in retaining the sub-communities of the network properties. In order to validate the outcome, we compare it with the state-of-the-art, InfoMap algorithm [32]. InfoMap algorithm optimizes *The Map equation*, which exploits the information-theoretic duality between finding community structure in networks and mini-mizing the description length of a random walker's movements on a network. InfoMap supports the two and multi-level partitioning while the core idea is similar to the Louvain algorithm. Implementing this algorithm on the Populite data set, we get the information on the network structure represented in Table 6.

A schematic view of the web-based network navigator[3] is depicted in Fig. 2. The communities are labeled according to the political groups existing in the Italian parliament. The representative nodes of each community are highlighted

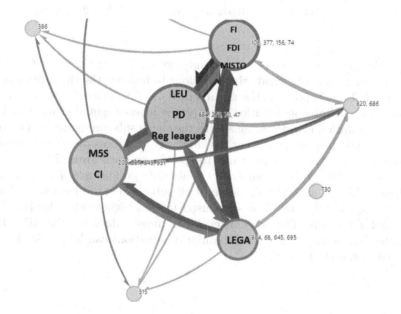

Fig. 2. Schematic view of infomap Algorithm [32] representing the Populite data set. The nodes with higher flow of information are demonstrated by each community. The information flow among each community is weighted and demonstrated by pointers.

---

[3] https://www.mapequation.org/infomap/.

in the figure. The thickness of links connecting the communities demonstrates the flow of information or in other words, the weight of the connection between two partitions.

Having at hand this information from InfoMap, we could find the most influential nodes in the flow of information which can be the interpretation of leaders, and nodes connected to these leaders construct the sub-communities, see Table 6 for details. On the other hand, leveraging the output vectors of AVPRA, as we discussed in the Sect. 4.2, the partitions extracted by state-of-the-art algorithms are in good accordance, more than 88%, with the partitions resulting from clustering the VLs by AVPRA, details in Table 2.

Table 6. The extracted information using the InfoMap algorithm on the Populite data set. **Flow** is the rate of received information to each communities, **in-flow** is the entering and **out-flow** is the rate of exit information. Number of nodes, links and the most involved nodes in the flow path are also mentioned.

Communities	Flow	In-flow	Out-flow	Nodes	Links	Representative nodes id
LEU/PD/REG	0.3898	0.07294	0.05730	184	11918	884,279,70,47
LEGA	0.1028	0.02777	0.03422	146	4999	904,68,645,695
FI/FDI/MISTO	0.1965	0.06379	0.06688	186	7366	106,377,156,74
M5S/CI	0.3105	0.03600	0.04211	256	15734	202,237,849,931

Considering each cluster as a community, we implement the $OPTIC$ clustering algorithm on the VLs inside the partitions to find out the similarities in the second level. Table 7, presents the mean VL, VL_P, for the involved nodes inside communities and sub-communities. Clearly, the most-weighted element of VL_P for the communities, is in accordance with the one in sub-communities. This approach also could help in measuring the similarity/distances of sub-communities in terms of measuring their tendency to specific political areas. Moreover, the distribution of the existing groups and the absolute prominence of a few of them are observable. For example, in cluster 0 all sub-clusters are catheterized by a high value in the PD label. The sub-cluster 0.0 has higher values for the FDI, $M5S$, and FI labels. The sub-cluster 1 has lower values for the $M5S$ label and higher values for the IV label. Similar observations can be provided for all clusters and sub-clusters.

Table 7. The mean weight of VLs located inside a cluster(communities) and sub-clusters (sub-communities). Two examples of clusters and some of the belonging sub-clusters mean weights of elements are represented. Each element refers to a political party a node may involved in. M5S: Movimento5 Stelle; GM: Gruppo Misto; Lega; IV: Italia Viva; PD: Partito Democratico; FI: Forza Italia; FDI: Fratelli D'Italia; CI: Coraggio Italia; LU: Liberi e Uguali; Pla: Per le autonomie

	Mean weight of VL (VL_p) of clusters/sub-clusters									
Cluster	M5S	GM	Lega	IV	PD	FI	FDI	CI	LU	Pla
0	0.10784001	0.066733	0.055306	0.02146	**0.660737**	0.107175	0.029693	0.022745	0.036151	0.005188
Sub-clusters	VL_p of sub-clusters									
0	0.1162275	0.068403	0.060062	0.020338	0.646582	0.112942	0.031678	0.023786	0.036209	0.005452
1	0.09068673	0.065458	0.05509	0.022798	**0.653536**	0.110606	0.029541	0.02258	0.035431	0.00496
2	0.08138816	0.061689	0.05185	0.023376	**0.674685**	0.104717	0.027103	0.021945	0.034635	0.004913
3	0.12472662	0.068516	0.061732	0.020404	**0.637912**	0.118537	0.034373	0.024205	0.03432	0.004864
4	0.10234745	0.064337	0.045815	0.022505	**0.691376**	0.09406	0.024516	0.021495	0.035897	0.005123
Cluster										
1	**0.746649**	0.111349	0.038724	0.003204	0.075565	0.044796	0.014362	0.030933	0.009983	0.001288
Sub-clusters	VL_p of sub-clusters									
0	**0.748093**	0.112028	0.038639	0.00308	0.072941	0.043236	0.013958	0.031057	0.00991	0.001257
1	**0.774574**	0.112761	0.03088	0.002101	0.047472	0.031561	0.010888	0.028511	0.007825	0.000872
2	**0.774678**	0.111601	0.024984	0.003139	0.071959	0.036025	0.010138	0.029971	0.009463	0.001004
3	**0.758054**	0.11416	0.035063	0.003208	0.070387	0.038875	0.013638	0.027245	0.009758	0.001030
4	**0.78523**	0.11601	0.02202	0.01803	0.04000	0.02840	0.00817	0.03110	0.00718	0.00075

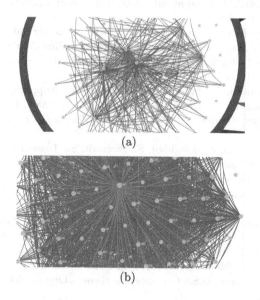

(a)

(b)

Fig. 3. Hierarchical representation of communities extracted from infomap Algorithm [32]. (a). The community of *M5S and CI* is zoomed in (b)The in-flow/out-flow of information of node 212 is depicted.

6   Conclusion

Due to the unbounded increasing size of networks representing a system of instances and interconnections, neither capturing structural nor domain-specific properties are feasible by using traditional network analysis tools. Leveraging tools to reflect domain-specific and structural properties of networks in the feature space digestible by ML algorithm for further exploration seems inevitable in real-life network studies. In our experiment, the AVPRA algorithm [37] has been proven to be able to capture the *structural properties* of the studied network on multiple *analytical tasks*, without disregarding the ability to retain its *domain-specific* features. The algorithm is also *incremental*, making it possible to update its results when the domain is evolving and supports a *transparent* analysis of the obtained results, explaining them in terms of the domain features embedded during the VLP procedure.

References

1. Abbas, A.M.: Social network analysis using deep learning: applications and schemes. Soc. Netw. Anal. Min. **11**(1), 1–21 (2021)
2. Azaouzi, M., Romdhane, L.B.: An evidential influence-based label propagation algorithm for distributed community detection in social networks. Proc. Comput. Sci. **112**, 407–416 (2017)
3. Azzini, A., et al.: Advances in data management in the big data era. In: Goedicke, M., Neuhold, E., Rannenberg, K. (eds.) Advancing Research in Information and Communication Technology. IAICT, vol. 600, pp. 99–126. Springer, Cham (2021). https://doi.org/10.1007/978-3-030-81701-5_4
4. Bader, D.A., Kintali, S., Madduri, K., Mihail, M.: Approximating betweenness centrality. In: Bonato, A., Chung, F.R.K. (eds.) WAW 2007. LNCS, vol. 4863, pp. 124–137. Springer, Heidelberg (2007). https://doi.org/10.1007/978-3-540-77004-6_10
5. Bellandi, V., Ceravolo, P., Maghool, S., Siccardi, S.: Toward a general framework for multimodal big data analysis. Big Data (2022)
6. Blondel, V.D., Guillaume, J.L., Lambiotte, R., Lefebvre, E.: Fast unfolding of communities in large networks. J. Stat. Mech: Theory Exp. **2008**(10), P10008 (2008)
7. Bonner, S., Brennan, J., Kureshi, I., Theodoropoulos, G., McGough, A.S., Obara, B.: Evaluating the quality of graph embeddings via topological feature reconstruction. In: 2017 IEEE International Conference on Big Data (Big Data), pp. 2691–2700 (2017). https://doi.org/10.1109/BigData.2017.8258232
8. Borgatti, S.P., Halgin, D.S.: On network theory. Organ. Sci. **22**(5), 1168–1181 (2011)
9. Cao, S., Lu, W., Xu, Q.: Grarep: learning graph representations with global structural information. In: International Conference on Information and Knowledge Management (CIKM), pp. 891–900 (2015)
10. Chiesi, A.: Network analysis. In: Smelser, N.J., Baltes, P.B. (eds.) International Encyclopedia of the Social & Behavioral Sciences, Pergamon, Oxford, pp. 10499–10502 (2001). https://doi.org/10.1016/B0-08-043076-7/04211-X,https://www.sciencedirect.com/science/article/pii/B008043076704211X

11. Emirbayer, M., Goodwin, J.: Network analysis, culture, and the problem of agency. Am. J. Sociol. **99**(6), 1411–1454 (1994)
12. Grando, F., Granville, L.Z., Lamb, L.C.: Machine learning in network centrality measures: tutorial and outlook. ACM Comput. Surv. (CSUR) **51**(5), 1–32 (2018)
13. Grando, F., Lamb, L.C.: On approximating networks centrality measures via neural learning algorithms. In: 2016 International Joint Conference on Neural Networks (IJCNN), pp. 551–557. IEEE (2016)
14. Gregory, S.: Finding overlapping communities in networks by label propagation. New J. Phys. **12**(10), 103018 (2010)
15. Grover, A., Leskovec, J.: node2vec: Scalable feature learning for networks. In: ACM SIGKDD International Conference on Knowledge Discovery and Data Mining (KDD), pp. 855–864 (2016)
16. Hamilton, W., Ying, Z., Leskovec, J.: Inductive representation learning on large graphs. In: Conference on Advances in Neural Information Processing Systems (NIPS), pp. 1024–1034 (2017)
17. Hasan, M.A., Zaki, M.J.: A survey of link prediction in social networks. In: Social network data analytics, pp. 243–275. Springer (2011). https://doi.org/10.1007/978-1-4419-8462-3_9
18. Jokar, E., Mosleh, M.: Community detection in social networks based on improved label propagation algorithm and balanced link density. Phys. Lett. A **383**(8), 718–727 (2019)
19. Kipf, T.N., Welling, M.: Semi-supervised classification with graph convolutional networks. arXiv:1609.02907 (2016)
20. Li, Q., Zhou, T., Lü, L., Chen, D.: Identifying influential spreaders by weighted leaderrank. Phys. A **404**, 47–55 (2014)
21. Lim, M., Abdullah, A., Jhanjhi, N., Khan, M.K.: Situation-aware deep reinforcement learning link prediction model for evolving criminal networks. IEEE Access **8**, 16550–16559 (2019)
22. Martínez, V., Berzal, F., Cubero, J.C.: A survey of link prediction in complex networks. ACM Comput. Surv. (CSUR) **49**(4), 1–33 (2016)
23. McDaid, A.F., Greene, D., Hurley, N.: Normalized mutual information to evaluate overlapping community finding algorithms. arXiv preprint arXiv:1110.2515 (2011)
24. Mendonça, M.R., Barreto, A.M., Ziviani, A.: Approximating network centrality measures using node embedding and machine learning. IEEE Trans. Netw. Sci. Eng. **8**(1), 220–230 (2020)
25. Nurek, M., Michalski, R.: Combining machine learning and social network analysis to reveal the organizational structures. Appl. Sci. **10**(5), 1699 (2020)
26. Opitz, J., Burst, S.: Macro f1 and macro f1. arXiv preprint arXiv:1911.03347 (2019)
27. Ou, M., Cui, P., Pei, J., Zhang, Z., Zhu, W.: Asymmetric transitivity preserving graph embedding. In: ACM SIGKDD International Conference on Knowledge Discovery and Data Mining (KDD), pp. 1105–1114 (2016)
28. Palmonari, M., Minervini, P.: Knowledge graph embeddings and explainable ai. Knowl. Graphs Explain. Artifi. Intell. Found. Appli. Challenges **47**, 49 (2020)
29. Perozzi, B., Al-Rfou, R., Skiena, S.: Deepwalk: online learning of social representations. In: ACM SIGKDD International Conference on Knowledge Discovery and Data Mining (KDD), pp. 701–710 (2014)
30. Perozzi, B., Kulkarni, V., Chen, H., Skiena, S.: Don't walk, skip! online learning of multi-scale network embeddings. In: International Conference on Advances in Social Networks Analysis and Mining (ASONAM), pp. 258–265 (2017)

31. Rossi, A., Barbosa, D., Firmani, D., Matinata, A., Merialdo, P.: Knowledge graph embedding for link prediction: a comparative analysis. ACM Trans. Knowl. Discovery Data (TKDD) **15**(2), 1–49 (2021)

32. Rosvall, M., Bergstrom, C.T.: Maps of information flow reveal community structure in complex networks. arXiv preprint physics.soc-ph/0707.0609 (2007)

33. Salehi Rizi, F., Granitzer, M.: Properties of vector embeddings in social networks. Algorithms **10**(4), 109 (2017)

34. Silva, T.C., Zhao, L.: Machine Learning in Complex Networks. Springer, Cham (2016). https://doi.org/10.1007/978-3-319-17290-3

35. Sun, H., Huang, J., Zhong, X., Liu, K., Zou, J., Song, Q.: Label propagation with-degree neighborhood impact for network community detection. Comput. Intell. Neurosci. **2014**, 130689 (2014)

36. Traag, V.A., Waltman, L., Van Eck, N.J.: From louvain to leiden: guaranteeing well-connected communities. Sci. Rep. **9**(1), 1–12 (2019)

37. Bellandi, V., Ceravolo, P., Damiani, E., Maghool, S.: Agent-based vector- label propagation for explaining social network structures. CCIS, vol. 1593 (2022). https://doi.org/10.1007/978-3-031-07920-7_24

38. Wang, X., Cui, P., Wang, J., Pei, J., Zhu, W., Yang, S.: Community preserving network embedding. In: Thirty-First AAAI Conference on Artificial Intelligence (2017)

39. Xie, J., Szymanski, B.K., Liu, X.: Slpa: uncovering overlapping communities in social networks via a speaker-listener interaction dynamic process. In: 2011 IEEE 11th International Conference on Data Mining Workshops, pp. 344–349. IEEE (2011)

40. Xing, Y., Meng, F., Zhou, Y., Zhu, M., Shi, M., Sun, G.: A node influence based label propagation algorithm for community detection in networks. Sci. World J. **2014**, 627581 (2014)

41. Xu, X., Yuruk, N., Feng, Z., Schweiger, T.A.: Scan: a structural clustering algorithm for networks. In: Proceedings of the 13th ACM SIGKDD International Conference on Knowledge Discovery and Data Mining, pp. 824–833 (2007)

42. Zhu, X., Ghahramani, Z.: Learning from labeled and unlabeled data with label propagation (2002)

Research in Progress Papers

Generating Plugs and Data Sockets for Plug-and-Play Database Web Services

Arihant Jain[1] , Curtis Dyreson[1]([✉]) [iD], and Sourav S. Bhowmick[2] [iD]

[1] Department of Computer Science, Utah State University, Logan, UT, USA
curtis.dyreson@usu.edu
[2] Nanyang Technological University, Singapore, Singapore
assourav@ntu.edu.sg
https://www.usu.edu/cs/people/CurtisDyreson/,
https://personal.ntu.edu.sg/assourav/

Abstract. We propose a novel system for creating data plugs and sockets for plug-and-play database web services. We adopt a plug-and-play approach to couple an application to a database. In our approach a designer constructs a "plug," which is a simple specification of the output produced by the service. If the plug can be "played" on the database "socket" then the web service is generated. Our plug-and-play approach has three advantages. First, a plug is *portable*. A plug can be played on any data source to generate a web service. Second, a plug is *reliable*. The database is checked to ensure that the service can be safely and correctly generated. Third, plug-and-play web services are *easier to code* for complex data since a service designer can write a simple plug, abstracting away the data's real complexity. We describe a system for plug-and-play web services and experimentally evaluate the system.

Keywords: Web services · Databases · Plug-and-play

1 Introduction

Web services are a common technology for transferring data between a web server and an application. As shown in Fig. 1 a web service is a bridge between an application and a database with a coupling on both ends. The *application coupling* is between the code in the application and the web service. A web service provides (or accepts) data formatted in a specific *shape*, which is usually a *hierarchy* since the data is typically formatted in JSON or XML, and could be further transformed using GraphQL. The second coupling is between the web service and the back-end database, which we will call the *database coupling*. The database coupling maps flat, relational data in the database to the shape (hierarchy) used by the service; it is typically an object-relational mapping (ORM).

We observed that the design and construction of the application and database couplings could be improved in (at least) three ways. First, the application coupling is *rigid*. The web service constructs data to a specific shape. We will call

M. Sellami et al. (Eds.): CoopIS 2022, LNCS 13591, pp. 279–288, 2022.
https://doi.org/10.1007/978-3-031-17834-4_16

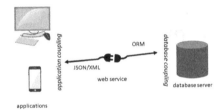

Fig. 1. Couplings in a web service

this shape a *data socket*. An application also needs data in a specific shape, which we will call a *data plug*. If the data plug does not fit the data socket then the application is unable to couple to the web service. Rigidity reduces application portability. Second, both couplings are *brittle*, changes to a data plug or data socket, *i.e.*, changes to the database, application, or web service, may break an existing coupling. Brittleness "pins" both the database *schema* (how the data is organized) and the application (which uses the schema to construct queries), limiting their evolution. Third, the application and database couplings are *static*. That is, an application can only choose among the data sockets pre-defined by the database coupling. Complicating the problem is that the application coupling and database coupling are specified using separate technologies.

This paper proposes a plug-and-play approach to web service construction to make the couplings more flexible, resilient to change, and dynamic. We call our plug-and-play web service creator AUTOREST. Suppose that a biodiversity application wants visualize a taxonomic hierarchy from data stored in a biodiversity database. There are many such databases [1] hosted by various biodiversity platforms such as Symbiota2, Specify, or Arctos, to which the application could couple. The databases have the same kinds of data but different schemas. The designers of the taxonomic hierarchy viewer application describe its data needs as a set of data plugs. AUTOREST either constructs data sockets from the database to fit each of the data plugs or describes how the construction will fail (lose information).

As an example, suppose that as part of the visualization of the taxonomic hierarchy the application consumes data about journal articles related to scientific names, grouping titles and DOIs of articles below the names. Additionally the application would like to translate the keys in the key/value pairs in the data (this translation is optional) from English to Spanish. The application designer would give the data plug specification shown in Fig. 2 for growing a new web service to provide the data. The GET service endpoint for providing the data would (if possible to construct) provide data formatted as shown in Fig. 3.

```
[{  "el nombre cientifico" : "scientific name",
    "los articulos" : [{"titulo": "title",
                        "DOI": "DOI"}] }]
```

Fig. 2. A plug-and-play web service specification

```
[ { "el nombre cientifico" : "Canis lupus",
    "los articulos" : [ { "titulo" : "From the Past to the Present: Wolf Phylogeography",
                          "DOI" : "10.3389/fevo.2016.00134" },
                        { "titulo" : "..." ,
                          "DOI" : "..." },
                        ... ] },
  { "el nombre cientifico" : "..." ,   ... }, ... ]
```

Fig. 3. Data returned by the constructed service

2   AUTOREST Architecture

In this section we describe the architecture of AUTOREST. This section describes each step in the generating a data plug and socket.

2.1   Getting Started

AUTOREST has a GUI written in Python, though AUTOREST is primarily written in Java. The code is publicly available from github: https://github.com/cdyreson/autorest.AUTOREST provides an interface to connect to a database and harvest the metadata, *e.g.*, the schema, from the database.

2.2   Association Multigraph Construction

AUTOREST next creates an *association multigraph*. An edge in the graph is a foreign key relationship (it is undirected since the edge can be traversed in either direction) and a node is a table. Attributes for a table are associated with the node. We use foreign keys because they are available in the schema.

2.3   Parsing the Plug

The plug is parsed, creating an abstract syntax tree (AST). We use ANTLR to parse the plug and walk the AST to perform other actions. AUTOREST matches the plug to the association multigraph by first matching names in the plug to attributes associated to nodes in the graph. A name may match multiple nodes. For each match, AUTOREST builds the spanning tree from the leaves of the plug (the plug specifies a hierarchy) to the root using the principle of *closeness* to associate parents with children. Closeness can be described as the property that two data items are *related* if they are connected (by a path) and that no shorter paths that connect items of the same *type* exists [6,16]. In the context of relational databases the *type* of a datum is the domain (an attribute in a

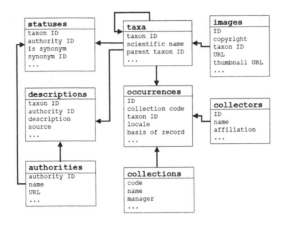

Fig. 4. Reduced schema of the Symbiota2 database

relation) to which it belongs. This matching creates a closest spanning tree, which is traversed using an inorder walk to generate a *path* that connects the data. Since a name may match multiple nodes in the graph and multiple edges could connect a pair of nodes, there could be several paths for a plug. The next step determines the *best* path.

2.4 Finding Closest Paths

There can be several possible paths between two tables in a database. To find the closest path we use a modified breadth-first search algorithm to find all the shortest paths between the two tables. There are several cases of how queries are processed as described in the remainder of this section.

Case: Single Table Plug. Suppose we want to create a simple web service that returns an orders key and status information from the Symbiota2 database using the plug shown in Fig. 5. We process the plug as described previously. After processing, we have data for the SELECT and ORDER BY keywords. To create a query we need to find the join conditions between the columns in the database. In this section, we will discuss the algorithm we use to process queries to generate paths or join conditions for the query.

For a given search query we first begin with the first column and then we find the relation to the next column. For the example query, it is locale and basis of record, respectively. Looking at the schema in Fig. 4 we see that both columns are in the same table. To get the data for the FROM keyword, all we need is the name of the table. Our algorithm generates the SQL query shown in Fig. 6. Similarly, if the query had more columns from the same table then we would only need to add the column names to the SELECT and ORDER BY clauses.

```
[ { "where": "locale", "basis": "basis of record" } ]
```

Fig. 5. Simple, single table plug

```
SELECT DISTINCT locale, 'basis of record'
FROM occurrences
ORDER BY locale, 'basis of record'
```

Fig. 6. SQL for the single table plug shown in Fig. 5

Case: Multi-table Plug. Suppose we want to create a web service to find the scientific names of taxa and information about the images for each taxon, then we would use the plug given in Fig. 7. Again we get the data for SELECT and ORDER BY from the initial processing stages of the search query. Next we need to find the relation among the different columns in the query. As described earlier we start with finding the relation for scientific name and the next column URL. These columns are from different tables. So we build the join condition between tables, taxa and images and create a query-specific path resulting in the SQL query shown in Fig. 8. The reason we are use left joins is if there were taxa that do not have any images then we would not get their scientific names in the result set.

Case: Multi Hierarchy Plug. Suppose that the plug is as given in Fig. 9. Finding paths in a hierarchical query differs from a flat query since we need to find paths between parents and children in the plug. For the example query, we find the relation between scientific name and locale, and similarly after than between scientific name and URL. The query generated for this plug is shown in Fig. 10. We create the hierarchical structure from the result set after executing the query. Since the result is ordered by nodes higher in the hierarchy, the hierarchy can be constructed in a streaming fashion from the result.

Case: Multiple-path Plug. There could be multiple shortest paths connecting two relations, for example for the plug given in Fig. 11 one path is

```
taxa - descriptions - authorities
```

while another is given below.

```
taxa - statuses - authorities
```

Such a situation is quite likely to occur in a database with several relationship types between a pair of entity types.

To enable the user to choose the best path, AUTOREST visualizes the paths. In this visualization on the full Symbiota2 schema (rather than the reduced and simplified schema used previously) there are seven paths that connect the authorities and taxa tables. The visualization enables a developer to choose

```
[ { "taxon": "scientific name",  "image": "URL",
    "copyright": "copyright", "thumbnail": "thumbnail URL" } ]
```

Fig. 7. Multi-table plug

```
SELECT DISTINCT taxa.'scientific name', images.URL,
                images.copyright, images.'thumbnail URL'
FROM taxa LEFT JOIN images USING ('taxon ID')
ORDER BY taxa.'scientific name', images.URL,
               images.copyright, images.'thumbnail URL'
```

Fig. 8. Generated SQL query for plug in Fig. 7

a path other than the one AUTOREST deems as best (lowest cost/most information retained).

We measure the desirability of the web service on the basis of rows returned, which is an indicator of the completeness of the plug computation. The more rows being returned from a query implies that less data is being lost with the join condition. The rows can be either counted by executing the query and then counting the rows (*e.g.*, using EXPLAIN ANALYZE) or by estimating the number of rows (*e.g.*, using EXPLAIN). AUTOREST shows the estimated number of rows and also presents the user with a graphical representation of the path of the join condition in the database.

Finally, to maximize completeness a user can choose to perform the *union* of alternative paths. We do not automatically detect when a union will improve the completeness since the query subsumption problem (figuring out if a query produces a subset of another query) is also NP-complete. Rather we leave it to the designer to choose to union alternatives.

2.5   Creating the Service

In our implementation, we auto generate a Python script using the Flask framework to create the web service.

3   Evaluation

In this section we describe the results of several experiments to evaluate AUTOREST. The evaluation measures the *feasibility* of plug-and-play web services. We explore two alternatives in cost estimation in an SQL query compiler while creating a web service using AUTOREST.

We performed our experiments on a desktop machine with an i7-4770 CPU with a clock speed of 3.40 GHz and 16GB of DDR3 memory. The OS used is Ubuntu 18 LTS, 64-bit and the Java version used is version 11. We performed the experiments using the Postgres DBMS version 12. We used an out-of-the box version of both Postgres and Java, with no adjustments made for performance

```
[ { "taxon": "scientific name", "occurrences": [ { "locale" : "locale" } ],
    "images": [ { "URL" : "URL"} ] } ]
```

Fig. 9. A multi-hierarchy plug

```
SELECT DISTINCT taxa.'scientific name', occurrences.locale, images.URL
FROM taxa LEFT JOIN occurrences USING ('taxon ID')
          LEFT JOIN images USING ('taxon ID')
ORDER BY taxa.'scientific name', occurrences.locale, images.URL
```

Fig. 10. SQL for the multi-hierarchy plug of Fig. 9

tuning, such as increasing cache memory size. The experiments used a standard relational benchmark database, TPC-H [15]. We used TPC-H rather than Symbiota2 since we wanted to experiment with different database sizes (in a later experiment).

For the first experiment the TPC-H database generator was used to generate a database 10 MB in size. We manually created seven plugs based on TPC-H queries, which are in the test section of the implementation package. The experiment measures the total time to create the web service, from input of the plug to completion of code creation. We tested using EXPLAIN vs. EXPLAIN ANALYZE to resolve shortest paths queries. The difference between EXPLAIN vs EXPLAIN ANALYZE is that the former estimates the cost of a query from database statistics, while the latter runs the query capturing the actual cost. Estimating query cost is much faster than running a query and measuring the cost. Figure 12 plots the cost of generating the web service for each plug. The plugs increase in complexity from plug one to plug seven, and therefore in cost. The experiment also shows that using EXPLAIN ANALYZE is more expensive for complex plugs, for plugs six and seven it is more than double the cost.

EXPLAIN ANALYZE takes more time, but it is unclear if it is producing a "better" result. The quality differences between EXPLAIN and EXPLAIN ANALYZE can be measured by examining how close the former comes to estimating the number of rows in the query result, which is what we use for gauging completeness and ranking paths. Figure 13 shows the percent difference in the queries corresponding to the seven plugs. The query size estimator in Postgres accurately predicts the size of the result for most of the queries, only query 2 shows significant differences. We observed that sometimes the query estimator overestimates the number of output rows for queries that involve DISTINCT, which eliminates duplicate rows from the query result.

We also measured the time to produce the first result. Pagination is typically used for web services, so the time to the first result is essentially the time to produce the first page. Figure 14 shows the difference in the cost of computing the first result vs. the complete result using EXPLAIN.

```
[ { "scientific name": "scientific name", "editors": "editors" } ]
```

Fig. 11. A multiple path plug

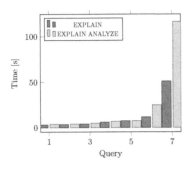
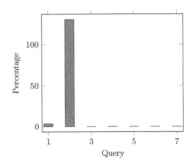

Fig. 12. Timing `EXPLAIN` vs. `EXPLAIN ANALYZE` on seven plugs of increasing complexity

Fig. 13. Percentage difference of number of rows in EXPLAIN vs EXPLAIN ANALYZE

The previous experiments used a relatively small database, so we were interested in determining how the size of the database impacted the time taken. Figure 15 plots the time difference between `EXPLAIN` and `EXPLAIN ANALYZE` for the seven plugs on databases of increasing size. The results show that as the database size increases, the time difference also increases, which means that `EXPLAIN ANALYZE` takes longer with larger databases. We have only included results from the initial five queries as the time difference in the last two queries is extremely large.

4   Related Work

Related work falls into two categories, existing tools for web services creation and peer-reviewed research. We cover the tools first.

There are API-side tools to create or document a client's view of a web service, that is, a program interface and documentation *e.g.,* the Swagger User Interface editor [13]. API-side tools like GraphQL can be further applied to process the data returned by a web service, but lack the database construction of the service as described in this paper. There are also tools to create the *DBMS-side of the web service.* A canonical tool in this category is Doctrine [5]. AUTOREST combines the API-side and DBMS-side construction.

Plug-and-play web services are a technique for easing the burden of constructing a hierarchy from a database, which has been investigated previously in various ways. The problem of constructing a hierarchy from relational data is simplified by storing the hierarchical data in a relational database [11,14] or key/value store, such as MongoDB. The main challenge addressed in this paper is how to transform (flat) relational tables to hierarchical data (JSON),

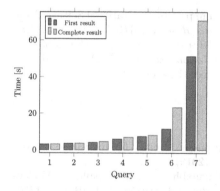

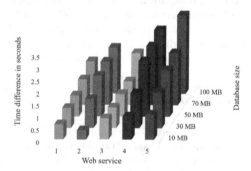

Fig. 14. Timing first result vs complete result set

Fig. 15. Difference between EXPLAIN and EXPLAIN ANALYZE

which is a different problem than how to transform hierarchical data to hierarchical data [6,10,12,16]. Codd famously proposed transforming hierarchical data to relational data [4], which is the paradigm that has dominated much of the database literature. Web service composition [3] is another way of changing the shape, through the process of composing existing web services. Such compositions are prone to brittleness [8]. AUTOREST grows a web service rather than composing existing services; composition does not address how to create a hierarchy from tables.

Data can be integrated from one or more source schemas to a target schema by specifying a mapping to carry out a specific, fixed transformation of the data [2]. Once the data is in the target schema, there is still the problem of queries that need data in a hierarchy other than the target schema. In some sense schema mediators integrate data to a fixed schema, which is the starting point for what plug-and-play web services aims to do. The different problem leads to a difference in techniques used to map or transform the data. For instance tuple-generating dependencies (TGDs) are a popular technique for integrating schemas [7,9]. Part of a TGD is a specification of the source hierarchy from which to extract the data. Specifying the source will not work for plug-and-play web services, which must be agnostic about the source.

5   Conclusion

We built a system called AUTOREST to provide plug-and-play web services. AUTOREST generates a web service from a simple JSON specification of the output of the service. We described how the specification is used to compute the hierarchical output from relational tables and how attributes are related in a association multigraph. AUTOREST essentially eliminates the need for any prior coding knowledge to create a web service, and also enables fast web service creation. This paper describes how AUTOREST is implemented and gives an experimental evaluation.

Acknowledgements. This work was supported in part by the National Science Foundation under Award No. DBI-1759965, *Collaborative Research: ABI Development: Symbiota2: Enabling greater collaboration and flexibility for mobilizing biodiversity data.* Opinions, findings and conclusions or recommendations expressed in this material are those of the author(s) and do not necessarily reflect those of NSF

References

1. Ball-Damerow, J., et al.: Research applications of primary biodiversity databases in the digital age. PLoS ONE **14**, e0215794 (2019)
2. Bhide, M., Agarwal, M., Bar-Or, A., Padmanabhan, S., Mittapalli, S., Venkatachaliah, G.: XPEDIA: XML processing for data integration. PVLDB **2**(2), 1330–1341 (2009)
3. Chan, P.P.W., Lyu, M.R.: Dynamic web service composition: a new approach in building reliable web service. In: AINA, pp. 20–25 (2008)
4. Codd, E.F.: A relational model of data for large shared data banks. CACM **13**(6), 377–387 (1970)
5. Doctrine: Object relational mapper (2019). https://www.doctrine-project.org/projects/orm.html. Accessed 23 July 2019
6. Dyreson, C.E., Bhowmick, S.S.: Querying XML data: as you shape it. In: ICDE, pp. 642–653 (2012)
7. Fagin, R., Haas, L.M., Hernández, M., Miller, R.J., Popa, L., Velegrakis, Y.: Clio: schema mapping creation and data exchange. In: Borgida, A.T., Chaudhri, V.K., Giorgini, P., Yu, E.S. (eds.) Conceptual Modeling: Foundations and Applications. LNCS, vol. 5600, pp. 198–236. Springer, Heidelberg (2009). https://doi.org/10.1007/978-3-642-02463-4_12
8. Hu, T., et al.: MTTF of composite web services. In: ISPA, pp. 130–137 (2010)
9. Jiang, H., Ho, H., Popa, L., Han, W.S.: Mapping-driven XML transformation. In: WWW, pp. 1063–1072 (2007)
10. Krishnamurthi, S., Gray, K.E., Graunke, P.T.: Transformation-by-example for XML. In: PADL, pp. 249–262 (2000)
11. Liu, Z.H., Hammerschmidt, B., McMahon, D.: JSON data management: supporting schema-less development in RDBMS. In: SIGMOD, pp. 1247–1258. ACM (2014)
12. Pankowski, T.: A high-level language for specifying xml data transformations. In: ADBIS, pp. 159–172 (2004)
13. Swagger.io: Swagger UI (2019). https://swagger.io/tools/swagger-ui/. Accessed on 23 July 2019
14. Tatarinov, I., Viglas, S., Beyer, K.S., Shanmugasundaram, J., Shekita, E.J., Zhang, C.: Storing and querying ordered XML using a relational database system. In: SIGMOD Conference, pp. 204–215 (2002)
15. TPC.org: TPC-H (2019). https://tpc.org/tpch/. Accessed 22 July 2019
16. Zhang, S., Dyreson, C.E.: Symmetrically exploiting XML. In: WWW, pp. 103–111 (2006)

Design and Implementation of Education and Training Management System Based on Blockchain

Ran Chen, Xiaoming Wu(✉), Xiangzhi Liu, and Junlong Liang

Qilu University of Technology (Shandong Academy of Sciences), Shandong Computer Science Center (National Supercomputer Center in Jinan), Jinan 250014, China
cr576612@163.com, {wuxm,liuxzh}@sdas.org, 13223054558@163.com

Abstract. Ensuring the quality of education and training has always been the focus of social concern. Traditionally, many chain education and training institutions have adopted a centralized management platform, which will lead to a lack of effective supervision among institutions. If the training records of trainees have problems such as data falsification/tampering, it is not easy to trace back, so that the security and credibility of the training data cannot be guaranteed. Moreover, due to the influence of geographical, economic and other factors, there is a lack of unified assessment standards in various regions, which makes it difficult to guarantee the training quality of trainees. In this context, this paper proposes an education and training management system (ETS) based on Hyperledger Fabric blockchain technology to provide a safe and reliable traceability solution for education and training management. In this system, we define some rules through smart contracts to implement different business logic. Using the characteristics of decentralization and high credibility of the blockchain, it solves the problems of uneven training quality and untraceable training records in the traditional education and training process. The system we built enables reliable sharing and privacy protection of training data. In addition, this paper provides an effective network configuration idea to obtain the best performance of the blockchain system. The performance of the proposed system is evaluated by experiments.

Keywords: Education and training · Hyperledger fabric · Access authorization · Data security · Smart contract

1 Introduction

In the context of national learning, the scale of the training market for educational institutions is also expanding. These institutions need to standardize the management of various data in the training process and record them in the database [1]. A reliable system can greatly improve office efficiency and ensure data security. But in the traditional education and training system, all

© The Author(s), under exclusive license to Springer Nature Switzerland AG 2022
M. Sellami et al. (Eds.): CoopIS 2022, LNCS 13591, pp. 289–298, 2022.
https://doi.org/10.1007/978-3-031-17834-4_17

training-related data are stored in a single database through web and network technologies to meet the needs of managers for supervision and storage [2]. This centralized management model cannot guarantee the security and reliability of data. If there is a problem with the system center, it will cause a lot of damage. In addition, traditional databases have the risk of data tampering and data leakage [3]. If the training records of trainees are false, it is difficult for relevant departments to trace them, which makes the data lack credibility.

In the era of rapid development of the education institution, the application of blockchain technology meets the decentralized learning needs and models of today's social educational institutions [4]. Applying it to the education institution can help effectively solve some existing problems that cannot be solved online and offline [5]. Among them, we can prevent the falsification of training data by comparing the hash values [6]. Data transparency is ensured through sharing mechanisms, and system security is enhanced through authentication [7]. At the same time, transactions that occur in ETS can be automatically verified and executed by using pre-designed smart contracts. To reduce the workload of managers, and to ensure the security of ETS data.

The goal of this paper is to research, develop and implement a platform centered on training institutions using blockchain technology. Provide a safe and high-quality training method to standardize the system of the entire training assessment process to ensure the training quality of trainees. The main contributions of this study are as follows:

- We propose an education and training management system based on Hyperledger Fabric, which provides a comprehensive plan for the design of training assessments in the education and training process. Authorized personnel can understand the training records of each trainer at a glance, improve the transparency of training data and maintain reasonable privacy.
- In this system, the identity verification stage of each role is designed in the alliance chain, and reasonable smart contracts are developed to prevent illegal personnel from falsifying information during the management process, and improve the security and reliability of the system.
- The system adopts four data storage methods of CouchDB, PostgreSQL, MySQL, and Redis to realize the optimal "on-chain and off-chain" data storage solution.
- The developed prototype system is evaluated, and the optimal network configuration and transaction size are obtained through comparative experiments.

2   Background

2.1   Blockchain

In recent years, with the development of blockchain technology, decentralized systems centered on blockchain technology have become more and more common. Blockchain is essentially a distributed database [8]. It is a series of encrypted data blocks, each data block contains transaction information in the network for a period of time, the digital certificate verifies the validity of its information, and the next data block is continuously generated [9]. Features of blockchain technology: uniqueness; data transparency; irreversibility of records; traceability [10]. The characteristics of blockchain allow it to effectively solve the problem of trust between parties. Although third-party protection measures are common at present, the market demand for data fraud and information traceability has been increasing [11]. These characteristics of the blockchain make it very promising and have been affirmed in many applications.

2.2 Blockchain Education

At present, with the continuous improvement and expansion of blockchain technology, many international educational institutions have begun to discuss the application of blockchain technology in the field of education. They hope that blockchain technology can help build a safe and reliable education platform to promote the efficient development of the future education field [12]. Woolf University is a blockchain university announced by former Oxford University academics. The school's overall management model relies on blockchain technology. Use blockchain technology to record students' attendance and learning progress in real time and store them on the blockchain. The researchers also explored the application mode of blockchain in the field of education by analogy to the application scenarios of blockchain in other fields. In response to the new needs of the development of the education field, Fedorova et al. [13] proposed some scenarios for the application of blockchain technology in the field of education, including the degree certificate system and data management system, and clarified the advantages of applying blockchain in the field of education. Ayub Khan and others [14] proposed a blockchain-based educational credential verification framework to avoid document fraud and abuse. At the same time, in order to solve the deficiencies in data storage and management, the industry has also tried to combine blockchain technology with cloud storage technology to improve the controllability of data [15].

In general, the application of blockchain technology in the field of education is more complex, and faces problems such as difficulties in promotion and operation, limited data storage space, and insufficient transaction throughput. Therefore, there are still many challenges for the implementation of blockchain training in educational institutions.

3 Platform Model Design

This section mainly discusses the architecture of the platform, including platform architecture and design.

3.1 Platform Architecture

The platform simulates three education and training branches to form a consortium chain, and forms an education and training management system based on Hyperledger Fabric with the platform management interface. And ETS can provide a complete interface and SDK to integrate with other existing systems. The platform architecture is shown in Fig. 1.

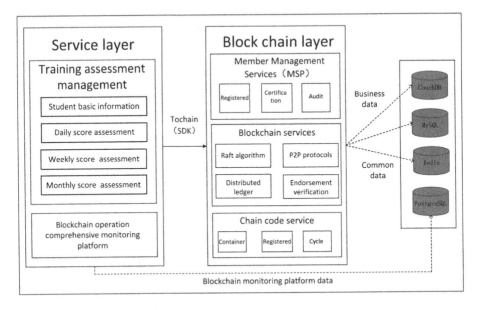

Fig. 1. The platform architecture.

ETS is divided into three layers: service layer, blockchain layer and data storage layer. The service layer includes two business modules: training management and integrated monitoring platform for blockchain operation. The backend of the service layer provides a RESTful API for the web side to call. The web side uploads the requested data (student information, assessment records, etc.) to the backend, and the backend calls the corresponding function through routing to execute specific business logic. Interact with the blockchain network by encapsulating the Hyperledger Fabric SDK to complete operations such as connecting to the blockchain network, selecting channels, sending transaction proposals, and writing to the ledger. The JSON data of the response is sent back to the front end, and the front end processes the response and displays it to the administrator.

The blockchain layer provides MSP member management services, blockchain services and chain code services based on the Hyperledger Fabric framework. After connecting to the blockchain gateway, the user will select the designated channel and initiate a transaction proposal to the blockchain network. The designated endorsement node in the network will call the smart contract to simulate the execution of the transaction and return the transaction response, and then the ordering node will use a specific consensus algorithm to sort the transactions and package them into blocks. The block synchronization is performed between the accounting nodes through the P2P protocol, and the blocks are verified and written into the distributed ledger.

The data storage layer keeps data persistent. In this network, business data such as identity information and training records are stored in the CouchDB database. System management related data is stored in a MySQL database. Connect to the Redis cache database through the specified API and store common data to improve the high performance of data storage. The PostgreSQL database is used to provide the data required for the blockchain to run the comprehensive monitoring platform to ensure the integrity of the system data in a more secure way.

The integrated monitoring platform for blockchain operation provides platform monitoring functions to monitor and operate nodes on the entire blockchain platform. The monitoring includes functions such as the entire network block information, deployed contract information, the number and working status of nodes, and transaction query.

3.2 Platform Solution

Based on the complexity of educational scene nodes, we propose a basic educational blockchain network architecture. There are 6 "roles" in the ETS management chain process framework diagram. However, our solution is scalable, and new nodes can be added dynamically according to demand to ensure the flexibility of the system.

- Educational Institution (EI): Provide all-round support for trainee training. To establish a branch of an educational institution, you need to apply to the headquarters. Only after the application is approved can they join the alliance chain of the institution.
- Student (S): Students must be certified by the institution before proceeding to subsequent training courses. After the certification, the basic information of the trainee can be entered into the blockchain network, and trainees who have not entered the information are not eligible for training.
- Level C Administrator (LC): There are different levels of administrators in each EI, and they all need to be authenticated and qualified before they can join the network. LC will judge the results of the day based on the daily performance of the students, and write the information into the ledger.
- Level B Administrator (LB): According to the performance of each student for a week, the grades obtained for the week are judged, and the assessment information is written into the ledger.
- Level A Administrator (LA): The grades obtained for the month are judged based on the comprehensive performance of each student for the month. After the training, it will be determined whether the student's grades meet the graduation standards according to the comprehensive results.
- Third Party (TP): At each stage of the assessment, all assessment results can be accessed through the blockchain network, and all information can be used to detect false grades to ensure the quality of training for trainees.

The specific process is as follows: In the process of education and training, from the beginning of the training institution receiving trainees to the end of the training, it needs to go through the following stages.

1) This step is the registration phase for each role in the system. All participants (EI, S, LA, LB, LC, TP) must be authenticated in the Hyperledger Fabric network, and only after the authentication is passed, can transactions and information be exchanged in the network channel.

2) When a new S needs to register for training, the corresponding institution will first confirm the personal information related to the name, age, training courses and plans of the S. After confirming that the information is correct, the corresponding EI will upload the information to the blockchain center through the sorting node for accounting.

3) At the end of each day's training, LC will give a reasonable score to all trainees on the performance of the day according to the pre-established assessment standards. And upload the assessment information of each S to the blockchain network, in which the smart contract will automatically detect the uploaded information, and the unqualified information will not be recorded in the blockchain network. For example, the assessment score of the day exceeds the standard score. After confirming that the information is correct, the ledger will be updated.

4) After the weekly training, LB will conduct weekly scores based on the scores of each trainee for the week and upload them to the blockchain network.

5) After the monthly training, LA will conduct monthly scoring according to the score of each student in that month. And LA will conduct assessment and certification after the S training. Through the monthly assessment information, it is decided whether the S has passed the education and training.

6) TP will review the corresponding transaction information in the blockchain network according to the applicant's request. When there is an unqualified S, the appraiser will be traced back to the transaction records to find out the problem.

4   System Implementation

This section mainly describes the configuration environment and implementation of the platform.

4.1   Configuration

In this study, the entire blockchain network consists of three servers of Ubuntu 18.04 system. They simulate three different educational institutions, each of which contains an orderer node and a peer node. In ETS, we use the version of Hyperledger Fabric 2.2, and the consensus is the Raft algorithm. Its advantage is that it can provide a stable ordering service even if some nodes are down. The service is similar to a cluster device, and each node interacts through Raft.

4.2 Implemention

In ETS, we implement smart contract through Node.js. And the contract is installed on the selected peer nodes in the network to provide services for transactions between various organizations in the network. The contracts designed in this paper are mainly divided into application contracts and transaction contracts. The application contract mainly provides registration, query and other operations for the system, and traders can search based on the specified fields. In the transaction contract, we mainly implement the business logic in ETS, and provide services for managers to perform assessment, recording and other functions. We have pre-established policies in access control management that define the permission rules for different participants in the blockchain network. The main functions of ETS are described below.

Student Registration: First, obtain the basic information of students (student_id, student_name, student_age, base_score). Taking the information as input and submitting it to the system through the corresponding SDK, the server will find a matching method in the chaincode after receiving the registration request, and check the parameters in the request method body. After it is determined that the information meets the description rules, the student information is uploaded to the blockchain network and a unique identity is created for the student. The registration process of EI, LA, LB, and LC in this system is similar to the registration process of students.

Assessment of the student: Institution managers can perform transactions to record the assessment results of each student. According to the level of managers, their assessment authority is also different. For example, LA can evaluate the student's performance for one month, and LC can only record the student's performance for the day. When the manager scores a student, the request parameters will be uploaded to the chaincode, and the contract will be used to judge whether the transaction is legal. For example, "score" cannot be a non-negative number. After being confirmed by the contract, this piece of information will generate a new key-value pair and save it in the blockchain. Algorithm 1 describes the process.

Obtain student training records: In ETS, the Couchdb database is used, which can support rich query operations. When we trace student assessment records, we can use "student_id" and "administrator_id" as input. Submit the application through the specified API, and the network will first judge the user's permissions. After passing, the node will search for the corresponding method in the chaincode and get all the parameters in the request body. The data in the request body is checked according to the custom rules, and the corresponding assessment record information of the students is returned.

5 Performance Analysis

To ensure the viability of the system, we performed some tests. And in this section, the corresponding results will be given through experiments.

Algorithm 1: Assessment of the student

---

  input : Student ID, Administrator ID, Date,Score
  output: Accept or reject this transaction

1   Generate composite key by input information;
2   Transactions are obtained by composite key;
3   **if** *(Administrator=LA)* **then**
4 | Result← Operate the daily, weekly and monthly assessment scores of student;
5   **else**
6   **if** *(Administrator=LB)* **then**
7 | Result← Operate the daily and weekly assessment scores of student;
8   **else**
9 | Result← Operate the daily assessment scores of student;
10   **end**
11 **end**

We use Intel(R) Core(TM) i5-10500 CPU @3.10 GHz processor, running on Ubuntu18.04. We perform operations on a specific HTTP interface, sending mock requests through Apache Bench 2.3 to test the server. Because the SDK we connect to the blockchain network is written with node, and node is single-threaded, there are concurrency issues. In the process of on-chain, a lot of hash calculations are required, resulting in slow on-chain speed and low efficiency. In order to solve this problem, we adjust the best network configuration according to the situation. Improve hash computing power by starting multi-threaded services and make full use of CPU resources. In this experimental environment, after our comparison, it is found that enabling 8 services is the best case. After the network configuration is modified (am), the efficiency of query and creation operations will be significantly improved.

Query operation: Fig. 2(a) shows a comparison of the time required to complete different transaction sizes before (bm) and after (am) network configuration modification. After testing, we can find that the response time of the query operation is significantly shortened after the configuration modification. In ETS, the performance of query operations is evaluated by response time (ms).

Create operation: Due to the existence of the consensus mechanism, the creation operation will be more complicated, and the throughput of the system will be affected by the configuration of the ordering service. In this paper, we take parameters such as Batch Timeout and Message Count as fixed values, mainly to analyze the impact of block size on system performance to obtain the best blockchain network efficiency. In our system, the size of each on-chain data is controlled at around 6 k to 8 k, and transactions that take place in the network support this range. In ETS, the throughput of a create operation is evaluated by the number of requests processed per second (RPS), which is the speed at which requests are completely processed.

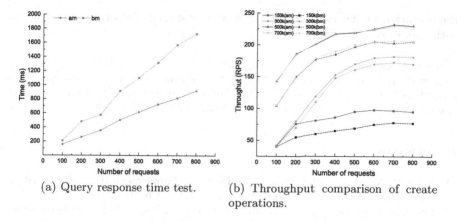

(a) Query response time test.

(b) Throughput comparison of create operations.

Fig. 2. Tests for query and creation operations

As can be seen from Fig. 2(b), after the network configuration is modified (am), the throughput of the creation operation has been significantly improved. And when the block size is configured as 500 k, the performance of the system is optimal, and the creation throughput of ETS can reach about 230 RPS. When the block size exceeds 500 k, the system performance can no longer be increased. From the test results, the work efficiency of our system has a good response to the needs of practical applications.

6   Conclusions and Future Research

In view of the current problems of decentralization, data fraud, and leakage in education and training management in educational institutions, we designed a blockchain education and training management system based on Hyperledger fabric. In this paper, the three-layer blockchain architecture of the system is proposed, and the implementation details of the system are discussed. Using the core advantages of blockchain, it ensures the traceability and transparency of information, meets the needs of traditional education and training systems in terms of information islands and data tamper resistance, and improves the training quality of trainees. Finally, this paper explores the optimal network configuration of the system through experiments and evaluates the performance of the system, confirming the feasibility and effectiveness of ETS.

In future studies, we plan to do further research on data normalization. It is necessary to combine the views and opinions of various stakeholders such as the Education Bureau and government agencies. These views and opinions may lead to conflicting data standardization, which is also a limitation of future research. In addition, it is necessary to further integrate more relevant institutions to jointly promote the development of the education field. Investigate the interoperability between the platform and related blockchain-based devices. Facilitate the evolution of the platform into a new educational platform in conjunction with various educational.

Acknowledgements. This work is supported by National Key Research and Development Project (No. 2021YFF0901300), Major Scientific and Technological Innovation Projects of Shandong Province, China,No. 2019JZZY010132, Key Research and Development Program of Shandong Province, China(No. 2021RKY02021).

References

1. Yuan, P., Xiong, X., Lei, L., Zheng, K.: Design and implementation on hyperledger-based emission trading system. IEEE Access **7**, 6109–6116 (2018)
2. Liu, X., Barenji, A.V., Li, Z., Montreuil, B., Huang, G.Q.: Blockchain-based smart tracking and tracing platform for drug supply chain. Comput. Industr. Eng. **161**, 107669 (2021)
3. Zhang, S., Yao, L., Sun, A., Tay, Y.: Deep learning based recommender system: a survey and new perspectives. ACM Comput. Surveys (CSUR) **52**(1), 1–38 (2019)
4. Bhaskar, P., Tiwari, C.K., Joshi, A.: Blockchain in education management: present and future applications. Interact. Technol. Smart Educ. (2020)
5. Alammary, A., Alhazmi, S., Almasri, M., Gillani, S.: Blockchain-based applications in education: a systematic review. Appl. Sci. **9**(12), 2400 (2019)
6. Denis González, C., Frias Mena, D., Massó Muñoz, A., Rojas, O., Sosa-Gómez, G.: Electronic voting system using an enterprise blockchain. Appl. Sci. **12**(2), 531 (2022)
7. Kakarlapudi, P.V., Mahmoud, Q.H.: Design and development of a blockchain-based system for private data management. Electronics **10**(24), 3131 (2021)
8. Alnssayan, A.A., Hassan, M.M., Alsuhibany, S.A.: Vacchain: a blockchain-based EMR system to manage child vaccination records. Comput. Syst. Sci. Eng. **40**(3), 927–945 (2022)
9. Iftekhar, A., Cui, X., Yang, Y.: Blockchain technology for trustworthy operations in the management of strategic grain reserves. Foods **10**(10), 2323 (2021)
10. Chen, C.L., et al.: An anti-counterfeit and traceable management system for brand clothing with hyperledger fabric framework. Symmetry **13**(11), 2048 (2021)
11. Zhang, J., Zhong, S., Wang, T., Chao, H.C., Wang, J.: Blockchain-based systems and applications: a survey. J. Int. Technol. **21**(1), 1–14 (2020)
12. Liang, X., Zhao, Q., Zhang, Y., Liu, H., Zhang, Q.: Educhain: A highly available education consortium blockchain platform based on hyperledger fabric. Concurrency Comput. Pract. Exp. e6330 (2021)
13. Fedorova, E.P., Skobleva, E.I.: Application of blockchain technology in higher education. Europ. J. Contemp. Educ. **9**(3), 552–571 (2020)
14. Ayub Khan, A., Laghari, A.A., Shaikh, A.A., Bourouis, S., Mamlouk, A.M., Alshazly, H.: Educational blockchain: a secure degree attestation and verification traceability architecture for higher education commission. Appl. Sci. **11**(22), 10917 (2021)
15. Li, J., Wu, J., Jiang, G., Srikanthan, T.: Blockchain-based public auditing for big data in cloud storage. Inf. Process. Manag. **57**(6), 102382 (2020)

Conformance Checking for Trace Fragments Using Infix and Postfix Alignments

Daniel Schuster[1,2]([envelope]) [ORCID], Niklas Föcking[1] [ORCID], Sebastiaan J. van Zelst[1,2] [ORCID],
and Wil M. P. van der Aalst[1,2] [ORCID]

[1] Fraunhofer Institute for Applied Information Technology FIT,
Sankt Augustin, Germany
{daniel.schuster,niklas.foecking,sebastiaan.van.zelst}@fit.fraunhofer.de
[2] RWTH Aachen University, Aachen, Germany
wvdaalst@pads.rwth-aachen.de

Abstract. Conformance checking deals with collating modeled process behavior with observed process behavior recorded in event data. Alignments are a state-of-the-art technique to detect, localize, and quantify deviations in process executions, i.e., traces, compared to reference process models. Alignments, however, assume complete process executions covering the entire process from start to finish or prefixes of process executions. This paper defines infix/postfix alignments, proposes approaches to their computation, and evaluates them using real-life event data.

Keywords: Process mining · Conformance checking · Alignments

1 Introduction

Information systems track the execution of organizations' operational processes in detail. The generated *event data* describe process executions, i.e., *traces*. *Conformance checking* [2] compares traces from event data with process models. *Alignments* [8], a state-of-the-art conformance checking technique, are widely used, e.g., for quantifying process compliance and evaluating process models.

Most conformance checking techniques relate complete traces, covering the process from start to finish, to reference process models. Processes are often divided into stages representing different logical/temporal phases; thus, conformance requirements can vary by stage. Conformance checking for trace fragments covering conformance-critical phases is therefore useful. Also, event data often needs to be combined from various data sources to analyze a process holistically. Thus, conformance checking for trace fragments is valuable as complete traces are not required. While there is the notion of prefix alignments [1], definitions and calculation methods for infix/postfix alignments do not yet exist.

This paper defines infix/postfix alignments and presents their computation. Figure 1 outlines our contributions. The computation of infix/postfix alignments

© The Author(s), under exclusive license to Springer Nature Switzerland AG 2022
M. Sellami et al. (Eds.): CoopIS 2022, LNCS 13591, pp. 299–310, 2022.
https://doi.org/10.1007/978-3-031-17834-4_18

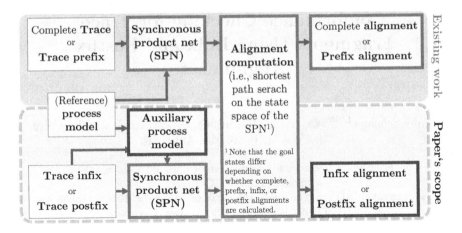

Fig. 1. Overview of our approach regarding infix/postfix alignment computation

builds on existing work on calculating (prefix) alignments [1]. For (prefix) alignment computation, the *synchronous product net (SPN)* [1] is created that defines the search space of the corresponding alignment computation, i.e., a shortest path search. In this paper, we modify the SPN to adapt it for infix/postfix alignment computation by using an *auxiliary process model* (cf. Fig. 1) as input instead of the reference process model. The actual search for the shortest path in the state space of the SPN remains unchanged compared to (prefix) alignments apart from different goal states. We propose two approaches to derive an auxiliary process model. One assumes sound workflow nets [7], i.e., a subclass of Petri nets often used to model business processes, and the second assumes block-structured workflow nets, i.e., process trees, a subclass of sound WF-nets.

In the remainder of this paper, we present related work (Sect. 2), preliminaries (Sect. 3), define infix/postfix alignments (Sect. 4), present their computation (Sect. 5), and evaluate the proposed computation (Sect. 6).

2 Related Work

We refer to [2,3] for overviews on conformance checking. Subsequently, we focus on alignments [1,8], which provide a closest match between a trace and a valid execution of a given process model. In [1,2] it is shown that alignment computation can be reduced to a shortest path problem. Further improvements by using alternative heuristics during the search are proposed in [11]. However, the state space of the shortest path problem can grow exponentially depending on the model and the trace [2]. Therefore, approaches for approximating alignments exist, for example, divide-and-conquer [6] and search space reduction approaches [10].

Alignments [1,8] are defined for complete traces that are aligned to a complete execution of a given process model. Additionally, prefix alignments exist [1], which are, for example, utilized for online conformance checking [5]. In this paper, we define infix/postfix alignments and demonstrate their computation. To the best of our knowledge, no related work exists on infix/postfix alignments.

3 Background

Given a set X, a multiset B over X can contain elements of X multiple times. For $X = \{x, y, z\}$, the multiset $[x^5, y]$ contains 5 times x, once y and no z. The set of all possible multisets over a base set X is denoted by $\mathcal{B}(X)$. We write $x \in B$ if x is contained at least once in multiset B. Given two multisets $b_1, b_2 \in \mathcal{B}(X)$, we denote their union by $B_1 \uplus B_2$. Finally, given two sets containing multisets, i.e., $B_1, B_2 \subseteq \mathcal{B}(X)$, we define the Cartesian by $B_1 \times B_2 = \{b_1 \uplus b_2 \mid b_1 \in B_1 \wedge b_2 \in B_2\}$. For example, $\{[a^2, b], [c]\} \times \{[d^3]\} = \{[a^2, b, d^3], [c, d^3]\}$.

A sequence σ of length $|\sigma| = n$ over a set X assigns an element to each index, i.e., $\sigma \colon \{1, \ldots, n\} \to X$. We write a sequence σ as $\langle \sigma(1), \sigma(2), \ldots, \sigma(|\sigma|) \rangle$. The set of all potential sequences over set X is denoted by X^*. Given $\sigma \in X^*$ and $x \in X$, we write $x \in \sigma$ if $\exists_{1 \leq i \leq |\sigma|} (\sigma(i) = x)$, e.g., $b \in \langle a, b \rangle$. Let $\sigma \in X^*$ and let $X' \subseteq X$. We recursively define $\sigma_{\downarrow_{X'}} \in X'^*$ with: $\langle \rangle_{\downarrow_{X'}} = \langle \rangle$, $(\langle x \rangle \cdot \sigma)_{\downarrow_{X'}} = \langle x \rangle \cdot \sigma_{\downarrow_{X'}}$ if $x \in X'$ and $(\langle x \rangle \cdot \sigma)_{\downarrow_{X'}} = \sigma_{\downarrow_{X'}}$ if $x \notin X'$. For a sequence $\sigma = \langle (x_1^1, \ldots, x_n^1), \ldots, (x_1^m, \ldots, x_n^m) \rangle \in (X_1 \times \ldots \times X_n)^*$ containing n-tuples, we define projection functions $\pi_1^*(\sigma) = \langle x_1^1, \ldots, x_1^m \rangle, \ldots, \pi_n^*(\sigma) = \langle x_n^1, \ldots, x_n^m \rangle$. For instance, $\pi_2^*(\langle (a, b), (c, d), (c, b) \rangle) = \langle b, d, b \rangle$.

Event data describe the execution of business processes. An event log can be seen as a multiset of process executions, i.e., traces, of a single business process. We denote the universe of process activity labels by $\mathcal{A}$. Further, we define a *complete/infix/postfix trace* as a sequence of executed activities, i.e., $\sigma \in \mathcal{A}^*$.

3.1 Process Models

Next, we introduce formalisms to model processes: Petri nets [7] and process trees. Figure 2 shows an example Petri net. Next, we define accepting Petri nets.

Definition 1 (Accepting Petri net). *An accepting Petri net* $N = (P, T, F, m_i, m_f, \lambda)$ *consists of a finite set of places* P, *a finite set of transitions* T, *a finite set of arcs* $F \subseteq (P \times T) \cup (T \times P)$, *and a labeling function* $\lambda \colon T \to \mathcal{A} \cup \{\tau\}$.

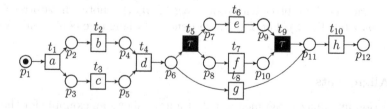

Fig. 2. Example Petri net, i.e., a sound WF-net, modeling a process consisting of activities $a, \ldots, h$. The initial marking $m_i = [p_1]$, and the final marking $m_f = [p_{12}]$.

We denote the initial marking with $m_i \in \mathcal{B}(P)$ and the final marking with $m_f \in \mathcal{B}(P)$.

In the remainder of this paper, we say Petri nets when referring to accepting Petri nets. Given a Petri net $N = (P, T, F, m_i, m_f, \lambda)$ and markings $m, m' \in \mathcal{B}(P)$, if a transition sequence $\sigma \in T^*$ leads from m to m', we write $(N, m) \xrightarrow{\sigma} (N, m')$. If m' is reachable from m, we write $(N, m) \rightsquigarrow (N, m')$. Further, we write $(N, m)[t\rangle$ if $t \in T$ is enabled in m. We let $\mathcal{R}(N, m_i) = \{m' \in \mathcal{B}(P) \mid (N, m_i) \rightsquigarrow (N, m')\}$ denote the state space of N, i.e., all markings reachable from m_i. In this paper, we assume that process models are sound workflow nets (WF-nets) [7].

Process trees represent *block-structured WF-nets*, a subclass of sound WF-nets [4]. Figure 3 shows an example tree modeling the same behavior as the WF-net in Fig. 2. Inner nodes represent control flow operators, and leaf nodes represent activities. Four operators exist: sequence ($\rightarrow$), parallel ($\wedge$), loop ($\circlearrowleft$), and exclusive-choice ($\times$). Next, we define process trees.

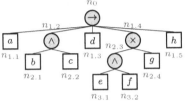

Fig. 3. Process tree T modeling the same process as the WF-net in Fig. 2

Definition 2 (Process Tree). *Let $\bigoplus = \{\rightarrow, \times, \wedge, \circlearrowleft\}$ be the set of operators. A process tree $T = (V, E, \lambda, r)$ consists of a totally ordered set of nodes V, a set of edges $E \subseteq V \times V$, a labeling function $\lambda : V \rightarrow \mathcal{A} \cup \{\tau\} \cup \bigoplus$, and a root node $r \in V$.*

- *$(\{n\}, \{\}, \lambda, n)$ with $dom(\lambda) = \{n\}$ and $\lambda(n) \in \mathcal{A} \cup \{\tau\}$ is a process tree*
- *given $k > 1$ trees $T_1 = (V_1, E_1, \lambda_1, r_1), \ldots, T_k = (V_k, E_k, \lambda_k, r_k)$ with $r \notin V_1 \cup \ldots \cup V_k$ and $\forall i, j \in \{1, \ldots, k\}(i \neq j \Rightarrow V_i \cap V_j = \emptyset)$ then $T = (V, E, \lambda, r)$ is a tree s.t.:*
  - *$V = V_1 \cup \ldots \cup V_k \cup \{r\}$*
  - *$E = E_1 \cup \ldots \cup E_k \cup \{(r, r_1), \ldots, (r, r_k)\}$*
  - *$dom(\lambda) = V$ with $\lambda(x) = \lambda_j(x)$ for all $j \in \{1, \ldots, k\}, x \in V_j$, $\lambda(r) \in \bigoplus$, and $\lambda(r) = \circlearrowleft \Rightarrow k = 2$*

$\mathcal{T}$ denotes the universe of process trees. We refer to [4] for a definition of process tree semantics. Given $T = (V, E, \lambda, r) \in \mathcal{T}$, the child function $c^T : V \rightarrow V^*$ returns a sequence of child nodes, e.g., $c^T(n_0) = \langle n_{1.1}, \ldots, n_{1.5} \rangle$, cf. Fig. 3. The parent function $p^T : V \nrightarrow V$ returns a node's parent; e.g., $p(n_{2.4}) = n_{1.4}$. For $n \in V$, $T(n) \in \mathcal{T}$ denotes the subtree with root n; e.g., $T(n_{2.3})$ denotes the subtree rooted at node $n_{2.3}$ (cf. Fig. 3). For $T \in \mathcal{T}$, we denote its language-equivalent WF-net by N^T.

3.2 Alignments

This section introduces alignments [1,2]. Figure 4 shows an example for the WF-net shown in Fig. 2 and trace $\sigma = \langle d, a, e, h \rangle$. An alignment's first row, i.e., the trace part, equals the given trace if the skip symbol $\gg$ is ignored. The second row, i.e., the model part, equals a sequence of transitions (ignoring $\gg$) leading from the initial to the final marking. An alignment is composed of moves, for instance, each column in Fig. 4 represents a move; we distinguish four:

- **synchronous moves** indicate a match between the model and the trace,
- **log moves** indicate a *mismatch*, i.e., the current activity in the trace is not replayed in the model,
- **visible model moves** indicate a *mismatch*, i.e., the model executes an activity not observed in the trace at this stage, and
- **invisible model moves** indicate *no* real mismatch, i.e., a model move on a transition labeled with τ.

Since we are interested in an alignment finding the closest execution of the model to a given trace, the notion of optimality exists. An alignment for a model and trace is *optimal* if no other alignment exist with less visible model and log moves.

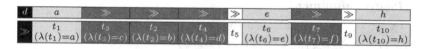

Fig. 4. Optimal alignment for the WF-net shown in Fig. 2 and $\sigma = \langle d, a, e, h \rangle$

4   Infix and Postfix Alignments

This section defines infix and postfix alignments. Infix alignments align a given trace infix against an infix of the WF-net's language. Thus, the model part of an infix alignment starts at some reachable marking from the given WF-net's initial marking and ends at an arbitrary marking. Figure 5 depicts two infix alignments for the WF-net shown in Fig. 2. As for alignments, the first row of an infix alignment corresponds to the given trace infix (ignoring $\gg$). The second row corresponds to a firing sequence (ignoring $\gg$) starting from a WF-net's reachable marking.

Postfix alignments follow the same concept as infix alignments. A postfix alignment's model part starts at a reachable marking but ends at the WF-net's final marking. Figure 5 shows examples of postfix alignments for the WF-net shown in Fig. 2. As for alignments, the notion of optimality applies equally to infix and postfix alignments. Next, we define complete, infix, and postfix alignments.

Definition 3 (Complete/infix/postfix alignment). *Let $\sigma \in \mathcal{A}^*$ be a complete/infix/postfix trace, $N = (P, T, F, m_i, m_f, \lambda)$ be a WF-net, and $\gg \notin \mathcal{A} \cup T$. A sequence $\gamma \in \left((\mathcal{A} \cup \{\gg\}) \times (T \cup \{\gg\}) \right)^*$ is an complete/infix/postfix alignment if:*

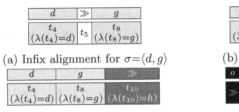

(a) Infix alignment for $\sigma = \langle d, g \rangle$

(b) Infix alignment for $\sigma = \langle b, d, f \rangle$

(c) Postfix alignment for $\sigma = \langle d, g \rangle$

(d) Postfix alignment for $\sigma = \langle a, d, g \rangle$

Fig. 5. Optimal infix and postfix alignments for the WF-net shown in Fig. 2

.1. $\sigma = \pi_1^*(\gamma)_{\downarrow A}$

2.   – **Complete alignment:** $(N, m_i) \xrightarrow{\pi_2^*(\gamma)_{\downarrow T}} (N, m_f)$
   – **Infix alignment:**
   $$(N, m_i) \rightsquigarrow (N, m_1) \xrightarrow{\pi_2^*(\gamma)_{\downarrow T}} (N, m_2) \rightsquigarrow (N, m_f) \text{ for } m_1, m_2 \in \mathcal{R}(N, m_i)$$
   – **Postfix alignment:**
   $$(N, m_i) \rightsquigarrow (N, m_1) \xrightarrow{\pi_2^*(\gamma)_{\downarrow T}} (N, m_f) \text{ for } m_1 \in \mathcal{R}(N, m_i)$$
3. $(\gg, \gg) \notin \gamma \;\wedge\; \forall_{a \in \mathcal{A}, t \in T}\big(\lambda(t) \neq a \Rightarrow (a, t) \notin \gamma\big)$

5   Computing Infix/postfix Alignments

The given reference process model cannot be immediately used to compute infix/postfix alignments because it requires starting in the initial marking m_i. Thus, our approach (cf. Fig. 1) constructs an *auxiliary process model.*

Reconsider the second requirement of the infix/postfix alignments definition. For both infix/postfix alignments, the model part starts with a transition enabled in marking m_1 that is reachable from the initial marking m_i. Hereinafter, we refer to candidate markings for m_1 (cf. Definition 3) as *relevant markings.* The central question is how to efficiently calculate relevant markings that might represent the start of an infix/postfix alignment in its model part. Below, we summarize our overall approach for infix/postfix alignment computation.

1. Calculate *relevant markings* in the given WF-net that may represent the start of the infix/postfix alignment in the model part, cf. m_1 in Definition 3.
2. Create the auxiliary WF-net using the relevant markings (cf. Definition 4).
3. Create the SPN using the *auxiliary* WF-net and the given trace infix/postfix.
4. Perform a shortest path search on the SPN's state space with corresponding goal markings, i.e., goal states regarding the shortest path search.
   – **Infix alignment:** goal markings contain the last place of the SPN's trace net part
   – **Postfix alignment:** standard final marking of the SPN [1,2]
5. Infix/postfix alignment post-processing: removal of the invisible model move that results from using the auxiliary WF-net instead of the original WF-net.

The first two steps are essential, i.e., the generation of the auxiliary WF-net. The subsequent SPN generation remains unchanged compared to alignments [1,2]. Likewise, the shortest path search on the SPN's state space is unchanged compared to alignments; however, the goal marking(s) differ, see above. Subsequently, we present two approaches for constructing the auxiliary WF-net.

5.1   Baseline Approach for Auxiliary WF-net Construction

This section presents a baseline approach for constructing the auxiliary WF-net. This approach assumes a sound WF-net $N = (P, T, F, m_i, m_f, \lambda)$ as reference process model. As sound WF-nets are *bounded* [9], their state space is finite. Thus, we can list all reachable markings $\mathcal{R}(N, m_i) = \{m_1, \dots, m_n\}$; the baseline approach considers all reachable markings as relevant markings. Given N, the baseline approach adds a new place p_0, representing also the new initial marking $[p_0]$, and n silent transitions allowing to reach one of the markings $\{m_1, \dots, m_n\}$ from $[p_0]$. Thus, when constructing the corresponding SPN using the auxiliary WF-net, it is possible from the SPN's initial marking to execute a transition representing an invisible model move that marks the model part at some reachable marking m_1 (cf. Definition 3). Figure 6 shows the auxiliary WF-net of the WF-net shown in Fig. 2. Below we generally define the auxiliary WF-net for a given set of relevant markings. Note that for the auxiliary WF-net constructed by the baseline approach, the set of relevant markings $\{m_1, \dots, m_n\} = \mathcal{R}(N, m_i)$.

Definition 4 (Auxiliary WF-net). *Let $N = (P, T, F, m_i, m_f, \lambda)$ be a WF-net and $\{m_1, \dots, m_n\} \subseteq \mathcal{R}(N, m_i)$ be the given set of relevant markings. We define the auxiliary WF-net $N' = (P', T', F', m_i', m_f', \lambda')$ with:*

- $P' = P \cup \{p_0'\}$ *(assuming $p_0' \notin P$)*
- $T' = T \cup \{t_j' \mid 1 \le j \le n\}$
- $F' = F \cup \{(p_0', t_j') \mid 1 \le j \le n\} \cup \{(t_j', p) \mid 1 \le j \le n \wedge p \in m_j\}$

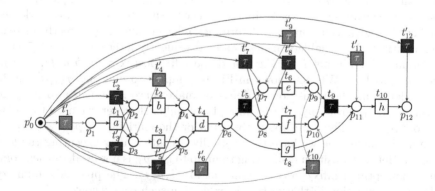

Fig. 6. Auxiliary WF-net constructed using the baseline approach (Sect. 5.1) of the WF-net shown in Fig. 2. Red elements are not contained if the baseline approach with subsequent filtering is used (for the example infix $\sigma = \langle b, d, f \rangle$). (Color figure online)

- $m_i' = [p_0']$ and $m_f' = m_f$
- $\lambda'(t_j) = \lambda(t_j)$ for all $t_j \in T$ and $\lambda'(t_j') = \tau$ for all $t_j' \in T' \backslash T$

When creating the SPN using the auxiliary WF-net and a given trace infix/postfix, the added transitions in the auxiliary WF-net correspond to invisible model moves. For example, reconsider the infix alignment in Fig. 5a. The infix alignment for $\sigma = \langle d, g \rangle$ and auxiliary WF-net shown in Fig. 6 returned after step 4 contains an invisible model move on t_5'. As this invisible model move on t_5' is the result of using the auxiliary WF-net instead of the original WF-net for which we calculate an infix/postfix alignment, we must remove it, i.e., Step 5.

Improved Baseline by Subsequent Filtering. Instead of considering all reachable markings as relevant markings, we filter markings not enabling transitions whose labels are contained in the given infix/postfix σ. Reconsider the auxiliary WF-net shown Fig. 6; red elements are not included if subsequent filtering is used for the example infix $\sigma = \langle b, d, f \rangle$. For instance, t_1' is not included, as the marking reached $[p_1]$ only enables t_1 with $\lambda(t_1) = a \notin \sigma$. Below, we define the relevant markings for a WF-net $N = (P, T, F, m_i, m_f, \lambda)$ and infix/postfix σ.

$$\{m \in \mathcal{R}(N, m_i) \mid \exists_{t \in T} ((N, m)[t\rangle \wedge \lambda(t) \in \sigma)\} \cup \{m_f\}$$

Note that the auxiliary WF-net constructed by the baseline approach without filtering is independent of the provided trace infix/postfix. However, the auxiliary WF-net constructed by the baseline plus subsequent filtering depends on the provided model *and* the trace infix/postfix.

5.2   Advanced Auxiliary WF-net Construction for Process Trees

This section introduces an advanced approach for constructing an auxiliary WF-net from a given *block-structured* WF-net, i.e., a process tree. Compared to the baseline, the advanced approach aims to reduce the number of relevant markings. Further, the advanced approach determines relevant markings directly instead of computing all reachable markings and subsequently filtering (cf. Sect. 5.1).

Assume the WF-net from Fig. 2 and the infix/postfix $\sigma = \langle b, d, f \rangle$. Reconsider the auxiliary WF-net shown in Fig. 6; jumping to marking $[p_2, p_3]$ within the model using the transition t_2' does not make sense if we can also jump to marking $[p_2, p_5]$. From $[p_2, p_3]$ we can replay b and c. However, we need to replay b according to σ. Thus, we would always favor the marking $[p_2, p_5]$ over $[p_2, p_3]$ since in the latter one we have to eventually execute c after executing the b to proceed. Hence, transition t_2' allowing to jump to $[p_2, p_3]$ is not needed when computing an optimal infix/postfix alignment for $\langle b, d, f \rangle$. The proposed auxiliary WF-net construction in this section is exploiting such conclusions.

Figure 7 shows the auxiliary WF-net that is generated by the advanced approach. The shown auxiliary WF-net is specific for the WF-net shown in Fig. 2 and the infix/postfix $\sigma = \langle b, d, f \rangle$. Compared to the auxiliary WF-net generated by the baseline approach (cf. Fig. 6), the one shown in Fig. 7 contains less silent transitions; leading to a reduced state space of the corresponding SPN. To compute the relevant markings, the advanced approach systematically traverses the given process tree as specified in Algorithm 1, which internally calls Algorithms 2 and 3.

Restriction to Submodel. In addition to the described approach, we can further reduce the size of the auxiliary WF-net if we compute *infix alignments*. For a process tree T, we determine the minimal subtree that contains all leaf nodes whose labels are contained in the given trace infix. Since the other subtrees do not contain leaf nodes relevant for the given infix, we can ignore them[1]. Next, we call Algorithm 1 for the determined subtree and execute the auxiliary WF-net for the determined subtree and the corresponding relevant markings.

6   Evaluation

This section presents an evaluation of the infix alignment computation. We use real-life, publicly available event logs. We sampled 10,000 infixes per log. Further, we discovered a process model using the entire log with the inductive miner infrequent [4]. The implementation and further results can be found online[2].

Regarding the correctness of the proposed approaches: Baseline, Baseline + subsequent filtering and the Advanced approach, we compare the cost of the computed infix alignments. As the baseline approach considers all reachable markings as relevant, it is guaranteed that no other relevant markings exist. Per trace infix, we find that all approaches yield infix alignments with identical costs.

Figure 8 shows the overall time spent for the alignment computation, i.e., Step 1 to 5 (cf. Sect. 5). We find that using the advanced approach significantly shortens the overall alignment calculation time compared to the baseline approaches

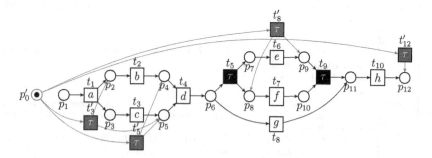

Fig. 7. Auxiliary WF-net constructed using the advanced approach (cf. Sect. 5.2) for the block-structured WF-net shown in Fig. 2 and the infix $\sigma = \langle b, d, f \rangle$

---

[1] Note that if the determined subtree is placed within a loop, the subtree containing the highest loop and the initial determined subtree has to be considered.

[2] https://github.com/fit-daniel-schuster/conformance_checking_for_trace_fragments.

Algorithm 1: Calculating relevant markings for process trees

> **input** : $T=(V,E,\lambda,r){\in}\mathcal{T}$, $\sigma{\in}\mathcal{A}^*$
> **output:** $M \subseteq \mathcal{B}(P^T)$
> **begin**
> 1 $M \leftarrow \{\}$;   // initialize the set of markings for the auxiliary WF-net
> 2   let $N^T = (P^T, T^T, F^T, m_i^T, m_f^T, \lambda^T)$ be the corresponding WF-net of T;
> 3 $A \leftarrow \{a \mid a{\in}\mathcal{A} \wedge a{\in}\sigma\}$;   // store all activity labels from σ in the set A
>   **forall** $n \in \{\overline{n} \mid \overline{n}{\in}V \wedge \lambda(\overline{n}){\in}A\}$ **do**   // iterate over leaves whose label is in σ
> 4 $\lfloor$ $M \leftarrow M \cup BuMG(T, n, null, N^T, \emptyset, A)$;   // call $BuMG$ for each leaf n
> 5   **return** $M \cup \{m_f^T\}$;   // m_f^T is needed for postfix alignments to ensure that the
>   entire model is skippable (i.e., postfix alignment contains log moves only)

Algorithm 2: Bottom-up marking generation ($BuMG$)

> **input** : $T=(V,E,\lambda,r){\in}\mathcal{T}$, $n{\in}V$, $n'{\in}V$, $N^T=(P^T,T^T,F^T,m_i^T,m_f^T,\lambda^T){\in}\mathcal{N}$,
> $M{\subseteq}\mathcal{B}(P^T)$, $A{\subseteq}\mathcal{A}$
> **output:** $M{\subseteq}\mathcal{B}(P^T)$
> **begin**
> 1   **if** $\lambda(n) \in \mathcal{A}$ **then**   // n is a leaf node of T
> 2 $\lfloor$ let $t \in T^T$ be the transition representing $n \in V$;
> 3 $M \leftarrow \{[p \in {\bullet}t]\}$;   // initialize M with a marking enabling t
> 4   **else if** $\lambda(n) = \wedge$ **then**   // n represents a parallel operator
> 5 $S \leftarrow \langle s_1,\ldots,s_k \rangle = c^T(n)_{\downarrow V \setminus \{n'\}}$;   // $S \in V^*$ contains the siblings of n'
> 6   **forall** $s_j \in S$ **do**
> 7 $\lfloor$ $M_{s_j} \leftarrow TdMG(T(s_j), N^{T(s_j)}, A, true)$;
> 8 $M \leftarrow M \times M_{s_1} \times \cdots \times M_{s_k}$;   // Cartesian product because $\lambda(n) = \wedge$
> 9   **if** $r = n$ **then**   // node n is the root node of T
> 10 $\lfloor$ **return** M;
> 11 $M \leftarrow BuMG(T, p^T(n), n, N^T, M, A)$;   // call $BuMG$ on n's parent

---

Algorithm 3: Top-down marking generation ($TdMG$)

> **input** : $T=(V,E,\lambda,r){\in}\mathcal{T}$, $N^T=(P^T,T^T,F^T,m_i^T,m_f^T,\lambda^T){\in}\mathcal{N}$, $A{\subseteq}\mathcal{A}$,
> $addFinalMarking{\in}\{true, false\}$
> **output:** $M{\subseteq}\mathcal{B}(P^T)$
> **begin**
> 1   **if** $\lambda(r) \in \mathcal{A}$ **then**   // r is a leaf node
> 2   let $t \in T^T$ be the transition representing r;
> 3 $M \leftarrow \emptyset$;
> 4   **if** $\lambda(r) \in A$ **then**
> 5 $\lfloor$ $M \leftarrow M \cup \{[p \in {\bullet}t]\}$;   // t's label is in the given trace infix/postfix
> 6   **if** $addFinalMarking = true$ **then**
> 7 $\lfloor$ $M \leftarrow M \cup \{[p \in t{\bullet}]\}$;
> 8   **return** M;
> 9   **else**   // r represents an operator
> 10 $S \leftarrow \langle s_1,\ldots,s_k \rangle = c^T(r)$;   // S contains all children of the root node r
> 11   **if** $\lambda(r) = \rightarrow$ **then**
> 12 $\lfloor$ **return** $TdMG(T(s_1), N^{T(s_1)}, A, false) \cup \cdots \cup TdMG(T(s_{k-1}), N^{T(s_{k-1})}, A,$
> $false) \cup TdMG(T(s_k), N^{T(s_k)}, A, addFinalMarking)$;
> 13   **if** $\lambda(r) = \wedge$ **then**
> 14 $\lfloor$ **return** $TdMG(T(s_1), A, N^{T(s_1)}, true) \times \cdots \times TdMG(T(s_k), N^{T(s_k)}, A, true)$;
> 15   **if** $\lambda(r) \in \{\circlearrowleft, \times\}$ **then**
> 16 $\lfloor$ **return** $TdMG(T(s_1), N^{T(s_1)}, A, addFinalMarking) \cup TdMG(T(s_2), N^{T(s_2)},$
> $A, false) \cup \cdots \cup TdMG(T(s_k), N^{T(s_k)}, A, false)$;

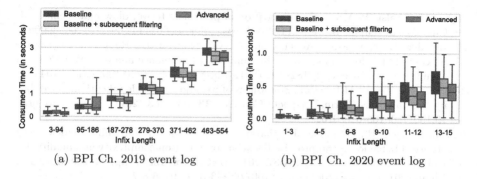

(a) BPI Ch. 2019 event log   (b) BPI Ch. 2020 event log

Fig. 8. Time spent for computing infix alignments, i.e., Step 1–5 (cf. Sect. 5)

because the auxiliary WF-net produced by the advanced approach contains fewer silent transitions than the one created by the baseline approach.

7 Conclusion

This paper extended the widely used conformance checking technique alignments by defining infix and postfix alignments. We presented two approaches for computing them, i.e., a baseline approach and an advanced approach assuming process trees as a reference model. Our results indicate that the advanced approach outperforms the baseline if the reference process model is block-structured.

References

1. Adriansyah, A.A.: Aligning observed and modeled behavior. Ph.D. thesis (2014). https://doi.org/10.6100/IR770080
2. Carmona, J., van Dongen, B., Solti, A., Weidlich, M.: Epilogue. In: Conformance Checking, pp. 261–263. Springer, Cham (2018). https://doi.org/10.1007/978-3-319-99414-7_13
3. Dunzer, S., Stierle, M., Matzner, M., Baier, S.: Conformance checking: a state-of-the-art literature review. In: Proceedings of the 11th International Conference on Subject-Oriented Business Process Management. ACM Press (2019). https://doi.org/10.1145/3329007.3329014
4. Leemans, S.J.J.: Enhancement & inductive visual miner. In: Robust Process Mining with Guarantees. LNBIP, vol. 440, pp. 423–447. Springer, Cham (2022). https://doi.org/10.1007/978-3-030-96655-3_9
5. Schuster, D., van Zelst, S.J.: Online process monitoring using incremental state-space expansion: an exact algorithm. In: Fahland, D., Ghidini, C., Becker, J., Dumas, M. (eds.) BPM 2020. LNCS, vol. 12168, pp. 147–164. Springer, Cham (2020). https://doi.org/10.1007/978-3-030-58666-9_9
6. Taymouri, F., Carmona, J.: A recursive paradigm for aligning observed behavior of large structured process models. In: La Rosa, M., Loos, P., Pastor, O. (eds.) BPM 2016. LNCS, vol. 9850, pp. 197–214. Springer, Cham (2016). https://doi.org/10.1007/978-3-319-45348-4_12

7. van der Aalst, W.M.P.: The application of petri nets to workflow management. J. Circ. Syst. Comput. **8**, 21–66 (1998). https://doi.org/10.1142/S0218126698000043

8. van der Aalst, W.M.P., Adriansyah, A., van Dongen, B.: Replaying history on process models for conformance checking and performance analysis. WIREs Data Mining Knowl. Discov. **2**, 182–192 (2012). https://doi.org/10.1002/widm.1045

9. van der Aalst, W.M.P., et al.: Soundness of workflow nets: classification, decidability, and analysis. Formal Aspects Comput. **23**, 333–363 (2011). https://doi.org/10.1007/s00165-010-0161-4

10. van Dongen, B., Carmona, J., Chatain, T., Taymouri, F.: Aligning modeled and observed behavior: a compromise between computation complexity and quality. In: Dubois, E., Pohl, K. (eds.) CAiSE 2017. LNCS, vol. 10253, pp. 94–109. Springer, Cham (2017). https://doi.org/10.1007/978-3-319-59536-8_7

11. Dongen, B.F.: Efficiently computing alignments. In: Daniel, F., Sheng, Q.Z., Motahari, H. (eds.) BPM 2018. LNBIP, vol. 342, pp. 44–55. Springer, Cham (2019). https://doi.org/10.1007/978-3-030-11641-5_4

An Experimental Study of Intuitive Representations of Process Task Annotations

Myriel Fichtner[1]([✉])(iD), Urs A. Fichtner[2](iD), and Stefan Jablonski[1]

[1] University of Bayreuth, Bayreuth, Germany
{myriel.fichtner,stefan.jablonski}@uni-bayreuth.de
[2] Section of Health Care Research and Rehabilitation Research, Institute of Medical Biometry and Statistics, Faculty of Medicine and Medical Center, University of Freiburg, Freiburg im Breisgau, Germany
urs.fichtner@uniklinik-freiburg.de

Abstract. Business process modeling languages support enterprises in visualizing workflows in a graphical representation. Many studies provide recommendations about which modeling language to choose and how to represent models in terms of usability. However, there is no support in how to present detailed instructions regarding the execution of process tasks. We denote such instructions as task annotations which have to be considered during process execution to ensure process success. Integrating this information in an understandable way into process models is challenging and has not been sufficiently researched. This paper describes a novel study to address how task annotations can be presented in process models intuitively. In an experimental setup, we compare different representation formats for different task settings and evaluate them regarding the aspects effectiveness, mental efficiency and satisfaction. We found empirical support that image- and diagram-based representations are intuitively comprehensible across all task settings regardless of the user's level of experience or education. Furthermore, we could statistically prove inferiority of textual task annotations.

Keywords: Business process modeling · Intuitiveness · Process model comprehensibility · Understandability · Task representation formats

1 Introduction

Business process models describe internal or external workflows of enterprises in a graphical representation. To create such models, different business process modeling languages are available, e.g., Business Process Model and Notation (BPMN) or Event-driven Process Chain (EPC). They mainly differ in the set of modeling elements and their representations. The languages are applied depending on the use case and preferences of the modelers or process participants. In

M. Sellami et al. (Eds.): CoopIS 2022, LNCS 13591, pp. 311–321, 2022.
https://doi.org/10.1007/978-3-031-17834-4_19

general, such models aim at supporting a common understanding of organizational processes [16]. This aspect is a precondition to ensure successful implementations of tasks and thus of successful process executions. Therefore, process models must be understandable by all involved participants. The comprehensibility of a model is directly related to its usability [7], while the ability of a modeling language to support the translation between the viewer's cognitive and visual model is a decisive criterion [4].

Studies that compare the usability of process modeling languages, e.g., [4, 20], provide recommendations about which modeling language to choose for a use case. However, they do not suggest how to represent detailed process instructions regarding usability. For certain tasks, it is essential to integrate concrete execution instructions into a model, e.g., exact placement information for an object that is manipulated within a task. We denote such execution instructions as *task annotations* which do not refer to the general process flow, but define detailed, fine-grained actions within a process task. Depending on the task, such instructions can become very complex. Due to the limitations of modeling languages, they cannot be represented appropriately in a model. Integrating them into process flows would lead to large and overloaded models containing hundreds of elements. For this reason, non-textual representations of instructions are suggested, e.g., pictures or videos [21]. Following [3], a task annotation can be linked to a task as i) text, ii) medium or iii) diagram. Although process models can benefit greatly from different representation formats for task annotations, no empirical investigation of their intuitive usability (IU) in different application setups and for different user groups has been conducted so far.

This work evaluates the IU of textual, pictorial and diagrammatic task annotations for BPMN process models within an experimental study. We give recommendations on how to represent task annotations or to extend process models by such instructions in a user-oriented and intuitively comprehensible way. We provide a reusable questionnaire framework and show its exemplary application enabling process designers to evaluate the intuitiveness of their models.

2   Theoretical Background and Related Work

Usability is the ease of use when interacting with a system [13]. ISO 9241-11 suggests that system usability should be assessed by measuring *effectiveness*, *efficiency* and *satisfaction*. Effectiveness includes the user's ability to complete assigned tasks, efficiency results from the resources required to complete them and satisfaction is derived from user feedback [18]. Many systems aim to be usable by naïve users that have no prior knowledge, i.e., the usability of a system must be intuitive and self-explanatory. From this requirement, IU has emerged as sub-concept of usability. In contrast to the definition of usability, IU focuses on low mental effort and the subconscious application of prior knowledge [10] and is assessed by three sub-aspects *effectiveness*, *mental efficiency* and *satisfaction*.

A usable process modeling language has to support the creation and understanding of models [6]. Among the work on understandability of process models we distinguish between (1) approaches examining the impact of individual modeling elements on process comprehensibility (e.g., [9,15]) and (2) work that compares different modeling languages and process representations in terms of understandability. The majority of these focus on usability, e.g., [2,4], only a few evaluate the intuitive usability of modeling languages, e.g., [8,20]. Of our particular interest are approaches that examine different representations of processes independently of a modeling language. In [17], purely textual forms of representation are compared to diagrams. It is shown that the use of textual or diagrammatic instructions does not influence process understandability for non-experts and experts but graphic notations are easier to understand by experts. The comprehensibility of each representation type was evaluated with ten comprehension questions. Another approach examines whether task requirements have an influence on which representation format process participants prefer [5]. Three types of representations are considered: textual, structured text, and diagrammatic. Each type is evaluated with and without icons. Prior knowledge is evaluated in terms of modeling experience and modeling familiarity. Subjects are asked to judge four task settings regarding their preferred representation format through pair-wise comparisons. For all tasks, diagrams are rated best, and structured text was consistently preferred over text.

3 Research Method

3.1 Study Design

In our study, we evaluate the intuitiveness of different representations of task annotations. Similar to [5,9,17,20], we evaluate prior knowledge of study participants regarding process modeling. In contrast to previous approaches, we evaluate the three sub-aspects of IU (effectiveness, mental efficiency, satisfaction) separately. Thereby, a presentation is intuitive if it achieves high scores in all aspects. This approach allows us to identify the origin of potential usability problems. In [19] a questionnaire toolbox regarding the three sub-aspects is provided. The toolbox is developed as a generally applicable instrument for evaluating software, apps, and technical products. The questionnaires have been proven to be applicable in many different research areas (e.g., interaction with mobile devices [12], robot programming [14]) what inspired us to use them for the evaluation of process models as well.

According to [6], comprehensibility can only be measured indirectly either by comprehension tests or by performing problem-solving tasks. Encouraged by [5] that suggest the latter for future work, we evaluate comprehensibility in an experimental setup. The used questionnaire toolbox is specifically designed for experimental studies. The authors propose that other formats besides **textual** and **diagram**-based representations should be evaluated. Following the ideas of [3] and [21], we provide a novel approach to exploratively evaluate **image**-based process descriptions as further representation format. In contrast to previous work we do not evaluate representation types of process models but focus on user preferences regarding presentations of task annotations.

The results in [20] state that the level of education has an influence on the comprehensibility of process models. For this reason, we decided to measure the educational degree of study participants.

We aim on answering the following research questions (RQ):

RQ1. Which representation format of task annotations is most intuitive? Based on the findings of [17, 20] our hypotheses towards this RQ are:

Hypothesis 1a. Diagrammatic representations of task annotation are more intuitively comprehensible than textual representations.

Hypothesis 1b. Prior knowledge in process modeling and execution has an impact on the intuitive comprehensibility of diagram-based task annotations.

Hypothesis 1c. Depending on the level of education, a certain representation format is more intuitively comprehensible compared to others.

RQ2. Are there representation formats of task annotations that are more intuitively comprehensible than others for a particular task setting? Following the work of [5], we hypothesize that:

Hypothesis 2. Depending on the task setting, task annotations are more intuitively comprehensible in certain representation formats.

3.2 Study Procedure and Materials

The study comprises three parts, while one interview including the experiments took about 23 min. We conducted 50 interviews. For detailed information on materials, questionnaires, instrumentation and content, see our repository[1]. In the following we shortly describe the overall study procedure, while a supporting visualization is uploaded in the repository.

First, prior experience, preferred representation format of instructions and demographics were surveyed. Afterwards, basic BPMN elements were briefly explained within max. 2 min and an exemplary BPMN diagram was shown.

Second, subjects were presented a BPMN diagram that contained a task with an annotation in a specific representation format. Then, the subjects were asked to execute the depicted process model. Time of execution was measured and the result was evaluated in terms of effectiveness. Afterwards, efficiency was evaluated by having participants rate their mental effort. Then, open questions were asked about the execution results to find out how the task annotation has been interpreted in detail. Finally, the subjects received feedback on execution success and were asked to rate the task annotations, resulting in an assessment of the satisfaction aspect. Afterwards, this procedure was repeated for the other two representation formats, each with a different task setting.

Last, after participants executed three diagrams and assessed all sub-aspects, they were asked to rank three process models with different representations of task annotations according to their preference in terms of understandability.

3.3 Task Settings and Representation Formats

In this study, we focused on the use of process models from a manufacturing and production perspective. In such environments, process descriptions often con-

---

[1] https://www.ai4.uni-bayreuth.de/en/research/tools_res/index.html

tain instructions to manipulate objects in the work space. Inspired by [14], we designed three simple tasks that reflect common activities from real processes in industry: placing, stacking, and sorting. For example, in the metal injection molding process, components have to be placed from one plate to another before they are put into the sintering oven. In other scenarios, items must be stacked without breaking or interfering with each other. Sorting objects is also often part of process executions, for example in warehouse management. For a realistic setup, we used materials from real process environments: metal components of different sizes and shapes (e.g., gears or timing belt pulleys), industrial storage bins of different colors and a metal plate (cf. repository). We labeled each component with a sticker showing a character (A-H) to facilitate their identification.

Motivated by [3], we defined process steps describing only roughly the type of activity to be performed and the objects that have to be manipulated within this step. Afterwards, we attached task annotations to all three tasks, which contained more precise instructions to be followed during task execution (cf. Table 1).

Each task setting focused on different instruction aspects: positioning of an object in the work space (placing), positioning of objects relative to each other (stacking) and sequencing and assignment of objects (sorting). We created one BPMN diagram for each task setting, resulting in three models. We decided to use BPMN as it is the current standard for business process modeling, having a high usability. In order to ensure comparability of the process models, each model is structured in the same way. Each of them consisted of three tasks, while the second task is deviating depending on the task setting: t_1) *take all components from the carton*, t_2) place, stack or sort components with corresponding task annotation (cf. Table 1) and t_3) *put remaining components back into carton.*

From previous work, we learned that the task setting has an impact on the preferred process representation format [5]. In their study, task settings are related to the understanding, communicating, executing and improving of one specific process, i.e., the process of selecting a Nobel Prize winner. Although, in contrast to our work, the study investigates processes on control flow level, we learned from their study design. We created different representation formats for the annotations per task setting (placing, stacking, sorting) to examine possible correlations in terms of IU. Overall, we examined three representation formats of task annotation: i) text, ii) image and iii) diagram. For each process model per task setting, we created three additional models, each containing the task annotations in different representation formats. In total, we ended up with nine

Table 1. The three task settings with process steps and annotations.

	Process step	*Task annotation*
Placing task	Place components **A, B, D, E, G** and **H** on the metal plate	Place component **A** in the upper or lower quarter of the metal plate
Stacking task	Stack components **D, E, F** on metal plate and components **B, G** on metal plate	Place component **E** on metal plate, on it **D** and on it **F** and place component **B** on metal plate, on it **G**
Sorting task	Sort components **A, B, C, D, F, G** in boxes	Sort component **A, F** in blue box, **B, C** in red box and **D, G** in green box

process models to cover all combinations of task setting and annotation representation format. All process models can be found in the repository.

4 Analysis and Results

4.1 Descriptive Statistics

Detailed descriptive statistics on the 50 study participants can be found in the repository. Since data was collected in presence of the investigator, we could avoid missing values. We classified subjects having already created or read process models as having prior knowledge, regardless of the modeling language used.

4.2 Statistical Methods

We computed linear mixed models (LMM) using the R package lme4. For significance testing, we estimated the degrees of freedom via the Satterthwaite method (R package lmerTest). Since every study participant executed three tasks (repeated measures), we modeled person ID on level 2 as cluster variable. We modeled each outcome variable (effectiveness, efficiency, satisfaction) on level 1. As predictors, we included the representation format, task setting, level of experience and educational degree. We calculated fixed effects and marginal R^2 according to [11]. To estimate, which representation format is best suited for which task setting, we applied pairwise comparisons (R package emmeans). Hereby, the Tukey method was used to correct for multiple testing.

4.3 Hypothesis Testing

Hypotheses 1a, 1b, 1c. For all sub-aspects of intuitiveness, we found a significant relationship with the representation formats (cf. Table 2). In all three LMM, text-based annotations (T) performed worst. In terms of effectiveness (LMM1), we found smallest values for T, contrasting significantly to image-based annotations (I), but not significantly to diagram-based annotations (D). D and I were not significantly different to each other. Similar patterns were found for efficiency and satisfaction. T were significantly inferior to I and D in LMM2 and LMM3. I and D showed no significant difference to each other. Considering the mean values for each model, I performed best regarding effectiveness ($M = 95.2$) and D achieved best values regarding efficiency ($M = 31.2$) and satisfaction ($M = 4.5$).

To test the effect of expertise and educational degree, we extended each LMM by including the relevant predictor and an interaction term (cf. Table for Hypothesis 1 in the repository). We found neither a significant main effect, nor a significant interaction effect for level of expertise. For educational level, the pattern is similar, except for the efficiency scale (LMM2). Here, significant differences in the outcome in relation to the educational level were found, however, they disappeared after correcting for multiple testing.

Table 2. Fixed-effect models with pairwise comparisons on the three aspects.

	LMM 1			LMM 2			LMM 3		
	Effectiveness			*Mental Efficiency*			*Satisfaction*		
	Mean values	(SD)		Mean values	(SD)		Mean values	(SD)	
I	95.2	(22.8)		32.4	(36.3)		4.4	(0.9)	
D	93.6	(13.0)		31.2	(24.0)		4.5	(0.6)	
T	86.8	(15.2)		45.3	(24.5)		3.9	(0.6)	

Contrasts	Estimate	SE	p-value	Estimate	SE	p-value	Estimate	SE	p-value
I - D	1.60	3.34	0.88	1.26	4.71	0.96	−0.04	0.13	0.94
I - T	8.40	3.34	0.04	−12.84	4.71	0.02	0.49	0.13	0.00
D - T	6.80	3.34	0.11	−14.10	4.71	0.01	0.53	0.13	0.00

p-value	0.03			0.01			0.00		
Marginal R^2	0.04			0.05			0.10		

Hypothesis 2. We used pairwise comparison to test whether certain representation formats are more suitable for a specific task setting than for others in terms of intuitive comprehension (cf. Figs. for Hypothesis 2 in repository).

For effectiveness, we found no significant superiority of any task annotation representation for the placing and sorting task. For the stacking task, however, we found significant inferiority of T ($M_{T_{st}} = 78$) in comparison to the other representations ($M_{I_{st}} = 100$, $M_{D_{st}} = 98$). The mean values for the placing task were highest for I and D ($M_{I_p}, M_{D_p} = 89$), while for the sorting task, the highest mean value was found for T ($M_{T_{so}} = 100$). The examination of the efficiency dimension resulted in the same pattern as for effectiveness: For the stacking task, significant inferiority (represented by higher values) of T ($M_{T_{st}} = 68$) was found in comparison to the other representations ($M_{I_{st}} = 33, M_{D_{st}} = 31$). The other task settings showed no significant differences across the representation formats. For satisfaction, the pattern follows the other two sub-aspects: Significant inferiority of T was found for the stacking task, while the other two task settings showed no clear differences related to the representation format. However, D showed highest mean values for placing and sorting ($M_{D_p} = 4.2, M_{D_{so}} = 4.7$) and I showed the highest mean value for stacking ($M_{I_{st}} = 4.6$).

Comparing the task settings that performed best for each representation format in terms of all sub-aspects, we found the following significant differences: There is a significant advantage of the sorting task compared to the others for T in terms of effectiveness. For efficiency, we found a significant advantage of the placing and sorting task for T in comparison to the stacking task. For satisfaction, we found significant differences between all three task settings within T. There is a significant advantage of the sorting task compared to the others, while placing is significantly better than stacking. We found a significant advantage of the sorting task compared to the placing task within I and D.

5   Discussion

5.1   Summary of Findings

First, we want to discuss if there is a particular representation format which supports designers in presenting a task annotation in an intuitively understandable way. A representation format is intuitively comprehensible, if all three sub-aspects score high values. We summarize that text-based representations are inferior to the other two representation formats for each sub-aspect. Especially the satisfaction value in case of textual annotation significantly differs compared to the other representation formats. Further analysis reveals that the perceived error rate of the text-based annotations differs most from the values of the diagrammatic and pictorial representation. We deduce that the success of the execution of the process model has an impact on the study participants' satisfaction. Also for textual representations, this sub-aspect is the main cause of low intuitiveness.

In contrast to [17], stating that diagrammatic process presentations are more comprehensible for experienced users, the level of prior knowledge has no impact on the intuitive comprehensibility of a certain representation format in our study. Moreover, text-based annotations perform worse across all levels of prior knowledge. Due to our small sample size, we are not able to confirm the findings in [20], stating that academic education has an impact on the obtained total scores. The expressive power of our results is limited while we conclude that the educational level has no additional explanatory effect.

Second, we want to discuss whether there is a preferred representation format regarding a certain task setting. In our study, we found a clear inferiority of the text-based annotations to the other representation types in the stacking task. Here, the process step description contained the components that had to be stacked in alphabetical order. The task annotation then described the assembly in another order. For the textual annotation, this issue was assessed as significantly more demanding compared to the other formats. This led to high values regarding mental effort and therefore to a poor rating of the efficiency. For the other two task settings, placing and stacking, we did not identify any differences between the representation formats. However, our results confirm the findings in [5] that the suitability of a representation format depends on the task setting.

In sum, we conclude that diagrammatic and pictorial annotations are generally preferable for presenting task annotations in context of manufacturing processes. For tasks including many objects and dependencies between them, textual annotations should be avoided. Furthermore, within international process environments, it should be pointed out that textual task annotations have a further disadvantage since they have to be translated properly. For many tasks this results in a high amount of work associated with considerable costs [1]. When using images, process designers have to be careful how they present the task annotation. In images depicting positive examples (cf. stacking and sorting task), study participants often tried to reproduce the shown scene. Even if this does not have an impact on the process success, it greatly restricts the possible solution space. Therefore, we recommend more abstract images that consider this aspect and show only relevant details (cf. placing task). Finally, study participants preferred image-based annotations in direct comparison to the other formats across all task settings. The execution time analysis shows that instructions can be processed about 20 seconds faster when they are presented as images or diagrams instead of texts.

5.2 Threats to Validity

The explanatory power of our LMMs is limited due to small sample sizes. However, since we were able to find significant differences, we can assume that there is a real inferiority of textual information which would be contrasted even more having a larger sample size. For hypothesis 1c, the small sample size led to weak-performing statistical models, which should be addressed in future studies.

Another threat is the transferability of results that were produced in controlled experimental setups with study investigators present to real-life working environments. Motivational aspects, personality traits, job satisfaction and cognitive capacities might play a role in determining whether a representation format is the most suitable for a specific task.

In our study, we examined the influence of different task settings on the comprehensibility of task annotations. For this purpose, we adapted common activities from real process environments. However, when considering concrete process tasks from manufacturing contexts, activities, and hence execution instructions, can become very complex. We propose that for such tasks, the level of experience in terms of process modeling and execution might have an impact on the intuitive comprehensibility of task annotations. In order to verify this assumption, future studies should consider task settings from real process environments comprising different complexities.

6   Conclusion

In this work, we present the results of an experimental study regarding the intuitiveness of different representations of task annotations. Our study contributes to process modeling research by providing an empirical investigation of how to present task annotations intuitively considering different task settings. We recommend that regardless of a task setting, image- or diagram-based task annotations should be preferred in order to reduce the mental effort while maintaining high effectiveness and satisfaction. We show a novel approach on how to examine the intuitive usability of process modeling aspects by providing a questionnaire framework for further studies. Since image-based annotations have proven as intuitively comprehensible, future research could extend this work by examining different types of image representations.

References

1. Batoulis, K., Eid-Sabbagh, R.-H., Leopold, H., Weske, M., Mendling, J.: Automatic business process model translation with BPMT. In: Franch, X., Soffer, P. (eds.) CAiSE 2013. LNBIP, vol. 148, pp. 217–228. Springer, Heidelberg (2013). https://doi.org/10.1007/978-3-642-38490-5_21
2. Fahland, D., et al.: Declarative versus imperative process modeling languages: the issue of understandability. In: Halpin, T., et al. (eds.) BPMDS/EMMSAD -2009. LNBIP, vol. 29, pp. 353–366. Springer, Heidelberg (2009). https://doi.org/10.1007/978-3-642-01862-6_29
3. Fichtner, M., Schönig, S., Jablonski, S.: How LIME explanation models can be used to extend business process models by relevant process details. In: ICEIS 2022, Vol. 2, pp. 527–534. SciTePress (2022)
4. Figl, K., Mendling, J., Strembeck, M.: Towards a usability assessment of process modeling languages. In: 8th GI-Workshop Geschäftsprozessmanagement mit Ereignisgesteuerten Prozessketten (EPK), CEUR-WS, pp. 138–156. Citeseer (2009)
5. Figl, K., Recker, J.: Exploring cognitive style and task-specific preferences for process representations. Requirements Eng. **21**(1), 63–85 (2014). https://doi.org/10.1007/s00766-014-0210-2
6. Gemino, A., Wand, Y.: A framework for empirical evaluation of conceptual modeling techniques. Requirements Eng. **9**(4), 248–260 (2004)
7. Houy, C., Fettke, P., Loos, P.: On the theoretical foundations of research into the understandability of business process models. In: ECIS 2014, Tel Aviv, Israel (2014)
8. Jošt, G., Huber, J., Heričko, M.: An empirical investigation of intuitive understandability of process diagrams. Comput. Stand. Interf. **48**, 90–111 (2016)
9. Mendling, J., Reijers, H.A., Cardoso, J.: What makes process models understandable? In: Alonso, G., Dadam, P., Rosemann, M. (eds.) BPM 2007. LNCS, vol. 4714, pp. 48–63. Springer, Heidelberg (2007). https://doi.org/10.1007/978-3-540-75183-0_4
10. Mohs, C., Hurtienne, J., Kindsmüller, M.: IUUI-intuitive use of user interfaces: Auf dem Weg zu einer wissenschaftlichen Basis für das Schlagwort "Intuitivität." MMI-Interaktiv **11**(11), 75–84 (2006)
11. Nakagawa, S., Johnson, P., Schielzeth, H.: The coefficient of determination R 2 and intra-class correlation coefficient from generalized linear mixed-effects models revisited and expanded. J. Royal Soc. Interface **14**(134), 20170213 (2017)
12. Naumann, A., Hurtienne, J.: Benchmarks for intuitive interaction with mobile devices. In: MobileHCI 2010, pp. 401–402 (2010)
13. Nielson, J.: Usability 101: introduction to usability (2009)
14. Orendt, E., Fichtner, M., Henrich, D.: Robot programming by non-experts: intuitiveness and robustness of one-shot robot programming. In: RO-MAN 2016, pp. 192–199. IEEE (2016)
15. Palash, B.: Does cognitive overload matter in understanding Bpmn models? J. Comput. Inf. Syst. **52**(4), 59–69 (2012)
16. Recker, J., Safrudin, N., Rosemann, M.: How novices model business processes. In: Hull, R., Mendling, J., Tai, S. (eds.) BPM 2010. LNCS, vol. 6336, pp. 29–44. Springer, Heidelberg (2010). https://doi.org/10.1007/978-3-642-15618-2_5
17. Rodrigues, R. et al.: An experiment on process model understandability using textual work instructions and BPMN models. In: 29th Brazilian Symposium on Software Engineering, pp. 41–50. IEEE (2015)

18. Shackel, B.: Usability - context, framework, definition, design and evaluation. Interact. Comput. **21**(5–6), 339–346 (2009)
19. Wegerich, A., Löffler, D., Maier, A.: Handbuch zur IBIS Toolbox-Evaluation Intuitiver Benutzbarkeit. Bundesministerium für Bildung und Forschung (2018)
20. Weitlaner, D., Guettinger, A., Kohlbacher, M.: Intuitive comprehensibility of process models. In: Fischer, H., Schneeberger, J. (eds.) S-BPM ONE 2013. CCIS, vol. 360, pp. 52–71. Springer, Heidelberg (2013). https://doi.org/10.1007/978-3-642-36754-0_4
21. Wiedmann, P.: Agiles Geschäftsprozessmanagement auf Basis gebrauchssprachlicher Modellierung. PhD thesis, University of Bayreuth, Germany (2017)

A Method for Integrated Modeling of KiPs and Contextual Goals

Zeynep Ozturk Yurt[1]([✉])[iD], Rik Eshuis[1][iD], Banu Aysolmaz[1][iD],
Anna Wilbik[2][iD], and Irene Vanderfeesten[1,3][iD]

[1] Eindhoven University of Technology, Eindhoven, The Netherlands
z.ozturk.yurt@tue.nl
[2] Maastricht University, Maastricht, The Netherlands
[3] Open Universiteit, Heerlen, The Netherlands

Abstract. Knowledge-intensive processes (KiPs) progress in a flexible way towards the achievement of process goals. Contextual factors like location and regulations affect how these goals are achieved in KiPs. Conventionally, a context is considered to be either static or dynamic. For some KiPs part of the context can be dynamic, meaning that the context can change during the execution of the KiP as a result of the decisions and interpretations of the knowledge-worker based on the information gained throughout the process. A holistic approach linking dynamic context, goals and processes is vital for modeling such KiPs. This paper presents a method, based on enterprise models, for integrated modeling of KiPs with contextual goals under dynamic contexts. With our method, we guide business analysts in modeling complex, flexible KiPs under dynamic contexts.

Keywords: Knowledge-intensive process · Enterprise modeling · Goal modeling · Process modeling · Context

1 Introduction

Knowledge-intensive processes (KiPs) are executed in a flexible way by knowledge workers to achieve goals. Flexible process models support knowledge-workers in executing the KiPs [5]. However, goals are implicit in process models. The relation between the processes and goals is even more evident for KiPs than traditional activity-centered business processes, since KiPs are by definition goal-oriented [5]. It is crucial that the goals and the KiP models are aligned well to make sure the goals are satisfied properly throughout the process execution.

The context of a business process covers any information that affects the design and execution of a business process and how the process goals are achieved [19]. Values taken by a combination of one or more contextual factors e.g., weather or location, define the business process context, e.g., rainy weather or location as city center. A process context is typically assumed to be either static or dynamic. In a single execution of a process, static context is fixed and predefined, e.g., the season for an airline booking process. The context can also be

M. Sellami et al. (Eds.): CoopIS 2022, LNCS 13591, pp. 322–332, 2022.
https://doi.org/10.1007/978-3-031-17834-4_20

dynamic, so change during the process execution, e.g., the weather for an airline booking process.

The dynamism of the context of a business process usually originates from the changes in the environment. But in a KiP, context can also dynamically change based on the interpretations and decisions made by the knowledge workers throughout the process execution. For example, in a medical diagnosis process, the process goal is to come up with a diagnosis by doing some tests. Depending on which diseases are suspected, the clinician should perform different tests to decide upon the final diagnosis and achieve the process goal. Therefore, the set of suspected diseases defines the context of the diagnosis process. But the results of a test may be such that the clinician decides to investigate a new disease, so the clinician can dynamically change the context of the diagnosis process.

Conventionally, context-awareness in business processes deals with adapting processes to unexpected or uncontrolled changes in the context due to a change in the environment. However, like in a medical diagnosis process, the change in the context can be an inherent part of the business logic rather than being unexpected or uncontrolled. For such KiPs, knowledge workers need to cater for changing goals as a result of controllable changes in dynamic context during the process execution. Failing to do so results in KiPs where goals are not satisfied properly. Therefore, integrated modeling of goals, the dynamic context, and the processes is essential to support knowledge workers in executing these process.

Several related works focus on the link between goals, processes, and context. However, they either focus on procedural process models that are not suitable for KiPs [6,9,13,21], consistency analysis rather than process modeling [7,8] or they do not cover all of these three aspects (i.e., goals, processes, and context) in an integrated and holistic manner [10–12,15,16,19].

To fill this gap, we present *a method based on process and goal models for integrated modeling of contextual goals and KiPs*, when the context is dynamic and controllable.

The method enables the representation of the contextual goals on KiP models and supports the alignment of KiP models with goals in dynamic contexts. We have followed the design science research (DSR) methodology [18] to develop our method and investigated its use in a real-life case study. The results indicate that the method can be used to build a link between a KiP and its contextual goals and support effective execution of KiPs under dynamic contexts.

The paper is organized as follows. Section 2 presents the design of our method. Section 3 briefly discusses the evaluation. Lastly, Sect. 4 concludes our paper.

2 Method for Integrated Modeling of KiPs with Contextual Goals

In this section, we describe our method on a running example on Abdominal pain treatment process inspired from [14] (See appendix[1] for background knowledge).

---

[1] https://sites.google.com/view/methodintegratedkipmodeling/home.

The Abdominal pain treatment process is a KiP where the clinicians, as experts, have the discretion over how the process is executed to achieve the goals of the process. The clinician first aims to determine the disease causing the abdominal pain (Final diagnosis determined), and then to treat the patient (Treatment finalized). Final diagnosis determination requires an iterative process of information gathering. First, based on the information provided by the patient and physical examination, the clinician determines a working diagnosis (Working diagnosis identified), i.e., a potential diagnosis explaining the patient's symptoms. Usually, clinicians come up with a list of working diagnoses and refine this list as more information is gathered, through tests done throughout the differential diagnosis process. Each suspected disease requires different tests to be confirmed as the final diagnosis. The clinician performs these tests to achieve the Differential diagnosis examined goal in Fig. 1. Therefore, each suspected disease is a contextual factor defining the context for the Abdominal pain treatment process. That context is dynamic since throughout the process, the suspected disease that is investigated by the clinician can change until the final diagnosis is made.

Our method takes a contextual goal model as input. Contextual goal models are introduced in requirements engineering literature [1]. Existing approaches can be used to derive the input contextual goal model [1,17]. First, the goals that will be modeled in the process model are selected. Then, in the second step, goals are modeled as milestones in the process model. Next, milestone sentries are specified. At this point, a draft process model is obtained that does not yet consider the effect of context. Simultaneously in the fourth step, taking the contextual goal model as input, different goal model variants for different dynamic contexts are derived. Using the goal model variants and the draft process model as input, the milestones in the process model are contextualized and a final draft process model with contextual goals is obtained. Table 2 in the appendix (see footnote 1) summarizes the steps and their inputs and outputs. Each step in our method is further elaborated in the following subsections.

2.1   Selecting Goals

Our method starts with the selection of goals that will be modeled in the process model from the goal model. This selection is done based on different goal types proposed in [4]. Our method assumes that the goals in our input goal model are already classified using this taxonomy and proposes a selection strategy. Figure 1 is the goal model of our example on healthcare services. For this goal model, we focus on the goals of the Abdominal pain treatment process, as explained in the following paragraphs.

First, fundamental, means-ends, process, and activity goals are investigated. Fundamental goals do not have a direct link to the process but are related to the process by their means-ends goals [4]. Next, the lowest level means-ends goals are investigated and the processes they relate to are identified. For instance, in our example, we select the means-ends goal Patient with abdominal pain treated as the goal of the Abdominal pain treatment process. From this point on, our scope is this means-ends goal and its sub-goals. Means-ends goals can have more

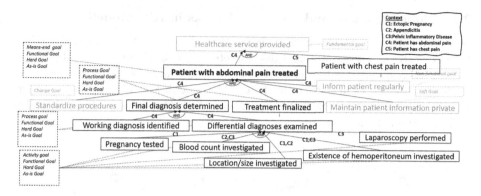

Fig. 1. Contextual Goal Model for Healthcare Services (Goals to be modeled in the process model in bold

refined goals like process and activity goals. Next, process or activity goals are also selected to be modeled in the process model.

Opposed to [4], we believe both functional and non-functional goals can be related to processes. For instance, the goal Inform patient weekly is a non-functional goal, yet can be selected and modeled in Abdominal Pain Treatment process, if required. Therefore, a business analyst can decide to select both functional and non-functional goals.

Next, hard goals and soft goals are investigated. While modeling goals as milestones in a CMMN model, the expressions stating when such a goal is achieved should be modeled in a clear-cut manner. This is very challenging for soft goals as they are subjective. Although soft goals can be related to a business process or activity [4], modeling them as achievable targets within a process model is not feasible. Therefore, soft goals are not selected to be modeled in the process model in our method.

The goals are also classified with respect to their temporal aspect, as goals of the current process (as-is goal), motivations for change (change goal), or a future goal to be aimed in an improved business process (to-be goal) [4]. Our aim is to model the current goals in a process model such that the achievement of goals through process activities can be depicted and traced. Therefore, change and to-be goals are not selected.

Lastly, for the process goals, restricted scope or broad scope goals are investigated. Restricted scope goals are achieved within a single execution of one business process, whereas a broad scope goal requires multiple executions of one or more business processes to be achieved. Our aim is to model the goals in a process model such that we can trace them throughout a single execution. Therefore, we leave out broad scope goals.

2.2   Modeling Goals and Associated Tasks in KiP Models

Next, we turn our attention to modeling the selected goals in the KiP model. Since milestones represent achievable targets in a CMMN model [2], there is a natural correspondence between goals and milestones. Hence, in our method, goals are modeled as milestones in the CMMN model. For this step, we consider regular goal models. In Sect. 2.5, we discuss how to model contextual goals, building upon the models we derive in this section.

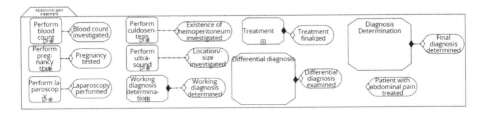

Fig. 2. Activity, process and means-ends goals modeled as milestones, abdominal pain treatment process (See Fig. 1 in the appendix (see footnote 1) for a bigger picture.)

Figure 3 depicts the draft process model obtained as output of this step. First, milestones corresponding to the goals selected in the previous step are created. Activity goals are modeled as milestones. Related activities are modeled as tasks and linked to these milestones. Process goals are modeled as milestones and related processes are modeled as stages attached to these milestones, as process goals refer to goals achieved by a set of activities. For instance, we modeled the activity goal Blood count investigated and the process goal Working diagnosis determined as milestones and we next identified the task Perform blood count and the stage Working diagnosis determination, respectively, and linked them to these milestones.

If the process goal is decomposed into more refined goals, its milestone is attached to an expanded stage, e.g., the milestone Differential diagnosis examined. If the process goal is not decomposed into sub-goals, it is attached to a collapsed stage, indicating that the goal model does not provide further information for modeling this goal in the process model, e.g., the milestone Treatment finalized. The milestone corresponding to the selected means-ends goal is modeled as a separate milestone, e.g., the milestone Patient with abdominal pain treated. Figure 2 show the draft process model of our running example at this point.

Next, the following patterns are applied to the milestones in the process model to represent the goal relations in the goal model. Note that, M1 is the milestone representing goal G1, M2 is the milestone representing goal G2 etc.

Pattern-1: If a process goal, G1, is decomposed into more refined (sub)process goals, G2, or activity goals, G3, then its corresponding milestone, M1, is attached to a stage containing a sub-stage, an activity and their milestones M2 and M3. If G1 is AND(OR)-decomposed into G2 and G3, then M2 and M3 are linked to M1 on the same (different) sentry.

Pattern-2: If multiple process goals, G1 and G4, are decomposed into more refined (sub)process goals and share some of their sub-goals, G2 and/or G3, then M2 and M3 are either contained in the stage that owns M1 or M4. Then the milestone of the stage that contains M2 and M3 is linked to the other milestone that requires M2 and M3.

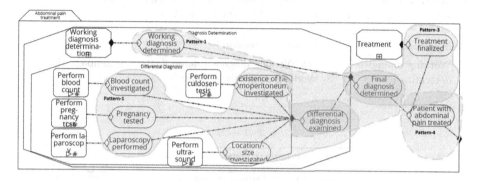

Fig. 3. Draft process model, abdominal pain treatment process

Pattern-3: If G1 and G2 are activity or process goals AND(OR)-decomposed from the same means-ends goal, G3, M1 and M2 are linked to M3 on the same (different) sentry.

Pattern-4: When the milestone corresponding to the selected top-level means-ends goal is achieved, the case is completed. Therefore, this milestone is linked to the case exit sentry.

Figure 3 shows the draft process model we get at this point with patterns 1, 3, and 4 applied.

2.3   Modeling Sentries

Depending on the goal modeling notation used, the goal models may be specified in different levels of detail regarding the achievement of goals e.g., goal outcomes in Archimate [20] or plans in TROPOS [3]. Our method assumes that the detailed information regarding the achievement of goals do not exist on the goal model and should be derived manually. In this step, the draft process model is extended with sentry expressions of each milestone, as depicted in Table 1.

When modeling the goals as milestones, tasks and processes were already linked to related milestones (activity or process goals). This shows that the milestone requires completion of the activity/process attached to it to be achieved; the ON-part of the sentries can be derived based on such relations. The IF-part of the sentries should be manually derived by the business analyst.

Lastly, milestones are also linked to each other to represent the hierarchy on the goal model. A sentry on a milestone that is linked to other milestones checks the occurrence of other milestones linked to it. Therefore, this is also included in the ON-part of the related sentry.

2.4 Deriving Goal Model Variants

Up to this point, a draft CMMN model is derived using a goal model as input. In this subsection, we introduce the notion of contextual goals in a CMMN model.

Table 1. Milestones and sentry expressions, abdominal pain treatment process (See Table 3 in the appendix (see footnote 1) for the full table.)

Milestone	Sentry Expression
Working diagnosis determined	ON Working diagnosis determination is complete IF Working diagnosis is found
...	...

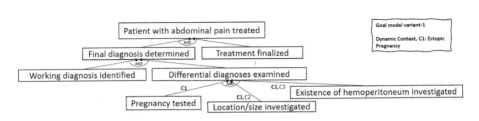

Fig. 4. Goal model variants, abdominal pain treatment process

First, goal model variants are derived from the input contextual goal model. Since context identifies the goals that should be achieved by the business process, different contexts refer to different goal models, which we refer to as goal model variants [1]. Goal model variants are derived from the contextual goal model by choosing the relevant context. We differentiate between static and dynamic context. In a single execution of a process, static context is fixed and can be predefined. In our goal model in Fig. 1, C4 and C5 are static contexts. The current static context is C4, patient with abdominal pain. This is a fixed context, which can be determined before the diagnosis process starts and does not change during the diagnosis process.

By setting the static context, the contextual goal model is reduced to a smaller goal model that contains only dynamic context annotations. Our aim is to cover the effect of dynamic contexts in a process model.

In our example, the suspected diseases define the context since each disease requires different tests to be confirmed as the final diagnosis. At the beginning, the clinician might suspect multiple diseases, but the final diagnosis, or the final context, is determined by looking at the results of the tests obtained throughout the diagnosis process. Therefore the context is not fixed and changes throughout the process as the suspected diseases investigated by the clinician change.

Then, for each mutually exclusive dynamic context, a goal model variant is derived. In our example, we have three mutually exclusive dynamic contexts;

C1,C2 and C3. Therefore we have three goal model variants. Figure 1 shows the goal model variant for the context C1 (See Fig. 2 in the appendix (see footnote 1) for other goal model variants). Note that, in this example we assume that the patient suffers from only a single disease causing the abdominal pain.

Table 2. Sentry expressions for contextual milestones, abdominal pain treatment process (See Table 4 in the apppendix for the full table.)

Milestone-Context	Sentry Expression
Differential diagnosis examined-Context-1	ON Perform pregnancy test is complete $\land$ Perform culdosentesis is complete $\land$ Perform ultrasound is complete
...	...

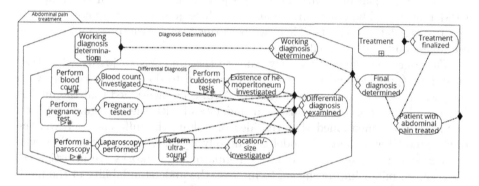

Fig. 5. Draft process model with contextual goals, abdominal pain treatment process

2.5   Contextualizing the Milestones

In this subsection, we explain how the goal model variants are expressed in a single CMMN model by contextualizing the milestones. On the goal model variants, the parent goals (means-ends goal decomposed into more refined process or activity goals OR process goals decomposed into sub-process/ activity goals) are investigated. Sentries are added to the corresponding milestone of the parent goal, such that there is a separate sentry for each goal model variant where this parent goal has a different set of sub-goals.

In our example, the goal Differential diagnosis examined has a different set of sub-goals in each goal model variant. Therefore, it has three different sentries representing three different ways of its achievement under different dynamic contexts. Then, we update Table 1, adding the expressions for the new sentries in Table 2.

Lastly, the links between tasks/stages and milestones in the draft process model are updated based on the expressions of the newly added sentries. The final draft of the process model of our example is shown in Fig. 5. Note that this draft process model should be further refined by the business analyst to derive a complete process model as part of the standard process analysis activities.

3   Evaluation

We evaluated our method through demonstration (See Sect. 3 in the appendix (see footnote 1)) on a case study about medicinal product development process in the iPSpine project. We presented our method and the models to domain experts consisting of six senior biomedical scientists and two regulatory experts in a meeting. The experts inspected models and we performed semi-structured interviews on usefulness. The experts indicated that they are positive about the usefulness of the process and goal models and our method for integrated modeling of processes and contextual goals in practice. Next, we implemented the models in a prototype platform[2] for the EU project iPSpine, based on the Flowable BPM Platform. The platform was used by three junior, three senior scientists and two regulatory experts. Then, we performed semi-structured interviews on usefulness and understandability.

The users mentioned that they can use these models to justify what they have done (process) and identify what they need to do to better comply with the chosen regulatory framework (goals). Also, they mentioned that the models and the platform are easy to use and understand with the user guide we have provided. They mentioned that the idea of linking the different contexts, the process model and the goal model is definitely useful when the scientific development is at the stage where different regulatory frameworks are investigated. We received minor improvements to increase the understandability of the models, e.g., adding additional explanations to the platform. Currently, we continue improving our models and the method based on the feedback we get from users, and we are evaluating with other domain experts.

4   Conclusion

In this paper, we have presented a method for the modeling KiPs with contextual goals under dynamic contexts. The contribution of this paper is the structured guideline that supports business analysts in modeling the contextual goals in a CMMN model.

The demonstration of the method on a real-life complex KiP and evaluation with the stakeholders confirm the usefulness of the models. The users commented that the explicit modeling of goals and the link to the process in goal models is useful for their job. Furthermore, introducing the effect of context to the models helps them investigate the effect of context on the process efficiently. One limitation of our method is that the evaluation is carried out by model inspection rather than method application by users. However, the evaluation on

---

[2] https://sites.google.com/view/ipspinepmp/ipspine-process-management-platform.

the models provided positive insights on the usefullness of the models generated by our method. As a next step, we plan to extend our evaluation such that the method is applied by users and apply our method to model different KiPs.

Acknowledgment. The work presented in this paper is part of iPSpine project that has received funding from the European Union's Horizon 2020 research and innovation programme under grant agreement No. 825925.

References

1. Ali, R., Dalpiaz, F., Giorgini, P.: A goal-based framework for contextual requirements modeling and analysis. Requirements Eng. **15**, 439–458 (2010)
2. BizAgi, et al.: CMMN, v1.1(dec 2016). OMG Document Number formal/16-12-01, Object Management Group (2016)
3. Bresciani, P., Perini, A., Giorgini, P., Giunchiglia, F., Mylopoulos, J.: Tropos: an agent-oriented software development methodology. Auton. Agents Multi Agent Sys. **8**, 203–236 (2004)
4. Cardoso, E., Guizzardi, R., Almeida, J.P.: Aligning goal analysis and business process modelling: a case study in healthcare. Int. J. Bus. Process. Integr. Manag. **5**, 144–158 (2011)
5. Di Ciccio, C., Marrella, A., Russo, A.: Knowledge-intensive processes: characteristics, requirements and analysis of contemporary approaches. J. Data Semant. **4**(1), 29–57 (2014). https://doi.org/10.1007/s13740-014-0038-4
6. Cortes-Cornax, M., Matei, A., Letier, E., Dupuy-Chessa, S., Rieu, D.: Intentional fragments: bridging the gap between organizational and intentional levels in business processes. In: Meersman, R. (ed.) OTM 2012. LNCS, vol. 7565, pp. 110–127. Springer, Heidelberg (2012). https://doi.org/10.1007/978-3-642-33606-5_8
7. Czepa, C., et al.: Supporting structural consistency checking in adaptive case management. In: Debruyne, C. (ed.) OTM 2015. LNCS, vol. 9415, pp. 311–319. Springer, Cham (2015). https://doi.org/10.1007/978-3-319-26148-5_19
8. Eshuis, R., Ghose, A.: Consistency checking of goal models and case management schemas. In: Polyvyanyy, A., Wynn, M.T., Van Looy, A., Reichert, M. (eds.) BPM 2021. LNBIP, vol. 427, pp. 54–70. Springer, Cham (2021). https://doi.org/10.1007/978-3-030-85440-9_4
9. Guizzardi, R., Reis, A.N.: A method to align goals and business processes. In: Johannesson, P., Lee, M.L., Liddle, S.W., Opdahl, A.L., López, Ó.P. (eds.) ER 2015. LNCS, vol. 9381, pp. 79–93. Springer, Cham (2015). https://doi.org/10.1007/978-3-319-25264-3_6
10. Haarmann, S., Seidel, A., Weske, M.: Modeling objectives of knowledge workers. In: Marrella, A., Weber, B. (eds.) BPM 2021. LNBIP, vol. 436, pp. 337–348. Springer, Cham (2022). https://doi.org/10.1007/978-3-030-94343-1_26
11. Heravizadeh, M., Edmond, D.: Making workflows context-aware: a way to support knowledge-intensive tasks. In: Proceedings APCCM, pp. 79–88 (2008)
12. Hewelt, M., Pufahl, L., Mandal, S., Wolff, F., Weske, M.: Toward a methodology for case modeling. Softw. Syst. Model. **19**(6), 1367–1393 (2019). https://doi.org/10.1007/s10270-019-00766-5
13. Horita, H., Honda, K., Sei, Y., Nakagawa, H., Tahara, Y., Ohsuga, A.: Transformation approach from KAOS goal models to BPMN models using refinement patterns. In: Symposium on Applied Computing, pp. 1023–1024 (2014)

14. Knechtel, M.A.: Formulating a Differential Diagnosis for the Advanced Practice Provider. Springer Publishing Company (2017)
15. Kueng, P., Kawalek, P.: Goal-based business process models: creation and evaluation. BPM J. **3**, 17–38 (1997)
16. Mattos, T.D.C., Santoro, F.M., Revoredo, K., Nunes, V.T.: A formal representation for context-aware business processes. Comput. Ind. **65**, 1193–1214 (2014)
17. Ozturk Yurt, Z., Eshuis, R., Wilbik, A., Vanderfeesten, I.: Context-aware process modelling for medicinal product development. In: Serral, E., Stirna, J., Ralyté, J., Grabis, J. (eds.) PoEM 2021. LNBIP, vol. 432, pp. 168–183. Springer, Cham (2021). https://doi.org/10.1007/978-3-030-91279-6_12
18. Peffers, K., Tuunanen, T., Rothenberger, M.A., Chatterjee, S.: A design science research methodology for information systems research. MIS **24**, 45–77 (2008)
19. Rosemann, M., Recker, J., Flender, C.: Contextualisation of business processes. Int. J. Bus. Process. Integr. Manag. **3**, 47–60 (2008)
20. The Open Group: ArchiMate® 3.0.1. Tech. rep. The Open Group (2018)
21. de la Vara, J.L., Sánchez, J., Pastor, O.: On the use of goal models and business process models for elicitation of system requirements. In: Proceedings of CAiSE, pp. 168–183 (2013)

Author Index

Printed in the United States
by Baker & Taylor Publisher Services

Printed in the United States
by Baker & Taylor Publisher Services